Using Superheroes and Villains in Counseling and Play Therapy

Through rich and research-grounded clinical applications, *Using Superheroes and Villains in Counseling and Play Therapy* explores creative techniques for integrating superhero stories and metaphors in clinical work with children, adolescents, adults and families. Each chapter draws on the latest empirically supported approaches and techniques to address a wide range of clinical challenges in individual, family and group settings. The chapters also explore important contextual issues of race, gender, culture, age and ethnicity and provide case studies and practical tips that clinicians can use to support clients on their healing journey.

Lawrence C. Rubin, PhD, ABPP, LMHC, RPT-S, is Professor of Counselor Education at St. Thomas University, where he directs the Mental Health Counseling Program, and Adjunct Professor of Counselor Education at the University of Massachusetts, Boston. He maintains a private practice as a psychologist, counselor and play therapist, specializing in children, teens and families, and is widely published on the subjects of counseling and popular culture. Dr. Rubin is also the editor of Psychotherapy.net.

D1595898

Using Superheroes and Villains in Counseling and Play Therapy

A Guide for Mental Health Professionals

Edited by Lawrence C. Rubin

Routledge
Taylor & Francis Group

NEW YORK AND LONDON

First published 2020
by Routledge
52 Vanderbilt Avenue, New York, NY 10017

and by Routledge
2 Park Square, Milton Park, Abingdon, Oxon, OX14 4RN

Routledge is an imprint of the Taylor & Francis Group, an informa business

Library of Congress Cataloging-in-Publication Data
Names: Rubin, Lawrence C., 1955– editor.
Title: Using superheroes and villains in counseling and play therapy : a guide for mental health professionals / edited by Lawrence C. Rubin.
Description: New York, NY : Routledge, [2019] |
Includes bibliographical references and index. |
Identifiers: LCCN 2019011575 (print) | LCCN 2019020614 (ebook) |
ISBN 9780429454950 (eBook) | ISBN 9781138613263 (hardback) |
ISBN 9781138613270 (pbk.) | ISBN 9780429454950 (ebk)
Subjects: LCSH: Play therapy. | Heroes. |
Superhero films. | Children–Counseling of.
Classification: LCC RJ505.P6 (ebook) | LCC RJ505.P6 U85 2019 (print) |
DDC 618.92/891653–dc23
LC record available at https://lccn.loc.gov/2019011575

ISBN: 978-1-138-61326-3 (hbk)
ISBN: 978-1-138-61327-0 (pbk)
ISBN: 978-0-429-45495-0 (ebk)

Typeset in Minion
by Newgen Publishing UK

This book is dedicated to my loving wife Randi, my superhero.

Contents

About the Editor

Lawrence "Larry" C. Rubin, PhD, ABPP, LMHC, RPT-S, is Professor of Counselor Education at St. Thomas University in Miami, Florida, where he directs the Mental Health Counseling Program. He is also Adjunct Professor of Counselor Education in the Mental Health Counseling Program at the University of Massachusetts, Boston. Dr. Rubin is the past president of the Florida Association for Play Therapy, as well as past Board Chair of the Association for Play Therapy. He is in private practice as a psychologist, counselor and play therapist, specializing in children, teens and families. Dr. Rubin's research and writing interests lie at the intersection of psychology and popular culture. His textbook, *Diagnosis and Treatment Planning Skills: A Popular Culture Casebook Approach* with Dr. Alan Schwitzer is widely used in Counselor Education programs across the country. Other books by Dr. Rubin include *Handbook of Medical Play Therapy and Child Life: Interventions in Clinical and Medical Settings*; *Play-based Interventions for Children and Adolescents with Autism Spectrum Disorder* with Loretta Gallo Lopez; *Mental Illness in Popular Media: Essays on the Representation of Psychiatric Disorders*; *Food for Thought: Essays on Eating and Culture*; *Popular Culture in Counseling, Psychotherapy and Play-based Intervention*; *Using Superheroes in Counseling and Play Therapy* and *Psychotropic Drugs and Popular Culture: Medicine, Mental Health and the Media*. Dr. Rubin is on the editorial boards of the *International Journal of Play*, the *Journal of Popular Television* and the *Journal of Child and Adolescent Counseling*. He lives in Florida with his wife Randi and two children Zachary and Rebecca, six cats and a dog named Lily.

About the Contributors

Sophia Ansari, LPCC, is a Licensed Professional Clinical Counselor. She is the coordinator for the Midwest Play Therapy Institute in Chicago, IL. She provides workshops on play therapy to mental health professionals all over the country. Sophia earned her Bachelor of Science degree in Biology from Wright State University and her Master of Arts in Mental Health Counseling from the University of Cincinnati. She co-hosts Hero Nation, a podcast which celebrates diversity in the media and explores how to use geek culture in therapy. Sophia enjoys attending Comic-Cons with her equally geeky husband, Wamiq, and son, Humza.

Joyce Arendt, MSW, LICSW, RPT-S, EPT-D, SEP, graduated with a Bachelor of Science degree from the University of Minnesota majoring in Child Development and Emphasis in Criminal Justice. She received her graduate degree in Social Work from the University of St. Thomas, College of St. Catherine. Joyce has been trained and trains other therapists in many models of play therapy. She specializes in trauma work and volunteers her time assisting around the country for the Somatic Experiencing Trauma Institute that trains health professionals in Somatic Experiencing˚. Joyce is the owner and founder of Family Connections Counseling Center, Inc. In her free time, she enjoys the outdoors with her partner; hiking, biking, camping and kayaking. She also enjoys performing arts and has season tickets to the Minnesota Opera.

Josué Cardona, MS, is a design researcher and strategist. As a mental health counselor, he formed the Geek Therapy community which celebrates how people can use their interests and passions to do good in the world. You can learn more about him and his work at josuecardona.com

Roz Casey, Dip. Couns, Dip. Comm Services, B. Ad. Voc. Ed., Grad. Dip. Psych., M Spec. Ed., is accredited with the Australian Counselling Association, and is in private practice in Melbourne, Australia. She has had extensive experience with adults, teens and children in both education environments and various therapeutic contexts. Roz uses a range of modalities when counseling, including CBT, motivational interviewing, art and play therapy and applied behavior analysis. Roz currently practices in Victorian primary schools, providing therapy for children with a range of disabilities. She was a co-author in a paper about raising resilient adults with Autism, at the 2018 Australian Counselling Association's annual conference. The paper will be published in the *Australian Counselling Journal* in 2019. Roz is also a co-author for a paper about how individual practitioners can deliver trauma informed practice, in using a learning needs analysis framework, with three other international psychologists and mental health professionals. This paper will also be published in the *Australian Counselling Journal* in 2019. Roz is a sessional academic for the Masters of Education (Special Education, Advanced) at Torrens University Australia and the Bachelor of Community Services program at BoxHill Institute. Roz is also about to embark on a PhD about how play therapy can assist children to overcome childhood trauma.

Yoav Cohen-Manor, MA, is an expressive-arts therapist specializing in Bibliotherapy. A graduate of the University of Haifa from the Department of Counseling and Human Development, with an under-graduate education in literature, culture and creative writing, he lives and works in Israel. Yoav practices in the public schools and in private practice with children, adolescents and young adults. As a child, he recalls waiting for the five o'clock Spider-Man cartoons. Nowadays Spidey and other friends regularly come to the rescue in his therapy room—and as always, help save the day.

LaTrice L. Dowtin, PhD, LCPC, NCSP, RPT, is a native of the DC/Maryland area who believes in the ongoing pursuit of cultural humility. Dr. Dowtin is a specialist-level nationally certified school psychologist and a licensed clinical professional counselor who specializes in trauma and infant mental health for culturally, racially and linguistically diverse families. She is currently adjunct faculty at Gallaudet University in the Infant, Toddler and Families graduate program, while finalizing her clinical psychology training as a Child Psychology Postdoctoral Fellow at Stanford University's School of Medicine in the neonatal intensive care unit (NICU) psychology program. Dr. Dowtin has presented regionally and nationally and has conducted research on topics regarding racial and cultural inequities among infant care settings, childcare classrooms, schools and mental health providers.

Larisa A. Garski, MA, LMFT, is a psychotherapist and the Clinical Director at Empowered Therapy in Chicago, IL. She specializes in working with individuals, families and young adults who identify as outside the mainstream—such as those in the geek and LGBTQIA communities. She regularly appears at pop culture conventions, speaking on panels related to mental health and geek wellness. Her work as a clinical writer and researcher has appeared or is forthcoming in a variety of pop psychology and video game psychology books including but not limited to *Supernatural Psychology: Roads Less Traveled*, *Westworld Psychology: Violent Delights* and *Daredevil Psychology: The Devil You Know*.

Brenna Hicks, PhD, RPT, LMHC, is a licensed private-practice play therapist, author, speaker and parenting expert. Working exclusively with children and their families, she founded The Kid Counselor to offer play therapy, parent training and education. Brenna has been featured in *The New York Times*, and on CNN and iVillage. She earned her PhD from the University of South Florida, where she also teaches courses in counseling. Brenna is working on an upcoming book about Play Therapy. A native Floridian, she loves the beach, the sun and baseball. She lives in the Tampa Bay Area with her husband and son.

Rachel Hutnick, MA, LPC, RPT, is an attachment-based family play therapist and a mother. She is a Licensed Professional Counselor and Registered Play Therapist in the state of New Jersey, and counsels children of all ages, adolescents, adults, families and couples in a private practice setting. Rachel is a graduate of Arcadia University's Masters in Counseling Program, and in addition to attachment work and play therapy, she has extensive experience with Cognitive Behavioral Therapy, specifically Exposure and Response Prevention for the treatment of OCD. She also received advanced training in Dyadic Developmental Psychotherapy (DDP), Eye Movement Desensitization and Reprocessing (EMDR), Emotionally Focused Therapy for couples (EFT), Theraplay and Sand Play Therapy, and completed a Certificate in Adoption Studies at Rutgers University.

Lara Taylor Kester, MA, LMFT, holds a Master's degree in counseling psychology as well as a certificate in traumatology and treatment from Holy Names University. A registered Associate Marriage and Family Therapist in California at the time this chapter was written, all that stands between her and her MFT license is the final clinical examination. She currently works with at-risk and foster youth in the San Francisco Bay Area. Lara is also a co-host on GT Radio podcast (originally the Geek Therapy Podcast), and contributes chapters to books in the Popular Culture Psychology series such as *Wonder Woman Psychology: Lassoing the Truth*, *Game of Thrones Psychology: The Night is Dark and Full of Terrors* and *Captain America vs. Iron Man: Freedom, Security, Psychology*.

Carol Kirby, MS, NCC, attained a Master's degree in Clinical Mental Health Counseling and has been certified by the National Board of Certified Counselors as a National Certified Counselor. Carol has had a long career in financial industry regulation and, after her own experience with trauma, made a late life decision to pursue a degree in mental health. Carol is winding down her lengthy regulatory career with plans to pursue her avocation of helping others.

Justin D. Kruse, MS, LMFT, RPT, NCC, graduated with a Bachelor of Science degree from the University of South Dakota majoring in Psychology with minors in Sociology and Criminal Justice. He received his graduate degree in Mental Health Counseling from Minnesota State University, Mankato. Justin's clinical experience and treatment of childhood difficulties has ranged from the developmental impact of trauma and attachment to the use of multi-sensory forms of psychotherapy, including play therapy. In his work with children who have experienced trauma, Justin's dog companion, Buddy, is a friendly face greeting the children on their journey. Justin is a co-founder of the Journeys Toward Healing Counseling Center. In his free time, he enjoys playing board games with his family, spending time outdoors and painting.

Steve Kuniak, PhD, NCC, ACS, LPC, is a ranked faculty member in a graduate counseling program. He has earned a PhD in Counselor Education from Duquesne University, is a Board Certified Counselor, Approved Clinical Supervisor, and Licensed Professional Counselor. He specializes in incorporating his passion for video games, science fiction, fantasy and other geeky interests into his practice. He has helped hundreds of students and developing counselors to begin uncovering their own unique forms of practice. His research focuses on exploring Gamers and Geeks as a unique culture, and his research and clinical practice has led to many interviews in national publications, radio shows and podcasts. Dr. Kuniak also presents at mental health and pop culture conventions.

Judith Lester, LISW-S, RPT, ACTP, has a Master of Social Work degree from the Ohio State University, and is a licensed independent social worker supervisor in the state of Ohio. Judy is an Advanced Certified Trauma Practitioner and Certified Agency Trainer for the National Institute of Trauma and Loss in Children (TLC). She is a

Registered Play Therapist and Early Childhood Mental Health Consultant. Judy leads an innovative team of mental health professionals as the Treatment Director for SAFY Behavioral Health, providing play therapy, trauma treatment and other therapeutic mental health intervention services to children, their families and adults in west central Ohio. Judy has developed three TLC trainings and has presented trainings to hundreds of mental health professionals, teachers, early childhood professionals, foster parents and community members in an effort to create more trauma informed communities. She is a graduate of the Association of Play Therapy's Leadership Academy 2012. Judy has authored blogs for TLC and a Play Therapy magazine article. She likes to share her love of play and words with others.

Kory Martin, MA, LMFT, is a licensed Marriage & Family therapist with experience working in various clinical settings within the Minneapolis/St. Paul metro area including intensive day treatment, crisis response treatment, school-based services and outpatient care. In each of these settings, he values the balance between providing individual and family therapeutic services and he engages his clients with empathy and authenticity and dedicates himself to culturally reflective clinical practice. He approaches his work with the belief that his clients bring abilities into the therapeutic relationship that they employ daily to adapt to their various stressors, systemic patterns, and presenting issues and they benefit from strength-based intervention that empower them to parlay those abilities into lasting change.

Justine Mastin, MA, LMFT, LADC, E-RYT200, is the owner/founder of Blue Box Counseling, a private practice in Minneapolis. Justine specializes in working with clients who self-identify as being outside the mainstream—such as those in the geek, secular and LGBTQIA communities. Justine is also the fearless leader of YogaQuest, a yoga organization that blends geek narratives with yoga to reach this underserved population. In addition to her work in the office/studio, Justine appears at pop culture conventions around the country where she teaches yoga and speaks on geek wellness topics. Justine contributed chapters to *Supernatural Psychology: Roads Less Traveled*, *Daredevil Psychology: The Devil You Know* and *Westworld Psychology: Violent Delights* in the Popular Culture Psychology Series.

April D. Pachuta, AA, has an Associate's degree in Business and is a medical insurance specialist. She is one year away from completing her Elementary Education degree with a minor in English from Bethany College. She was sorted into Ravenclaw. Her favorite class would have been Transfiguration and she would have been a library regular.

Robyn Joy Park, MA, LMFT, is a Marriage and Family Therapist who wholeheartedly dedicates her practice to serving children, adolescents and families at The Center for Connection, in private practice and at community-based organizations in Los Angeles. Her clinical training at agency and school-based settings has served children, adolescents and families, as well as individual and group counseling services. Her experience includes working within various in-home, educational, agency, residential and therapeutic settings. Robyn received her undergraduate degree in Justice and Peace Studies at the University of Saint Thomas and is a graduate of Antioch University where she received her Master of Arts in Clinical Psychology, specializing in both Child Studies and Applied Community Psychology. Robyn provides community trainings, workshops and presentations both locally and nationally and is experienced in the treatment of foster care and adoption-related issues, anxiety, depression, grief and loss, trauma and maternal mental health. In her free time she can be found completing her Play Therapy certification, globetrotting, training for marathons, and preparing for the Zombie Apocalypse.

Aimee Loth Rozum, ATR-BC, LMHC, is a Board Certified Art Therapist and budding Play Therapist. Her clinical work focuses on children and adolescents dealing with mood disorders, trauma and bereavement. She was trained at Loyola Marymount University and spent a decade of her life working in community mental health in Los Angeles and MA before branching out into Bereavement and Impending Loss work with children and families with another decade working in hospice. She has contributed to various art therapy texts, is a supervisor and an Adjunct Instructor in the graduate program in Expressive Therapies at Lesley University, and has a full time private practice. She is married to a comic book writer and lives in New England.

Janina Scarlet, PhD, is a Licensed Clinical Psychologist, a scientist and a full-time geek. A Ukrainian-born refugee, she survived Chernobyl radiation and persecution. She immigrated to the United States at the age of 12 with her family and a year later, inspired by *the X-Men*, wrote *Superhero Therapy* to help people with anxiety, depression and PTSD. She currently works at the Center for Stress and Anxiety Management in San Diego. Dr. Scarlet's books include: *Superhero Therapy, Harry Potter Therapy, Therapy Quest* and *Dark Agents*, as well as numerous contributions to the Psych Geeks Books Series, such as *Star Wars Psychology, Star Trek Psychology, Wonder Woman Psychology, Supernatural Psychology*, and many others.

Christina M. Scott, MEd, LPCC, NCC, is a school-based mental health therapist who lives and works in rural Ohio. She sees clients ranging from pre-school age to seniors in high-school. Graduating in 2015, Christina has had experience providing therapy services to adult and youth populations, and she has worked in both the mental health and substance abuse realm. During the writing of this book, she became independently licensed and looks forward to becoming a supervisor as well as becoming a Registered Play Therapist. She is always trying to find ways of incorporating expressive arts, pop culture and anything "geeky" in her practice. Her favorite superhero is Buffy the Vampire Slayer. Since the unfortunate realization that she cannot spend her nights slaying vampires, Christina has instead devoted her life to helping kiddos navigate the trials of high school like Buffy had helped her.

Mawule A. Sevon, MA, NCSP, BCBA, has earned recognition for her unique contributions to the field of education and mental health. Having earned a specialist's degree in School Psychology and national board certification as a Behavior Analyst, she uses her behavioral approach to impact the racial disparity in the educational system. Her primary focus is inequity within disciplinary practices for preschool and elementary aged children. Working to increase the cultural competencies of clinicians in the field, Mawule has presented and spoken at professional conferences and academic events on topics related to culture, race, diversity and inclusion. She now sits on the Association of Professional Behavior Analysts' Ad Hoc committee of Diversity and Inclusion and the National Association of School Psychologists' Multicultural Affair Committee's African American subcommittee.

Michael Smith, MS, NCC, has been a life-long lover of comic books and superheroes. He attained a Master's degree in Clinical Mental Health Counseling and has been certified by the National Board of Certified Counselors as a National Certified Counselor. He traveled to London and participated in a 40-hour training course to receive a Level 1 certification in Narrative Therapy from the Institute of Narrative Therapy in England. He currently works as a co-occurring substance use counselor at an inpatient substance use rehabilitation center where he uses his training as a counselor, his training in Narrative Therapy, and his love of comic books and superheroes to work with his clients to begin healing from the impact of substance use disorders.

Meridith Nealy Starling, MSSW, ED.S., RPT-S, is a Licensed Clinical Social Worker and Registered Play Therapist. She is a proud mom who enjoys building Legos and hunting for Pokémon with her son. She worked as a pediatric oncology social worker for two world renowned health systems until her family relocated to a small Midwest town. Intrigued by the power of play she pursued an Educational Specialist degree in Play Therapy from The University of Mississippi in 2014. Since then she has volunteered extensively, organized fundraisers, and owned/operated a small private practice. She eventually decided to close her practice to spend more time with her family. When she is not writing she enjoys traveling the globe with her family and spending time with her amazing super-hero mom friends.

Sarah D. Stauffer, PhD, LPC, NCC, NCSC, RPT-S, is a psychologist in Lausanne, Switzerland working with sexually maltreated children and their families at the Association ESPAS. She is a counselor educator, researcher, presenter and author, and teaches courses in play therapy and the effects of trauma on children and adolescents. She is the Clinical Editor for *Play Therapy*™ Magazine. She was sorted into Gryffindor, and likely would have taught Defense Against the Dark Arts at Hogwarts and would have spent her spare time in the library.

Foreword
Superheroes Matter, Villains Too

I've loved comic books and superheroes all my life. It's how I connected with my parents and friends. Fictional characters formed my worldview, so when I became a Mental Health Counselor in 2010, I couldn't help but think that fictional characters might be just as important to my clients.

It turns out I was right. When I encouraged clients to explain how they felt using stories they were familiar with and loved, they were more comfortable expressing themselves. Sometimes we don't have the words to describe how we feel and in those cases, sometimes, a fictional story can help us do that.

Unfortunately, my supervisors and co-workers did not agree, and I was discouraged from bringing fictional stories into therapy, especially video games, comic books and cartoons. That experience motivated me to start GeekTherapy. com and build a community of people who knew what I knew. I began to meet other people who agreed that beloved fictional characters were an opportunity to reach clients in a meaningful way, but it wasn't until I found Larry Rubin's book *Using Superheroes in Counseling and Play Therapy* that I was certain I was onto something.

The book was incredibly validating because it wasn't just Larry who wrote about how superheroes could be helpful in clinical work, he had many authors talking about *Lord of the Rings, Star Trek, Batman, Hulk, Star Wars, Superman* and more. The book served as inspiration for me and many others to whom I recommended it. It was practical and thought-provoking thanks to the many examples it provided.

In the years since I found Larry's book, after many conversations with members of the Geek Therapy Community, I realized that villains are just as, and sometimes even more, relatable than the heroes. Their stories are easier to relate to and empa-thizing with villains feels like an accomplishment because it's something we don't practice enough with the "villains" in our lives. This is why I'm so excited that the book you're reading focuses on the benefits of using both heroes and villains.

Although the most popular heroes and villains are timeless, the world has changed a lot since 2010. That's why I'm so glad to see that this book is written by a new generation of mental health practitioners who love and understand these characters as much as their clients. Most importantly, they know that these characters matter to their clients. And if they matter to our clients, they should matter to us.

Whether you are a student or a seasoned mental health professional, I hope you'll learn from and be inspired by *Using Superheroes and Villains in Counseling and Play Therapy* as much as I was by the original.

Josué Cardona, Founder of Geek Therapy

Introduction: Superheroes, Past, Present and Future

Lawrence C. Rubin

It was a dark and stormy night. Nah, too melodramatic! The city was in chaos and it desperately needed a savior. Nope, too hackneyed. No one knows when they got here, but for certain, the Earth was in danger! I'm not even sure where that one came from.

Look up in the sky! It's a bird, it's a plane! Ah, there it is; nothing like an old favorite, tried and true.

Okay, you get the message, and the message is bigger and better than it was when I first gathered a super team of therapists, researchers and educators for my *Using Superheroes in Play Therapy and Counseling* (Rubin, 2006). Welcome to the next installment—the adventure promises to be worth the trip, or 'the read' in this case.

Over this last decade since my first volume, or should I say, "our first volume," superheroes and supervillains of all sizes, shapes, races, ages, nationalities, sexual preferences and gendered identities have burst onto the scene—Green Lantern, Wonder Woman, Hellboy, Green Hornet, Spider-Woman, Wasp, Ant-Man, Aquaman, Ghost Rider, Ironman, Punisher, Thor, Captain America and Black Panther, to name a few. And then there are the superhero teams and families, those gatherings of giants that include the Avengers, Guardians of the Galaxy, Justice League and Watchmen. And this list, far from exhaustive, doesn't include all of the heroes, superheroes and supervillains whose origin stories can be found on the small screen as well as in the pages of comic books and graphic novels.

While the television, movie and comic book worlds have clearly been hotbeds of everything superheroic, the scholarly/academic world has done more than its share in studying the nature and impact of superheroes and supervillains on the broader culture. Scholarly articles have appeared in a range of humanities journals such as *Children's Literature Association Quarterly* (Hager, 2008), *YC Young Children* (De-Souza & Radell, 2011), *Childhood Education* (Lilja, 2012), *Sex Roles* (Coyne et al., 2014; Pennell & Behm-Morawitz, 2015), *Journal of American Culture* (Mills, 2015) *Cinema Journal* (Atchison, 2015), and the *Journal of Modern Literature* (King, 2016).

However, and more germane to this volume, scholarly attention has also come from the clinical/psychological sector including *PLOS One* (Rosenberg, Baughman, & Bailenson, 2013), the *Journal of Experimental Social Psychology* (Young, Gabriel and Hollar, 2013) and *Body Image* (Dour & Theran, 2011). These superhero-based journal articles have been paralleled by a proliferation of related books including *The Psychology of Superheroes: An Unauthorized Exploration* (Rosenberg & Canzoneri, 2008), *Even a Superhero Needs Counseling: What Superheroes and Super-villains Teach Us about Ourselves* (Bates, 2016), and *Superhero Therapy: Mindfulness Skills to Help Teens and Young Adults Deal with Anxiety, Depression, and Trauma* (Scarlet, 2017).

What has all of this to do with the title of this volume, *Using Superheroes and Villains in Counseling and Play Therapy: A Guide for Mental Health Professionals*? As it turns out, quite a bit! I will begin with an anecdote from a fellow clinician, a marriage and family therapist by day, and super-parent by night (C. Silitsky, 2018, Personal Communication).

> *Having repeatedly failed his school hearing tests, my son, age six, was finally diagnosed with EVA, a condition characterized by an enlargement of the ves-tibule housing the auditory nerve. A person can live their whole life with this condition without being aware of it and with no repercussions. However, if there is any kind of head trauma, the inter-cranial pressure rises and the chemicals that transmit sound can damage the nerve, causing irreversible and permanent hearing loss. He has had two concussions through normal child play, resulting in moderate loss on one side and now must wear a hearing aid. He must also avoid any possibility of further head trauma so cannot partake in typical sports and recreational activities.*
>
> *Adjustment was and continues to be difficult for my husband who comes from a traditional Mediterranean culture that sees this vulnerability as a stigma. He tells him to take it off in front of others, so that they won't "ask questions." I took a more positive approach. Our son is a super fan of Superman. He has costumes, action figures, themed birthday parties and has seen all of the movies. I framed the hearing aid as his having the new found power of super-hearing. On his first day wearing it, I showed him how I could whisper in the downstairs kitchen and he could hear me all the way upstairs. We talked about how people thought of Superman as "different," but in a good way.*
>
> *On his first day wearing it to school, he asked the teacher if he could show it to the class. He told his classmates that they could no longer keep secrets from him because he would be able to hear them, that they would probably want one but they could not have one because they were so expensive, and that he now had super-human abilities that they would not be able to comprehend.*
>
> *Oh, and did I mention that our audiologist's name is Dr. Metropolous?*

Since the publication of my first book, I have received countless emails and calls from fellow therapists, much like this one, who were excited to share their personal and clinical anecdotes. Superheroes and supervillains had populated their playrooms and therapy spaces in strange, unexpected but typically useful ways with their clients—of all ages. I was encouraged to know that the metaphor of the superhero was sufficiently robust and flexible to stretch and be stretched in a multitude of creative ways for the many clinical challenges for which they were summoned.

In this volume and largely because of the proliferation of supervillains in popular culture and the clinical anecdotes I accumulated, I have expanded the metaphor to include them. The essays and examples in this volume by a very talented team of clinicians, scholars and clinical educators will demonstrate just how robust the superhero/supervillain metaphor can be when applied by a creative and informed clinician. Welcome to the journey.

Part I, entitled *Superheroes, Super Theories*, explores the clinical intersection of selected theories and the superhero mythos. In Chapter 1, "Flourishing after the Origin Story: Using Positive Psychology to Explore Well-being in Superheroes and Supervillains," Sophia Ansari and Christina M. Scott invoke Seligman and Csikszentmihalyi's core elements of resiliency and positivity along with the wisdom of superheroes and villains to help children in play therapy connect with their inner strengths. In Chapter 2, "Alter Egos and Hidden Strengths: The Powers of Superheroes in Child-Centered Play Therapy," LaTrice Dowtin takes us on a tour through the superhero universe, stopping along the way to share her clinical experience with children with whom she utilized these characters in client-centered play therapy (CCPT). In Chapter 3, "Control, Corruption and Destruction. Oh My!: The Role of Villains in Experiential Play Therapy," Justin D. Kruse and Joyce Arendt take us step by step through their work with a troubled 15-year-old traumatized boy on the Autism spectrum who finds his way out of the darkness through his imaginative play with the concept and character of the villain. In Chapter 4, "The Healing Power of Superhero Stories: Bibliotherapy and Comic Books," Yoav Cohen-Manor takes us to the intersection of psychoanalysis, bibliotherapy and superhero comic books as he demonstrates their healing power with a young troubled teen.

Part II, entitled "Using Heroes and Superheroes to Treat Specific Disorders," turns the beam of knowledge on the use of superheroes to work clinically with particular forms of pathology. In Chapter 5, "I Like Them Because They Are Fast and Strong: The Use of Superheroes in Play Therapy with a Latency-Age Boy with Developmental Coordination Disorder," Aimee Loth Rozum helps a young boy come to terms with his unique challenge while playing out effective ways to wrestle it into submission. In Chapter 6, "Using Spidey Senses During the Storm of Anxiety," Janina Scarlett calls on comic book heroes Spider-Man and Storm, along with a tool belt full of cognitive behavioral strategies including systematic desensitization and self-regulation to help two of her anxiety-ridden clients stand up to and conquer their fears. In Chapter 7, "Superhero or Villain? Merging Play Therapy with CBT for Children with Autism," Roz Casey brings her own brand of creativity, CBT and play therapy to bear in helping children on the autism spectrum learn to balance out their inner world with the demands of the world around them. In Chapter 8, "Superheroes and Villains in the Treatment of Substance Use Disorder," Michael Smith and Carol Kirby tap into the power of the timeless tale of Dr. Jekyll and Mr. Hyde, superheroes and White and Epston's narrative therapy to teach us how to work effectively with clients diagnosed with substance use disorders.

Part III, entitled "Strength in Numbers: Superhero Teams," explores the ways in which the hero/superhero team can work therapeutically for individual clients and families. In Chapter 9, "I Can Be a Super Friend! Using Scripted Story to Promote Social Emotional Skills for Young Children with Problem Behaviors," Judith Lester brings us right into the early education classroom to show us how to use the Super Friend program developed at the Center on the Social and Emotional Foundations for Early Learning at Vanderbilt University to help children with social and behavioral challenges. In Chapter 10, "Stronger Together: The Family as a Super Hero Team," Steve Kuniak brings together family systems theory and narrative therapy to demonstrate how to help families battle their own demons and overcome the forces that divide them. In Chapter 11, "El Diablo: What His Role in the Suicide Squad Teaches Children about Emotion Regulation and the Power of Connection," Rachel Hutnick engages an improbable and perhaps inappropriate role model of El Diablo from the Suicide Squad, to help a young boy begin to master the challenging task of self-regulation and interpersonal connection. In Chapter 12, "Using the Avengers to Influence the Self-Actualization Process for Children," Brenna Hicks deftly shows us how each of the Avengers can be harnessed to aid a young client overcoming inner villains through client-centered play therapy.

Part IV, entitled "Villains Rise to the Challenge of Helping," addresses the ways that popular villains and monsters can be utilized by the clinician to help children and teenagers with their own unique struggles. In Chapter 13, "No Joking Matter—Villains are People Too: Working with the School Bully," Meridith Nealy Starling demonstrates the use of both at Adlerian and client-centered play therapy in the treatment of a boy who has been identified as the school bully and who yearns to be accepted by others. In Chapter 14, "Brain Food: Integrating IPNB and Zombies with Diverse Populations," Robyn Joy Park utilizes individual and group counseling and play therapy to help dysregulated children and teens avoid the coming zombie apocalypse within. In Chapter 15, "How Secrets Influenced Relationships for Harry Potter Heroes and Villains: Parallels in Family Therapy," by Sarah D. Stauffer and April D. Pachuta, we sit in on a masterful reading of the narrative and sub-narratives in the Harry Potter series, and how they inform and are informed by the theoretical and clinical principles of Bozsormenyi-Nagi's Contextual Therapy.

Part V, entitled "Superheroes at the Intersection," explores ways in which clinicians use the superhero metaphor to explore issues of diversity with their clients. In Chapter 16, "Female Superheroes: Raising a New Generation of Girls and Boys," Lara Taylor Kester encourages us to explore and challenge gender binaries that have unduly and unjustly influenced media depictions of super heroes/heroines; and then takes us into the clinical space to see how these stereotypes have been shattered through her clinical work with teens. In Chapter 17, "Beyond

Canon: Therapeutic Fanfiction and the Queer Hero's Journey," Larisa A. Garsky and Justine Mastin explore the fascinating intersection of the queer trope, narrative therapy and fanfiction to help a young adult client who painfully finds himself at a precarious juncture in his own queer journey. In Chapter 18, "The Black Panther Lives: Marveling at the Internal Working Models of Self in Young Black Children Through Play," LaTrice L. Dowtin and Mawule A. Sevon deconstruct the stereotypes of the Black experience in order to help a 7-year-old boy embrace his racial and cultural identity with the assistance of the characters from the Black Panther film through psychodymanically-oriented play therapy. In Chapter 19, "Un-Masking the Alter Ego: Fear and Freedom in the Affirmation of the Inner Hero," Kory Martin combines Narrative and Strategic therapies with Critical Race Theory to help young clients of color make sense of and peace with their burgeoning yet conflicting identities.

References

Atchison, C. (2015). Superheroes and identities. *Cinema Journal, 55*(1), 192–199.

Bates, D. (2016). *Even a superhero needs counseling: What superheroes and super-villains teach us about ourselves*. D. B. Press (audio book).

Coyne, S. M., Linder, J. R., Rasmussen, E. E., Nelson, D. A., & Collier, K. M. (2014). It's a bird! It's a plane! It's a gender stereotype! Longitudinal associations between superhero viewing and gender stereotyped play. *Sex Roles, 70*(9–10), 416–430.

De-Souza, D. & Radell, J. (2011). Superheroes: An opportunity for prosocial play. *YC: Young Children, 66*(4), 26–31.

Dour, H. J. & Theran, S. A. (2011). The interaction between the superhero ideal and maladaptive perfectionism as predictors of unhealthy eating attitudes and body esteem. *Body Image, 8*(1), 93–96.

Hager, L. (2008). Saving the world before bedtime: The Powerpuff Girls, citizenship, and the little girl superhero. *Children's Literature Association Quarterly, 33*(1), 62–78.

King, Z. (2016). The superhero historicized, theorized, and read. *Journal of Modern Literature, 39*(2), 167–170.

Lilja, E. (2012). Prioritizing voices in teacher research: Learning to listen to my students' voices over my own. *Childhood Education, 88*(6), 391–393.

Mills, A. R. (2015). What is a superhero? *The Journal of American Culture, 38*(2), 201–202.

Pennell, H. & Behm-Morawitz, E. (2015). The empowering (super) heroine? The effects of sexualized female characters in superhero films on women. *Sex Roles, 72*(5–6), 211–220.

Rosenberg, R. S., Baughman, S. L., & Bailenson, J. N. (2013) Virtual superheroes: Using superpowers in virtual reality to encourage prosocial behavior. *PLOS One, 8*(1): e55003.

Rosenberg, R. S. & Canzoneri, J. (2008). *The psychology of superheroes: An unauthorized exploration*. Dallas, TX: Benbella Books

Rubin, L. (Ed.). (2006). *Using superheroes in counseling and play therapy*. New York: Springer.

Scarlet, J. (2017). *Superhero therapy: Mindfulness skills to help teens and young adults deal with anxiety, depression, and trauma*. Oakland, CA: Benbella Books.

Young, A. F., Gabriel, S., & Hollar, J. L. (2013). Batman to the rescue! The protective effects of parasocial relationships with muscular superheroes on men's body image. *Journal of Experimental Social Psychology, 49*(1), 173–177.

PART I

Superheroes, Super Theories

In this section, we will consider how some of the dominant psychosocial and clinical theories have been harnessed to bring the superhero into the therapeutic domain.

CHAPTER 1

Flourishing After the Origin Story: Using Positive Psychology to Explore Well-being in Superheroes and Supervillains

Sophia Ansari and Christina M. Scott

Our origin stories, the moments that change us and define us, are often born from our battles and our hardships rather than from our splendor and glory. After witnessing the murder of his parents, a young Bruce Wayne is faced with not only the enormity of his loss, but a decision—either allow the tragedy to destroy him or; instead, grip on to his relationships, connect with his inner strengths and find meaning and purpose in life. This would allow him to not bounce back from his trauma but—bounce *forward*. He ultimately chooses to take his hardship and heartache and channel them through eudemonic passages which lead to the birth of the vigilante, Batman. His transition into serving something greater than himself and finding conviction from his loss teaches us that tragic pasts do not necessarily have to lead to tragic futures. Batman's story of resilience and courage show us that one *can* thrive after devastation. It is possible to unearth our passion, purpose and maintain the joy we once experienced before the trauma, before the loss, before the depression and anxiety monsters reared their forbidding heads. Resilience is not some unattainable superpower; it is universal, and it can be harnessed (Letamendi, 2013).

Powering Up with Positive Psychology!

An area of psychology that focuses on cultivating strengths, relationships and finding meaning is positive psychology. Positive psychology is "the scientific study of what makes life worth living" (Peterson & Park, 2014, p. 2). For decades, the field of psychology was focused on pathologizing and centered on the question, "What is wrong with you?" Mental health professionals became preoccupied with repairing what was broken. Positive psychology's origin story thus began in response to this fixation of human weakness over human strengths (Seligman & Csikszentmihalyi, 2000). Martin Seligman and Mihaly Csikszentmihalyi, the pioneers of positive psychology, asserted that the question we should instead be asking is, "What is *right* with you?" Seligman and Csikszentmihalyi emphasized that our attention needed to be redirected on building upon what was working.

It is just as important to build on the best things in life as to repair the worst (Seligman, 1999).

In his book, *Flourish: A Visionary New Understanding of Happiness and Well-Being*, Seligman describes his theory of well-being and the five core pillars that are all worth cultivating to thrive or *flourish* (Seligman, 2011). These five elements allow individuals to connect with their positive emotions, strengths, purpose, accomplishments and build authentic relationships (Seligman, 2011). They include the following core elements, which will each then be elaborated:

- Positive Emotion. Feeling positive emotions, pleasure, gratitude, mindfulness, optimism.
- Engagement. Being fully absorbed in activities that use your strengths, are challenging and have a clear goal (flow).
- Relationships. Social connections, love. Fundamental to well-being.
- Meaning. Having a purpose, finding meaning in life. Belonging to and serving something you believe is bigger than yourself.
- Accomplishment. Mastery, ambition, pursuing success, achievement, pride in yourself.

Positive Emotion: World Domination is Overrated

The positive emotion element describes happiness as primarily sought through the senses (having tasty food, vacations, fast cars). Research has shown that feeling positive emotions contributes to our well-being in that it can result in a decrease in stress hormones and pain as well as elevate mood (Fredrickson, 2001). In fact, there is growing support that a propensity for humor and the implementation of laughter therapy groups can bring relief to physical and emotional pain (Kuru & Kublay, 2017). So, does that mean mercurial supervillains like the thrill-seeking Joker are happy? After all, he interprets everything as insanely funny (even when no one else gets the punchline). Seligman notes that worldly pleasures and indulgences make us feel good but so do positive interactions with others and cultivating gratitude, hope, optimism and utilizing mindfulness skills (Seligman, 2011). These elements are also an integral part of positive emotion and are skills that supervillains are not known to cultivate.

Larfleeze (also known as Agent Orange) is a supervillain hell-bent on the pursuit of all things pleasurable. His sole mission is to gain material wealth and power. Part of the Orange Lanterns Corps, Larfleeze is the wielder of the orange light of avarice. The emotional electromagnetic spectrum of the Lantern Corps is fueled by emotions of all sentient beings. Each color is unique to an emotion (White/Life; Red/Rage; Orange/Greed; Yellow/Fear; Green/Willpower; Blue/Hope; Indigo/Compassion; Violet/Love; Black/Death) ("Emotional Spectrum," n.d.). The Lantern Corps is comprised of many members; however, Larfleeze is the *only* member of the Orange Lantern Corps because of his unwillingness to share the power of the orange light. Greed at its finest and a lonely existence!

Pleasurable activities can be fine in moderation; however, supervillains tend to seek out pleasure in excess. Supervillains like the Joker and Larfleeze seek revenge and power at all costs necessary because it *feels good,* and they value the pleasure and put more weight on feeling good rather than feeling pain. After all, their origin stories most certainly involve a lot of pain and so they cling to the belief that pain is bad and pleasure is good (because it feels safer). This dark path inevitably leads to *experiential avoidance.* Experiential avoidance is the effort to avoid negative emotions, thoughts and bodily sensations by engaging in temporary acts of pleasure (Hayes, Strosahl, & Wilson, 1999). The avoidance serves as a coping and emotional regulation shield for feeling emotions, especially fear and sadness. Due to the unwillingness to experience these hurtful thoughts and feelings, supervillains cling to anger which serves as a protective agent from becoming hurt again. Never fully embracing their emotions, supervillains are easily led to the *dark side.* By resisting pain, they ultimately suffer.

Another drawback to the supervillain mind-set of solely seeking pleasure is that it habituates rather quickly, and we are confronted with a phenomenon known as the "hedonic treadmill" (Gilbert, 2006). This phenomenon, also known as hedonic adaptation, asserts that human beings easily become bored of the activities that once brought them happiness (Fritz, Walsh, & Lyubomirsky, 2017). Seligman warns that when we focus solely on pleasure and ignore the realm of meaning and discount our relationships and strengths, that we instead live a rather empty life (Seligman, 2002). Encapsulated by greed, no matter how much Larfleeze obtains it is never enough.

Engagement: The Superpower of Flow

Positive psychologists assert that pleasure is only one component of well-being and that we should also invest in our strengths, relationships, ambitions and find our purpose. *Engagement, Relationships, Meaning* and *Accomplishment* are all eudaimonic pillars to well-being. When we focus on these pursuits of personal growth, we avoid the empty life and consequently are more in line with our values, have a greater sense of efficacy and self-worth and live a very full life. Superheroes choose not to focus on hedonic motivations; rather, they choose to focus on eudaimonic motives such as contributing to something bigger than themselves. Instead of evaporating his inheritance, Bruce Wayne pours his wealth and resources into the creation of Batman to better Gotham City. In the film *Iron Man* (Feige, Arad, & Favreau, 2008), Tony Stark imbues hedonism, but as his story unfolds, we see a very different man. He begins to recognize how futile the pursuits of power, fame and big explosions had become after the loss of innocent civilian lives. We witness Tony's personal growth as he declares, "I had my eyes opened. I came to realize that I had more to offer this world than just making things that blow up" (Feige, Arad, & Favreau, 2008).

If we can identify our strengths and utilize them in our work, relationships and day to day lives, we can ultimately engage in our superpower of "flow." Flow is a phenomenon introduced by Csikszentmihalyi who became fascinated when artists became lost in their work. He described flow as a sense of time almost standing still when one is completely absorbed in whatever task they are engaged in (Csikszentmihalyi, 1997). The individual is so completely unified with the experience that they are in complete awe, they ignore all biological needs and time feels as though it is standing still. Flow, a great extension of our amazing human capabilities, is analogous to Dr. Strange's superpower of time manipulation through heightened and intense awareness and focus.

To experience flow, the individual must be employing their signature character strength (more on that later!). The activity should pose somewhat of a challenge and have clear, defined goals (Csikszentmihalyi, 1997). Engagement is not as raw as the feeling of pleasure but instead brings intrinsic value and reward. In the film *Iron Man* (Feige, Arad, & Favreau, 2008), Tony Stark is seen spending hours upon hours creating and perfecting the flight mechanics of the Mark II suit that he completely misses several calls made to him by his secretary. Tony was clearly engaging in his signature strengths of *creativity, love of learning* and *perseverance*. His goal of achieving sustained flight was eventually successful, but not without a few explosions and bruises along the way!

Positive Relationships: The Sidekicks Who Teach Us about Love

Positive relationships are the *most* fundamental element to well-being (Seligman, 2011). Bruce Perry, one of the world's leading experts on childhood trauma, has spent his career studying the mental, emotional and physiological effects of trauma in children, adolescents and adults. His research and experience in the field of trauma have shown that one of the key ingredients to overcoming adversity and trauma and building resilience is *relationships* (Perry & Szalavitz, 2017). How you are responded to by those around you will determine whether you are an individual who overcomes the trauma. Imagine for a moment if instead of asking the hurt child or adult, "What's wrong with you?" we asked, "What happened to you?" By instilling in them that their stories matter, we build trust and safety and offer compassion which are all ingredients to posttraumatic growth (PTG). Posttraumatic growth is the positive change that can occur after adversity (Calhoun & Tedeschi, 2013).

Now imagine for another moment some of the origin stories of our well-known supervillains. Let's take for example the story of Scarecrow, one of Batman's well-known adversaries. In the graphic novel *Batman: The Dark Knight, Vol. 2, No. 12* (Hurwitz & Finch, 2012), we learn about the origin story of Scarecrow. Born Jonathan Crane, Scarecrow grew up in a house where he was constantly subjected to cruel experiments by his father. His mother had died when he was very young, and his father was distant, cruel and obsessed with controlling fear. He would repeatedly lock Jonathan in a room filled with fear-inducing toxins. Jonathan was also relentlessly bullied at school. He had no social support. No one to talk to.

Nowhere had he felt safe. During one of the experiments, his father dies unexpectedly leaving young Jonathan trapped in the room for days. Jonathan grows up to become a man obsessed with controlling and creating fear. His traumatic childhood leads him on a trajectory to performing cruel experiments on others (including Batman) much like his father did unto him. It is well-known that "hurt people hurt people."

Attachment theory emphasizes that for healthy social and emotional development to occur, a child must have a positive relationship with at least one primary caregiver (Holmes, 2014). By securing this relationship the child is better able to learn to regulate emotions and grow up to secure other healthy relationships. When children are abused by a caregiver, that trust is drastically altered and a sense of safety and connection to others is severed. When attachment is insecure, children can grow up to experience a wide range of cognitive, behavioral, emotional, social and physiological disorders (Cassidy, Jones, & Shaver, 2013). Most origin stories of supervillains show a life of instability, loss, exposure to pain and trauma. Life perspectives are radically re-engineered. If we can engage in a conversation within the context of compassion and strength, we can reach out to the bullies and the bullied. If we ask, "What happened to you?" and point out strengths whenever we see them, we send the message that we see the superhero within and he/she can be accessed.

In the film *Logan* (Parker, Kinberg, Donner, & Mangold, 2017), we are given a unique glimpse into the relationship between Wolverine and Professor Xavier. Professor Xavier has long served as a mentor to Wolverine, always seeing through his tough exterior and reminding Wolverine of his inner strengths. He bestows wisdom to Wolverine on embracing love, stating "You know, Logan this is what life looks like. A home, people who love each other. Safe place. You should take a moment and feel it" (Parker, Kinberg, Donner, & Mangold, 2017). Batman's greatest ally, Alfred, provided a young Bruce with support and compassion. This allowed Bruce to experience a secure attachment. One that would help him channel his grief and access his inner hero. Without this relationship, both his civilian life and superhero life would probably implode. Superman's secure relationship with his parents and the values they instilled in him are brought forth in his relationships. Spider-Man's humor and optimism are a result of his nurturing upbringing by Aunt May. Scarecrow, however, had no such person to embrace him with love and empathy during those formative years when his worldview was transforming and moving into a downward spiral. What would have happened if he had his own Alfred or Aunt May? Things may have turned out differently for that young and afraid boy. As poignantly said by Kamala Khan in *Ms. Marvel, No. 17* (Wilson, Miyazawa, & Blake II, 2015), "Imagine what would happen if compassion were normal. Imagine how many people would still be here."

Superheroes must often figure out a balance between "superhero-ing" and their relationships. In the Netflix series *Daredevil* (Goddard, 2015), Matt Murdock tries to balance his life as a vigilante and as a lawyer. His best friend and law firm partner,

Foggy, is often left hanging out to dry at court depositions and trials when Matt goes off to thwart the bad guys. Karen, a woman who he develops feelings for (who also works at the law practice) is in a constant state of disappointment when Matt is nowhere to be found at work or during dinner dates. His vigilantism ends up pushing away Foggy and Karen. Even after learning of Matt's vigilante life, Foggy still fails to understand Matt's need to be Daredevil. At one point in the series, Matt states that he and the Daredevil are the same person and he refuses to apologize for being his true authentic self. Foggy views Matt's decision more as reckless behavior than a noble cause. Matt is left feeling unheard and isolated. He becomes depressed and pushes everyone away. Relationships are built on acceptance and trust; both lacking in Daredevil's complicated relationships. Karen, hiding dark secrets of her own, also alienates herself from Matt. Their secrets keep them apart. Matt does go on to eventually reveal his identity to Karen. A peace offering of trust to remove the distance between them.

Research has shown that when one individual in a relationship experiences Posttraumatic Growth (PTG), that the other individual in the relationship also reports an equivalent level of PTG (Tedeschi, Blevins, & Riffle, 2017). After tragedy, communities come together to support and enhance psychological growth of its members. We see unity and comfort provided in supergroups such as the X-Men, Avengers and Guardians of the Galaxy. In *Guardians of the Galaxy, Vol. 2* (Feige & Gunn, 2017), various relationships and group dynamics are explored and the recurrent theme is love. Interpersonal relationships between Rocket and Groot; Drax and Mantis; Star-Lord and Yondu; Gamora and Nebula, to name a few, show us how a group of misfits ultimately forge a unique bond of love and trust beyond the adversities they have each had to overcome.

Meaning: The Superhero Mission

Meaning encompasses belonging to and serving something greater than yourself (Seligman, 2011). By becoming outward focused (philanthropy, doing good in the world) we gain a sense of fulfillment and purpose in life which allows us to go on even after difficult circumstances. Viktor Frankl chronicles how he found meaning and purpose even as a prisoner in a Nazi concentration camp in his book, *Man's Search for Meaning* (Frankl, 1959). Frankl's heroic story teaches that we all have a choice in how we respond to tragedy. We can allow it to destroy us or we can vow to grow, move forward and find meaning. If we do not seek meaning, we will ultimately fill the void with hedonistic pursuits. A profound concept emphasized by Frankl is that "life has meaning under all circumstances, even the most miserable ones" (Frankl, 1959, p. 12).

Superheroes are intrinsically motivated to use their abilities and resources for good even after tragic life events. Superheroes exemplify altruism by fighting evil and standing up for justice, equality and peace. Rather than pursuing pleasure and material objects, billionaire superheroes like Batman, Iron Man and Green Arrow are philanthropists who give back to their communities and use their wealth to support their vigilante lifestyle (the Batmobile isn't cheap!). The positive relationships that superheroes have, offer love and comradery but also help to develop and instill values of compassion, courage and humility. These values drive superheroes to fight to give others a second chance much like they were given. This capacity for tapping in to personal strength and inner wisdom after trauma, loss and adversity show us that superheroes are meaning makers. As famously stated in the graphic novel which first introduced Spider-Man, *Amazing Fantasy, No. 15*, "With great power, there must also come—great responsibility!" (Lee & Ditko, 1962).

The supervillain Lex Luthor is also a well-known philanthropist. However, Lex Luthor is *not* intrinsically motivated. His obsession with vengeance and power stems from his jealousy of Superman, who is worshipped by the citizens of Metropolis. Resentment due to his own problematic relationships, especially with his father, lead him to become obsessed with destroying Superman. His highly intelligent mind is clouded with vengeance and his strengths are overshadowed by his neurotic obsession with power. Poison Ivy, who at first glance does appear to have altruistic intentions, values the environment; however, she is fueled by her hatred for those who destroy the planet, namely humans. Other villains like Vandal Savage are driven by boredom. Supervillains possess unique strengths and capabilities, but because they place the most value on feeling happy (focused on positive emotions only) they live a life unsatisfied and unfulfilled.

Accomplishment: Hanging Up the Cape for the Day Job

Accomplishment occurs when individuals pursue achievement, success and mastery for its own sake (Seligman, 2011). Setting goals and achieving them provides a sense of accomplishment. Not all superheroes need a second job. The billionaire superheroes certainly do not need the second income! What greater way to prove to yourself that you are more than just your cape, mask and super abilities than achieving or mastering a skill that takes brains over brawn? She-Hulk is a lawyer who defends superheroes as well as the poor, mentally ill and those who have had their civil liberties infringed upon. Spider-Man has mastered the art of photography. Beast offers his brilliance by teaching the youth at the Xavier Institute. Spectrum's leadership skills are demonstrated when she is leading the Avengers and serving as a police officer. She challenges herself by training to become an excellent swimmer and becomes a nautical expert and a skilled markswoman. This mindset of goal setting and perseverance must certainly give superheroes a competitive edge when facing new challenges and foes.

Unlocking Our Powers Through the VIA Inventory of Strengths

The VIA Inventory of Strengths supports all five elements (PERMA) of Seligman's and Csikszentmihalyi's model of well-being. Engaging in your character strengths leads to more positive emotions, flow, healthier relationships, meaning and accomplishments (Seligman, 2011). The VIA Classification is a cross-cultural common language describing the best qualities in human beings (Niemiec, 2017). Christopher Peterson and Martin Seligman collaborated with a team of scientists and traveled the world and spoke with people from all cultures, religions and backgrounds and what they found were six commonly valued virtues: Wisdom, Courage, Humanity, Justice, Temperance and Transcendence (Niemiec, 2017; Peterson & Seligman, 2004). The "pathways" to these virtues consist of 24 character strengths (Niemiec, 2017). Virtues, character strengths and their descriptions are included in Table 1.1. The historical analysis on character strengths is presented in the text written by Peterson and Seligman titled, *Character Strengths and Virtues: A Handbook and Classification* (Peterson & Seligman, 2004). Research has shown that when they are applied, they have a strong potential to boost well-being, improve relationships and foster resilience (Proyer, Ruch, & Buschor, 2013). The VIA Survey is a free, valid and reliable self-assessment tool. It is used globally and has been translated in over 37 languages.

The VIA lends itself beautifully to superhero work in that it assists individuals in grasping a better understanding of their true inner powers. Unlocking our character strengths allows us to power up our productivity and evolve into self-accepting, flourishing beings! The survey can be found at www.viacharacter.org. The VIA Survey for adults consists of 120 questions and the youth version (ages 10–17) includes 96 questions. Individuals rate the degree to which each statement represents them on a five-point scale (i.e., "I do the right thing even if others tease me for it."). A free report, which ranks the order of character strengths, is available immediately after taking the VIA Survey. All 24 character strengths exist in each human being and are expressed in varying degrees (Niemiec, 2017). The top five strengths are called "signature strengths" and are strengths an individual frequently uses. The signature strengths are core to our superhero identity. When we are engaging in these strengths we are energized and being our authentic selves. Think of a moment when you are passionate, your eyes light up and others are captivated by your enthusiasm and energy—that is a moment in which you are utilizing a signature strength! It is empowering to identify our signatures strengths in that it allows us to feel validated, seen and heard.

For those who do not have access to a computer or internet connection, an alternate option is to instead provide the client with a list of character strengths and their definitions and to ask the question, "Which of these strengths is most core to who you are and defines you as a person?" (Niemiec, 2017, p. 24). Ultimately you are asking, "Which strengths represent your core superpower?" The character strengths can be understood by children as young as 4 years old and have been utilized in preschools and elementary schools (Fox Eades, 2008). There are invaluable tools and resources on the VIA website including resources on how to support and implement the VIA Survey for youth with intellectual and developmental disabilities (Niemiec, Shogren, & Wehmeyer, 2017). To download kid-friendly definitions of the character strengths as well as strengths-based games visit: www.allourstrengths.com/resources/.

Table 1.1 VIA Classification

VIA Classification of Character Strengths and Virtues

Virtue of Wisdom

Creativity: Original, adaptive, ingenuity, seeing and doing things in different ways
Curiosity: Interest, novelty-seeking, exploration, openness to experience
Judgment: Critical thinking, thinking through all sides, not jumping to conclusions
Love of Learning: Mastering new skills and topics, systematically adding to knowledge
Perspective: Wisdom, providing wise counsel, taking the big picture view

Virtue of Courage

Bravery: Valor, not shrinking from threat or challenge, facing fears, speaking up for what's right
Perseverance: Persistence, industry, finishing what one starts, overcoming obstacles
Honesty: Authenticity, being true to oneself, sincerity without pretense, integrity
Zest: Vitality, enthusiasm for life, vigor, energy, not doing things half-heartedly

Virtue of Humanity

Love: Both loving and being loved, valuing close relations with others, genuine warmth
Kindness: Generosity, nurturance, care, compassion, altruism, doing for others
Social Intelligence: Emotional intelligence, aware of the motives and feelings of oneself and others, knows what makes others tick

Virtue of Justice

Teamwork: Citizenship, social responsibility, loyalty, contributing to a group effort
Fairness: Adhering to principles of justice, not allowing feelings to bias decisions about others
Leadership: Organizing group activities to get things done, positively influencing others

Virtue of Temperance

Forgiveness: Mercy, accepting others' shortcomings, giving people a second chance, letting go of hurt when wronged
Humility: Modesty, letting one's accomplishments speak for themselves
Prudence: Careful about one's choices, cautious, not taking undue risks
Self-Regulation: Self-control, disciplined, managing impulses, emotions, and vices

Virtue of Transcendence

Appreciation of Beauty and Excellence: Awe and wonder for beauty, admiration for skill and moral greatness
Gratitude: Thankful for the good, expressing thanks, feeling blessed
Hope: Optimism, positive future-mindedness, expecting the best and working to achieve it
Humor: Playfulness, bringing smiles to others, lighthearted—seeing the lighter side
Spirituality: Connecting with the sacred, purpose, meaning, faith, religiousness

Strengths-Based Interventions

Strengths-Spotting: Using Super Strengths Vision

The information gained from the VIA Survey can be used to create strengths-based interventions using our favorite heroes and villains. An exercise known as "strengths-spotting" involves identifying character strengths in others and in one-self (Niemiec, 2017). The client can be asked to identify character strengths that are present in a superhero or supervillain (using comics, books or scenes from television or film).

The film *The Hunger Games* (Jacobson, Kilik, & Ross, 2012) shows us a dystopia which consists of the wealthy, hedonistic Capitol of Panem, which rules over 12 impoverished districts. Every year children from the 12 districts are selected to participate in an obligatory annual televised death match. Katniss Everdeen finds herself volunteering to take the place of her younger sister, Primrose, who was selected to participate in the Hunger Games. This action alone demonstrates Katniss's *love* for her sister as well as *bravery, self-regulation, leadership* and *kindness*. In the games, her strengths of *perseverance, judgment* and *creativity* are apparent as she maneuvers and overcomes challenges presented to her. A substantial number of scenes in this film alone would lend itself beautifully to a strengths-spotting exercise!

To further the discussion of character strengths, the clinician can pose questions such as, "What character strengths would you need to survive the Hunger Games?" The conversation can then focus on the client's own strengths, allowing the individual to identify and list when he/she has demonstrated his/her signature strengths in specific times or through challenges. When has their inner superhero shone through? What were some ways that they demonstrated *bravery, hope, forgiveness*, etc.? Who is someone in their life that demonstrates these strengths? Strengths-spotting encourages a deeper level of understanding of the character strengths and reminds us that we utilize them daily in our lives. In the book, *Positive Psychology at the Movies: Using Films to Build Virtues and Character Strengths*, Ryan Niemiec and Danny Wedding provide a rich and in-depth discussion of character strengths and positive psychology themes in cinema as well as invaluable resources for the classroom and therapy (Niemiec & Wedding, 2014). A must-have for the pop culture loving positive psychologist!

Not all superheroes and supervillains possess extraordinary super abilities or magical powers. Batman's *spirituality* is demonstrated in his ability to find purpose (protecting the citizens of Gotham city) after suffering the tragic loss of his parents. His *love of learning* is demonstrated through his acquiring a breadth of knowledge in several areas of study such as sociology, psychology, geography, computer science, physics, criminology, the martial arts and so much more! He must rely on his strength of *bravery* which he uses to speak up in the face of injustice. Other heroes are given magic and gadgets but must still learn to harness their innate strengths to successfully and responsibly wield the powers given to them. Hal Jordan, a human who is part of the Green Lantern Corps, must utilize his *self-regulation* to wield the power of willpower via the Green Lantern ring. All heroes and villains, whether mortal or immortal, embody paragons of strengths and virtues and bring them forth in their missions and challenges.

Henry's evolution of strengths. Henry began seeing me (CS) for counseling services at the age of nine, following an unexpected loss of a close friend at his school. Henry had an extensive history of loss in his young life. He constantly expressed worry that he would also lose his mother. In our early sessions, it was clear that Henry was avoidant of any topics related to grief and loss. The one element in his life that was constant was his fervent passion for the game of Pokémon which was unmatched to any other interest he had. I knew then, that if I wanted to reach Henry and provide him with the guidance he needed to manage his fears and process his loss, I would need to do so with the help of Pikachu and Charizard. An important theme in the world of Pokémon is strengths utilization. These supernatural creatures use the strengths inherent within them to triumph in challenges and forge meaningful relationships through teamwork. Henry deeply resonated with Bulbasaur, Charmander, Pikachu and Pikachu's trainer, Ash.

We began the basics of emotional insight and awareness through creating Pokémon cards. With the character cards representing emotions and the energy cards symbolizing coping skills, Henry was able to face his difficult emotions and identify the impact his thoughts had on his daily functioning. Henry created cards to represent the intensity of his sadness and created character attacks and identified the hit points (HP) to convey the extent to which he felt affected by sadness. In his energy cards, Henry was able to explore safe places such as "school" and coping activities such as "playing with my dog." Due to Henry's cognitive limitations and level of functioning, I did not complete the VIA Survey with him. Instead, I implemented a list of strengths and replaced the terms with "Pokémon Natures," which I had learned from Henry were the equivalent of the Pokémon character strengths. From these Pokémon Natures, Henry chose his top strengths and was asked to create his own Pokémon based on these strengths. Included in the activity were the client's identified attacks (or ways he could utilize his strengths) and his weaknesses (or overutilization of his strengths). We also discussed where to find the Pokémon, in which Henry was asked to choose where he felt the most belonging. Through the lens of his favorite game/ television series, Henry identified using his "brave shield" which would protect him and applying his "honest blast" to others in which he could "blast someone with honesty" to discuss difficult topics.

As we continued our weekly Pokémon adventures, I began to observe a profound change in Henry's confidence and demeanor. During Henry's initial presentation, he appeared timid and anxious and he expressed self-doubt and uncertainty regarding his abilities. Through speaking the language of play, I was able to teach about character strengths and ultimately witness Henry flourish. He brought forth his Pokémon Natures (strengths) to his daily life and I had the profound honor of witnessing his real-life *evolution* into a healing and thriving superhero.

The adventures of Batman and Derrick. Derrick came to therapy with low self-esteem and a high regard for all things "superhero." His two favorite superheroes were Batman and Spider-Man. Our (CS) work together was centered on self-esteem building and working toward effectively processing and resolving the residual effects of grief earlier in the client's childhood. After contacting Derrick's parents to request permission to administer the survey, as the survey records all answers for research purposes, we planned a 45-minute session to complete the survey and process the experience. Using the youth version, I assisted in reading to him the questions and marked his chosen responses on the computer-based survey. For a student who had, on multiple occasions, expressed his dislike for academic activities, I expected some resistance in administering the survey. Derrick, however, responded well and maintained focus, sharing that he found the self-reflective experience enjoyable.

As we reviewed the results of the survey, Derrick expressed self-doubt and skepticism regarding his signature strength of *bravery*. I worked with Derrick in exploring his conceptualization of bravery, encouraging him to expand his perspective outside of the obvious superhero acts of bravery. "How do superheroes show strengths in their day jobs?" Derrick identified examples of Peter Parker taking care of his family and Bruce Wayne managing his stress level in a fast-paced work environment. Derrick eventually accepted the idea that he too possessed the strength of *bravery*, sharing that he would stand up for others who were being bullied; he wouldn't accept, however, that *bravery* was his top strength; instead he identified with *humor* and *creativity*. Derrick shared that one of his everyday villains is boredom and he fights this with his strengths of *creativity* and *humor*.

During one session when Derrick appeared particularly frustrated due to a recent math exam, he shared with me that he felt discouraged and unable to manage his negative self-talk. To provide him an ability to create a self-defined narrative which would highlight his strengths, Derrick was asked to create his own superhero. He created an intricate comic centered on his superhero self as he fought the evil nemesis called "Math Man." As Math Man aimed to paralyze his victims with debilitating fear of their math scores, Derrick's superhero was able to overcome these attempts at instilling fear and discouragement by using his inner strengths to defeat Math Man.

In the course of our work together, Derrick seemed to be having some social anxiety and low self-esteem. I helped him find a picture of his favorite superhero, Batman. I asked Derrick to explore all the strengths that Batman possessed and to write them on the picture. Derrick identified not only strengths Batman demonstrated (e.g., brave, strong, awesome) but also wrote down obstacles that Batman faced (e.g., lonely, isolated). As we processed this activity, Derrick shared that he identified with each of these traits, both positive and negative, and that he understood that if the great Batman could deal with occasional feelings of loneliness and social stressors, he could too! I encouraged Derrick to take some time to reflect on the compassion he showed for the complex character of Batman and turn that compassion inward to accept and care for himself (the healing power of self-compassion!).

Supergroups: Character Strengths in Numbers

Superheroes and supervillains demonstrate the importance of sharing their unique strengths to accomplish a task that may be difficult to accomplish individually. Supergroups such as the X-Men, Justice League, Avengers, Guardians of the Galaxy and Fantastic Four are prime examples of how different superheroes come together to serve a common mission. It is not enough to focus on their superpowers of flight, super strength and magic alone as these supergroups also bring their innate character strengths to each mission which allows the team to *flourish*. Group work and family sessions can include discussion and comparison of each group/family member's top five strengths as well as a discussion of the strengths they all have in common. Exploring how the X-Men come together or even struggle to embrace their roles due to inflated egos and miscommunications can serve to help illuminate the importance of teamwork and highlight various family dynamics.

Nina joins forces with her mom. As I (CS) worked with 10-year-old Nina, it became apparent that there was significant conflict in the home, between Nina and her mother. Nina had trouble with emotional regulation and would often act out and display volatile outbursts. Nina's mother reported a history of depressive symptoms and appeared overwhelmed and unmotivated to engage with Nina during these outbursts. The relationship between mother and daughter seemed to center on faults and problems.

I explained the VIA Survey to Nina and her mother during a family session, educating the two on the importance of maintaining an awareness and staying cognizant of our personal strengths. I had assigned Nina's mother the task of completing the survey for herself, while I worked with Nina in completing the youth survey during an individual session. When the three of us met for the following family session, we processed the results of both Nina's and her mother's surveys, exploring how we could use this insight to help build their mother-daughter relationship. It turned out that both Nina and her mother had as their top strength, *appreciation of beauty and excellence*. This provided them with a common ground and helped direct them toward shared interests and activities in which they could engage and build upon.

Subtract a Signature Strength: When Superman Loses His Powers

There have been several occasions when Superman has found himself no longer the Man of Steel, but simply, a man. Whether it be caused by Kryptonite or the use of his solar flare which drains him of his powers, Superman is no longer able to fly or hurl the bad guys through the air effortlessly without breaking a sweat. To add insult to injury, this powerlessness has even lead to the Fortress of Solitude not being able to recognize him and stripping him of his costume (who is Superman without the cape and tights?!)! When we look at our signature strengths, the core of who we are, we are reminded that without these qualities we would have great difficulty in sustaining our relationships, careers and our physical and mental health. Think for a moment if you could not use your signature strength for one day, month or year! What would that be like for you? Probably completely devastating! You would probably lose your job, relationships and be in despair. In his book, *Character Strengths Interventions: A Field Guide for Practitioners*, Ryan Niemiec discusses this intervention, known as "Subtract a Signature Strength" (Niemiec, 2017, p. CSI 5). In posing this question, individuals gain a deeper gratitude and appreciation for their signature strengths (Niemiec, 2017).

Overusing and Underusing Strengths: Finding a Balance of Power

Storylines involving our favorite heroes and villains also offer immense opportunities to observe and reflect on what happens when our favorite heroes and villains overuse and underuse their character strengths. What happens when Spider-Man loses his character strengths of *humility, gratitude, honesty* and *kindness* (underuse of strengths)? In the film *Spider-Man 3* (Ziskin, Arad, Curtis, & Raimi, 2007), Peter Parker's personality shifts after an extraterrestrial symbiote, known as Venom, attaches itself to his body. His Spidey suit turns black and causes Peter Parker/Spider-Man to act brash and arrogant. This malevolent version of himself results in a rift in his relationship with Mary Jane and affects him in his professional life, alienating him from his colleagues. Doc Ock, a genius engineer and inventor, and one of Spider-Man's greatest foes is a prime example of what can go wrong when one *overuses* a strength. Doc Ock's overuse of his strength of *love of learning* ultimately results in his detriment when he turns to a life of crime in order to finance his experiments (Ziskin, Arad, & Raimi, 2004). When a strength is overused an imbalance occurs and the strength is no longer a strength. Even being too brave can result in fatality!

   Abby's quest for balance. Teachers described 10-year-old Abby as impulsive and lacking focus. This "what's wrong" attitude inspired me (CS) to take a strengths-based approach with this young client. Abby would come to sessions excited to share with me stories about her week, shenanigans of her pet kitten as well as an eagerness to ask questions on a myriad of topics. Whereas I could have seen a young girl with impulsivity and distractibility, I saw a child who flourished in her *zest* for life, her *curiosity* of the world, and her *appreciation of beauty and excellence* in her experiences. It appeared that Abby overused these strengths to the point that other strengths were lowered (e.g., *judgment* and *self-regulation*). During administration of the survey (which can prove lengthy and challenging to some), we made a deal that Abby would stay focused long enough to complete a page of questions and would then be given an opportunity to tell one story. She responded well to this technique, and we completed the last several pages without any need to stop and refocus. Not to my surprise, the survey revealed that Abby's top strength was *appreciation of beauty and excellence*, which was illustrated in all her fun and enthusiastic story-telling. In processing the results of the survey, Abby explored how she could boost her lower strength of *self-regulation* to balance her top strengths of *zest* and *appreciation of beauty and excellence* in a way which would allow her to focus and still maintain her enthusiasm.

Using Your Superpowers in New Ways: The Sorting Hat Ceremony

Research has found that people who use one of their signature strengths in a new way each day for one-week experience an increase in happiness for six months (Gander, Proyer, Ruch, & Wyss, 2013). A fun and interactive intervention to allow the use of strengths in new ways is to write the signature strengths on slips of paper and place them in a jar or hat. For clients who embrace the world of Harry Potter, a witch hat can be used to imitate the sorting hat ceremony. Before the client leaves the session, he/she can be instructed to randomly draw a piece of paper from the hat. Whatever strength is picked will be the strength to focus on for the week. For example, if *kindness* is chosen the client will use that strength in a new way every day for a week (helping the teacher, sharing with a sibling, eating lunch with a student who eats alone). The client should observe and make note of how using the strength has benefited them at home or school, in their academics and in their relationships. This intervention can also be used with lower strengths to assist in "boosting" those strengths.

The superhero transformation of Anna. For some kids it's Superman, Batman and Wonder Woman; for others it's Dean and Sam Winchester from the television series *Supernatural* (Kripke, 2005). When my (CS) 17-year-old client, Anna, was having a difficult time with making friends and building confidence, we found a strengths-based approach in therapy to be most helpful. She was a fan of the television series *Supernatural* which revolves around two brothers who take on the forces of evil and are motivated to do so because of the value they place on love and family. During our sessions, we explored personal strengths through the lens of the show and found ways for Anna to fight her "demons" of social anxiety and self-doubt.

Through a strengths-spotting exercise using video clips from the show, we were able to identify Sam and Dean utilizing their strength of *bravery* in battling villains and in forming new and meaningful relationships. Anna was able to boost her strength of *bravery* and apply it to building her own social connections. We worked on social skills training to assist her in bringing forth the strength of *bravery* in new ways and practiced stepping outside of her comfort zone and into social circles. Anna reported improved confidence in her social interactions and was able to make new friends when she transferred to another school district. *Supernatural* helped to elevate Anna's self-acceptance and motivated her to expand her support system, and in doing so, she became the brave superheroine of her own story.

Personal Reflections

Making the superhero leap from a "What is wrong?" mentality to a "What is right?" mentality poses its challenges since this is not a model we are exposed to early on in our education and training. In helping clients identify and level up in their strengths, I (CS) too had to be mindful of my own strengths as a clinician. Oftentimes after a session, clinicians may fall in to an all familiar trap of focusing on what we could have said or done differently that would have provided greater insight. I began to realize that this supervillain mindset which revolves around focusing on my own insecurities and self-doubt took away focus from the meaningful work I do with my clients. Our ability to transform suffering in to healing and to sit with individuals in their pain and help them feel heard and validated is real superhero work! Let's remember that!

Rigid thinking or over-focusing on a client's top strengths can become an unintended effect when using a strengths-based approach. Initially, I (CS) had found myself solely focused on a client's signature strengths, realizing that in doing so, I had overlooked the client's other strengths as well as her less developed strengths—the superpowers that she needed extra help in boosting. I had to be mindful of not fixating on my clients' signature strengths as this would lead me down the road of labeling my clients as "the funny one," "the curious one," "the creative one." Ryan Niemiec offers insight and tips on how to avoid labeling our clients and reminds us that if we go down this road, we could lose sight of the entire picture that makes up our client (Niemiec, 2017).

In my (CS) work with a client I found myself challenging aspects of countertransference in that I could relate with the client's top strengths, as they mirrored my own. Due to that similarity, I found myself over-focusing on the client's top strengths, later realizing that I was placing my own eagerness to build these strengths. Maintaining self-awareness, doing your own strengths work outside of the sessions and striving for a balance can assist the therapist in correcting that overcompensation and make the healthy shift to a strengths-based approach.

When I (CS) was growing up (and still to this day), the superhero I looked up to the most was Buffy the Vampire Slayer. She didn't wear a cape and she didn't always look the part, but Buffy was the epitome of female empowerment. Buffy taught me that whether you're wearing leather and pummeling vampires or wearing pig-tails and trying to pass geometry, you are powerful. While Buffy and her Scooby Gang would fight against "the vampires, the demons and the forces of darkness" (Whedon, 1997), they would also go to battle in their relationships, in dealing with loss and rejection, and in finding their strengths. When I completed the VIA Survey and saw that my signature strengths were *kindness, creativity* and *humor*, I could easily see the earlier influences these characters had on me then and now. When Rupert Giles showed *kindness* to a young slayer and her group of eccentric friends, he provided the group with guidance and acceptance. Willow Rosenburg used *creativity* in her wit and resourcefulness to help defeat the villains time and time again. Xander Harris brought *humor* to a world that would otherwise stay dark. I developed, through this show and these characters, my own strengths and I can attest that through the therapeutic power of authentic storytelling, we too can become more aware of our own superpowers.

Conclusion

Adversity, trauma, loss and grief are inherent themes in superhero and supervillain stories. The Punisher bears witness to horrifying events abroad at war and then faces a much more devastating war at home, one that no one can win—his wife and two children are murdered. Storm was left orphaned after her parents are killed during war. Wolverine was brainwashed and weaponized by the government. Scarecrow was mentally and emotionally abused by his father. The Joker's wife and unborn child were killed. The Green Lantern, Simon Baz, faced Islamophobia. Batgirl became a paraplegic after being shot by the Joker. Origin stories serve a greater purpose than just providing the reader with a defining moment of when a character gains his/her superpowers or abilities. These origin stories and how they unfold teach us that loss and adversity can be debilitating and isolating and that there are varying ways adversity and trauma can radically transform our life perspective. Why do some characters turn inward and become enveloped in rage and revenge while others strike outward by saving others from a similar fate? The answer may lie in positive psychology's study of well-being.

Positive psychology aims to study positive experiences, the psychological state of flow, relationships, strengths of character and meaning and purpose. These elements also make up the healing potion of Posttraumatic Growth (PTG). For transformation and growth to occur, we must be able to count on our sidekicks, much like Batman who turns to Alfred Pennyworth for love and support. We must feel safe and accepted, much like if we were attending The Xavier School for Gifted Youngsters, an institute founded on fostering a safe environment for the X-Men. And we must engage in our inner strengths that will ultimately help us to focus on what we have gained rather than what we have lost.

In exploring well-being through the lens of superheroes and supervillains, it can be posited that superheroes live fuller lives than supervillains. Supervillains seek hedonic fulfillment while superheroes pursue more eudaimonic life paths. Superheroes and supervillains both have character strengths, yet the difference lies in how they use those strengths. Superheroes use their strengths to live a life of meaning by contributing to something bigger than themselves. While supervillains tend to be driven by pleasure, power and revenge. Some villains try to solve the world's problems, but morals and ethics are usually not the guiding force behind their decisions. While maintaining relationships can be difficult for superheroes, they do understand the importance of positive relationships and value their sidekicks, family and team members. Character strengths are key elements to well-being and superhero and supervillain stories lend themselves to strengths-spotting work. We can spot character strengths in our favorite heroes and then spot those same strengths within ourselves, leading to greater self-acceptance and connection to these characters we greatly admire. By reminding ourselves of our strengths (superpowers) and connecting with others (our sidekicks), we too can create our own stories of triumph and beauty.

Questions for Clinical Discussion

1. Take the VIA Survey at www.viacharacter.org. Reflect on your results. How do you/will you use *your* strengths in your professional and personal life?
2. Who is your favorite superhero? How does this superhero embody some of your signature strengths?
3. A clinician can demonstrate the strengths-spotting intervention by showing video clips of movies/TV shows to increase a client's understanding of strengths. What movie/TV show/comic book scenes can you think of which might be helpful in demonstrating each of the character strengths?
4. "The 24 character strengths, as a group, are a common language that describe what is best in human beings" (Niemiec, 2017, p. 2). How can you begin to utilize and spread this language within your practice or organization?
5. What positive psychology themes of well-being (PERMA) can you identify in your favorite superhero and supervillain stories?

References

Calhoun, L. G. & Tedeschi, R. G. (2013). *Posttraumatic growth in clinical practice*. New York: Routledge.

Cassidy, J., Jones, J. D., & Shaver, P. R. (2013). Contributions of attachment theory and research: A framework for future research, translation, and policy. *Development and Psychopathology, 25*, 1415–1434. http://doi.org/10.1017/S0954579413000692

Csikszentmihalyi, M. (1997). *Finding flow: The psychology of engagement with everyday life*. New York: Basic Books.

Emotional Spectrum. (n.d.). Retrieved June 8, 2018 from the Comic Vine Wiki: https://comicvine.gamespot.com/emotional-spectrum/4015-49955/

Feige, K. (Producer) & Gunn, J. (Director) (2017). *Guardians of the Galaxy, vol. 2* [Motion picture]. Burbank, CA: Walt Disney Studios Motion Pictures.

Feige, K., Arad, A. (Producers), & Favreau, J. (Director) (2008). *Iron Man* [Motion picture]. Hollywood, CA: Paramount Pictures.

Fox Eades, J. (2008). *Celebrating strengths: Building strengths-based schools*. Warwick, UK: CAPP Press.

Frankl, V. (1959). *Man's search for meaning*. New York: Simon & Schuster.

Fredrickson, B. L. (2001). The role of positive emotions in positive psychology: The broaden-and-build theory of positive emotions. *American Psychologist, 56*, 218–226. http://doi.org/10.1037/0003-066x.56.3.218

Fritz, M. M., Walsh, L. C., & Lyubomirsky, S. (2017). Staying happier. In: M. D. Robinson & M. Eid (Eds.), *The happy mind: Cognitive contributions to well-being* (pp. 95–114). Cham, Switzerland: Springer.

Gander, F., Proyer, R. T., Ruch, W., & Wyss, T. (2013). Strength-based positive interventions: Further evidence for their potential in enhancing well-being and alleviating depression. *Journal of Happiness Studies, 14*, 1241–1259. http://doi.org/10.1007/s10902-012-9380-0

Gilbert, D. (2006). *Stumbling on happiness*. New York: Alfred A. Knopf.

Goddard, D. (Creator) (2015). *Daredevil* [Television series]. New York: Netflix.

Hayes, S. C., Strosahl, K., & Wilson, K. G. (1999). *Acceptance and commitment therapy: An experiential approach to behavior change.* New York: Guilford Press.

Holmes, J. (2014). *John Bowlby and attachment theory* (2nd edn.). London: Routledge.

Hurwitz, G. & Finch, D. (2012). *Batman: The dark knight, Vol. 2, No. 12.* Burbank, CA: DC Comics.

Jacobson, N., Kilik, J. (Producers), & Ross, G. (Director) (2012). *The Hunger Games* [Motion picture]. Santa Monica, CA: Lionsgate Films.

Kripke, E. (Producer) (2005). *Supernatural* [Television series]. British Columbia, Canada: Warner Bros. Television Distribution.

Kuru, N. & Kublay, G. (2017). The effect of laughter therapy on the quality of life of nursing home residents. *Journal of Clinical Nursing, 26*(21–22), 3354–3362. http://doi.org/10.1111/jocn.13687

Lee, S. & Ditko, S. (1962). *Amazing Fantasy, No. 15.* New York: Marvel Comics.

Letamendi, A. (2013, May 21). Superheroine recovery: An interview with Batgirl's therapist (T. Langley, Interviewer). *Psychology Today.* Retrieved from www.psychologytoday.com/us/blog/beyond-heroes-and-villains/201305/superheroine-recovery-interview-batgirls-therapist

Niemiec, R. (2017). *Character strengths interventions: A field guide for practitioners.* Boston, MA: Hogrefe Publishing.

Niemiec, R. M., Shogren, K. A., & Wehmeyer, M. L. (2017). Character strengths and intellectual and developmental disability: A strengths-based approach from positive psychology. *Education and Training in Autism and Developmental Disabilities, 52*(1), 13–25.

Niemiec, R. M. & Wedding, D. (2014). *Positive psychology at the movies: Using films to build character strengths and well-being* (2nd edn.). Boston, MA: Hogrefe Publishing.

Parker, H., Kinberg, S., Donner, L.S. (Producers), & Mangold, J. (Director) (2017). *Logan* [Motion picture]. Los Angeles, CA: 20th Century Fox.

Perry, B. & Szalavitz, M. (2017). *The boy who was raised as a dog: And other stories from a child psychiatrist's notebook—What traumatized children can teach us about loss, love, and healing.* New York: Basic Books.

Peterson, C. & Park, N. (2014). Meaning and positive psychology. *International Journal of Existential Psychology & Psychotherapy, 5*(1), 2–8. Retrieved from http://journal.existentialpsychology.org/index.php/ExPsy/article/view/196

Peterson, C. & Seligman, M. E.P. (2004). *Character strengths and virtues: A handbook and classification.* New York: Oxford University Press; Washington, DC: American Psychological Association.

Proyer, R. T., Ruch, W., & Buschor, C. (2013). Testing strengths-based interventions: A preliminary study on the effectiveness of a program targeting curiosity, gratitude, hope, humor, and zest for enhancing life satisfaction. *Journal of Happiness Studies, 14*(1), 275–292. http://doi.org/10.1007/s10902-012-9331-9

Seligman, M. E. P. (1999). *Transcript of a speech given by Dr. Martin E. P. Seligman at the Lincoln Summit in September of 1999.* Retrieved from www.sas.upenn.edu/psych/seligman/lincspeech.htm

Seligman, M. E. P. (2002). *Authentic happiness.* New York: Free Press.

Seligman, M. E. P. (2011). *Flourish: A visionary new understanding of happiness and well-being.* New York: Free Press.

Seligman, M. E. P. & Csikszentmihalyi, M. (2000). Positive psychology: An introduction. *American Psychologist, 55*(1), 5–14. http://doi.org/10.1037/0003-066X.55.1.5

Tedeschi, R. G., Blevins, C. L., & Riffle, O. M. (2017). Posttraumatic growth: A brief history and evaluation. In: M. A. Warren & S. I. Donaldson (Eds.), *Scientific Advances in Positive Psychology* (pp. 131–163). Santa Barbara, CA: Praeger.

Whedon, J. (Producer) (1997). *Buffy the Vampire Slayer* [Television series]. Los Angeles, CA: 20th Century Fox Television.

Wilson, G. W., Miyazawa, T., & Blake II, N. (2015). *Ms. Marvel, No. 17*. New York: Marvel Comics.

Ziskin, L., Arad, A. (Producers), & Raimi, S. (Director) (2004). *Spider-Man 2* [Motion picture]. Culver City, CA: Columbia Pictures.

Ziskin, L., Arad, A., Curtis, G. (Producers), & Raimi, S. (Director) (2007). *Spider-Man 3* [Motion picture]. Culver City, CA: Columbia Pictures.

CHAPTER 2

Alter Egos and Hidden Strengths: The Powers of Superheroes in Child-Centered Play Therapy

LaTrice L. Dowtin

Introduction

Children are powerful creatures who are often underestimated because of their inclination to play. Often, adults regard play as frivolous and without purpose. However, play is how children learn. Play allows children to engage in the rehearsal of their immediate surroundings, recall recent events and transfer them from short-term to long-term memory (Hamilton, Reas, & Mansfield, 2017; Narimani, Soleymani, Zahed, & Abolghasemi, 2014). While play increases learning potential, it can also help heal children who have been through difficult and traumatic events. Specifically, child-centered play therapy (CCPT) provides children with the unique opportunity to access skills, powers and resources through the support of a skilled play therapist so that they can re-write their own story. Play therapists equipped with the ability to follow their client's lead and needs, and who are guided by CCPT principles, need the assistance of toys. Therefore, play therapy rooms that are stocked with superheroes and superheroines encourage children's expressions of their daily exterior shells, as well as their hidden inner strengths. This chapter lays the foundation for the selection, usage, and potential therapeutic interpretations of superheroes from a CCPT framework. Characters such as Supergirl, Iron Man, the Flash, Captain America and Wonder Woman are considered in this chapter as catalysts to a discussion on representation. Moreover, the author explores significant considerations for gender, culture, and ability as they impact, benefit and influence young children through a CCPT lens.

Child-Centered Play Therapy

According to the seminal work of Carl Rogers (1959), person-centered theory was built on the premise that all people want to be fully functioning; however, sometimes they are missing relational aspects in their lives that cause conflict, stir their anxiety and that damage their functionality. Thus, the relationship between client and therapist can be a foundation of healing. With the relationship as the foundation, person-centered therapy identifies three therapeutic factors; empathy (empathic understanding), congruence (also sometimes referred to as genuineness), and unconditional positive regard (Sharf, 2012). Person-centered therapists use these therapeutic factors as facilitators while they figuratively walk alongside their client, as they emerge from injured to restored beings. The belief is that the client is the only one who internally knows what the client needs to heal. While the client may be blind to what is dangerous, they are often the expert in what is safe. Thus, the therapist's job is to be *with* the client, be a companion and reflection of the client on their journey so that the person can experience genuine acceptance (Rogers, 1959).

Child-centered play therapy (CCPT) is guided by the early work of Rogers' person-centered and client-centered theories (Rogers, 1951) and blossomed through the teachings of play therapists such as Virginia Axline and Garry Landreth (Hartwig, 2017). Similar to Rogers, CCPT has three curative factors: the person, the phenomenal field, and the self (Landreth, 2012). That is, behaviors, feelings, ideas, and physical being are the *person*—the child. The child works or plays toward a goal to satisfy a need. Play meets the child's psychological needs. Children reveal their experiences, their perceptions of reality, their self-concept and their internal desires when engaged in CCPT (Landreth, 2012). Therapists often want to interpret the child's play. However, interpretation is not necessary for children to feel at peace with what they have experienced; the safe relationship is needed.

The *phenomenal field* is the child's more readily available environment, both internally and externally (Landreth, 2012). Therefore during play, the therapist's experience is constitutionally different from the child's reality. For the therapist, the child is playing in a make-believe world. For the child, in the moment of play, make-believe is fact. Still, the person and the phenomenal field are not enough to create a healthy child; the child needs the *self* to be complete (Landreth, 2012; Rogers, 1951). The hypothesis is that the *self* grows due to direct interaction with the phenomenal field (Landreth, 2012). Many present-day play therapists believe that this is the link between person-centered and CCPT, such that the child directs the therapist's journey through the child's internal psychological world.

A competent CCPT practitioner demonstrates the capacity to sometimes ignore a sense such as sound and increase their use of sight. The active play therapist understands the heightened value of their eyes in this therapeutic approach. The words that children use during their play therapy session are often internal speech made audible. This speech is not necessarily for the consumption of others, but rather for the internal processing and understanding of the speaker—the child. What is important for the play therapist is knowing that play is how the child communicates in session (Landreth, 2012). That means a child's play is powerful, much more so than verbal expression. A therapist who is watchful and thoughtful will notice that the child's actions tell their story. The therapist is to show acceptance of the child's expressed thoughts, feelings and desires (Landreth, 2012). This acceptance builds the capacity of trust within the relationship between therapist and child. The child learns that they are safe to express what has happened to them and to demonstrate how they feel about it.

In CCPT, the therapist engages in affect reflection of the child's emotions. The therapist wonders aloud with the child and empowers the child using unconditional positive regard and the fervor of the child-therapist relationship (Landreth, 2012). In that respect, CCPT is like a dance; a conversation using the child's natural language of play, rather than like a precise mirror. Child-centered play therapists understand that play is an active ingredient in the therapy for a child because words fall short on providing an outlet for the child whose language is still developing. Play is universal, while spoken and signed languages are not (Dowtin, 2018). This key point is important when considering Deaf (children and adults who are cultural members of the Deaf community are denoted with a capital "D," while the medical classification of being deaf is written with a lowercase "d," Leigh, Andrews, & Harris, 2016) and hard-of-hearing children. In CCPT, the nonverbal impact, the use of space and facial expressions have the strongest power over the child's ability to heal (Landreth, 2012). Research has suggested that some play therapists believe that when working with Deaf children, verbal language, both spoken and signed, can interfere with the nonverbal aspects of CCPT (Dowtin, 2018). Therefore, a play therapist's capacity for observation, a deep understanding of trauma, a strong conceptualization of child development, their guiding theoretical orientation and an appreciation for the specific child in the play therapy room outweighs the play therapist's talent for interpreting verbal language.

As therapists demonstrate their superpowers with helping young traumatized children express themselves and regain their strength, children engaged in CCPT frequently find themselves needing the external support of other superheroes. The toys that line our shelves as play therapists provide children with opportunities to fight battles, win and lose, as superheroes do. Therefore, it is vital that CCPT therapists understand the storylines of dominant, and sometimes minor, superheroes. No child deserves to share a story, traumatic or otherwise, with a CCPT therapist who does not understand enough of the backstory to truly immerse themselves in the journey.

Character Analyses

America Under Attack: The Boy Who Saves Us

Currently, one of the most popular superheroes is Captain America (Ranker Comics, 2018). He was born out of the desperation of World War II (WWII) when American children needed something to smile about during the hard times of the war. The first Captain America comic book was published in 1941 (*Captain America Comics*, 2018), which was almost the middle of WWII. At that time, it seemed like the war was never going to end with it lasting from 1939–1945 (the original comic series ceased in 1950). Looking back, it is clear why he was such a popular superhero; he was the ideal soldier saving North America from invaders.

It is palpable that boys can still hang their hearts on Captain America and dream that they, too, will grow into big and strong men. He has a classic backstory that many young boys can relate. He was the small, weak boy who grew into a fearless leader and hero. His alter ego, or original self, Steven "Steve" Rogers, was fragile and often sick as a child (Feige et al., 2011). He was a White male who was insignificant in size when compared to others his age, and his peers bullied him. He did not have many friends but had a kind heart and wanted to help. For Steve, joining the military was a way to help his country and show that he had grown into a man. Through experimental testing, Steve eventually emerged as Captain America, fearless, mighty, capable, healthy, tall, and even handsome (Feige et al., 2011).

Captain America can provide children with the power to play their story using a character who has seen two sides to their life and lives to tell about it. He lived as an almost invisible person who was only detectable when being teased. Anyone who saw Steve before he became Captain America would likely agree that he had a difficult social life. However, he has also seen the side of life where he is respected and powerful. That is the side of life that some boys long to realize for themselves. Sometimes, young boys who enter the play therapy room and select Captain America as their alter ego are trying to tell their story. They are trying to experience life in the manner that they presume Captain American experiences life, with resilience and fury. However, beneath that fury, there is a tiny boy who is struggling through social situations, has difficulty making and maintaining relationships in his peer group, and perhaps, needs moments during CCPT when he feels empowered and victorious. While clinical diagnoses are not at the forefront of CCPT, in today's managed healthcare, diagnoses are a relative component of mental health treatment. Sometimes social struggles are associated with diagnoses of attention-deficit hyperactivity disorder (ADHD), which is something to consider when children enter the play therapy room (Panksepp, 2007).

In a Flash: Saved by the Boy Next Door

Similar to Steve, Barry Allen (not to be confused with the original Flash, Jay Garrick released in 1940; *Flash Publication History*, 2018) was a White male who was a kind and unassuming child. He lived through traumatic events such as partially witnessing his mother's murder (Berlanti, Johns, & Kreisberg, 2014). Barry experienced another traumatic event when his father was arrested and sentenced to a life term for allegedly murdering Barry's mother. He was smarter than he was swift as a child. As Barry grew, he became described as the good-natured boy next door who fights crime using science. Barry is a crime scene investigator or forensic scientist (*Flash Publication History*, 2018) who is wickedly devoted to solving crimes. However, he is slow and clumsy. Then, he is struck by lightning from a particle accelerator and left in a coma for nine months. (Berlanti, Johns, & Kreisberg, 2014). Soon after he wakens from his coma, his alter ego awakens. Barry discovers that he is the fastest man alive. He is a speedster. He is the Flash. As the Flash, Barry has endless potential and can decide how to use his powers. He chooses to use them to solve crimes and imprison criminal meta-humans (humans who have exceptional powers resulting from the same accident that awarded Barry his speed). Even more astonishing is that becoming the Flash allows Barry to build self-confidence. He is no longer this slow, clumsy and somewhat awkward person. He is quick, agile and witty.

There are several reasons that a child may gravitate towards the Flash in the play therapy room. A child may want to experience his speed. Some children are expressing that they are trying to quickly run away from or run toward something that is presently not within their reach. Children with diagnoses of ADHD (any type), posttraumatic stress disorder (PTSD), social anxiety disorder, selective mutism and adjustment disorder based on the diagnostic statistical manual 5th edition (DSM-5) criteria may select the Flash as their alter ego in the play therapy room, the Flash may allow them to practice the skills that frighten them or they may choose to express the characteristics that they share with him. For example, Barry Allen is shy and socially awkward, while the Flash is fearless and outgoing.

Iron Man: Heroes Are Not Born, They Are Built

From a different angle but along the same path as Barry Allen's intelligence, we meet Iron Man whose alter ego is Tony Stark (Pearce, Black, & Feige, 2013). In Tony, we find nearly unmatched intellect. He introduces readers and viewers to a man who is so brilliant that he invents means to successfully operate on himself, save his own life, and remarkably turn himself into one of the fiercest superheroes that the world has ever seen—Iron Man. While Tony has a backstory, much of what is known about him is that before he became Iron Man, he was one of the wealthiest men in the world (Pearce, Black, & Feige, 2013). He inherited some of his riches and the rest he acquired through his technological inventions at Stark Enterprises. This makes Iron Man unique in that his alter ego's story is not riddled with hardship and agony in the way most often conceptualized for superheroes. Tony was already wildly successful before he assumed the role of Iron Man.

Tony shows children that they can be smart and have brawn. He reinforces the stereotype that boys are great at science, technology, engineering and mathematics. In essence, his message is that if you cannot physically fight on your own, you can invent a piece of technology that can do it for you. Unlike most of the other superheroes, Iron Man can fly and fire missiles. He is a one-man military unit. He is also massively destructive when he fights. It is fathomable that a child who identifies with Iron Man may admire his ability to save the day, while also relishing in his tendency to cause colossal explosions. Research suggests that children with complex trauma histories either have over or under controlled emotional and behavioral regulation (Cook et al., 2017). Re-enacting explosions and destruction through the imagery of Iron Man missiles may be revealing of a child who feels little control over many aspects of their life. In the play therapy room, these children may need help practicing assertiveness and may need to feel empowered and in control when appropriate.

Minority Uprising: An Ongoing Revolution

To the observant play therapist, there has been a theme in the characters discussed thus far in this chapter. We met the kind and stoic White American male who saves us all; the intelligent boy next door, White male speedster, who dashes to fight crime; and the genius White male billionaire who can destroy anything in his wake. All three of these characters provide children and CCPT therapists with cavernous dimensions for understanding, processing and healing from trauma and challenging events. However, characters such as these seem to imply that only White men have strength. In their silver screen versions, all of these characters have minority sidekicks, though, to date, there has only been one movie with a racial and cultural minority cast with a leading superhero of non-White origin (Jao, 2018). Statistically, the most popular superheroes to make it to mainstream media have traditionally been White males (Jao, 2018). If one were to review all of the major superhero movies from 1978 when the first Superman hit the silver screen to 2014, the revelation would be that over 90% of them had a White male as the main hero (Aucoin, 2014). That revelation, though perhaps shocking given North American racial and ethnic demographics, makes sense because comic book credits reveal that approximately 70% of comic book contributors are white and over 90% of comic book credits are men (Hanley, 2016). Furthermore, it was not until 2017 when Wonder Woman hit the silver screen (Dockterman, 2017) during a resurgence of feminism in the United States. After Wonder Woman produced record-breaking numbers in the box office (Hughes, 2017) and took a stance for girls and women, a groundbreaking major motion picture in the superhero genre was released on February 16, 2018, The Black Panther. The Black Panther superhero movie was comprised of an almost entirely Black, African and African-American cast and characters (Grant, Feige, & Coogler, 2018). Interestingly, the Black Panther character made his silver screen debut in one of the Captain America movies, which provided the platform to launch the Black Panther into its own movie.

Children are greatly influenced by what is and what is not portrayed in the media. Young children use representations of their images in media to show what is possible for them to dream for themselves. Children who read comic books or watch superhero movies spend time fantasizing over what could be true for them. The wonder and amazement that occurs when a child becomes absorbed into witnessing a marvelous character save the day has endless possibilities for a positive impact on their self-image. Black psychologist Amos Wilson (1978/2014) stated, "more important than the comic themselves is what the child brings to the comic book reading situation and what he takes away from it" (p. 121). The notion that the media impacts childhood experiences and interpretation of self is demonstrated in the numbers. With the release of each superhero movie, society experiences an increase in the particular superhero's paraphernalia and children pretending to be those characters. Statistics show that the popularity of US Halloween costumes can be predicted, to some reasonable extent, based on the most recent release of a superhero movie (Ho, 2016).

The children who enter our playrooms do not exist within bubbles. They are complex and emotionally rich people who deserve to be seen and treated as such. That means it is important to consider complete selves including gender and cultural expression. It can be argued that these components of children's personalities are so germane to who they are that they should be at the forefront of thought among clinicians when beginning case conceptualizations, when setting up their play therapy rooms and when interacting with children and caregivers.

Supergirl: The Sister and the Fighter

Supergirl was arguably the first female character in modern-day media to remind audiences that women can be supers too. She debuted in a television series in October 2015 with much hype and campaigning for girls and women to watch (Rosenberg, 2015). Not since the Wonder Woman television series in the 1970s, had America rallied around to watch a female superhero take over their screens on a weekly basis. Supergirl's induction into the small screen presence was a step in the right direction. However, the fact that it took 63 years following the first airing of the original Superman television series for Supergirl to obtain a television show demonstrates the preference placed on male superheroes.

Cousin to Superman, Supergirl is brave, strong, has X-ray vision, and can fly, while maintaining her femininity in her attire, flowing golden hair and makeup. As Kara Danvers, her alter ego, she is clumsy, kind and meek. She rarely asserts herself and never shows aggression (Grassi et al., 2016). However, once she finds her hidden strength, she releases her powers for the first time to save her human sister. Kara fades as Supergirl emerges to live a double life often sacrificing Kara's happiness for Supergirl's responsibilities as National City's savior and protector. Supergirl cares about the greater good. She works tirelessly daily to protect the people in the city that she loves. She often fails the first time and is known to turn evil when drugged or controlled by villains. When this happens, Supergirl expresses immense guilt for not being strong enough to initially fight off powers of mind control or for realizing too late that she had been drugged.

Supergirl brings somewhat uncomplicated interpretations to the playroom. She lives in her cousin's shadow but only slightly. While Supergirl is able to exert her independence as a formidable superheroine, doing so causes her sadness in her personal life when she is Kara. With each episode, Kara and Supergirl are learning to co-exist. This turmoil uniquely shows audiences, girls and women, that it is not only acceptable to make mistakes, but it is always permissible to try again. Supergirl often fails on her first and second attempts at defeating a supervillain and occasionally she considers giving up, but she never actually quits. Therefore, in many ways she is a representation of fortitude. Children who select Supergirl to share their story, may be struggling with feelings of guilt and may be trying to discover how to learn from their experiences to keep moving forward. Often, Supergirl wins. She is fierce and relentless in her pursuit to save those that she loves. Child-centered play therapists can use their knowledge of Kara and Supergirl to foster resilience in their child clients. She is an excellent example of the power of empathy. While Kryptonite is said to be her weakness, supervillains have often said that Supergirl's most predictable quality is her *big figurative heart* or her empathy and love for others (Grassi et al., 2016). Play therapists can highlight her empathy to empower clients. Empathy is a strength, not a weakness.

Wonder Woman: No Men Allowed

Diana Prince, or Princess Diana in the major motion picture, is an Amazonian warrior from an all-female kingdom on Paradise Island (Snyder, Snyder, Roven, Suckle, & Jenkins, 2017). Raised by strong warrior royalty, her mother and aunt, she is destined to take the helm after her mother dies in battle. Diana travels with a male soldier to help defeat a human villain and ends up battling a supernatural entity as Wonder Woman. Throughout the movie, initially people—men, leap to protect Wonder Woman and they continually assume that she is a frail woman when they first meet her; however, repeatedly she proves that she does not need defending. She recurrently saves male soldiers without fear and charges ahead to complete her mission.

Unlike any other female superheroines, supporting characters and sidekicks, Wonder Woman does not know what it is like to live in a patriarchal society. She knows nothing of condescending and harmful beliefs about the presumed inadequacies of women. Wonder Woman only knows the power that she possesses, and she believes that she can overcome anything; her self-concept and self-esteem are solidified in the fact that she *can*. She has never experienced self-doubt solely in relation to her gender. Therefore, Wonder Woman is different from any girl raised in America or in most other countries. She epitomizes confidence and redefines the terms superhero and superheroine.

When play therapists are trying to present examples of strength for their clients, Wonder Woman might not be a far reach. Both because of and regardless of gender, she has the potential to erupt in CCPT empowering those who tell part of their story through her eyes. Play therapists should watch carefully as children use Wonder Woman. She is a superhero who has had many reinventions and remains a character that women, girls, men, boys and others admire.

The tapestry of human existence. Characters such as Supergirl and Wonder Woman make a step in the direction of equality for women in powerful superhero roles. With occasional attempts to bring people of color and people with varying exceptionalities to the mainstream, the superhero genre in movie and television format leaves much room for inclusion. While Black Panther has made box office history, the comic book series Black Lightning that includes a father and two superhero daughters as the main superheroes has begun to dazzle audiences with an all-Black cast (Rose, 2018). This means that weekly, viewers can see images of themselves in all of the complexities of human relationships. This superhero show depicts Black people in roles of hope, triumph, destruction, villainy and all-powerful goodness. It is no doubt that Black Panther on the larger screen made way for Black Lightning on the small screen. Perhaps, Black Lightning has cracked the door open for other groups to be portrayed as superheroes.

Toy Considerations. As CCPT play therapists, it is important to consider the needs of all children who may benefit from CCPT. This means considering their race, culture, gender, abilities, various family structures and children's multiple identities. Child-centered play therapists have a responsibility to ensure that the toys and miniatures available to the children in their playroom allow them to fully express the intricate nature of human experiences. Many play therapy rooms have toys related to the previously mentioned characters as they are well-known and readily available through many different sources. Equally, it is likely that just as many play therapy rooms are void of appropriate representations of diversity that use less commonly discussed characters.

Some comic book heroes have been depicted as differently abled such as deaf, blind, or using assistive devices to walk. Hawkeye, a comic book hero in the line of Marvel Avengers, becomes deaf. Depending on the version, he uses either a hearing aid or American Sign Language (ASL) to communicate and continue fighting evil supervillains. Marvel Comics also created Blue Ear who is a deaf superhero who prominently wears a blue hearing aid. Echo is a little-known superheroine who is Native American and deaf and sometimes assumes the role of Ronin. Most people think Ronin is a man until she reveals herself as Echo. She has made a new resurgence as she has appeared on the Netflix series, Daredevil, and potentially provides a space to include acceptance of the fluidity of gender expression. Similarly, Daredevil, although perhaps a character for older children and adult audiences, is also a character of different abilities. Daredevil is blind and learned to use his other senses to fight villains in the nights of New York City. These characters and what they symbolize for children, should be incorporated into the play therapy room. While it is important that CCPT play therapist remain current with some of the popular characters that are available in the present, it is equally important that play therapy rooms expose children to a broader range of experiences than they receive from mainstream media outlets. Additionally, while traditional client-centered play therapists do not utilize scripted characters or figures drawn from popular culture, play therapists who value the metaphor of the superhero may choose to incorporate these particular toys and symbols into their play therapy room.

Case Applications

When Supervillains Come to Play

In times of false empathy and uncertainty, children have the ability to find safety and healing in the special powers of unconditional positive regard, empathy, genuineness and superheroes. Equipped with their special—their super powers, children can battle and conquer their supervillains. Too often, supervillains present in forms of once trusted adults, family cars, cozy places in the home and so many other shapes.

Right in front of the child's eyes, these positive people, places and things sometimes morph into traumatic events. The once trusted adult fades, while the villain emerges from the darkness of his layer and touches the child in painful, seemingly unspeakable ways. The fun family car transforms into a beast that traps the child and nearly kills her mother. The one-car garage that serves as a perfect hiding place for a two-year-old child suddenly goes dark and there is no escape.

Now, with the reality that life can change in an instant, the traumatized child feels that nowhere will ever be safe again. The abused child erupts with aggression and sexual persuasion to get her needs met. The child who experienced the car accident tantrums every time she or her mother have to get into their new car; she cries for hours when her caregiver drops her off at preschool calling out for her return. Last, the child who was accidentally locked in a garage for hours now stands motionless and soundless in moments of fear, moments that occur too frequently.

A Wonderful Treasure. I remember working with a little girl who was Black American; her name was Treasure (a pseudonym). She had light brown skin, medium brown curly hair and big dark brown eyes. She was small for her age, shy at times and tended to exist in isolation. She was born in the United States as were both of her biological parents, but she was adopted by a family member who was born in an English-dominant country in South America. Her adoptive mother had a South American accent, but English was her only language. Treasure had a complex trauma history from birth to age two and a half, at which time she was removed from the care of her biological mother and eventually placed in kinship care in a family member's home at the age of 3-years-old. During that same year she was in a car accident with her primary caregiver. I met her shortly after her fourth birthday. She had a significant expressive language delay, but her receptive language was within age expectations. Treasure's primary method of treatment was CCPT.

Our playroom was stocked with a wide variety of toys and had some, though not many, toys that looked like people from minority races and cultures. However, there were no superheroes or superheroines of color in our playroom. One day, after she had just had her fourth birthday and had recently survived a significant car accident, Treasure was working through her trauma and started looking for a different toy to tell her car accident story when she came across Wonder Woman. In some ways, this felt like an appropriate selection for her as in essence, Treasure did not have biological parents and was often put in positions where she had to defend herself and others. In other ways, I wished that we had more toys visually representative of Treasure. Then it happened; she picked up the small toy and said, "she doesn't look like me, but let's pretend she does." I was a bit surprised that she had said this aloud in a clear and well-articulated sentence given her expressive language challenges. I reflected her statement to her, and she pointed to her hair and skin and then to Wonder Woman's hair and skin indicating that those things were different between her and the action figure. Such a powerful observation for 4-year-old Treasure. After the session, I thought about what her play might have been had there been superheroines who looked like her in our play therapy room, toys in the room that represented real strength, fearlessness, femininity and Blackness. Might she have felt more connected to her story and approached her healing sooner? Did having to pretend that a White character was, in fact, Black, say something to her about her genuine ability to conquer her fears and process her past? Research suggests that Black girls' identity formation is correlated with common media images and portrayal of Black femininity (Muhammad & McArthur, 2015). This supplicates the question of what happens to Black girls' identity development when there are limited or no representations.

Kaiyin Trapped in the Dark. Kaiyin (a pseudonym) was a 4-year-old deaf Asian American boy living with he biological hearing parents. His mother was a child of a Deaf adult (CODA). She was fluent in American Sign Language (ASL), and his father was proficient in the language. Kaiyin had a diagnosis of generalized anxiety disorder (GAD) and used ASL to communicate. Kaiyin was referred due to excessive tantrums at home and significant aggression toward his mother. Kaiyin's preschool teacher reported that when nervous, Kaiyin would often stand perfectly still and take several minutes before he would move. He literally displayed being frozen in fear. Kaiyin was engaged in CCPT to help decrease his GAD symptoms without a clear understanding of how his GAD developed. During his initial evaluation, his parents could not recall any events in Kaiyin's life that could contribute to GAD.

Upon meeting Kaiyin, it was clear that he loved specific items in the play therapy room. He enjoyed all things Star Wars, cars, trucks, planes and superheroes. His favorite superhero in sessions was the Flash. It was when he started playing out a game of hide-n-seek that his trauma was revealed. His mother then recalled that when Kaiyin was 2-years-old he was playing hide-'n-seek with his paternal grandmother when he accidentally got locked in the garage. The garage was completely dark and Kaiyin could not open the door. It took his grandmother minutes to realize where Kaiyin was hiding, but the garage door was jammed, and she could not open it. After about two hours of trying a multitude of entry points, the fire department cut open the garage door. Kaiyin's mother thought that Kaiyin was too young to remember the event and, therefore, she did not realize that it could have been traumatic for him. However, as Kaiyin shared through his play, he remembered and remained terrified of what he experienced as result of his game of hide-'n-seek.

Kaiyin used the Flash to share his story. The Flash has a power where he can vibrate his body so fast that he can move through objects; it is called phasing. If Kaiyin had that power when he was two years old, he would have been able to phase himself out of the garage or he would have been able to move quickly enough to escape before the garage door closed. He would also never feel frozen in fear. Through nearly a year of CCPT treatment, Kaiyin was able to address the underlying feelings of fear leading to his symptoms of GAD. He was able to channel the strength of the Flash while practicing his fearlessness and resilience.

Jimena and the Girl of Steel. Jimena (a pseudonym) was a four-and a half-year-old Latina girl with dark brown eyes and natural chestnut colored hair. She was living in foster care at the time she began seeing her latest therapist. She was initially referred for treatment due to excessive crying, night terrors, compulsive masturbation and attempting to perform sex acts on adults. She had seen her first therapist in dyadic child-parent psychotherapy (CPP) informed sessions with her foster mother. She saw that therapist for nearly two years before being transferred to a different therapist. Records indicated that CPP was initially chosen because it is an evidence-based treatment for infants and young children who have experienced trauma (Lieberman, Ippen, & Van Horn, 2015). Child-parent psychotherapy is delivered in dyadic and sometimes family models and incorporates CCPT principles of following the child's lead (Lieberman, Ippen, & Van Horn, 2015).

Background. Jimena had been in foster care since she was 18 months old. She was removed from the care of her biological parents due to confirmed acts of severe physical and sexual abuse by her father and other adult males at her father's request. It was reported that Jimena and all other biological siblings experienced similar acts of abuse. Her sexual abuse started when she was 9 months old and continued until her removal at 18 months. Initially, foster care social workers assumed that Jimena would not need treatment for her abuse because she was pre-verbal when her abuse began, and she was supposedly "too young to remember" her experience. However, soon Jimena's behaviors and fears revealed a different story. Before she turned two years old, she began to engage in excessive masturbation resulting in visits to a pediatrician. Initial treatment allowed Jimena to feel safe with her foster mother, build their relationship, and allow her foster mother to learn about Jimena's history from Jimena's perspective.

Child-Centered Play Therapy. As Jimena grew, she was beginning to need her own space to process and integrate some of her traumatic memories. Through CCPT, Jimena played with dolls, initially with reservation. She cared for them by feeding them, giving them baths, singing to them, and generally nurturing them while the play therapist reflected the babies' experiences and labeled Jimena's emotions. Over time, Jimena began to share snippets of her trauma in between her nurturing play until she was engaged in trauma play for the majority of her session. As some CCPT therapists often do, the play therapist frequently assumed the voice of the baby and Jimena would correct the therapist if or when the content of the message was inaccurate. Jimena's play presented themes of helplessness, fear, pain and confusion. While the baby could crawl and babble during moments of nurturing play, during sexual trauma play Jimena would remove the arms and legs of the baby and put tape over the baby's mouth to symbolize that the baby could not move and could not scream for help—could not escape. Jimena's play expressed that not only was the baby restricted from escape but also that no one came to save the baby, at least not initially. Jimena sometimes saw the baby as bad for doing something that the father told her was not permitted. She expressed her guilt and, in turn, demonstrated that it was the baby's fault that the father hurt her. Her play also revealed that she saw the baby as weak for not getting away. It was clear that although all of her abuse took place while she was an infant and early toddler, she blamed herself. Much of Jimena's play with her father as all-powerful, was similar to the Supergirl villain, Darkseid. In the comic, Darkseid is able to capture and nearly kill Supergirl on more than one occasion. Even though it takes the strength and power of several heroes to save Supergirl, sometimes she blames herself for being captured (Grassi, 2016).

Eventually, Jimena started to verbalize how much her body hurt when her father took care of her. As Jimena learned the vocabulary of body parts, she became able to use those words in her sessions. Part of sexual trauma work with young survivors is to either directly or indirectly teach the correct names of all body parts including sex organs (breasts, penis, vagina) instead of codenames or nicknames that induce shame (e.g., down there, privates, wee-wee, etc.; Cohen & Mannarino, 2015). Using CCPT, the therapist used the correct names of body parts when describing Jimena's play and when invited to take the voice of the baby. This is slightly different in traditional CCPT where the therapist tries to primarily use the words provided by the client. The clinician, in this case, understood that Jimena did not have the vocabulary to tell her story even when she wanted to use words because her trauma occurred preverbally.

Jimena started to add other toys to her CCPT sessions. The main staple that she added to her play was a Barbie-sized Supergirl toy. She left Supergirl intact, except she insisted on Supergirl wearing pants or shorts instead of the skirt that came with the toy. This was a parallel experience for Jimena because there was a time in her development when her pediatrician recommended that she only be allowed to wear pants or long shorts with belts to slow her access to her genitalia when she was masturbating to the point of vaginal injury. Jimena has since been allowed to wear skirts and dresses again, but obviously, she still needed to unpack that time in her life.

Supergirl started trying to save the baby by trying to fly and swoop in to pick it up. She also tried to fight off the baby's father when he was hurting it, but even when the baby was picked up, pieces of it were always left behind (i.e., one or more of the baby's limbs, diaper or clothes). Additionally, Supergirl would often be captured by the baby's father, the baby would get dropped from the sky, and all it could do was to lie on the ground listening to cries, thumps, grunts, and then silence. From what the therapist knew of Jimena's history, it was likely that the initial presentation of Supergirl was perhaps a representation of Jimena's biological mother or possibly one of Jimena's older sisters trying to save Jimena.

Outcome. Jimena's journey was neither smooth nor linear. She used Supergirl to play out her feelings of distress. As time progressed, there were times when Supergirl was successful in saving the baby, which became a reflection of Jimena's capacity for change. As Jimena grew in her verbal language and developed an understanding of what happened to her, she began to play scenes that allowed another female character to the help baby go to a new home that was safe. The therapist believed that the unnamed female character served as Jimena's foster mother.

Personal Reflections

Treasure, Kaiyin and Jimena each taught me something about the need for appropriate representation in the play therapy room. As a Black woman clinician, I aim to find examples of the children who enter my play therapy room because I know firsthand what is like to exist in a world that seems to be ignorant of my existence. I grew up viewing reruns of Wonder Woman in the late 1980s and early 1990s. I remember thinking that she was beautiful, and I wanted her powers. I was painfully aware that she looked nothing like the women in my family or like me. Now, fast forward to present times, and I find myself frustrated to see that while there have been some improvements in the representation of Black women, in other ways not much has changed. In 2016, Treasure pretended that the toys looked like her, while in the 1990s I found myself wishing that I looked more like the characters. Thankfully, Treasure had a strong sense of self. Though she had experienced a great deal of turmoil in her few short years, she was firmly rooted in embracing her power and beauty as a Black girl.

I remember the first day that Treasure wore meticulously created braids in her hair, cornrows, that ended with purple and pink beads. She enjoyed the clickety-clack sounds that the beads made as they tapped against one another when she shook her head. She radiated joy when she shook her hair. I remembered that feeling from my childhood. Growing up, it was a rite of passage for little Black girls to finally get beads in our hair. All of the girls in my neighborhood would compare beads and beam with effervescent smiles when we showed each other our newly restyled braids. Differently from Treasure, however, my early childhood was comprised of me being surrounded by multiple generations of people who looked like me. People with many shades of brown skin and a variety of kinky and curly hair textures. Treasure, on the other hand, was the only Black girl in her preschool classroom at that time. She had classmates who were Latinx, White, Black and multiracial. However, she was the only Black girl. No other girls had hair like Treasure's. Treasure also had a team of teachers and therapists (mental health and speech-language pathologists) who, until she met me, were all White. Outside of her family, Treasure had limited opportunities to see Black people. I often flash back to the day when Treasure's lead teacher shared in a meeting that she wanted to talk to Treasure's mother about not putting beads in her hair. My heart sank. I fought tears of anger and sadness. My thoughts raced as I struggled for words to say just how harmful I thought that would be for Treasure. The teacher explained that the beads were over stimulating to Treasure, in her opinion, and were distracting to the other children. So, in essence, she was saying that being a Black girl is an over stimulating distraction. In that moment, I did not know how to say words without dousing them in anger or carrying them in sadness. I also was not sure if my feelings were related to Treasure or if it was my countertransference and feeling like the little girl in me was under attack. Here Treasure was telling me that she has to pretend toys look like her to process her trauma, and her teacher wanted to strip away a cultural rite of passage and a developing Black identity. A supervisor that

I had at that time beautifully put it all into perspective for me when she said, "You may not be Treasure, but you are the only person at the table who can remember and speak to what it is like to be a 4-year-old Black girl. If you don't advocate for her in times when her caregivers are not invited to meetings, who will?"

In my experiences with Treasure, I failed her by not ensuring that the playroom had equal representations of Black people—Black superheroines and superheroes. But, I also failed her when I froze and could not find my words to help the teacher see the situation from another perspective. I have since learned to advocate for Black children in the same way that I aim to be an ally for other minority communities. In order to do that, I often have to shed that fear that my community of predominantly White play therapists will label me as an *angry Black woman* for shedding light on the areas within the field that have neglected minorities. Treasure taught me that my feelings are valid, that my ideas are important and that my role as a CCPT play therapist is to use my powers for the good of children and their families. She left me with those lessons and encouraged me to remain open to the process of learning.

I learned important lessons from my work with Kaiyin as well. Kaiyin was one of the few Deaf children whom I have had the honor to work with using CCPT as the primary treatment approach. Kaiyin's grandmother played an integral role in Kaiyin's healing. She was part of his primary support system. She was culturally Deaf, which meant that, like Kaiyin, she used ASL as her primary language. She adored Kaiyin, much in the same way that most grandparents adore their grandchildren. She also felt a special connection with him since he was her only grandchild and he was Deaf. However, since she was the person caring for him when he accidentally locked himself in the garage, she reported immeasurable guilt for Kaiyin, especially once she realized that the event likely contributed to his diagnosis of GAD. As it was explained to me by Kaiyin's mother, in their culture it is rare for elder members to express remorse toward children because it is believed that all actions by an elder are completed with good intentions and in the best interest of children. However, Kaiyin's grandmother wanted to join some treatment sessions with Kaiyin so that she could repair the ruptures that she felt existed within their relationship due to his garage experience. She wanted a safe space to apologize to him and to help him process his feelings. She acknowledged that since she was also terrified that day for his safety, they "were in it together."

In the playroom, Kaiyin found the Flash relatable even though the character did not look like him and did not know ASL. It was clear that Kaiyin was drawn to the Flash's speed. However, I also wondered if the fact that the Flash wore a full mask helped Kaiyin pretend that the Flash could look like anyone underneath his costume. While Kaiyin found comfort in the play therapy room, it was a foreign place for his grandmother. It was her, not Kaiyin, who commented on wanting more examples of their culture in the toys that were available to them. She provided suggestions for toys such as including a Chinese yo-yo, a mini Buddha, small kites, and shuttlecocks, which are badminton-shaped toys made from feathers. She reported that adding remnants of her childhood increased her capacity for expression and play with Kaiyin, while making her feel that her beliefs were honored even in sessions where she was not present. We held her in mind. In that way, Kaiyin and his grandmother invited me into their experience and showed me that even though I was not present on the day of their trauma, we were still *all in it together.*

Finally, there was Jimena. All trauma work is difficult. I have found that no matter how young a child is when they experience betrayal by a trusted adult, they remember. Jimena's prolonged trauma of physical and sexual abuse was a prime example of how profoundly and richly infants and young children can remember feeling terrified and helpless. Her experience was also a testament to the power of CCPT and allowing a child to tell their story. Her abuse was so pervasive that it had permeated crevices of her memory that CCPT reached well.

It was obvious that Jimena was purposeful in her selection of toys to aid her in CCPT. Superman was equally available to her, as were a wide range of other male superheroes that she never touched or even looked at for longer than a few seconds. She chose Supergirl even though Supergirl looked nothing like the girls and women in Jimena's biological family. They all had brown eyes, dark colored hair, and light brown or tanned skin. Jimena's foster mother had fair skin, but she was a brunette similar to Jimena. Jimena never called attention to the differences between herself and Supergirl. For Jimena, it seemed that the critical part was that there was a character who had the powers that she needed to fully share and process her story. It was more important for her that Supergirl's gender, strength, vulnerability and gift of flight were represented than physical characteristics such as skin tone and hair. In ways that mattered to Jimena, she was represented.

Conclusion

Child-centered play therapy is one of the earliest and fundamental forms of play therapy. It allows children to share their experiences without direct influence from adults. As a child engages in CCPT, they become engrossed in their make-believe play as it transforms into a manifestation of their reality. During CCPT, children's experiences come to life and become visible by CCPT therapists even when a full background history is unavailable as we learned with Kaiyin. Initial reenactments of a child's story exist both in the present and in the past as the child attempts to make sense of what happened. As children are engaged in affect reflection, receiving unconditional positive regard and acceptance from their CCPT therapists, they increase their capacity for resilience and healing. Children lead their CCPT therapist on the child's journey toward healing.

Children are strong and complicated. Therefore, they need powerful and equally complex characters who can withstand the forces that the child has experienced. The use of superhero and superheroine symbolism in CCPT builds children's capacity for expression. Sometimes children select characters due to the character's hidden strengths, and other times it is due to the character's alter ego. Regardless, children choose toys with purpose and meaning as we saw with Jimena. It is the CCPT therapist's onus to explore that meaning. Similarly, it is the therapist's responsibility to ensure that their play therapy rooms are supplied with toys that have the depth and breadth that children need without them having to add a layer of pretending as did Treasure.

Supergirl and Wonder Woman were discussed in this chapter as they are steps toward an effort to narrow the gender gap among prevalent superheroes. Each of them has produced ground-breaking results making room in television and movies for other casts led by females. It is worth noting that there are a few minority superheroes that were not covered in this chapter due to limitations of space and their limited relevance to children, not necessarily their import-ance in the larger context of gender or racial equality. However, among the existing superheroines, women of color are still missing in leading roles. Diverse characters of racial, cultural and ability groups are also habitually omitted in the television and movie versions of superhero expression. Play therapists should explore their inclusion practices to ensure that they are authentically providing children with safe spaces for processing their emotions. Every child deserves a chance to be incredible.

Questions for Clinical Discussion

1.   Why is it important to consider complex character analyses when children select superheroes while engaged in CCPT?
2.   How would you use the diversity considerations in this chapter to lead discussions of toy selection in your agency?
3.   Sometimes children of color seem to be unaware of race when they select toys to represent themselves in play. How much of that is a product of them habitu-ating to the experience that there are often few representations of themselves?
4.   What is your role, as a play therapist, in providing a variety of toys represen-tative of a wide range of gender, race, cultural, and ability?
5.   How might the inclusion of diverse characters support the development of children including children from majority groups?
6.   What therapeutic impact may available toy selection have on children who have experienced traumatic events?

References

Aucoin, J. (2014, October 24). The superhero diversity problem. *The Harvard Political Review.* Retrieved from http://harvardpolitics.com/books-arts/superhero-diversity-problem/

Berlanti, G., Johns, G., & Kreisberg, A. (Creators) (2014 to present). *The Flash* [*Television series*]. In: P. Producer (Producer). Vancouver, BC: Berlanti Productions DC Entertainment, Warner Bros.

Captain America Comics 1941 (2018). *Marvel.* Retrieved from www.marvel.com/comics/issue/7849/captain_america_comics_1941_1

Cohen, J. A. & Mannarino, A. P. (2015). Trauma-focused cognitive behavior therapy for traumatized children and families. *Child and Adolescent Psychiatric Clinics, 24*(3), 557–570.

46   *LaTrice L. Dowtin*

Cook, A., Spinazzola, J., Ford, J., Lanktree, C., Blaustein, M., et al. (2017). Complex trauma in children and adolescents. *Psychiatric Annals, 35*(5), 390–398.

Dockterman, E. (2017, June 19). Why Wonder Woman broke through. *Time*. Retrieved from http://time.com/4810489/why-wonder-woman-broke-through/

Dowtin, L., L. (2018). *The therapeutic power of play: Play therapy training experiences of mental health professionals with Deaf clients* [Doctoral Dissertation]. ProQuest Dissertations Publishing. Retrieved from http://search.proquest.com/docview/2030355360/

Feige, K., McFeely, S., Markus, C., Johnston, J., Evans, C., et al. Marvel Studios. (2011). *Captain America, the First Avenger* [Motion picture]. Hollywood, CA: Paramount Home Entertainment.

Flash Publication History (2018). *DC Database*. Retrieved from http://dc.wikia.com/wiki/Flash_Publication_History

Grant, D. J., Feige, K. (Producers), & Coogler, R. (Director) (2018, February 16). *Black Panther* [Motion picture]. Burbank, CA: Marvel Studios and Walt Disney Pictures.

Grassi, M., Sullivan, T., Berlanti, G., Adler, A., Kreisberg, A. et al. (2016). *Supergirl: The complete first season*. Warner Home Video (Firm).

Hamilton, C. M., Reas, H. E., & Mansfield, M. E. (2017). The safe space: An examination of the neurobiological benefits of play therapy with traumatized children. In: *Emerging Research in play therapy, child counseling, and consultation* (pp. 81–99). Hersey, PA: IGI Global.

Hanley, T. (2016, August 15). Gendercrunching and ethnobrunching comics for June 2016 – Marvel, DC, and Image. *Bleeding Cool*. Retrieved from www.bleedingcool.com/2016/08/15/gendercrunching-and-ethnocrunching-comics-for-june-2016-marvel-dc-and-image/

Hartwig, E. K. (2017). The child-centered approach to puppet play with children. In: C. Schaefer & A. Drewes (Eds.), *Puppets in play therapy: A practical guidebook* (pp. 77–85). New York: Taylor & Francis.

Hughes, M. (2017, November 2). "Wonder Woman" is officially the higher-grossing superhero film. *Forbes*. Retrieved from www.forbes.com/sites/markhughes/2017/11/02/wonder-woman-is-officially-the-highest-grossing-superhero-origin-film/

Ho, S. (2016, October 31). *Top 2016 Halloween costumes: Superheroes dethrone princesses*. Retrieved from www.nbcnewyork.com/news/local/Superheroes-Top-Princesses-Halloween-Costume-Trends-396780441.html

Jao, A. (2018, March 20). Before "Black Panther" movie, black comic creators spent years breaking down barriers. *NBC News*. Retrieved from www.nbcnews.com/news/nbcblk/black-panther-black-comic-creators-spent-years-breaking-down-barriers-n848461

Landreth, G. L. (2012). *Play therapy: The art of relationship* (3rd edn.). New York: Routledge/Taylor & Francis Group.

Leigh, I. W., Andrews, J. F., & Harris, R. (2016). *Deaf culture: Exploring deaf communities in the United States*. San Diego, CA: Plural Publishing.

Lieberman, A. F., Ippen, C. G., & Van Horn, P. (2015). *Don't hit my mommy! A manual for child-parent psychotherapy with young children exposed to violence and other trauma*. Washington, DC: Zero to Three.

Muhammad, G. E. & McArthur, S. A. (2015). "Styled by their perceptions:" Black adolescent girls interpret representations of Black females in popular culture. *Multicultural Perspectives, 17*(3), 133–140.

Narimani, M., Soleymani, E., Zahed, B. A., & Abolghasemi, A. (2014). The comparison the effectiveness of executive functionals and play therapy on improving of working memory, attention care and academic achievement in students with math learning disorder. *Journal of Clinical Psychology, 4*(20), 1–16.

Panksepp, J. (2007). Can PLAY diminish ADHD and facilitate the construction of the social brain? *Journal of the Canadian Academy of Child and Adolescent Psychiatry/Journal de l'Academie canadienne de psychiatrie de l'enfant et de l'adolescent, 16*(2), 57–66.

Pearce, D., Black, S., & Feige, K. (2013). *Iron Man 3*. Burbank, CA: Buena Vista Home Entertainment.

Ranker Comics (2018). Top 100 Most Popular Superheroes and Villains in Comic Books. *Ranker Comics*. Retrieved from www.ranker.com/list/superheroes-ranked-by-most-comic-book-appearances/ranker-comics

Rogers, C. (1951). *Client centered therapy*. Boston, MA: Houghton-Mifflin.

Rogers, C. (1959). A theory of therapy, personality, and interpersonal relationships, as developed in the client-centered framework. In: S. Koch (Ed.), *Psychology: A study of a science*. Study 1, Vol. 3: *Formulations of the person and social context* (pp, 184–256). New York: McGraw-Hill.

Rose, S. (2018, January 20). From Black Panther to Black Lightning: Black superheroes are go! *The Guardian*. Retrieved from www.theguardian.com/film/2018/jan/21/black-superheroes-punching-in-own-right-black-panther-marvel

Rosenberg, (2015, October 26). "Supergirl"s' creators lean into their show's feminism. *The Washington Post*. Retrieved from www.washingtonpost.com/news/act-four/wp/2015/10/26/supergirls-creators-lean-into-their-shows-feminism/?noredirect=on&utm_term=.e9dd31b41f4a

Sharf, R. (2012). *Theories of psychotherapy and counseling concepts and cases* (5th edn.). Belmont: Brooks/Cole Cengage Learning.

Snyder, Z., Snyder, D., Roven, C., Suckle, R. (Producers), & Jenkins, P. (Director) (2017). *Wonder Woman* [Motion picture]. Burbank, CA: Warner Bros.

Wilson, A. N. (1978–2014). *The developmental psychology of the Black child* (2nd edn.). New York: Afrikan World InfoSystems.

CHAPTER 3

Control, Corruption, and Destruction, Oh My! The Role of Villains in Experiential Play Therapy®

Justin D. Kruse and Joyce Arendt

Stealthily he crept toward the bank. His arms and legs mirrored a marionette. He stood behind a cracked door, listening, watching. He saw the guard pacing; slowing with each step. "Perhaps he will fall asleep." The guard sat. His eyes closed. The room was silent except for the snores of the guard who held pressed to his chest a small safe filled with fortunes. He opened the door and paused kneeling over the guard. His breathing was overcast by the deep thud of his heart. He slowed his breathing, matching the guard. He waited. He watched. He blew the guards hands who flicked the air away releasing the clenched safe. When the guard woke, he felt confused and hollow and instantly knew something was wrong, but what? Panic filled what was now empty, the unknown, and the villain remained all but a mystery.

This was the story scripted by a 7-year-old child who in infancy was sexually abused. Children play in many different ways. They stack blocks, ride bikes, put puzzles together, draw and play games. But children also can play in another way, via imagination. Through use of metaphorical expression, as in Experiential Play Therapy® (EPT®), the child above was able to use play to face his trauma—his monster, the villain who walked away with his soul (Norton & Norton, 2006, 2008; Norton, Ferriegel, & Norton, 2011).

With the infinite complexity of human nature, the understanding of the villain through a therapeutic lens provides an opportunity to acknowledge and integrate the fluidity of both good and evil qualities of the self. In play therapy, there presents an opportunity to capitalize on resources the villain role provides by experientially facing both sides of the power play equation. Through EPT® children can explore the villain role by having a safe avenue to express conscious or unconscious feelings, open untapped and undefined strengths, and begin a process of integration that shapes behavior and provides an opportunity to move toward change. We begin this chapter with an understanding of the EPT® model, the impact of trauma on children and how to track the trauma energy. The villain's pursuit follows with an examination of the therapist's role and a review of thematic play that embraces symbolism and metaphor through the lens of the child. Examples of how villains "show up" in the playroom will be integrated throughout the chapter as well as in a closing case study. Join us as we leave the protection of the bat cave and journey into the depth of the dark, the malicious and the injured.

Experimental Play Therapy*

The innate capacity of children to move toward wholeness and healing is at the cornerstone of the EPT* model of play therapy developed by Drs. Byron and Carol Norton in 1988 who later wrote *Reaching Children through Play Therapy: An Approach to Experiential Play Therapy* (2002). When traumatic events interrupt attachment and development, it alters the neurophysiology and challenges the child's sense of safety, thus, profoundly impacting his worldview. Fantasy play is a child's primary form of expression. Paley (2004) suggested, "Fantasy play, rather than being a distraction, helps children achieve a goal of having an open mind, whether in the service of further storytelling or in formal lessons" (p. 26). Paley also describes "play is the work of children" (p. 1). The EPT* model relies on fantasy play. It is designed to help children work through traumatic events and has four major constructs: (1) establishing trust; (2) expression of needs; (3) empowerment; and (4) closure and separation. These constructs contain five stages of the play therapy process: (1) exploratory; (2) testing for protection; (3) dependency; (4) therapeutic growth; and (5) separation.

Children's toys create an atmosphere of self-expression and this unique communication quickly conveys the child is in control. For example, when a child enters the playroom curiously looking around, the therapist might comment "looks like you are checking things out" or "you are looking at all the toys to see what you might want to play with." Additionally, something familiar may catch the child's eye and he may exclaim while running to retrieve it, "I have this Spider-Man at home." An appropriate EPT* response may include, "we like the same things" or "you are seeing things you play with at home." While simple reflections, these statements communicate interest, attunement and a sense of safety. With children's curiosity "What is this?" EPT* therapists are trained to respond with, "It can be anything you want it to be" suggesting freedom to play without the interference of others' (another child or adult) agenda.

Conceptualizing the child's life as they enter the playroom marks the beginning of the exploratory stage. This initial exploration of toys and the therapist are key ingredients and viewed as the window into their world and relationship dynamics. Children will often create some type of situation as a test in order to determine relative safety. For example, they may ask to use the bathroom, they may aggress on a toy or pretend to shoot a gun at the therapist and observe the therapist's reaction. When exploration and testing for protection have been successful, children will feel honored and validated. Conversely, unsuccessful interactions will hinder the establishment of trust and therapy will not progress or the child may simply comply. Neither of these outcomes is conducive for effective EPT*.

Transitioning to the dependency stage is where empowerment and ego strength are paramount. "Let's be cops and go get all the bad guys" or "let's wear these (helmets, armor, swords, guns, handcuffs, whistle)" are common exclamations during this stage which depict prolonged periods of preparing. It is often with high anxiety and rapid switching from one toy or idea to another that children desperately process their life experiences. Therapists become a vital part of the process as children borrow their ego strength until they can perform the task(s) solo. A therapist's reflections such as, "You are making sure you have everything you need to get the bad guys" or "You want to make sure you have all the protection you need" are ideal. This level of communication is aimed at addressing the themes of the play. In these examples, the thematic focus is on bad guy versus good guy, safety, and protection (Benedict, 2002).

The dependency stage is typically comprised of several months of high anxiety and abrupt changes. It is during this time the child gains an understanding of the self and the trauma narrative, permitting the play to deepen. With sustained safety and attuned interactions, children enter play sequences allowing them access to their defensive responses such as flight, fight and freeze. Additionally, progression toward victim/perpetrator role-play ensues which permits children to work through traumatic events. Initially, children play the role of the perpetrator (here on out referred to as "villain") and place the therapist in the role of the "victim" but the child will label the therapist's role as the "bad guy," thus, leaving the therapist often very confused as to what role they are playing. Accessing the villain initiates a level of strength and power as opposed to empowerment seen earlier in the establishment of trust and was inaccessible during the traumatic event. Conversely, placing the therapist in the role of the victim allows the child to re-experience traumatic events safely via the villain. Repeated sequences of villain play will occur until the child exhausts the painful experiences and feels validated.

The villain's empowered stance, validation and trust in the therapist shift the play, thus moving the child into states of vulnerability. They forgo and transfer the villain role by anointing the therapist as the new villain; the child the victim. Role-playing the victim, the child will orchestrate the therapist to act out the same play they perpetrated while the villain. However, they will prevent the therapist (villain) in successfully carrying out actions of harm. Rather, children access their defensive response system of flight and fight. A child might say to the therapist "ha-ha your bullets are just blanks" although the child may have instructed the villain to shoot. An EPT* therapist might respond after experiencing such a defeat with, "Oh man, I thought those were real bullets, you outsmarted me again. You just wait until next time!" Common encounters such as these during the dependency stage generates the power to fight or escape which was originally inaccessible.

As children repeatedly conquer the villain, the level of excitement and exhilaration grow exponentially. Therapists undoubtedly experience the exhilaration and join the child, further validating their pain and helping children move toward annihilation of the villain. Annihilation is the culmination of all their hard work and releasing the immobilized trauma energy stuck in the nervous system from the original event(s). The annihilation may or may not be grand. One example of an annihilation comes from a 4-year-old boy who rolled around endlessly on the inflatable bop bag and accidentally hit the air valve releasing all the air until completely flattened. He hurriedly blew it up again. Repeating this pattern for several sessions. Then one day rather than blowing it back-up, he picks up the now deflated bop bag, throws it out the playroom door and exclaims exuberantly "we don't need him anymore!" His hard work paid off allowing him to move into the next stage of therapy; therapeutic growth.

Another example of annihilation in the dependency stage is the case of 10-year-old Maria, who carried a knife in her backpack onto the school bus. A boy began teasing her and she stabbed him in the arm. Authorities appropriately referred her to play therapy rather than pressing charges. They knew the family and what she had been through. In her brief ten years, she had many painful experiences. Her mother was HIV positive and Maria witnessed all the medically invasive treatments. Additionally, her mother's boyfriend molested her at age six. Her mother reported it and he went to prison for five years. The culminating traumatic event occurred one Summer evening when a "wanted serial rapist" broke into their home, raping and assaulting her mother. Maria and her sister woke the next morning to find their mother in shock, tied up, naked, bloody and bruised. In the next sections, we will discover how this traumatic event for Maria thwarted her defensive flight/fight response which gave rise to fear and aggressive actions.

After six months of Maria recreating the horrific scene of finding her mother that morning, in which the bop bag was the villain (rapist), she used a plastic collapsible knife to stab him. Ironically, the knife did not collapse and popped the bop bag. The sound was deafening. Maria became elated. She found the xylophone and began to bang loudly while yelling in celebration. She noticed one of the small figurines used for Sand Tray Therapy in which a woman was covering her ears. In Maria's frenzy, she retrieved the figure and threw it across the room in what appeared to be anger for not honoring her celebration. When Maria's mother came back to the playroom for the parent check-in, Maria excitedly pointed to the bop bag and exclaimed: "Look, mom, look what I did to the man who hurt you!"

Once annihilation occurs, the play takes yet another big shift from dependency to therapeutic growth. The intense energy previously seen during play stops. It is unnecessary for children to continue working through traumatic events; their dignity is restored. Choice of toys and themes change, thus, transitioning to "rehearsal for life" play in the therapeutic growth stage. Following the rules becomes important as opposed to "cheating to win." Building structures and talking about friends and school become dominant. Engaging the therapist in collaborative and cooperative play is primary compared to being in control. Parents will begin reporting increases in grades, invitations for sleepovers, a decrease or elimination of symptoms, and sleep improvements. Essentially, significant decreases in all behaviors that led them to therapy is observed.

The separation stage of EPT® signals the end of therapy and should end as therapy began. Children need to say goodbye to the therapist and the playroom. Revisiting previous play or toys is their way of saying goodbye. Some therapists often misinterpret this to indicate termination should not occur. Or parents report similar behavioral issues that led to therapy. This minor "setback" is expected and is an important step for children as they terminate. They need to check with themselves to ensure all the work they did is real and can be sustained.

What Defines a Traumatic Event?

According to Peter Levine, (1997) "Traumatic symptoms are not caused by the 'triggering' event itself. They stem from the frozen residue of energy that has not been resolved and discharged; this residue remains trapped in the nervous system where it can wreak havoc on our bodies and spirits" (p. 19). Our complex neuro-physiology responds to threatening stimuli in the environment setting off a chain of events designed to protect us from the painful impact, injury or pending death. We continuously scan our environment (exteroception) and assess our internal states (interoception) via our sensory systems: vision, tactile, taste, olfactory and auditory, to determine threats of danger or safety. As stated by Kain & Terrell (2018),

> Psychologically speaking, moments of intense emotion activate the reptilian part of the brain, the first part of the brain to develop *in utero*. This is the root of our autonomic nervous system – the origin of our fight-or-flight response, which affects blood pressure, heart rate, breathing rate, body temperature, digestion metabolism, and multiple other bodily functions. This neurological response is powerful and easily triggered when threats are perceived, which is why it's so important for parents to step in and help children literally 'calm their nerves' during times of distress.
>
> (Kain & Terrell, 2018, p. 19)

When we detect a potential threat in our environment, we have access to crucial defensive responses; social engagement, flight and fight. If any of these defensive responses are utilized, we will be able to walk away from the event free from post-traumatic stress symptoms. Conversely, when these options fail we attempt to employ our final line of defense; freeze. When we freeze, we become immobilized and all the energy from the desire to act becomes immobilized and we stay "stuck" in inaction:

> In the case of a threat, the sympathetic nervous system (the energy-burning survival part) is activated. The pituitary gland, the master endocrine gland, is also activated and initiates the body's endocrine response. The pituitary gland, through the hormone *adrenocorticotrophic hormone* (ACTH), stimulates the adrenal glands to release cortisol, which puts a brake on norepinephrine, modulating the brain's future arousal response. In the event that the animal survives the immediate threat, cortisol also prepares the animal to manage ongoing stress through changes in its circulation, metabolism and immune response.
>
> (Scaer, 2005, p. 52)

The brain stem activates a primal action of survival preservation. During immo-bilization, our vagus nerve, especially the dorsal vagal nerve, shuts down our vitals: heart, vascular, respiratory, and digestive. The purpose is three-fold; one to dissuade a predator, two to minimize death from the injuries and three to not experience the pain.

Levine (1997) uses the example of how impalas feign death with perceived threat and how the body freezes in preparation to self-preserve. Once the threat is gone, animals "shake" off the trauma and move. Researchers and trauma experts unilat-erally conclude that when humans perceive a threat, their limbic system responds sending neurological signals to the brain stem allowing them access to the flight/ fight response system in order to prepare for self-preservation (Kain & Terrell, 2018; Levine, 1997; Perry & Szalavitz, 2006; Porges, 2004, 2011; Scaer, 2001, 2005; Van der Kolk, 2014; Ziegler, 2002).

If the unfortunate event of freeze occurs, developing post-traumatic stress dis-order (PTSD) symptoms is a likely outcome. The immobilization process halts typical brain activity stopping the neural processing connecting the event to actual survival (Levine, 1997, 2010; Van der Kolk, 2014). In other words, when we freeze our brain communicates to us that we were unable to prevent assault and our brain prepares us for death. The body and brain patterns remain "stuck" in a fear response and can be triggered in the future anytime the body re-experiences similar bodily sensations via our sensory systems. The fear is re-ignited as if the event is still occurring.

Experiencing traumatic events in our lives is unavoidable. How the traumatic events impact our lives is dependent on several factors. Whether the event is viewed as traumatic, or whether we utilized our defensive responses (flight/fight), or the type of event: shock or developmental (Van der Kolk, 2014). Shock trauma is a single incident event such as a car accident, death of a loved one, dog bite, fall from a ladder, medical or dental invasive procedure, witnessing something horrific or divorce. Developmental trauma results from abuse and neglect. However, devel-opmental trauma also results from less overt experiences such as emotional breaks and inconsistencies in the parent-child relationship, lack of parental attunement toward the child, and lack of reciprocity between parent and child through the first few years of life. Kain and Terrell (2018) assert the critical years are "from early fetal development through the third year of life, when the cognitive, thinking brain comes online" (p. 45).

The Four S's

Drs. Byron and Carol Norton discovered that through their education, experi-ence and witnessing thousands of play sessions, trauma is stored not only in the mind but in the body. As noted previously, the inability to properly discharge trau-matic energy at the time of an event is repeatedly re-experienced. They noticed during experiential play, a sequence of events occurs as children process traumatic events. They coined this sequence "the Four S's;" sensory, soma (body), surge and soothe. They also learned how play therapists, through careful observation of this energy and appropriate responses, can support the nervous system toward healing (Norton & Norton, 2002, 2006, 2008).

The sensory represents any memory entering our awareness via our sensory systems. It might be observed as a momentary dissociative response. Children may appear as if they are staring off into space or at a toy for a longer than normal period of time. It might also be viewed as some type of startle response or the child talking about a memory or an event.

Soma typically follows shortly after witnessing a sensory reaction. It is considered the entry point for traumatic events. The Soma indicates the sensory system and part on the body remembering the traumatic event. This can be observed in numerous ways and dependent on the particular child, the memories involved and the themes expressed. Some examples include a jerk or jolt. The child may let out a loud scream, screech or other sounds. They may use a swiping motion of their hand or other motions near an entry point of the trauma such as the mouth, genitals or buttocks. They may wiggle their bodies or move any part of the body impacted by the incident. They may even mention the name of the person responsible for causing the trauma.

This was observed in the case of Mathew, age seven. His father was incarcerated for physically abusing him and his sister. Mathew repeatedly created play scenes in which he and the therapist were deer hunters and when he shot at a deer he shot upward. He was shooting upward because he was small and his father was big. He was experiencing an implicit somatic memory of viewing his father as larger and looming over him. He needed to shoot upward in his fight response and attempted to protect himself which was something he was unable to do when the abuse was occurring (Norton, 2004). Additionally, Mathew frequently thrusted his head forward and down only while engaged in the above-described play. The mother confirmed Mathew's father regularly smacked the back of the children's heads as a way of maintaining control.

The surge is the action the body needs to take in order to complete the original traumatic event. When we are unable to access flight/fight as described above (e.g., being a small child or infant and too small to do anything, being trapped in some way, held at knife or gunpoint), the body becomes frozen and the traumatic event is frozen at the entry point in the body. Once the threat is gone, if humans do not "shake" off or "move," trauma is stored as implicit memory making post-traumatic stress more likely to develop (Levine, 1997, 2007, 2010, 2015).

Since we strive for self-determination and are propelled toward resolution of anything that overwhelms our systems, during EPT® sessions children are able to unconsciously recreate traumatic events in their life through the use of toys and imaginary play. Furthermore, if children can safely re-experience the trauma and allow energy to flow, they successfully move through the Four S's. The trauma and the emotionality tied to the trauma can be alleviated culminating toward mastery of these emotions. This process provides freedom for the child, resulting in the elimination of maladaptive behaviors.

Drs. Carol and Byron Norton contended children's maladaptive behaviors are the unfinished process of some traumatic event(s) in their life (Norton & Norton, 2002, 2006, 2008). Levine (1997) further attested we all experience traumatic events in our lives that overwhelm our systems and need not be catastrophic or life-threatening to generate havoc. However, we may not reach the level of developing post-traumatic stress disorder. Norton and Norton (2006) purported we recreate these traumatic events at an attempt toward resolution, but are often interrupted and suffer consequences due to continued inability to surge the energy stuck in the body. When children experience a surge in everyday life it might include such things as aggression, lying, stealing, tantrums, hyperactivity and inattentiveness. It is for this reason children are typically diagnosed with a myriad of disorders. Therapists trained in trauma work who understand the intricacies will appreciate children's symptoms and connect them to traumatic events rather than view the behaviors as children being "bad." Often therapists untrained in trauma work will prescribe interventions aimed at symptom reduction, which sadly often only leads to re-traumatizing the child.

During play sessions, the surge typically occurs shortly after the sensory. A surge, like the sensory, can be observed in numerous ways and depends on the particular child, the memories involved, and the expressed themes. Some examples of a surge response may be a crashing of items together, a burst of aggression such as hitting the bop bag or using a weapon, throwing themselves on a large soft object, or some type of large motor movement such as rolling around on the floor using kicking motions with the legs. Once the child has had the opportunity to complete the surge and move on to a soothing activity, healing is now possible. Repetition is crucial with increasingly more soothing time until a resolution is accomplished. A child's primary goal at this point is to make the feared object less scary. For example, if a child uses an aggressive toy such as a shark puppet to illustrate violence perpetrated upon them, they may then in subsequent sessions choose puppies rather than sharks, thus revealing the shift. The shift indicates dignity is being reclaimed because they were able to flee or fight against the shark which they were unable to do originally.

In their daily lives they have difficulty reaching the soothing stage because when they surge the immobilized energy from the trauma, the child receives a consequence whether it is a formal consequence such as a "time out" or a more informal consequence such as being yelled at, getting hit, or getting into trouble in some way. The result is that no one is available to provide a soothing response or an empathic statement calming the child's nervous system. Instead, the consequence inadvertently provides additional stimulation with increasingly higher levels of arousal which can lead to re-traumatization.

Through EPT®, children are able to use imaginary play without anyone imposing their agenda. They play out the sequences from the original traumatic event without consequences for their surges because they are disguised or embedded into the imaginary play. Thus, resulting in their ability to successfully move through the surge and achieve soothing. Soothing is often observed in play as sucking on a baby bottle, playing music softly, eating real food they bring in or pretend eating, smoothing, sifting or pouring sand or even just a calm quiet moment. The child should be allowed to soothe for as long as necessary with soft, calm, nurturing responses from the therapist. If this occurs at the end of a session, extending the session is ideal as this is the most critical time and should be honored. Connecting with the parents is necessary to ensure they continue extra soothing for the child at home. It is best to recommend bodily contact such as cuddling, holding or rocking, providing a bottle, backrubs or back scratches and as many verbal nurturing responses as possible. With an increase in soothing activities, the nervous system is allowed to finally calm down allowing for resolution and decreased need to surge in the "real world."

This process is naturally occurring during an EPT® session regardless if one is able to follow the energy. However, if one becomes adept at paying attention and following the child's energy, responses can deepen the play therapy process to move the child through the Four S's and the stages of EPT® toward resolution of the traumatic event.

The Villain's Pursuit

As the concept of villains is explored, we invite you to consider what villains showed up in your childhood play? Were you aware of the strengths the villain awakened in you? The depths it took you to? Enjoy the journey and be curious as without conflict there is no story; no transformation without sacrifice. The villain is a multilayered character and perhaps the best-known character apart from the hero who has the ability to provide conflict and serve as a lens into the child's world. Villains serve a purpose in children's play; an emotional confession displayed through symbolic form, and through this traffic the metaphor maintains the child's defense system. Through the play and containment of the therapist, the child is disclosing his story (Norton & Norton, 2006, 2008). In the playroom, villains are not just evil or antagonistic, nor are they simply a mere foil of the hero (the child); instead their metaphorical representations disguise the "painful realities of the child's life" (Norton and Norton, 2008, p. 194). By means of dynamic play, the villain is often as interesting and captivating as the hero and both are instrumental in understanding the play process. The storylines teach through agony and fear, lessons that prove revealing, extending an opportunity that when confronted stimulates the child's ability to release his constricted emotionality as he faces the monsters, his villains, under the bed.

Effective play often highlights the dramatic battles of villains and good characters and without these key roles, a child rightfully risks being unable to define his inner conflicts. With this in mind, the therapist must understand a villain is only as well imagined as the world and people he is fighting against. Saldana (2008) reported that when stories do not connect with the listener, the story withers away. With children's play, if the villainous plot does not vibrate between child and therapist, the child may be unable to move forward and instead will withdraw or act out (Norton and Norton, 2008). The child and therapist must build, support and feed one another.

The villain has been booed, hated and sometimes even cheered. However, through fantasies of combat, the child is able to feel capable, access their emotions, and take control of their anxieties (Jones, 2002). By understanding the motivations and purpose of the villain through the victim role, the villain becomes more than a cardboard cutout. Take time to appreciate the backstory and help make the villain as believable as the child needs. Through this understanding and use of aggressive play, children can transgress to new developmental levels by means of fighting through emotional challenges (Jones, 2002; Norton and Norton, 2008). In EPT* the role of the villain perpetuates this movement and repetitive play conveys "the internal pain or intrusion the trauma has imposed" (Norton & Norton, 2010c, p. 1).

Children's fantasy play introduces villains from all categories, human and non-human, with goals that often oppose the child, creating opposition and working directly against change. They may be intent on harming others, whether to further their own desires, to take revenge, or to simply cause chaos. Other times, the villain plots and plans to stop the child or derail him. What develops is sometimes a theme of light versus dark. The villain and its resulting narrative speak to our most basic human instinct; fear. To see this injury manifest and subsequently defeated, it can make for quite an intense experience. The villain's values and characteristics can include selfishness, greed and ambition and have developed symbolically from trauma experiences as experienced by the child. In her book, "A Short Defense of Villains," Agnes Repplier says,

> A villain must be a thing of power, handled with delicacy and grace. He must be wicked enough to excite our aversion, strong enough to arouse our fear, human enough to awaken some transient gleam of sympathy. We must triumph in his downfall, yet not barbarously nor with contempt, and the close of his career must be in harmony with all its previous development.
>
> (Repplier, 1890, p. 846)

Villainous casts from popular culture spanning from Disney films to Marvel comics, from Lego movies to Halloween classics, are seared into our minds. While not a definitive list, the villain can consist of characters of ancient evils, dark lords, witches, evil geniuses, tricksters, bullies and fanatics. Despite the villain that comes forward, Norton and Norton (2010c) highlight that "The child does not have the capacity to create a metaphor that did not have experiential meaning to them" (p. 2). Therefore, although a child watching Disney's Lady Tremaine may identify her as an evil step-mother or DC's Riddler as an intellectual mastermind, neither villain will translate through theme unless the child has made a symbolic connection (Norton and Norton, 2006, 2008). To the child, the role of villain is real but abstract. However, through play, the villain is represented in a manner that feared associations can be portrayed through expressive energies in several forms (Norton & Norton, 2002, 2006, 2008). The villain is the reason a hero is called to action; they are the reason puppies flee the seemingly invincible Cruella de Vil, or The Little Mermaid is convinced her voice is less important than beauty.

The villain acts and the hero reacts. The child's demise or continued limiting of power often seems the intent of the villain who combats against the child with deliberation. They often carry multiple characteristics including control, corruption and destruction. The villains tempt heroes and through the development of the storyline, the relationship between child and therapist, if nurtured, permits the child to "recapitulate his struggles, test them, watch them crumble, and rebuild them in such a way that he can tolerate, understand, and accept" (Norton & Norton, 2006, p. 30). In the child's play, the villain helps to take the child safely to the depths they otherwise may have been unable to express and the therapist provides a place of safety and protection where the child can learn to trust their strength.

Examples from the Playroom

An example of the villain metaphor is illustrated by 6-year-old Troy, who upon entering the playroom stated he was an evil scientist. It was only after several sessions that Troy found himself psychologically ready, trusting the therapist to contain the play. The therapist must be prepared to enter the child's fantasy play and assume assigned roles. Troy set the stage, reporting the therapist was "bad" having killed the evil scientist's mother and now had to undergo experiments and swallow poison, a clumpy brown mixture of clay while lying handcuffed on an operating table in a basement. While on the operating table, the therapist is told the conflicting message to resist and fight back. The therapist is told by the child that each time he fights back he could loosen the grip of the handcuffs. The child then pretended to push poison down the therapist's throat. Troy, who struggles to trust others, throws very large, violent tantrums when confined or cornered, is communicating through symbolic play his desire to engage his flight/fight response thereby loosening the handcuffs, freeing him from the torture he feels he is experiencing. Troy, as an evil scientist, focused on experimentation and use of poison in a role of power and control. To further understand this play dynamic, we can look at the meanings of the play to assess possible expression. Let's consider the symbolic meaning of the following roles, toys and environments.

Scientist: Analytical, formula, healing, discovery, brilliant, analyst, developer, creative, searching, remedy, methodical, solution, restorative, problem-solving, answers, resource, measurement, curative, logical, etc. Trauma response: revenge, poison, acid, painful, evil, sinister, menacing, vindictive, secret formula, and deadly formula (Norton & Norton, 2010b, p. 10).

Operating room: Crisis, pain, intense, internal, body concerns, vulnerability, change, etc. Trauma response: fright, anxiety, wounded, foreboding, panic, fear of pain, victim, helplessness, and fear of disability (Norton & Norton, 2010a, p. 6).

Basement: Fear, secret, hidden, uncomfortable, scary, threatening, intimidation, vulnerability, seclusion, dungeon, prison, captive, concealment, etc. Trauma response: fear, intimidation, seclusion, prison, violation, abuse, entrapment, isolation, and torture (Norton & Norton, 2010a, p. 1).

Clay: Creation, aggression, manipulation, self-esteem, resource, change, expression, contact, possession, etc. Trauma response: fear object, pressure, projection, control, need expression, manipulation, formidable, and intense feelings (Norton & Norton, 2010c, p. 6).

Handcuffs: Arrest, control, blame, perpetrator, power, constriction, containment, crime, violation, at fault, etc., Trauma response: in the dependency stage, guilty, personalized crime, should be in jail, violation, physical/sexual abuse, villain, protection, humiliation, brutality, victimization, and domestic violence (Norton & Norton, 2010c, p. 9).

One might surmise Troy was feeling controlled, violated, humiliated and victimized. Under such circumstances, the physiological consequence is constriction, dissociation and freeze/shock. The long-term consequences are likely to lead to depression, anxiety and post-traumatic stress disorder. Quite possibly abuse occurred and while these assumptions are only hypotheses further support is necessary, such as collaboration and intensity of themes, dynamics in the play and Troy's on-going behaviors. This one illustration should not stand alone but be a puzzle piece that when connected will present an image, the child's story: a metaphorical representation.

The Case Conceptualization of Jackson

With an understanding of villains, a review of EPT® and trauma, let us review a case. Jackson was 15 years old when he entered the community mental health clinic for treatment. His mental health history featured symptoms of an Autism Spectrum Disorder, anxiety and depression with interpersonal trauma in the context of a parental divorce and strained family interactions. Jackson's struggle in adjustment, as seen by his previous therapist and family, was best characterized as maladaptive daydreaming, a tangled undeniable byproduct of an overactive imagination along with characters, stories and plots. Having been only a year since his parents' separation and divorce, Jackson's unprocessed feelings were gridlocked. His father described feeling overwhelmed, acutely alone and while concerned about Jackson's behaviors and lack of social skills, he was most apprehensive about Jackson's elaborate daydreams involving characters, settings and other detailed features.

Jackson's adjustments were interpreted as disruptions with features of secure base distortion, hypervigilance and intrusive symptoms. With a developmental history suggestive of an overly sensitive response system, encapsulated by adjustment, Jackson appeared to withdraw from others and turn inward, having conversations with himself that quickly became identities with names, personalities and purpose. Jackson's therapist focused on the stages of EPT®, establishing a secure base relationship, and as Jackson became more relaxed, thematic play became a central part of the therapy. With toys as a manifestation of self, Jackson became acutely aware of the strength and power that emerged as he leaned into the experience. His narrative was full of epic clashes between the "good guys" and the "villains." His play commanded themes of anger and aggression as the villains emerged. Jackson symmetrically embraced the Wolverine's claw and Hulk's fist, both articulated as evil and corrupt, while capitalizing on the underdeveloped strength. It is important to highlight that while symbolism and metaphor can carry common themes, it is imperative that the child's perspective be embraced as was Jackson's portrayal of the Hulk and Wolverine as villains. In Killing Monsters, Jones (2002) commented that not only "By pretending to be them, young people are being strong" but that they also "need to tell the violent stories that are in them now" (p. 11–12). Working with a wounded child in this way is gentle, slow and enveloped in therapeutic safety. The storyteller becomes a helpful companion in the process of having and observing his feelings. This binocular viewpoint involved Jackson exercising the muscle to walk around something and having the relationship with it rather than just being in it. Caught in the excruciating storm of sensations, Jackson's quest to balance anger, fear and uncertainty was confronted symbolically through his trusting his pain "just enough" to explore it; allowing him to name the intertwined parts of his narrative, and in battles, untangle and assimilate.

Central to the therapist's work was his own self-awareness, his ability to remain regulated, and his capacity to empathically reflect Jackson's metaphorical expressions. At times, the therapist monitored his own emotions, for example, noticing that Jackson's aggressive behaviors induced some anxiety and frustration. He worked through these responses with a trusted senior colleague, reflected upon their significance, and prepared for sessions by increasing his mindfulness, ensuring he was therapeutically grounded. Additionally, the therapist kept mindful attention to Norton and Norton's (2010c) statement: "Toys may also be a repressed need or a deficit feeling, emotional state, or struggle for competency" (p. 3), which allowed for an emotional return of understanding even during the darkest and angriest of play.

Join us now as we walk through 14 sessions held with Jackson and his villainous cast from the perspective of EPT®. Please note, the conceptualization is our interpretation of the play, feel free to explore your own. As you read through the case below, sessions absent of symbolic play were not referenced due to a lack of relevance. Additionally, at the time of the case conceptualization, Jackson's father paused therapy until therapy appointments could be scheduled for Jackson after school. And as a result, therapy has not concluded and Jackson will likely continue to work toward therapeutic growth and separation.

No.	Client's Play	Conceptualization
1	Jackson began his play session by filling a two story dollhouse with multiple Lego people, including one he identified as "the killer." Significant time was spent exploring the therapist's toys and setting up the dollhouse. Jackson shared that he calls part of himself "Evil Jackson" and that he feels that while Evil Jackson has historically "not been nice" he feels that Evil Jackson is "starting to be nice but not always."	Multiple Lego people inside a dollhouse suggests the composition of individuals in his life with one being the "killer;" someone who has potentially harmed him. Through this play he introduces Evil Jackson who is "bad," most likely as a result of having been harmed. He reveals to the therapist he has a "bad side" and a "good side" with the bad side often prevailing but prefers to be good. While alluding to it here, we will see in the following sessions, Jackson also identifies with the role of "the killer" (a bad guy).
2	Jackson located the Lego characters used in the previous session and created "two homes." He said "the killer" was present. He noted that the characters in the two homes suspected the wrong individual as the killer and were being killed by "the killer" through surprise attacks. Jackson transitioned between play and talk. Between his acting out scenes he would pause and share information about himself. Jackson shared that when calm and relaxed, he is aware of the difference between his imagination and reality. He revealed that today's play was from his imagination and articulated that when anxious he shuts down.	"Two homes" implies the parents do not live together (which is the case with Jackson's family). Mentioning "the killer" again likely indicates it is a family member who is responsible for harming him. Jackson is demonstrating how the people in these two houses are blaming each other for Jackson's "bad" behavior and because they are wrong, "the killer" continues to do harm. And Jackson continues to act out impulsively. Jackson is caught off guard by the attacks from "the killer" because they happen suddenly and unexpectedly. "The more unexpected the wound, the longer it may take us to make peace with it" (Levine, 2005, p. 31). As a result, and in the role of the villain, he is "bad" and engages in "surprise attacks" too. Jackson sharing with the therapist that what he played was in his imagination insinuates it is too early in the therapeutic relationship and he is trying to conceal what might be happening at home.
3	Jackson noted he was having a "hard time" and was feeling frustrated with his mother. He stated that "Evil Jackson" has been present and was angry. He declared he wanted to battle.	Jackson is continuing to show how he is split into different people that are good and evil. "Like a bad guy," might indicate he does not completely commit to this idea and has some awareness that his behaviors are the result of being harmed, which are implied by his choice of the Wolverine claw.

He selected Wolverine claws for himself and handed the therapist Hulk fists. Jackson reported he is angry "kind of like a bad guy," followed with a laugh. Then he stated he could re-generate and that after he attacked the therapist five times, the battle would end. Jackson (the "bad guy") prevailed. He exclaimed "that was a lot of work" and asked to take a break.

Numbers are significant in children's play. It often signifies an age that abuse occurred, how often the abuse occurred, how many abusers, level of pain, or level of strength. Therefore, the idea that Jackson specifies that he will attack the therapist five times is important. However, it is too early in the play to determine meaning; continued assessment is necessary.

4   Jackson set up a scene of "bad guys" and "good guys" and reported he was part of the cast. He identified himself as "Jacksontron 2000." He also invited the therapist to participate and provided him the role of "Hulk." Jackson spent most of his time engaged in setting up the scene which left no time to engage in play.

Session four is early in the play and it is typically observed that children will spend a lot of time setting up a scene without ever following through with actual play. It is part of their anxiety and the titration necessary to face their pain. In this session, he is continuing to build on the good/bad guy theme. He has now morphed into Jacksontron 2000, which is probably more powerful than "Evil Jackson" and the Hulk. Jackson continues to place the therapist in the role of the Hulk. The Hulk is massive, aggressive, powerful, and destructive. As previously stated, in EPT* children will cast the therapist initially in the role of the victim ("good guy"), which is actually disguised as themselves and the child will be in the role of the villain to attack the victim from an empowered position. So essentially all roles, Hulk, Jacksontron 2000, Evil Jackson, and Wolverine are all aspects of Jackson as he gains the ego strength necessary to face the ultimate pain from trauma.

5   Jackson set up a scene of "good" versus "bad." Jackson reported he has superpowers and was on the "bad side" which prevailed during the battle. Jackson disclosed that he misses his mother. He shared that she will be getting married and that he was asked to attend. He noted he does not want to attend because, "I'm not ready to let her go."

Jackson is continuing to build ego strength from the villain role. Jackson begins to verbalize his feelings about the characters in his life that were earlier disguised in the Lego figures; mom and dad. He describes ambivalence toward them both. Here Jackson declares his dad is a "killer." While it is not stated specifically that his dad is "the killer," it is implied.

The therapist assisted Jackson as he processed his related feelings. He also shared that his father is "scarier than Slenderman" and that his father "has been involved in wars and has had to hurt and kill others for the USA." Jackson denied feeling fearful of his father but reported he is both "proud" and "scared" when he thinks of his father hurting others.

6   Jackson requested to battle. He selected one Wolverine claw and one Hulk fist for himself and provided the same to the therapist. Jackson directed he would play the "bad guy" and try to "teach" the therapist "how to fight back." He provided the therapist instruction on how to fight throughout the session.

The power differential has shifted toward equality, signifying he has now gained enough ego strength to begin facing his pain. Teaching the therapist how to "fight back" is essentially his way of teaching himself to "fight back" and prepare for the battle of reclaiming his dignity and self-worth. He is practicing re-engaging his defensive fight response because he was previously unable to fight back in real life. Now that Jackson has gained sufficient ego strength it denotes the onset of the dependency stage in which he will begin to play out the pain he experienced.

7   Jackson asked the therapist to play the role of a villain. Jackson was a "hero." Jackson reported that the therapist stole money and had to be attacked. After three "taps," the therapist was sent to jail. With Jackson's direction, the therapist attempted escape with provided supports. Jackson attacked the supports and then attacked the therapist. Jackson shared he too had supports and if the therapist received three side hugs, the therapist would then transition from villain to "good guy." By the end of the session, Jackson reported the therapist was a "good guy."

Stealing in play often indicates a loss of dignity and sense of self, which is commonly seen in those who have been abused and more specifically sexually abused. While it appears the therapist is playing the villain, the therapist is playing Jackson (the victim) but disguised as a villain. Jackson identifies his role as the "hero" but is the perpetrator (the true villain), disguised as the "good guy;" thus, allowing Jackson to play out his trauma from an empowered position, not a vulnerable position which would be too emotionally threatening. The metaphor for jail is confinement and being trapped, which is a way for Jackson to communicate how trapped he felt at the time of being harmed. Jackson taking out the "supports" might suggest that he has supportive people in his life or they are his altered parts, but he does not believe they are helpful or they are at the mercy of "the killer." He also communicates how necessary nurturance was and likely feels he never received so he further disguises his "needs" by suggesting "three side hugs" as a way to become good again.

8   Jackson selected the Wolverine claw and Hulk fist and directed more teaching was needed for the therapist. He noted he was the "bad guy" "like Evil Jackson." Jackson then proceeded to instruct the therapist how to fight back. He commented that the therapist seems to be getting better as he was able to fight back once.

More fighting lessons are necessary. He is acknowledging to the therapist that he is feeling stronger and is beginning to feel like he could fight back. We will see how this is a catalyst for later play where he is strong enough and actually fights back. It is also common during the early dependency stage that the roles become fluid and interchangeable as the client processes their trauma from different perspectives.

9   Jackson created a play scene with figurines on the floor depicting "good" and "evil" engaged in battle. He transitioned to fantasy play stating he was the therapist's teacher. Jackson reported, "We have to battle;" Jackson prevailed. He returned to floor play with the "good" and "evil" characters battling. He identified he was one of the characters in the play. He reported that he was learning to be "strong" and "fight back" but this was "hard" and that "sometimes Evil Jackson comes out." Jackson then asked to battle again with the therapist. He said "you need more practice … you fight like I used to and you need more practice but you're getting better." Jackson prevailed again and then returned to floor play where he also won.

Jackson is working very hard to develop power and strength. This type of play will typically take months. Children will engage in repetitive play frequently pendulating between opposites, such as good and evil (hence the fluidity with the roles) and between different mediums (i.e., floor/dollhouse/sand play with figurines or interactive role play), culminating into annihilation. Therapists often misinterpret this play to mean the child is "just playing" and therapists begin to get bored. It is actually critical that children have this opportunity during the dependency stage because improvements and gains are taking place often in miniscule ways. Through keen observation, therapists can access movement. Here Jackson states how hard it is and he is acknowledging his strength by telling the therapist he is getting stronger and used to fight like him, meaning the therapist is weak like he used to be. In actuality, Jackson is commenting on how he himself is getting stronger (remember the therapist is really Jackson).

Jackson continues developing more awareness that the bad part of himself that he has referred to as "Evil Jackson" comes out when he becomes too dysregulated and out-of-control.

10   Jackson informed the therapist "you have to train and engage in a battle." Today, nine attacks were necessary to win. Jackson prevailed but said the therapist is getting "stronger and smarter." Jackson switched his play and began working in the sand. While organizing items (superhero characters and villains) and placing them in rows, Jackson reported that sometimes he feels he is in his father's way. He denied his father ever saying this directly but reported, "I just feel this way sometimes."

The number of attacks is important to note. As stated above, during the dependency stage when play is repeated look for movement in the process. Session ten is a nice example. The therapist noted how Jackson wants nine attacks when three or five used to be the number of attacks or taps. Possibly something happened in Jackson's life between sessions and he is feeling weaker and needs more attacks to build back his strength. Or possibly it is because he is getting so strong he is able to fight more battles.

Jackson is also beginning to verbalize his feelings which is sometimes observed in the dependency play. Here he is verbalizing how he feels like he is in his father's way. When children bring up such random statements during play, the therapist should look at the previous play moments before to examine possible meaning. Jackson begins talking about his father proceeding this statement and the theme is about aggression, battles, power, control and bad vs. good. This likely indicates Jackson is struggling with all these issues and that the conflict is between him and his father. Furthermore, his father has probably been overly harsh possibly bordering on abuse toward Jackson. As children begin to play out their conflicts, they feel safer and stronger and they begin to develop better awareness of their internal environment, including conflicts. It is likely Jackson is engaging in these battles to develop a way of protecting himself against himself and/ or his father.

11   Jackson was quick to engage in imaginary play. He reported that his battle was between the "Injustice League" and the "Justice League." Jackson lined up figures and then paired them against each other. A battle ensued with the Justice League prevailing. A member of the Injustice League stated "the battle has only begun and will continue."

The "bad guy" versus "good guy" theme continues. There appears to be a slight change. He begins using characters from the Justice League and labels them as such with the opposing team being from the "Injustice League." It is likely he is gaining a belief that what is happening to him is unjust. While he continues getting stronger, he declares his internal battle continues.

12   Jackson reveals that "Evil Jackson is shifting to the good side but recently started to slide back to the dark side." Jackson proclaimed he has the ability to "bring Evil Jackson back to the good side" and that when he feels stressed out Evil Jackson is stronger. Jackson commented how there were three battles occurring and that each had one hero and two villains. After the heroes won their respective battles, a surprise villain attacked the heroes, many of which "died." Jackson expressed that the battle would continue next session.

Jackson is acknowledging progress and identifies how when he gets ahead, there always seems to be something that sets him back. It might be that he gets hurt again, and/or his bad behavior "all of a sudden" rises up and he gets aggressive.

13   Jackson selected a Hulk fist and Wolverine claw and provided the same to the therapist. He requested a battle. Jackson won and exclaimed "I'm getting stronger, Evil Jackson has been helped and was absorbed and is now part of me. I can use the strength of Evil Jackson to help in positive ways." However, Jackson noted that there are other "evils" that he must fight against but they are too hard to describe in detail today.

Integration of his villain part is occurring and he no longer feels out-of-control and can manage his bad behaviors. This is likely the result of the attacks described in session 12 in which many parts of him "died." In this session, he has begun to face his "shadow" (Jung, 1981). However, he acknowledges other "evil" parts still exist. With more strength and integration of self, Jackson approaches the deeper parts of his trauma.

14   Jackson selected a hulk fist and wolverine claw. Jackson says he is channeling "Evil Jackson." He handed the same play materials to the therapist. He announces after one receives "ten taps" the game ends. Jackson proceeded to direct

Jackson expresses "channeling Evil Jackson" because now Evil Jackson does not just appear, he has control over this part of himself but needs to call on the aggressive part of himself for the following annihilation play.

the therapist to tap him with the Wolverine claw ten times. Following the play, Jackson exhaustedly stated, "That was really hard" and hid in a covered chair reporting the chair was "uncomfortable."

Now it is ten taps, before it was three taps. It is likely he is engaged in the annihilation process. here is a need for ten taps because it indicates the higher-level pain from trauma and that this is going to be very hard work. Wanting to hide implies he feels vulnerable and possibly shame. He is likely scared to enter into the next aspect of the play. He needs the protection even when he might be too big to fit, but he accomplishes his task of hiding although unable to maintain because he did not fit well.

Jackson mentioned how he had been thinking about Batman, Superman and Spider-Man. He found these figures and placed them in the sand circling them with villains. One villain was approaching Spider-Man from behind with a gun. "The Punisher shot Spider-Man." Jackson exclaimed, "now he has a kryptonite bullet for, you guessed it, Superman." The Punisher knocks Superman to the ground, stands on his back and shoots.

Batman, Superman, and Spider-Man are three good guys that are being stalked by villians. These characters likely represent the "other evils" he mentions in session 13. He has been thinking about them because he has likely been configuring the play in his head prior to coming to session knowing more work is necessary and planning out the annihilation.

One of the villains approaching from behind combined with assessing the metaphor for gun (possible meanings of gun: "protection, assault, aggression, pain, anger, hostility, power, control, death, intrusion, impact, authority, boundaries") insinuates "surprise attack" but also might indicate sexual abuse (Norton & Norton, 2010c, p. 9). However, when interpreting such play as "fact" it can be a dangerous practice and instead should be viewed as a hypothesis only that needs further collaborating play. While similar play exists here in Jackson's sessions, there is an insufficient amount of play supporting sexual abuse thus far. The Punisher, a vigilante who employs violent behavior in his pursuit against crime, likely represents someone Jackson is punished by and/or someone Jackson views as enjoying violent behavior, which could possibly be his father. The shooting one of his good guy selves (Spider-Man) could be Jackson revealing the pain of abuse. Then the "Punisher" takes out the other hero with "kryptonite" which hurts Superman. Again, Superman is attacked from behind and is face down in the sand; thus, revealing once again a surprise attack. It really does not matter what type of abuse or if abuse occurred, the most important aspect of this process is to communicate to the child understanding what has happened to them in terms of pain. Acknowledging pain is primary.

Jackson adds various other images; a castle tower, Spider-Girl, Dark Batman, Drack, a Lego figure. "The bad guys might have control of everything right now. But that's only because they killed the good guys that were trying to stop them." A massive battle ensued; Spider-Girl was defeated. Batman and Dark Batman were both injured and removed. Spider-Man was successful in his battle and was replaced with a larger Spider-Man who then defeated the Punisher. The Lego guy tried to sneak under the ground and attack. Jackson announced, "Zombies can tunnel through the ground very fast." Jackson pushed the Lego guy through the sand and stated, "That's their (zombies) special capability—tunneling through the ground. They're always fast speeds." He brought back Spider-Girl and said "Spider-Girl is now actually over the water." Spider-Girl and the Zombie battle. Jackson announces, "Zombies can't swim so that was an easy beat, well sort of. Expect more villains are coming."

Now Jackson brings in a structure that he identifies as a "Castle Tower." The metaphor for castle is "home, authority, protection, impenetrable, boundary, defense, past, family, guarded, fortified, rigidity, power, safety." A trauma response includes "imprisonment, incest, isolation, strong, defenses, loneliness, distressful recollections, secretive, domination and captivity (Norton & Norton, 2010a, p. 2)." Here he is bringing in a structure likely representing his home and that it is "evil" or possibly that bad things happen at home. He is encircled by villains including "Dark Batman" which is a counterpart to the "good guy" Batman. Other villains are brought in and might indicate the level of fear he feels regarding what happens in the "castle tower" (home). He also brings in the good guys but has more villains and communicates how the villains are in control, which makes sense in terms of how he views his world and the need to fight.

Now he can begin the fight, starting with the good Batman and evil Batman, which both got hurt.

He gains a little strength when Spider-Man battles and is denoted by the increase in size of the figure. Now with some power, he is able to face one of the more dangerous figures "The Punisher."

Spider-Girl and Spider-Man both lose the battle and once again, Spider-Man is assaulted from behind. This is frenzied play which is typically observed when children approach the more painful aspects of their trauma due to high activation in the Sympathetic Nervous System.

He brings in a new type of villain. The metaphor for zombie is "emotionally constricted, detachment, monster, loner, depression, wounded, emotionally distorted, numbing, awkward, creature, seeks revenge, self-alienation." The trauma response is "freeze, or constricted mobility, flat affect or dysregulated affect, numbing and isolation" (Norton & Norton, 2010b, p. 13). Jackson viewed attacking zombies as not hard because they are not very powerful. Zombies might represent his mother.

He picked up a GI Joe figure and stated, "I feel like I didn't give this guy much of a chance earlier" and commented on how GI Joe was able to "mind control" the remaining figures.

Jackson brings in a soldier type of figure, GI Joe and now rather than just mere strength he is able to control the minds of the villains. It is possible the zombies represent those in his life who have harmed him as well but he is stronger than them and can overpower them. The GI Joe might represent his father (not only do children use many characters to represent the many aspects of self, children also use many characters to represent people in their lives and are interchangeable with themselves). As children face their trauma they begin to look at the individuals who have hurt them in a more favorable light or express wishful thinking. It might be that Jackson is able to see the good qualities of his father as well and is indicated by acknowledging that he has not given "GI Joe a chance" and can use the "mind control" to his advantage.

Jackson paused from the sandtray work and exclaimed, "Evil Jackson has been destroyed, Evil Dream Jackson is also gone, dead."

With these battles and the gaining of his strength, he is able to see how the bad parts of him are gone (Evil Jackson and Evil Dream Jackson); they killed each other.

He shared that that Dream Jackson and Evil Dream Jackson "killed each other" and that "they are part of me and sort of not. Jacksontron 2000 is still present. He is a good guy."

While he is able to verbalize and acknowledge the good and evil parts of himself, he still struggles with the ambivalence of being bad and internalizing the bad parts of himself. However, what has prevailed is the good part of himself, Jacksontron 2000.

With the introduction of many more villains suggests he is aware that more hard times are to come. He also seems to worry that his imagination is under attack which implies he worries he will lose his mind and his mind will become under control again, thus become "bad" again. It also suggests he knows he is getting stronger and more powerful which means the villains (and bad parts of himself) are going to be fighting back harder.

He noted that while battling at the start of session, "I was just a guy needing training. I think I was part good and part bad. My imagination is under attack—the good guys, the bad guys. These new guys are not taking any prisoners. What do they do? They kill only. But I've made a team of good guys that are trying to fight back."

He re-positioned the castle tower and commented, "Now it's basically nothing, almost nothing." He announced there was a "kryptonite bomb." A female character was introduced and began to battle the villains but was defeated by "Drack." Jackson commented how "Spider-Man just got brainwashed" and "That guy is actually holding a gun in his hand (referring to GI Joe)." Spider-Man then breaks free from the brainwash and defeats all remaining villains except Drack. He then adds a large T-Rex and noted, "Villains win today" and in reference to the GI Joe, "He is still trying to brainwash them."

With all his fighting, the castle tower (his home) has been diminished and has lost the negative power it once had, because it was bombed by kryptonite. He brings in again the loss of power he felt by losing his brain or his ability to think, which he now references as brainwashing. He is able to think more clearly. The gun is another reference to the abuse (and GI Joe has the gun). Spider-Man struggles in a fight and being brainwashed, but prevails. It is possible the brainwashing is something the "real villain" (dad) in his life tells him and he feels everything is his fault or is "bad." However, he no longer believes he is bad. He wins against all villains except one; Drack. Jackson will likely need to continue battling this guy in future sessions and needs to continue the fight against being brainwashed. Levine (2005) suggests, "In an attempt to overcome the feeling of having no control, the mind attempts to assert whatever power it hopes will hide the fear and sense of profound aloneness. Aggression toward others and ourselves is akin to the muscle fatigue of swimming as hard as we can and still being dragged farther out to sea" (p. 18).

Summary of Case Conceptualization

Trauma can shred our safety nets to increasing degrees and for Jackson, with each hurt and incessant change, the drawstrings pulled closer, his insecurity rose and his fantasy world grew more intense. Amazingly, he kept one foot grounded in reality. His transitions from the Hulk to Jackson and the retraction of Wolverine's claws at the end of each session reaffirmed this strength. Jackson seemed to accept that while softening to his anger and feeling hopeless, he was not helpless and symbolic play remained at his fingertips. While recognizing these struggles, Jackson made discoveries and through empowerment, a sense of internal protection and mastery started to occur naturally. With Jackson's perspective and capacity expanding, he was meeting his injury, the villainous role, with mercy. Jackson reported, "I can't get rid of Evil Jackson. I have to accept it because it's part of me but it doesn't control me." Levine (2005) states, "By opening into the possibilities of the heart, expanding the space that is able to absorb all that is let go of, we are able to find our own true compass of what is appropriate to our own healing and go mercifully on with our lives" (p. 23). Jackson was learning to trust himself and instead of masking his feelings through Evil Jackson, he was learning to integrate and that it was possible to face his villains while unified. While initially unmatched in relentlessness of the villain's campaign, Jackson manages to guide himself in skill development and tenacity, clinging to the ever-evolving sense of self. As therapy progressed, Jackson became more integrated and his father described Jackson as less controlling, more assertive, and showing more leadership across domains of functioning. His newly developed spaciousness permitted greater tolerated discomfort while EPT® provided the containment for Jackson to soften to the sensations and orchestrate himself. As Jackson continues his involvement in therapy, it is hoped this sense of self will further solidify as he learns the many strengths he possesses.

Conclusion

This chapter has explored ways in which EPT® embraces the "villain" in the child's approach to troublesome trauma content. In order for Jackson and others to balance their fear with courage, they must trust their pain enough to explore it (Levine, 2005). The containment of the therapist, use of play as a child's language, and understanding the role of "villain," result in the child safely externalizing fears, addressing distressing sensory impressions, and using metaphor to cope. Brody (2007) suggested that "Like myths and fairy tales, they provide an externalization of inner conflicts. The child can now see his inner difficulties more clearly and reflect on a variety of solutions" (p. 116). EPT® provides the theatrical stage necessary for children to begin a process of feeling understood in their language and generate solutions along the quest of empowerment.

There are many types of villains who bring out the many traits of heroes. We can learn valuable lessons from being present and containing a child's play. In EPT®, fantasy play can help the therapist understand the child's pain while providing them with the necessary skills for it to be used later as a template for empowerment. While the child continues to work on building ego strength, the villain is a reminder of the experience not to be forgotten but to integrate and rise above. With these villains, we must come to trust the process of healing enough to open our heart to the unknown. We must acknowledge its unpredictable unfolding with a sense of compassion for ourselves and others who tremble at the brink of what comes next, whether its tragedy or grace. And we must remember that somehow our heart has room for it all (Levine, 2005). Thank you for taking this journey with us but before you leave we share a series of questions for you to consider as you work to better understand the villain.

Questions for Clinical Discussion

1.   Which type of villain provides the best narrative for children's stories?
2.   What emotions does the villain evoke in you?
3.   What dark dreams do your villains satisfy?
4.   Why are we fascinated by villains?
5.   What makes a villain?
6.   How would you interpret Jackson's play?

References

Benedict, H. E. (2002). *Assessment play themes handout from workshop: Using research base theme patterns to enhance play assessment and therapy.* Presented at the National Association for Play Therapy Conference October 14–19, 2008, Dallas, TX.

Brody, M. (2007). Holy franchise! Batman and trauma. In: L. C. Rubin (Ed.), *Using superheroes in counseling and play therapy* (pp. 105–120). New York: Springer Publishing Company, LLC.

Jones, G. (2002). *Killing monsters: Why children need fantasy, super heroes, and make-believe violence.* New York: Basic Books.

Jung, C. G. (1981). *The collective works of C. G. Jung. Part 1: The archetypes and the collective unconscious* (2nd edn.). Princeton, NJ: Princeton University Press.

Kain, K. L. & Terrell, S. J. (2018). *Nurturing resilience: Helping clients move forward from developmental trauma: An integrative somatic approach.* Berkeley, CA: North Atlantic Books.

Levine, P. A. (1997). *Waking the tiger.* Berkeley, CA: North Atlantic Books.

Levine, P. A. (2007). *Trauma through a Child's eyes: Awakening the ordinary miracle of healing. Infancy through adolescence.* Berkley, CA North Atlantic Books; Lyons, CA: ERGOS Institute Press.

Levine, P. A. (2010). *In an unspoken voice: How the body releases trauma and restores goodness.* Berkley, CA: North Atlantic Books.

Levine, P. A. (2015). *Trauma and memory: Brain and body in a search for the living past.* Berkley, CA: North Atlantic Books.

Levine, S. (2005). *Unattended sorrow. Recovering from loss and reviving the heart.* New York: Rodale Books–Penguin.

Norton, B. (2004). Personal communication.

Norton, B., Ferriegel, M., & Norton C. (2011). Somatic expressions of trauma in experiential play therapy. *International Journal of Play Therapy, 20,* 138–152.

Norton, B. & Norton, C. (2006). Experiential play therapy. In: C. E. Schaefer and H. G. Kaduson (Eds.), *Contemporary play therapy* (pp. 28–54). New York: Guilford Press.

Norton, B. E. & Norton, C. C. (2010a). Symbolic meaning of environments expressed in experiential play therapy (EPT)* [Consultation handout]. Minnetonka, MN.

Norton, B. E. & Norton, C. C. (2010b). Symbolic meaning of roles expressed in experiential play therapy (EPT)* [Consultation handout]. Minnetonka, MN.

Norton, B. E. & Norton, C. C. (2010c). Symbolic meaning of toys expressed in experiential play therapy (EPT)* [Consultation handout]. Minnetonka, MN.

Norton, C. C. & Norton, B. E. (2002). *Reaching children through play therapy: An experiential approach* (2nd edn.). Denver, CO: White Apple Press.

Norton, C. C. & Norton, B. E. (2008). *Reaching children through play therapy: An experiential approach* (3rd edn.). Denver, CO: White Apple Press.

Paley, V. G. (2004). *A child's work: The importance of fantasy play.* Chicago, IL: The University of Chicago Press.

Perry, B. D. & Szalavitz, M. (2006). *The boy who was raised as a dog and other stories from a child psychiatrist's notebook.* New York: Basic Books.

Porges, S. W. (2004). Neuroception: A subconscious system for detecting threat and safety. *Zero to Three: Bulletin of the National Center for Clinical Infant Programs, 24* (5): 19–24.

Porges, S. W. (2011). *The polyvagal theory: Neurophysiological foundations of emotions, attachment, communication, and self-regulation.* New York: W. W. Norton & Company, Inc.

Repplier, A. (1890). A short defense of villains. *The Atlantic Monthly,* pp 841–846.

Saldana, L. (2008). Metaphors, analogies, and myths, oh my! Therapeutic journeys along the yellow brick road. In: L. C. Rubin (Ed.), *Popular culture in counseling, psychotherapy, and play-based interventions* (pp. 3–23). New York: Springer Publishing Company, LLC

Scaer, R. C. (2001). *The body bears the burden: Trauma, dissociation and disease.* Binghamptom, NY: The Hawthorn Press, Inc.

Scaer, R. C. (2005). *The trauma spectrum: Hidden wounds and human resiliency.* New York: W. W. Norton & Company, Inc.

Van der Kolk, B. (2014). *The body keeps the score: Brain, mind, and body in the healing of trauma.* New York: Viking Penguin Group.

Ziegler, D. (2002). *Traumatic experience and the brain: A handbook for understanding and treating those traumatized as children.* Phoenix, AZ: Acacia Publishing, Inc.

CHAPTER 4

The Healing Power of Superhero Stories: Bibliotherapy and Comic Books

Yoav Cohen-Manor

All superheroes share one main superpower—the power of healing. For all the superhero stories are essentially "healing stories." By setting examples of growth through the facing of hardship, difficulties and loss, their readers can draw inspiration from them, reflect on their own emotions and behavior and use the stories for self-transformation and healing. Bibliotherapy, as a creative arts therapy, incorporates stories and texts as an agent of transformation in the therapeutic process. In the following pages, I will present a psychodynamic theory of bibliotherapy, and show the unique healing properties of superhero comic books and how they can be used in the therapy session.

What is Bibliotherapy?

Bibliotherapy is a therapeutic methodology that is a part of expressive arts therapy. This particular therapeutic methodology uses text as part of the therapeutic process. The use of literature for therapeutic therapy dates back to ancient times. Over the doors of the ancient libraries of Alexandria and Thebes were inscribed the words "healing place of the soul," and Aristotle's conceptualization of catharsis revolves, in essence, around the healing effect he believed tragedy could have on the spectators (Zoran, 2009). We can find a more explicit and institutional use of literature for therapeutic purposes already in the beginning of the twentieth century, and by the 1930s, the therapeutic use of reading was already ubiquitous in the mental health professions (McKenna, Hevey, & Martin, 2010). Later in the 1960s, librarians began to recommend certain books that they believed could mentally help prisoners (Zoran, 2009). Today, an extensive body of research has confirmed the positive influences of the use of texts for therapeutic intervention in a variety of mental fields, from dealing with stress to coping with traumas (De Vries et al., 2017).

In Psychodynamic-Bibliotherapy, the text has an essential and crucial role both in the therapeutic process and the therapeutic relationship. The text is a "third object" located in the therapy room alongside the therapist and the patient. Similar to Ogden's conceptualization of the "analytic third" (Ogden, 1994) that holds the intersubjectively-generated experience of the analyst and the patient, the text, as a third object, is distinct from the therapist and patient, yet, at the same time, it is introjected into the patient's transference and projections: "the entire literary text is metaphorically affiliated to the patient's world, and hence constitutes a kind of artistic representation of this world in the therapeutic discourse" (Zoran, 2009 p. 59).

Israeli scholar Rachel Zoran, who conceptualized the theoretical foundation for Psychodynamic-Bibliotherapy, based her theorization of the therapeutic power of the text on the Donald Winnicott's concept of potential space (Winnicott, 2012). Winnicott theorized potential space as a liminal space between the baby and the object. This space is not part of the individual's self, nor is it part of the external world, rather it is between both. This psychic space links fantasy (the internal world) to reality (the external world), and contains playfulness, creativity, imagination and cultural experiences (Winnicott, 2012). The movement in the potential space is what makes the psychotherapeutic process possible.

In order for the text (be it a novel, poem or comic book) to function as a successful transitional object, it has to fulfill two conditions. The first condition is its autonomy, the text must be separate from the patient. This separation makes it possible to have a dialogue between the patient and the text. The second condition is a certain level of ambiguity, or ambivalence in the text. A literary text is characterized by an ambiguity stemming from information gaps in the text (Iser, 1978). In the process of reading, the reader fills these gaps with his imagination and experience. The text's ambiguity is the source of the reader's freedom in the creation of the story. In essence, the reader actively creates the story with his unique responses to the text. The text, in this scenario, is experienced as a part of the self that is also separate from it; thus it expands the potential space, which is essential for the ability to process inner content and conflict, and makes possible mental work from a safe distance that can bypass the patient's defenses and helps reach deeper levels of the psyche. The existence of the text as a potential space that links the patient's internal reality with the external reality, makes it possible for the text to function as a "third voice" in the bibliotherapeutic dialogue (Zoran, 2009).

Comic Books as a Third Voice

Superhero comic books present an interesting case of a "third voice" in the therapeutic setting, and have unique qualities for the therapeutic process. I shall try to explain the unique aspect of the language of comic books, and how it can be used as a "third voice," and will then focus on the case of superheroes, a unique genre in comic books.

While literature is made of verbal language, comic books construct their narrative through a mainly graphic medium, by juxtaposing images in a deliberate sequence (McCloud, 1994). This is why it is also called "sequential art" (Eisner, 1992). The comic book reader uses his imagination to merge the juxtaposed static images into a linearly progressing story. Hillary Chute underscores the function of the reader in comic books when she argues that "comics move forward in time through the space of the page, through its progressive counter-points of presence and absence: paced panels (also called frames) alternating with gutters (empty spaces)" (Chute, 2008, p. 452). The absence, those empty spaces between the panels constitute an unequivocal visual expression (though, of course, not the only one) of the literary gaps that are found in the language of comics. The reader has to use his imagination to fill the empty spaces between the painted panels; he imagines what took place between one panel and another and hence constructs for himself the relation between the panels. As Scott McCloud argues, the reader is not a passive or innocent consumer of the story, but is rather a partner in crime, so to speak (McCloud, 1994). These empty spaces do not only exist between the frames, but also operate on the level of the single picture. The framing of the picture will necessarily leave some of the information outside, leaving the reader with the task of completing it. For instance, a close up of a character's face will necessarily leave out the rest of its body as well as the surrounding in which his body is located, letting the reader complete this gap in his imagination. In the same manner, a more distant picture of the character may give the reader more information about the body of the character and the situation this character finds itself in, but it will not provide the character's facial expressions, and so he will have to complete them himself. One way or another, the gap is always necessarily there and the reader unconsciously completes the partial picture and hence imbues the frame with personal (that is, projected) contents.

Another dimension inherent to comics is the combination of visual language with verbal language, that is, images and text. Although according to McCloud's definition of comics, the graphic narrative can exist without a text (McCloud, 1994), comics, and especially superhero comics, usually combine images with text (Gavaler, 2018). Hillary Chute defines comics as "a hybrid word-and-image form in which two narrative tracks, one verbal and one visual register temporality spatially" (Chute, 2008, p. 452). The two channels, then, come together to create meaning, yet one does not substitute the other and the two are not identical. Text in comics can take on many forms—thought or speech bubbles or an independent separate text that belongs to the narrator. While in the early days of comics, their images usually functioned as illustrations of the text, as the genre developed, the relation between text and picture changed. Today, the visual channel has a much more developed and significant meaning, which is mainly separate from the text (Cohn, Taylor & Pederson, 2017). Thus, the text can add information or provide different information, yet the reader is responsible to connect this information to the image and fashion the hybrid meaning.

We can hence see that the comic language encapsulates three different loci of ambiguity. The first is the ambiguity of the visual language which exists in the absence in between and outside the image frames, but also in the images themselves as works of art that can be interpreted in many different ways. The second is the inherent ambiguity of the verbal channel, which necessarily leaves information gaps for the interpretation of the reader. And the third, the ambiguity that is created by the integration of the verbal channel with the visual. These three distinct loci of ambiguity make it possible for the comic to contain the meanings projected upon it by the reader or patient, and function as a transitional object and open a potential space.

Superhero Comics

Although comics were created before the twentieth century, they became popular in the 1930s (Chute, 2008). Moreover, it is customary to mark the birth of the superhero comics genre with the birth of the first superhero, Superman, in the late 1930s, that became a model for many other superheroes that soon followed (Gavaler, 2018). While there were those who believed the comic books would corrupt the youth and even lead to illiteracy (Chute, 2008), there were pioneers, even in the golden age of superheroes, such as Dr. Lauretta Bender, who argued that superheroes fulfill many "psychological needs of the child" (Lawrence, 2006,, p. xxv). And indeed, in a recent study (Betzalel & Shechtman, 2017), superhero stories were found to have much greater therapeutic effect on adolescents who deal with parental absence, than other (fairy tale or adventure) stories.

The positive ways in which superheroes can be used in therapy are discussed extensively in the various chapters of this book as well as in the editor's previous book (Rubin, 2006). I would like to focus on a few aspects that are specifically significant for bibliotherapy with comic books.

The Monomyth Model and the Movement from Conflict to Solution

Superhero comic book stories follow the monomyth model that Joseph Campbell presented in his book *The Hero with a Thousand Faces* (Campbell, 2008). Campbell conducted a constructionist analysis of myths and legends from around the world and found a repeating pattern with three main stages. In the first stage, the hero, who is a regular person, answers a calling for an adventure and passes over to a magic world, beyond the normal world. In the second stage, the hero faces challenges with the help of new powers and other helping characters; he withstands tests and overcomes these challenges and as a result is awarded with new powers or the discovery of inner strength. In the third stage, the hero returns to the regular world and is able to use his newfound abilities to contribute to his surroundings and community. The classical superhero model includes a regular person who becomes a superhero, or a man with powers who behaves like a regular person, and when needed takes upon himself the character of the hero, thereby marking the transition to another realm. Chris Gavaler (2018) notes that Campbell's book was published in the midst of the golden age of superheroes, and claims that since the monomyth model was created in a culture in which superhero comics flourished, it better describes superhero stories than ancient myths. While superheroes represent a complete monomyth (including the origin story, the discovery of the hero's powers or receiving them as a result of an accident or any other way), every single comic book unfolds the hero's struggle against certain threatening powers. Thus, every comic book depicts the middle part of the monomyth — encountering a threatening force, fighting it and overcoming it, even if temporarily (Gavaler, 2018). The therapeutic importance of the monomyth structure of superhero comics lies in the movement from conflict and resolution. The story contains a dynamic flow that does not fix the conflict in place. Through the story, the reader experiences a dynamic process of psychic movement. On one level, we can say that the reader is presented with a model in which the ego overcomes its difficulties and through it can come to the realization that through this it is possible to overcome his own difficulties. From a psychodynamic-bibliotherapeutic standpoint, when the reader projects his world into the story and experiences himself merged with the heroes, he experiences dealing with threatening elements and overcoming them. Thus, there is an experience of empowering the ego and an experience of movement and overcoming challenges.

I would like to argue that working with stories that have defined narratives of development and overcoming, with a significant change and permutation from one state to another, that is with an evolutionary change and not merely a transitional change, is an important psychological paradigm that can contribute to the therapeutic process.

Superheroes as Symbolic Characters

Superhero characters present their readers with ways of coping with psychological experiences and other difficulties. They can constitute role models for social skills and solving conflicts with intelligence and compassion (Gavaler, 2018). I would like to propose that the unique aspect of superheroes and supervillains in the therapeutic process does not stem from their complexity as characters but rather from their simplicity. Even though superheroes can present psychological complexity and depth of personality, they represent a very specific and distinct theme, and hence can be characterized as symbolic characters.

A first glance of a comic book already reveals how the graphic language distinguishes the superhero from other people (Brownie & Graydon, 2016) and marks him as a symbol. The superhero's colorful costume, the mask and the symbol on the chest brand the superhero. The role of the superhero's suit is not functional (who needs a cape during a fight) but rather symbolic. Thus, Captain America is painted in the colors of the American flag, Batman is dressed in black with the ears that endow him with a bat like appearance, Spider-Man is decorated with images of webs, and these are just some examples. Superheroes wear their role or persona openly. The fact that most superheroes are identified with a unique character or power that defines them and makes them memorable such as super speed, or powers of a certain animal (Gavaler, 2018), also adds the creation of the symbolism. In the same manner, the catchphrases that are identified with characters present them in an instance ("Is it a bird? Is it a plane? No, it's Superman" or Batman's "I am vengeance") are an example of their status as an icon-symbol.

From a bibliotherapeutic standpoint, superhero symbolism is significant first and foremost because it makes it possible for the reader to distance himself from the characters. A story can function as a transitional object on condition that it is at once familiar, so that the patient can identify materials of the self with the superhero, and experience the text as part of himself, yet he also has to maintain a measure of autonomy and distance so that the text will simultaneously be experienced as "not I," as part of the external reality. By distancing, the patient focuses on a character rather than himself and his defenses are hence lowered. Without this distance, the patient would feel that he is reading a story about himself, and would block himself from the story's emotional content. The fact that superheroes are "larger than life" separates them from the reader's daily existence. Thus, comics can directly deal with difficult content without threatening the reader.

Another important aspect of the superhero's symbolism is that characters distill an emotional and conceptual theme, making the story more easily palatable, especially for the younger patients: children and adolescents. The comics' painterly style tends more towards abstraction than realism and thereby underscores the essential details and makes it possible for the reader to place all his focus on an idea (McCloud, 1994), while the emphasis on the symbolic elements strengthens the same idea.

Superhero comics present us with a dichotomous division into "good" and "bad," and characters that can be reduced into a character trait or word: "The Avenger," "Wonder Kid," "Superman," and other palatable archetypal descriptions. They thus make it possible for the reader to quickly immerse himself in this strange world, since the basic essence of each character can be swiftly deciphered. When the patient reads about a character representing an archetype, and hence a certain principle in his psyche, the reading can be channeled into this aspect of the patient's personality. For instance, Spider-Man represents a conflict between strength and weakness, smallness and a sense of rejection. On the one hand, he is a "spider"—an anthropoid, which people instinctively reject, and on the other, a hero dedicated to saving lives (similarly, Peter Parker, the boy under the Spider-Man costume, deals with social rejection and a sense of not belonging). Thus, when a teen reads a Spider-Man story, he will read it through the lens of socially fitting in, since this is a theme the character introduces into every story by virtue of its symbolism. That is, the character's symbolism constitutes a kind of magnifying glass to certain aspects and makes it possible to focus the treatment on these aspects.

Like superheroes, supervillains are also symbolic characters. Thus, the struggle between the hero and the villain in the comic book's story is also a struggle between sets of ideas. The conflict is not between two characters but between themes, two different world views and values, two ideas symbolized in the comics by the hero and the villain. As stated, the character's symbolism makes it easy for the reader, and especially the young reader, to identify the conceptual theme, even if unconsciously, and experience the deeper symbolic struggle, which could even be his own inner-psychic struggle.

Hyperbole as an Emotional Metaphor

Like the colorfulness and exaggeration in the graphic design of the characters, the superhero plot is exaggerated. Ubiquitous images that can be found while sifting through comic books show a superhero fighting against a much larger monster, or forcibly thrown through a wall, or lifting a bus. These images go beyond our physical reality; however, their attractiveness points to their importance and centrality in the comic's visual language. I would like to propose that we read these hyperbolic images as emotional images or emotional metaphors. We can think of commonplace metaphors such as "carrying the world on his shoulders," which describe a psychic reality of difficulties and vulnerability via exaggerations of the physical. The comic book images could constitute a visual expression of these adages. That is, the visual plot of superhero comics depicts an autonomous emotional space. The reader accepts these images since in the world of the comic book they are not strange or foreign, and they follow the story of the superhero, who copes with challenges that match his super strengths. Since these images do not represent an action that the reader recognizes from his own reality, the identification operates on an emotional level. I would like to suggest that these images turn into emotional symbols and into an emotional-visual language that helps the patient-reader give shape to his otherwise internal emotional chaos. Thus, the patient receives both an echoing and identification, and a sense that he is not alone in his difficulties (of loneliness, helplessness, rage and so forth). Moreover, he gains an emotional-visual-narratological language through which he can understand his inner world. The fact that this language exists externally in the comic book makes possible a beginning of a dialogue and an internal psychic movement.

I would now like to demonstrate the theoretical overview through three case studies that demonstrate the therapeutic aspects of bibliotherapy. The first case study will be a reading of a Batman story named *The Killing Joke*. The second will focus on the experience of the reader through a story from a comic of Israeli writer Asaf Hanuka. While the third will include a clinical vignette.

First Case Study: a Reading of *Batman: The Killing Joke*

Batman: The Killing Joke is a graphic novel written by Alan Moore and illustrated by Brian Bolland, published in 1988 (Moore, Bolland, & Starkings, 2008). I chose this novel since its canonic status testifies to its quality and its ability to contain essential symbolic contents and also makes it more possible that the reader will know the book and its content. After presenting the plot of the novel, I will show how the bibliotherapeutic aspects outlined above help turn the comic book story into a space that may contain metaphorical representation of a therapeutic process.

Batman: The Killing Joke tells the story of a battle between Batman and The Joker and reveals The Joker's origin story. In the main plot line, The Joker escapes from Arkham Asylum—a mental institute for the criminally insane, where all the archvillains that Batman has captured in the past are held. He takes over an abandoned amusement park and plans to prove to Batman that any man can go insane, and that the difference between sanity and insanity is fragile and can hinge on "one bad day." The Joker kidnaps inspector Gordon, while also shooting and wounding his daughter, and then invites Batman to the amusement park so that Batman can witness how The Joker drives the inspector insane. Batman chases The Joker in the amusement park, which is turned into a nightmarish arena, until their final confrontation. In The Joker's origin story, we meet a failed comedian who has trouble providing for his pregnant wife. In his despair, he joins two criminals to rob a chemical plant. A moment before the robbery he discovers that his wife has died; however, the robbers make him go through the robbery nonetheless. The robbery goes bad, and as Batman charges toward him, he falls into the chemical plant's polluted water system. When he comes out of the water and removes his mask, the reader can see the physical (and mental) change that he has undergone in his encounter with the chemicals and his tragedy, and he becomes The Joker. In the concluding scene of the novel (in the present), Batman captures The Joker, who in turn, tells Batman a story about two lunatics in an insane asylum who try to escape the asylum but fail because of their own madness.

The Killing Joke is rich with multiple layers of meaning and significance. The main theme that I would like to underscore in my reading is trauma and the ways in which one can cope with it, or to put it differently, the strength and fragility of the human psyche. The story juxtaposes Batman with The Joker as mirror images of each other. While the two are usually perceived as completely antagonistic (good and evil, order and chaos), this story points toward their similarity (Doise, 2015). The Joker's origin story is structurally similar to Batman's origin and in a way parallel to it. The two characters offer different ways to cope with trauma. The Joker represents a possibility for the disintegration of the personality (the choice in madness from an inability to cope with his horrific psychic reality) while Batman represents post-traumatic growth, as he channels his grief and rage over his parent's death toward a sense of calling and helping others.

Since in the reading process the reader projects contents from his inner world to the external text, and as a result the contents that correspond to his internal reality are underscored and given a more prominent place in his reading experience, we should remember that different readers may be influenced by different specific contents in the comics more than with the main theme I pointed toward. For instance, a reader that faces questions of self-fulfillment and career choices, could be very sensitive to The Joker's origin story, since he left his regular job to follow his desire and try to have a career as a comedian. Through this prism, the entire story line echoes the way in which The Joker's identity is a manic denial of his failure as a comedian, an identity that infected him.

Like many other comic books, this story also follows Joseph Campbell's monomyth model (1949), and more precisely the middle stage in which the hero faces challenges and trials until he overcomes them and in the process is rewarded with new powers or understanding. Batman, the hero of the story, fights The Joker, is wounded in the process but eventually overcomes him. The meaning of the narratological structure is the existence of the narratological movement which, in the bibliotherapeutic process, can function as a paradigm of the psychic movement; rather than a fixation on a conflict there is development and growth. A deeper reading of *Batman: The Killing Joke* reveals that the narrative unfolds an emotional movement from conflict to solution through empathy. Batman attempts to reform The Joker while The Joker tries to drive Batman insane—or at least prove to him that he is just as insane as the Joker is. During the conflict between the two antagonistic forces (order vs. chaos, or in a more psychological iteration—resilience vs. madness) Batman is exposed to the similarity between them and this makes possible an ending in which The Joker tells Batman a joke and Batman laughs, thus creating a moment of empathy. This is a narrative in which the hero vanquishes the villain by acknowledging their resemblance and expressing empathy (while still maintaining his separateness). If we treat the conflict in the story as a model of an internal conflict, we can think of a therapeutic intervention that would make it possible for the patient to experience, in the transitional space, a model of containing the parts of the self through empathy. This is an experience of being in which the patient is not required to split, deny or repress chaotic parts or parts of the self that he perceives as negative, rather it provides a possibility to contain these parts without causing the self to collapse (just like Batman can show empathy to The Joker without ceding his identity as Batman or letting The Joker continue to wreak havoc and destruction). That is, the narrative constitutes a symbolic model of a psychic movement from conflict toward a complete self that can accept all his parts.

The story underscores the symbolic aspect of the characters of The Joker and Batman and hence their struggle is also charged with symbolism. In terms of the graphic novel's visual dimension, Batman is the picture of order. His suit is black and blue and he is draped in a cape, he exudes order and control. The Joker, on the other hand, with his green hair, white face and purple clothes exudes exaggerated colorfulness; this visual exaggeration of colors is similar to the chaos he wishes to bring into the world. In some of the images, The Joker is drawn with particularly big and round eyes, which makes him look like a skeleton. The blood pouring down from his eyes makes him look even more like a monster—an abomination from the natural order of things. He looks like something disturbing and nightmarish that should never have existed. The reader then can perceive the antagonistic relation between the two characters from the visual design alone. Another example is the face and the mask. While Batman is restrained, closed and hidden inside his mask, The Joker is a grotesque mask that cannot keep anything inside and expresses chaos. As stated above, the symbolic design of the superheroes and supervillains makes it possible for the readers, and especially the younger ones, to process them more quickly. In the framework of bibliotherapy, the characters' symbolism enables the reader-patient to experience the characters as symbols of themes or mental states; for instance, restraint, control and exercising judgment versus madness, the loss of boundaries and the loss of control. The symbol derives its importance from its inherent measure of ambiguity, thus, even though it focuses on a certain theme there is always, from its very nature, a space that is open to interpretation. For instance, a post traumatic patient can interpret the struggle between Batman and The Joker as a representation of an internal-mental struggle following a traumatic experience, between the desire to channel the mental diffi-culty toward growth and meaning and the wish to allow the mind to "fall apart." On the other hand, a patient dealing with an unstable and chaotic environment in his life, may read the story as a representation of facing threatening external forces. A bibliotherapeutic dialogue about the main characters and the relation between them can enable the patient, by distancing and projecting contents to the comic book that exists as an object in the transitional space, to process the nature of his difficulties, his coping mechanisms, as well as omnipotent fantasies (like Batman's omnipotence) and their mental price.

The chase scene toward the end of the novel presents a good example both of the way in which the visual language creates emotional metaphors and for the way in which the connection between the written texts and the images can produce interesting meanings and ambiguity. In the scene, Batman chases The Joker within a structure in the amusement park, which The Joker redesigned into a course of horrors. Throughout the chase, the reader sees Batman running surrounded by huge, laughing demonic faces. The image is an emotional and metaphorical hyper-bole reflecting a nightmarish experience of horror and persecution. One of the frames in the chase's frame sequence shows Batman falling into a trap, a hole in the floor filled with sharp spears coated with a certain liquid (which we can guess is poison), while he is holding on for his life with only one arm. This image offers another example of a metaphorical hyperbole. Even though in terms of its phys-ical dimensions, the image retains the natural style, its content is so symbolic that it is immediately turned into a general metaphor for danger and holding on by a thread.

I would like to use this image and the visual metaphor it encapsulates to demon-strate a fundamental element in the language of comics, the relation between the graphic medium and the verbal medium, and the way in which it can generate new significations. These significations are pivotal to the therapeutic process precisely because they are generated from a connection the reader-patient makes between the image and the text. Thus, the reader fashions these significations through his active interpretation and projections. The text that accompanies the sequence of images of the chase is The Joker's speech. The Joker tells Batman that what separates sanity from insanity is merely "one bad day." After all, Batman also had one bad day that changed him and made him "dress like a flying rat," only that Batman refuses to admit this, and continues to pretend that his struggle to keep sanity in check means something. We can see here a metaphoric identification between the image and the text. The image presents a physical trap into which Batman almost falls, while the text presents The Joker's mental trap—to pull away the stable ground of sanity beneath Batman's feet and make him give up. The Joker's text is written in speech bubbles without a source—this design choice blurs the source of the text and makes it possible to think of the text as an abstract iteration with which Batman has to cope. This frame is an excellent example for the manner in which the image and the text generate a third signification—in this case, Batman's emotional state. Batman is desperately holding onto stable ground and investing vast amounts of effort not to fall into a trap. The reader, then, can experience the theme reflected in the visual channel as Batman's psychic experience in the face of The Joker's emotional and mental attack. He is investing vast amounts of effort not to fall all the way into the trauma (the pit) and into mental disintegration, despite the temptation. That is, the metaphorical connection between the text and the image provides the reader with the tools to create Batman's emotional experience through his own imagination, as an experience he shares with him. Moreover, this image can also be perceived as a metaphor for emotions or existential experiences that he himself is experiencing. As stated before, this content exists as an interpretation of the reader, which can be formed because of the ambiguity of the text. And since the reader reaches these experiences and the emotion through his encounter with the story, they belong to the transitional space, the Winnicottian potential space. In other words, each reader has his own personal trap into which he is tempted to fall, and part of it is projected to the trap of the story, which hence makes it possible for the reader to process this content from a safe distance.

Second Case Study: the Experience of the Reader

To demonstrate the therapeutic potential that can be found in superhero comics, I will now turn my focus to the experience of the reader, through the poetic expression of an enthusiastic comic book reader turned comic book artist. Asaf Hanuka is an Israeli comic book artist, whose graphic novel "The Realist" (Habuka, 2015) contains comic strips that may be seen as meditations about his life. Asaf and his twin brother Tomer were both avid comic book readers as children, and both became comic book artists. The world of superheroes and its imagery is present in many of his comic strips, as part of his symbolic graphic language. The comic strip "Sambusak from Outer Space" is an autobiographical artistic representation of a childhood memory, in which Hanuka depicts the experience of reading a comic book and processing his own reality through the language of comics. A close analysis of this comic strip can shed light on the emotional processes that reading a comic makes possible. Moreover, this comic strip also exemplifies the way in which the world of the superheroes depicted in the comic opens a space for the creation of emotional images that make it possible for the psyche to process highly charged and emotionally complex experience.

"Sambusak from Outer Space" is a nine-frame comic story. I shall describe its outline frame by frame, and delve into depth afterwards as I analyze the story. The first frame shows the title of the story, set in the fashion of an opening titles of 1950s science fiction movies. The second frame shows two women (a mother and grandmother) baking in the kitchen and talking in Arabic. The next two frames show two kids (brothers) in their room. One of them is reading a comic book in his bed, and asks his brother if he understands anything that they overheard, to which the brother answers "No." The fifth frame, which is the frame in the center of the page, shows a close-up on the open comic book. In the page we see the back of Superman, and a green superhero alien in conversation. The green figure says "Earth will never be my home" and his eye shines green. In the next frames, the boy turns to his mother in the kitchen, and asks what language they were speaking. His mother answers that it doesn't matter. In the eighth frame the mother offers the kid a Sambusak and her eye shines green. In the last frame the kid is eating the Sambusak, pondering, and his eye also shines green.

The comic strip is constructed from two intertwining stories. In one story, Asaf and his twin brother are in their room, busy in the safe world of their childhood. Asaf is lying on the bed reading a Superman comic book, while his brother is drawing. In the second story, their mother and grandmother are baking "sambusak," a traditional baked dish while talking with each other in Arabic.

The conversation between Asaf's mother and her mother in Arabic is very significant. The dominant spoken language among Jews in Israel is Hebrew. Arabic has been marked as the language of the enemy—as a foreign language that should not be heard within Jewish home. Jews who migrated from the Arab world were required, in their socialization process, to separate from their Arab language and identity and adopt the new Israeli collective identity. That is, those who spoke Arabic, were a threatening "other." While the children studied Hebrew at school, and their parents spoke Hebrew with them, the generation of the parents and grandparents spoke amongst themselves, as immigrants do, in the language of the "old country."

This socio-political background explains why when the mother and grandmother speak Arabic amongst themselves, Asaf, the child, does not understand what they are saying or even what language they are speaking. When he asks his mother what language they spoke, the mother evades the question. That is, there is an element of secrecy.

The author of the comic strip left the letter in Arabic, so that a reader who is not familiar with the language will also experience the sense of foreignness and confusion. The Arabic conversation between mother and daughter revolves around baking. However, the details are not accessible from the point of view of the child, only their strangeness.

Let's take a closer look at the beginning of the story. Asaf the child is reading a Superman comic book, in which Superman is speaking with a green alien. The alien tells Superman that he cannot stay on Earth because he is a foreigner. The green sparkle in his eyes indicates his status as an alien. His foreignness is not only a fact, it is also his destiny; because of his foreignness he cannot be accepted as a citizen of Earth.

As Asaf is reading fantasy comic stories about aliens from outer space, that is, about a fictional world far removed from his own reality, the conversation between his mother and grandmother slowly reaches his consciousness. When the boy asks his mother what language she was speaking, it is unlikely that he is completely unaware of the matter before him. However, the way in which his mother avoids the question points toward a secret. There is an unspoken experience between the parents and the children. The comics provide the child with words (or images) for this nameless reality, for an experience he encounters yet does not have the tools to process. The next frame depicts the mother with a green sparkle in her eyes, like the alien in the comic book.

The child who experiences the foreignness of his family, but has yet to find a name for it, interprets the experience through the comic book he has just read. Like the alien, his mother also has a green sparkle in her eye. That is, she is like him—an alien, she does not belong "here." The green sparkle constitutes a visual metaphor that expresses the experience of the child in the story, the way in which he processes what he encounters, with the emotional vocabulary he received from the comic book. His way to understand what is taking place in his home is by seeing that it's just like the green alien from the Superman comic book.

On a basic level, we could say that the superhero comics contain elements that could be used as metaphors for the world of the reader, and help him build an emotional vocabulary (fashioned from the narratological or visual moments in the text). This emotional vocabulary helps the child mediate both his emotional internal world and external world.

Another way to view the process depicted in this comic strip is that the superhero comics constitute a transitional space for the child. According to Winnicott, the transitional space is simultaneously composed from what the child is and what he is not (Winnicott, 2012). That is, when Asaf the child reads the comics, he is simultaneously himself as he knows himself to be, and the character in the comics or, more precisely, while reading the alien he is both an external fictional character and Asaf. The identification that takes place in the transitional space makes it possible for Asaf to use the reading experience in order to internalize the complex issue of identity and foreignness, or rather to internalize the emotional aspect of this issue, and better understand the circumstances of his life.

Third Case Study: Father's Monster is Inside of Me

Noam (the names and details have been changed) was a 14-year-old teen. His school guidance counselor referred him to therapy because of his social difficulties, reclusive tendencies and difficulties in his studies. He almost never spoke with his classmates during school hours, and if one of the teachers addressed him, his answers would be curt at best, he would also usually role his eyes or get angry with the person who tried to communicate with him. Noam was closed in his world.

Noam's family life was complicated; he was an only child to a single mother. His father was a violent alcoholic, who was sent to prison when Noam was five and died three years later. Noam did not have any friends and spent his time playing computer games, watching television and reading comic books.

During our first meeting, Noam found it difficult to communicate with me, his answers were curt and he seemed very bored. However, when I asked him about his favorite superhero, the conversation suddenly took a turn, and an important channel in the therapy opened. Noam would not speak about himself, but was happy to dive into a long discussion on Manga shows, superhero movies he has seen and his favorite comics. I gradually received the impression that since his classmates thought that his favorite television shows were childish, he did not find anyone with whom he could share his emotional and cultural world, so he jumped at the opportunity to share it with me.

Noam came into our third meeting holding a copy of "Incredible Hulks" (Pak, Pelletier & Miki, 2011) comic book in his hand. I was surprised by his choice. The contrast between The Hulk and him was glaring. Noam was an especially skinny and weak-looking child, his body was slumped and always seemed to lack energy, and the only rage one could imagine running through his veins was expressed in his persistent resistance to talking about anything emotional in his life. I wondered why, out of all the other superhero characters, he identified with The Hulk. Was this a fantasy of possessing immense physical strength? Was it a fantasy of being able to take place and be present? I remembered that The Hulk was lonely and was chased by the army and wondered if Noam experienced his own loneliness through The Hulk.

When I asked Noam what he liked in The Hulk, he shrugged and said that he's just cool and that he likes it that he fights and destroys things. Since I knew that he had already read this comic book I decided to ask him to retell it. When a patient retells a story, he usually inadvertently changes it. He can add details or emphasize certain themes, thus indicating that these themes play a certain important role in his psychic array. On the cover of the comic was an image of The Hulk fighting another, much bigger green monster, who is holding or squeezing The Hulk in its hand. I asked Noam who the Hulk was fighting and he quickly answered "his father!" Noam began retelling the story, he quickly summarized the beginning and then began to describe in great detail the part in which Bruce Banner's (the scientist who became the hulk) parents Brian and Rebecca Banner appeared. Noam said that they rose from the world of the dead and the father blamed his son for being a monster. At that moment, Noam raised his eyes from the pages of the comic book.

"You know that The Hulk became that way because of his father?"

"Really?" I asked, "I thought it was because of an accident at his lab."

"Yes, but it was actually because his father was a scientist, and he was himself also affected by radiation. He thought that his son would become a monster like himself, so he tried to kill him, and killed his mother in the end."

Noam's words came out fast one after another, indicating how engrossed he was in the story—in stark contrast to the disengagement he usually displayed when we spoke about things "in the real world." He continued reading me the story, as if to prove his point to me.

The story in the comic book depicted The Hulk's struggle with the memory of his dead father. The father was human in the beginning but later turned into a huge monster who tried to destroy The Hulk. The more rage was directed at the father monster ("Devil Hulk"), the stronger it got. Other hulks, his new family (wives and sons), joined the fight, and together they managed to defeat the monster—his father. Noam's fascination with this story seemed to indicate that though his father died, Noam's conflict with him had yet to end.

The sequence of frames in which The Hulk suddenly looks smaller, since he is caught in the fist of an even bigger monster reminded me of Bruno Bettelheim's argument that giants in children's fairy tales emotionally represent adults (Bettelheim, 1975). This sequence represents an emotional experience of a child being abused by an adult. I thought of Noam's early life with his alcoholic father and the violent atmosphere at home. It seems that through these images Noam was able to process difficult emotional experiences from a very early age that might have been stored in his implicit memory, and were not accessible for him to explore in the conscious present. Given Noam's introverted character and my belief that the comics allowed him to safely touch upon difficult emotional experiences, that Noam was not yet ready to directly cope with the full emotional impact of these experiences without repressing them, I chose to continue discussing the comics with him, and thus keep him in the safe transitional space.

Two main themes surfaced in Noam's retelling of The Hulk's story, which Noam continued to underscore later in the treatment through other comics and stories he brought; the concern that evil passes down from fathers to sons and a family unit in which the father is violent or possesses super strength and as a result the mother is hurt. These themes led to me the conclusion that, other than the obvious childhood trauma, Noam had difficulties resolving the Oedipal conflict, since he rejected the classical solution—the identification with the father since, in his case, it proved too dangerous.

In The Hulk comic book, it is his female partners that save The Hulk from the eternal conflict with the memory of his violent father. That is, the new family connections that showed him that he himself was good, and thus different from his dad. In the beginning of the therapy, this possibility seemed unrelated to Noam's life, since he was completely unable to form social bonds. Perhaps that was because developing social skills is related to containing the Oedipal triangle. Nonetheless, the very presence of a conflictual movement in the story as well as the experience of catharsis as it is untangled during the reading, may have started an internal process of resolving the internal conflict.

After Noam finished reading the story and leafed through the comic book, I told him that it's terrible that The Hulk's father was the one who tried to hurt him so badly, and that Bruce was just a little child at the time. Noam answered that adults should not hit women and children, and after a moment added that the father's mutation actually also runs in Bruce's blood, and that the monster within him was there from the very beginning. "That's why he's also so dangerous—because when he turns into The Hulk, he sometimes doesn't know what he's doing and can hurt innocent people."

The theme of inheriting violence or evil and the hero's confrontation with a part of him that is evil or violent—sometimes as an inheritance from a father who was also a villain, played a central part in most of the stories Noam brought to our following meetings. Noam talked about movies that he saw and even brought more comics, like "Ghost Rider" and "Venom" and also talked about his favorite Manga television shows. By retelling the films and comics, Noam focused the prism through which he read the story; he underscored the themes of the inner conflict between the forces of good and evil and the question of whether a character is good or evil or if he has an evil part, and finally coped with the fact that strength comes from the darkest part in the personality. I was an active listener throughout most of our sessions—I would listen to the story just as he told it and asked him questions about the story and mainly about the protagonist and his experience. I was very careful to keep the gentle boundary of the transitional space, and let the conscious discourse remain focused on the characters rather than Noam himself.

Gradually and over time Noam began to spontaneously share significant events and conflicts and difficulties from his own life in therapy, and it seemed that the therapeutic room had become a safe emotional space for him. From the things he shared, and from conversations with his mother and his school staff, it became clear that Noam was gradually turning into a more optimistic teenager, who began to connect with children from his class and foster new friendships. He even stopped sulking in class when the teacher addressed him and found a way to communicate his wishes and difficulties.

By reading comics and retelling superhero movies, Noam created a safe potential space in which he could process questions touching on his very identity— what did he inherit from his father? And will this inheritance cause him to be as violent and dangerous as his father? The different heroes, whose stories Noam experiences, made him believe that his inheritance was not his destiny.

In order to carry out his identification with his father and untangle the Oedipal conflict, Noam had to know that he could, to put it in the language of The Hulk, control the Hulk within and accept it as a part of himself; a part that does not have to be destructive but can also prove positive.

Conclusions and Thoughts on Transference in Bibliotherapy

The bibliotherapeutic work with superheroes harnesses the healing power of heroic stories and fantasies, and uses it to help the transformation process and empowerment in the therapeutic room. There are many ways in which superheroes can be used in therapy. In this chapter, I attempted to discuss the psychodynamic process of working with superheroes as they are depicted in comic books. The theory of bibliotherapy treats written texts as a "third voice" (Zoran, 2009) in the therapeutic room that can help the therapeutic process. In this chapter, I examined the special case of comics and their hybrid language that combines texts with images, and explored some of the unique therapeutic qualities of Superhero comics.

For a conclusion, I would like to address the issue of choosing a text in the therapeutic setting, and hence touch on a central point in every psychodynamic therapy—the question of transference and counter transference. In the bibliotherapeutic process sometimes the patient brings the text and sometimes the therapist chooses a text, which he invites the patient to read, and to start a dialogue with. Whether the patient brings the text himself or whether the therapist chooses the text for the patient, the therapist needs to makes sure that the text is therapeutically suitable for the patient so that it will open the path for effective work. The process of choosing the story includes two steps: meditating and contemplating on the patient and examining the therapist's transference to the text.

Choosing a comic book for a patient requires the therapist to imagine both the patient's inner world and his potential responses to the text. The therapist needs to ask himself "what emotional experiences will this text make possible for the patient?" It is advisable to choose a comic book story that metaphorically touches on the main theme with which the patient is coping. This helps maintain the much-needed distance between the patient and the story, and helps the patient to remain in the potential space without turning the content to be concrete and about the patient himself. The comic book needs to be compatible with the patient's age, his personality, his cognitive abilities and personal inclinations.

The therapist needs to examine the plot and graphics of the stories, their complexity and content. It is advisable to choose relatively simple stories that are not too visually stimulating. A visual overload can create an experience of shock and confuse the patient, rather than simplify the themes with which he is coping. This becomes even more important when working with children. We need to treat the violence in the comics in a similar fashion. Excessive and overly blunt violence can be inappropriate for the treatment. For instance, in "Batman: The Killer Joke" the description of the violence toward the female character is quite realistic and is more compatible for working with adult patients; the therapist also needs to calculate whether there is a risk that this kind of realistic scene could trigger post-traumatic stress.

It is important to find out the extent of both patient and therapist previous knowledge with superhero stories. Not knowing the background of a story could lead to difficulties in understanding certain parts of it. In certain cases, the patient could react to things that are not even in the specific comics he is reading in therapy, but to things related to the character, which he knows from previous comics or movies.

After the therapist has chosen a suitable comic book for the therapy, he needs to examine his own transference to the text. In all psychodynamic therapies, a main emphasis is put on the therapist awareness of his counter-transference toward the patient, so that his own personal contents will not mingle with those of the patient. In bibliotherapy, the therapist also needs to be aware of his transferences toward the text so that he can filter them and prevent them from contaminating the therapeutic process. The therapist needs to be aware of feelings and thoughts that the text raises in him, personal experiences the text reminds him of, the function of the character of the superhero in his own life and childhood and what it symbolizes for him. Even though the process described above is based on a text which the therapist has chosen, these thoughts also accompany texts that the patient himself brings to the sessions.

To conclude the chapter, I would like to present a few questions regarding bibliotherapeutic work with comics for consideration and contemplation.

Questions for Clinical Discussion

1. We ought to address the violence painted in these comics and ask ourselves how it affects our young patients. By exposing them to this violence, might we lead to a certain emotional numbness?
2. And if so, how should this be dealt with?
3. When we work on a single comic that is a chapter in a series of a larger story, does this oblige us to continue working on the other chapters?
4. Will the patient experience this story as whole or will the "partiality of the story" have an unconscious effect of an uncompleted process?
5. How should a therapist work with children who can't read yet? If it is a case of learning disabilities—will confronting the difficulty in reading interfere with the therapeutic process?
6. New media raises further questions regarding the way we read comics, since reading a comic strip on a screen or on a tablet does not enable the random free skimming of images one experiences with a printed comic book page. This changes the way we read the stories. How will this and other techno-logical changes affect the bibliotherapeutic process?

These are just some of the questions that require our attention as we plan to make use of bibliotherapy with superhero comic books in the therapy room.

References

Bettelheim, B. (1975). *The uses of enchantment: The meaning and importance of fairy tales.* New York: Vintage books.

Betzalel, N. & Shechtman, Z. (2017). The impact of bibliotherapy superheroes on youth who experience parental absence. *School Psychology International, 38*(5), 473–490.

Brownie, B. & Graydon, D. (2016). *The Superhero costume: Identity and disguise in fact and fiction.* London: Bloomsbury Academic

Campbell, J. (1949). *The hero with a thousand faces.* Princeton, NJ: Princeton University Press.

Campbell, J. (2008). *The hero with a thousand faces* (3rd edn., Campbell, Joseph, 1904–1987, Works, 1993). Novato, CA.: New World Library.

Chute, H. (2008). Comics as literature? Reading graphic narrative. *PMLA, 123*(2), 452–465.

Cohn, N., Taylor, R., & Pederson, K. (2017). A picture is worth more words over time: Multimodality and narrative structure across eight decades of American superhero comics. *Multimodal Communication, 6*(1), 19–37.

De Vries, D., Brennan, Z., Lankin, M., Morse, R., Rix, B., & Beck, T. (2017). Healing with books: A literature review of bibliotherapy used with children and youth who have experienced trauma. *Therapeutic Recreation Journal, 51*(1).

Doise, E. (2015). Two lunatics: Sanity and insanity in *The Killing Joke*. *Image Text Volume 8, Issue 1*. Retrieved from www.english.ufl.edu/imagetext/archives/v8_1/doise/index.shtml

Eisner, W. (1992). *Comics and sequential art*. Amherst, MA: Kitchen Sink Press, Inc.

Gavaler, C. (2018). *Superhero comics*. London: Bloomsbury Academic.

Hanuka, A. (2015). *The realist*. Los Angeles, CA: Archaia.

Iser, W. (1978). *The act of reading: A theory of aesthetic response*. Baltimore and London: Johns Hopkins University Press.

Lawrence, J. S. (2006). Finding ourselves in our superheroes. In: L. C. Rubin (Ed.), *Using superheroes in counseling and play therapy* (p. xix–xxviii). New York: Springer Publishing Company.

McCloud, S. (1994). *Understanding comics: The invisible art*. New York: William Morrow.

McKenna, G., Hevey, D., & Martin, E. (2010). Patients' and providers' perspectives on bibliotherapy in primary care. *Clinical Psychology & Psychotherapy, 17*(6), 497–509.

Moore, A., Bolland, B., & Starkings, R. (2008). *Batman: The killing joke*. New York: DC comics.

Ogden, T. H. (1994). The analytic third—working with intersubjective clinical facts. *International Journal of Psychoanalysis, 75*, 3–20

Pak, G., Pelletier, P., & Miki, D. (2011). "Harrowed," *Incredible Hulks*, Vol. 1, No. 620. Marvel Comics.

Rubin, L. C. (Ed.). (2006). *Using superheroes in counseling and play therapy*. New York: Springer Publishing Company.

Winnicott, D. W. (2012). *Playing and reality*. London and New York: Routledge.

Zoran, R. (2009). *The third voice: The therapeutic qualities of literature and their application in bibliotherapy*. Jerusalem: Carmel.

PART II

Using Heroes and Superheroes
to Treat Specific Disorders

In this section, we shall see how superheroes and villains have come to the rescue in helping clinicians address the challenge of specific disorders

I Like Them Because They Are Fast and Strong: The Use of Superheroes in Play Therapy with a Latency-Age Boy with Developmental Coordination Disorder

Aimee Loth Rozum

Developmental Coordination Disorder

Developmental Coordination Disorder (DCD) or "Dyspraxia" occurs in roughly 6% of the population (American Psychiatric Association, 2013) with a higher prevalence in boys than girls. DCD is a poorly understood developmental condition with a stark impact on educational achievement (Harrowell, Hollen, Lingam, & Emond, 2018). Children are often late meeting coordination and motor milestones, and parents and caregivers often notice the child has difficulty with zippers, stairs, tying shoes, mastering bike riding and other fine and gross motor skills. The child may appear uncoordinated and have difficulties playing ball games, putting together puzzles and handwriting. Because children develop at different rates, a diagnosis of Dyspraxia/DCD is usually not given before age five (American Psychiatric Association, 2013). The issues with motor skills and coordination must persistently interfere with the activities developmentally associated with the age of the child. Children with Dyspraxia do not present with a distinct IQ profile and the disorder is not associated with a lower IQ for cognitive deficits (Sumner, Pratt, & Hill, 2016). Dyspraxia is distributed evenly across race, culture and economic status (Wuang, Wang, & Huang, 2012).

Dyspraxia is usually diagnosed when a child reaches school age and leaves the more relaxed environs of home or daycare-preschool settings for the structure and expectations of the school day. As the child advances, the academic and social work of school becomes more complicated and challenging. Children with Dyspraxia often write very slowly and have very poor penmanship and issues with working memory skills and processing speed (Sumner et al., 2016). The usual rate or task turn-over in the classroom can be very difficult for them, resulting in frustration. Dyspraxic children appear to be lazy, task-avoidant or defiant (Cairney, Rigoli, & Piek, 2013), when in fact they are simply struggling with the effects of the disability. Children who have DCD and are also deemed "gifted" in some areas face a double burden; they often struggle with perfectionism, learned helplessness and low motivation (Barnard-Brak, Johnsen, Hannig, & Wei, 2015). Teachers have identified significant emotional and behavioral problems in children with Dyspraxia (Hill & Brown, 2013; Van den Heuvel, Jansen, Reijneveld, Flapper, Boudien, Smits-Engelsman, & Bouwien, 2013), and children with Dyspraxia report lower self-efficacy and competence in physical and social domains, an increase in depression and anxiety and are more likely to experience social problems in school (Zwicker, Harris, & Klasses, 2012). There is a clear correlation between motor proficiency and psycho-social functioning in affected children (Wuang et al., 2012).

Dyspraxic children are identified by their peers as "not being good" at sports/games and are at risk from social ostracization. For young boys this becomes problematic early on when recess, a major socialization time, becomes an issue. Boys with Dyspraxia avoid team games and sports for fear of "letting down the team" or embarrassing themselves, or being teased (Cairney et al., 2013). Imagine being a fourth-grade boy at recess—if you are not lucky enough to find another "nonsporty" friend to play with, recess can become 30 minutes of anguish and loneliness. School-aged children with DCD experience increased rates of non-specific psychological distress and are at a greater risk of developing more persistent mental illness as they age, including panic disorder, social phobia and Obsessive-Compulsive Disorder (Pratt & Hill, 2011). Dyspraxic children are also associated with higher BMI and decreased levels of physical activity, which is directly linked to reports of low self-worth (Yao-Chuen, Kwan, Clark, Hay, Faught, & Cairney, 2018). Teachers report that students with DCD show an increased number of negative behaviors including those associated with ADHD (Crane, Sumner, & Hill, 2018). In addition, there is a strong association between DCD, ADHD and Autism Spectrum Disorders (Gillberg & Kadesjo, 2003) and DCD and ASD can present with broadly similar coordination difficulties (Hannant, Cassidy, Van de Weyer, & Mooney, 2018) and be considered too often as co-occurring (Cacola, Miller, & Williamson Ossom, 2017). Considering the prevalence of these comorbidities, it is important to do thorough diagnostic testing on children presenting with movement disorders.

Dyspraxia negatively impacts the quality of life of these children, affecting academic, social, emotional and family spheres. Parents of children with DCD report higher levels of anxiety due to worry. This may pertain to the fact that children with DCD are usually placed in mainstream school settings (appropriate to their cognitive abilities) where they are competing with typical children and may not have access to suitable accommodations (Wuang et al., 2012). As in most cases, parent impact is mediated by education level, culture, ability to access services for their child, and financial security. Parents of DCD children reported more psychosocial problems with their children, and the symptoms of the child interfered with family activities and cohesion (limiting physical pursuits, etc.).

Play Therapy as a Modality to Support Children with DCD

Play therapy is a natural choice for children with Developmental Coordination Disorder. Child-centered play therapy (CCPT) is based on Carl Rogers' person-centered theory (Rogers, 2012), and the focus is the child client's innate ability to move toward growth. The theory is based on the therapist conveying the following core conditions: genuineness, empathy, and unconditional positive regard. CCPT is a non-directive approach (Perryman & Bowers, 2018) and is a developmentally appropriate and responsive intervention as children communicate so well through play (Guest & Ohrt, 2018). Like psychotherapy with adults, the therapeutic relationship is key when working with children. In play therapy the genuineness, unconditional regard, empathy and warmth are key factors is setting an environment that is productive for therapeutic growth (Crenshaw & Kenney-Noziska, 2014). Unlike art, music and other expressive therapies, play therapy does not tax the Dyspraxic child with the need to use fine motor skills. The child is free to enter a world of their own making and shape it at will to improve their sense of efficacy and mastery. The essence of play involves multimodal integration, using moment-by-moment physical and emotional processing and response. It integrates sensory inputs, motor responses, reflective thought and emotional engagement (Levy, 2011), and this combination can be especially helpful for children with DCD who are affected in these very areas. The goal of play therapy is to provide an intervention that honors children's feelings and perceptions through a warm, non-judgmental and accepting relationship (Wan, Williams, Shahaeian, & Harrison, 2018). The playroom offers sensory, motor and imaginary interventions to facilitate the processing of affect.

Case Vignette: Ben

Ben was referred to me for services at the age of eight. His mother reported that Ben had been having an increasingly hard time at school, was easily frustrated and beginning to make statements indicating a decrease in his sense of self-worth and general happiness. At the time he had an IEP for fine motor skills, social vulnerabilities and organizational deficits. Ben also used two desks, because he needed the space to organize his work comfortably. At the time his parents felt that the school was meeting Ben's needs academically, but they were very concerned about his emotional health. Ben had been diagnosed with Developmental Coordination Disorder and received in-school and out-of-school Occupational Therapy services, as well as behavioral support at school. The goals of individual psychotherapy were to increase esteem, support the positive emotional expression skills Ben was learning at school and supplement those with cognitive behavioral and dialectical behavioral therapy interventions.

Ben lived with his parents, and his older siblings who were neurotypical and good students. Ben's parents both held advanced academic degrees. The family was financially secure, very close and supportive, and could offer Ben a secure, structured and creative homelife. Ben was polite and open with this therapist, and quickly brought in his own toys to play with, amassing a large collection of super-hero figures over the first year, which he gifted to the playroom. In addition to giving doubles of characters he already had, Ben also picked out and asked his mother to purchase specific toys (dragons, knights) he thought other children would enjoy. "I get a lot of help here, it is very relaxing, and I want other kids to like it too." This statement indicates that Ben experienced the playroom as pleas-urable and productive. While Ben never played with these himself, he expressed pleasure to hear that other children were using and enjoying them.

Because I was using a child-centered approach, I offered Ben several options of ways to interact, including art, games and sand tray. Ben gravitated toward unstruc-tured free play, using the superhero toys he donated to the playroom. Rather than use the sand tray as a base, Ben worked on the floor, usually laying down on the play rug. He always removed his shoes (usually a slip-on clog style) and remained barefoot or in his socks. He removed any outer jackets or sweatshirts, so that he was in the least restrictive clothing possible. He did not ask me to participate dir-ectly, but was always engaged with me verbally, describing the organization of the play and the tableau, as well as playing near me. Ben was very knowledgeable about the origins and powers of the various superheroes, as well as the movies they featured in, and how well the films did at the box office. Because Ben was receiving behavior-based interventions at school, our play work continued to be non-directive as I continued to frame our time together as a place Ben could relax, discuss his feelings and experiences, and maybe get some feedback. "Your job," he said, "is to give me great ideas!"

In the first year of our work, while Ben was in fourth grade, his superhero play consisted of staged battles between large groups, usually the villains against the superheroes, with other characters added to flesh out the story (like animals or people). In the beginning of our work, his mother would bring up any events or conversations that she thought Ben should talk about and this modeled good use of therapeutic support. This also allowed Ben to see his mother and I discussing difficulties of the week in a matter-of-fact and problem-solving manner, without judgment. After this check in, Ben and I would go off to the playroom. Soon Ben did not need this prompt from his mother and came up the stairs to the office prepared with what he wanted help with. Ben and I set up a routine where Ben would bring me his "worry list." The Worry List comprised any thoughts, ideas or situations he had encountered that he needed support on. These focused on the difficulties Ben was having at school dealing with his mounting frustrations and anxieties, his power struggles with teachers and incidents where he responded critically to his peers. Ben had entrenched negative thinking about school, that it was "terrible," "the worst part of my life, ever." We worked together to help him identify when he was "on a negative thought highway" and various thought stopping techniques, so that he felt that he had some skills to help him survive the school day. I also collaborated closely with the school Adjustment Counselor, so our work used similar language. Ben also seemed pleased and comforted that his

In School and Out of School "Feelings Team" worked together, and this collaboration also avoided any triangulation between Ben and his providers.

Ben and I met weekly and followed our routine. He would come in cheerfully, take off his shoes and outer clothes (in the winter), pick out his toys and lay on the floor. I would sit close by (maybe two feet from his play space) and watch his play. Ben was not interested in me reflecting what I was seeing but he would answer any questions I had about the play. The play formed a safe background to the cognitive interventions I offered, and occasionally we would set up a scenario specific to an issue he was struggling with. One week, when Ben was having a hard time with anger management and saying "I have anger issues," we set up a group therapy circle with the characters he felt had the most trouble with anger management (the Hulk and Wolverine featured prominently in the session). Ben role played all the clients and I played the counselor, and this gave him an opportunity to absorb new skills (as taught by the group therapist), always staying with the metaphor of the superheroes. In this way he could practice the interventions he was learning at school and use the play to help understand and integrate his feelings, using the struggles of the superheroes as metaphor for his own struggles with affect management.

As Ben moved from fourth grade to fifth grade, his school-based issues escalated. This move also meant moving to the middle school in town. During the end of summer vacation the focus became helping him prepare, and his superhero play took on a new level of aggression, mirroring his increased anxiety. His play started to involve fewer figures, and he chatted less during session. Adjusting to a new building, new teachers and a new academic schedule was very challenging for Ben. He had increasing bouts of anxiety and frustration in school, often appearing defiant to his teachers and rude to his peers. More academic supports were put into place, including extended OT experiences to help him reintegrate; however, his unhappiness continued, and his behaviors escalated. These included slamming books, making challenging statements and leaving the classroom without permission. It was at this point that a shift happened in Ben's play: he moved from large group interactions (including other characters such as animals) to single combat scenarios. Where before he would set up complicated scenes and narrate them, he now lay on the floor and his characters fought silently. I asked him why he always chose superheroes and he replied "I like them because they are fast and strong," two characteristics that Ben lacks. The hand-to-hand combat seemed to reflect the me-against-them themes of Ben's thinking. School had become a space where he was continually in defensive mode, wary and hyper alert, expecting bad things to happen.

Midway through fifth grade Ben was moved into a contained classroom for children with severe emotional difficulties (SED) that impacted their ability to learn in the mainstream classroom. Although this setting provided Ben with a smaller class and better student to teacher ratio, he found the other students reactive and annoying. His academic work began to suffer. More supports were put in place, including noise cancelling headphones and a secluded work space, so Ben could better focus. Once he adjusted to the highly structured point system in the class and learned the routine, Ben began to improve. He came to session reporting that while he was still "very aggravated" by his peers, having a slower paced classroom and more teacher support was helping him learn, and he was having fewer outbursts in school. His play in session continued to be hand-to-hand combat between two foes, but his energy was softer, and he appeared more flexible. In session he spent more time talking and less in process-play, also reflecting his reduced anxiety about school. As Ben's confidence and successes in school grew, we reduced his visits to twice a month, as we acknowledged he needed the play visits less now that he was feeling more confident and strong, like his favorite superheroes.

Discussion

Ben used superheroes to work through his anger and frustration about his academic and social struggles at school. The "fast and strong" superhero could be a way that Ben coped with the hurdles that his disability presented. In play, Ben was able to sublimate his negative feelings into expressions of aggression by the characters he had control over. In addition, the play space provided him with a 100% safe, empathetic and supportive place that could contain his feelings, reflect his emotions and provide unconditional regard. The playroom became a bridge between his very supportive home environment and the challenges of school. Ben felt strong and competent at home and in public but thwarted and frustrated at school. In this way he had two identities, much like the Hulk, Iron Man, Batman and Spider-Man. We had long and detailed discussions about how these guys navigated the stressors of their dual worlds.

Recent testing diagnosed Ben with Autistic Spectrum Disorder (high functioning). This had probably been missed due to Ben's superb verbal skills and very outgoing personality. As I noted earlier, many of the symptoms of DCD and ASD overlap, but detailed testing revealed that the anxiety and rigidity Ben exhibited, along with sensory issues and some difficulties with interpreting social cues, could be attributed to ASD. His mother reports that now that Ben's anxiety is under control he is doing fine academically. Ben's next hurdle will be transitioning to Junior High (yet another move, into a larger building with a new class schedule that more closely mirrors what students will encounter at the local high school). In the playroom I will be observing and following Ben's lead, to see what he accesses as support as he continues to mature. The superhero archetype is a rich one, well able to continue to support Ben as he navigates the power surges of adolescence.

Questions for Clinical Discussion

1. What are some other ways Super Heroes and Villains can be used to help children with movement disabilities?

2.   Many superheroes have enhanced physical abilities following some sort of accident or enforced medical procedure. How can this metaphor be used to help children with medical conditions that impair their physical lives?
3.   How can the architype of the Hero and the Hero's Journey be used to support children and teens with disabilities?
4.   Although male super heroes and villains outnumber female ones, which of the female comic book characters could be introduced to girls struggling with physical or emotional barriers?
5.   Ben would love to create his own comic book, but his fine motor skills do not allow him to produce something he could feel proud of. What assistive graphic technologies could help Ben create a visually pleasing story?
6.   Who are the comic book characters with disabilities? Are they handled sensitively?

References

American Psychiatric Association (2013). *Diagnostic and statistical manual of mental disorders* (5th edn.). Washington, DC: Author.

Barnard-Brak, L. Johnsen, S. K., Hannig, A. P., & Wei, T. (2015). The incidence of potentially gifted students within a special education population, *Roeper Review, 37,* 74–83.

Cacola, P., Miller, H., & Williamson Ossom, P. (2017). Behavioral differences in autism spectrum disorder and developmental coordination disorder: A systematic literature review. *Research in Autism Spectrum Disorders, 38,* 6–18.

Cairney, J., Rigoli, D., & Piek, J. (2013). Developmental coordination disorder and internalizing problems in children: The environmental stress hypothesis elaborated. *Developmental Review, 33,* 224–238.

Crane, L., Sumner, E., & Hill, E.L. (2017). Emotional and behavioral problems in children with developmental coordination disorder: Exploring parent and teacher reports. *Research in Developmental Disabilities, 70,* 67–74.

Crenshaw, D. & Kenney-Noziska, S. (2014). Therapeutic presence in play therapy. *International Journal of Play Therapy, 23,* 31–43.

Gillberg, C. & Kadesjo, B. (2003). Why bother about clumsiness: The implications of having developmental coordination disorder. *Neural Plasticity, 10,* 59–68.

Guest, J. D. & Ohrt, J. H. (2018). Utilizing child-centered play therapy with children diagnosed with autism spectrum disorder and endured trauma: A case example. *International Journal of Play Therapy, 27*(3), 157–165.

Hannant, P., Cassidy, S., Van de Weyer, R., & Mooney, S. (2018). Sensory and motor difference in autism spectrum disorder conditions and developmental coordination disorder in children: A cross syndrome study. *Movement Science, 58,* 108–118.

Harrowell, I., Hollen, L., Lingam, R., & Emond, A. (2018). The impact of developmental coordination disorder on educational achievement in secondary school. *Research in Developmental Disabilities, 72,* 13–22.

Hill, E. & Brown, D. (2013). Mood Impairments in adults previously diagnosed with developmental coordination disorder. *Journal of Mental Health, 22*(4), 334–340.

Levy, A. (2011). Neurobiology and the therapeutic action of psychoanalytic play therapy with children. *Clinical Social Work, 39,* 50–60.

Perryman, K. & Bowers, L. (2018). Turning the focus to behavioral, emotional, and social well-being: The impact of child-centered play therapy. *International Journal of Play Therapy, 27*(3), 227–241.

Pratt, M. & Hill, E. (2011). Anxiety profiles in children with and without developmental coordination disorder. Developmental Coordination Disorder: Mechanisms, assessment and intervention. *Research in Developmental Disabilities, 32*(4), 1253–1259.

Rogers, C. (1951). *Client centered therapy: Its current practice, implications and theory.* New York: Houghton Mifflin.

Sumner, E., Pratt, M., & Hill, E. (2016). Examining the cognitive profile of children with developmental coordination disorder. *Research in Developmental Studies, 56*, 10–17.

Van den Heuvel, M., Jansen, D., Reijneveld, S., Flapper, C.T., et al. (2016). Identification of emotional and behavioral problems by teachers in children with developmental coordination disorder in the school community. *Research in Developmental Disorders, 51–52,* 40–48.

Wan, C., Williams, K. E. Shahaeian, A., & Harrison, L .J. (2018). Early predictors of escalating internalizing problems across middle childhood. *School Psychology Quarterly, 33,* 200–212.

Wuang, Y-P., Wang, C-C., & Huang, M.O. (2012). Health-related quality of life in children with developmental coordination disorder and their parents. *Occupation, Participation and Health, 32*(4), 142–150.

Yao-Chuen, L., Kwan M. Y. W., Clark, H., Hay, J., Faught, B. E., & Cairney, J. (2018). A test of the environmental stress hypothesis in children with and without developmental coordination disorder. *Psychology of Sports and Exercise, 37,* 244–250.

Zwicker, J. G, Harris, S. R., & Klasses A. F. (2012), Quality of life domains affected by children with developmental coordination disorder: A systematic review. *Child Care, Health and Development, 39*(4), 562–580.

CHAPTER 6

Using Spidey Senses During the Storm of Anxiety

Janina Scarlet

I would like to say that it began on a dark and stormy night, although, I cannot be sure of that particular night's weather. There may or may not have been a storm.

But there was an explosion.

The Chernobyl nuclear power plant disaster affected thousands of lives, including mine. My family and I lived a few cities away, and like the many people residing in Ukraine and nearby countries, we experienced acute radiation poisoning. Despite the iodine treatments, my immune system was severely compromised. I spent many months in and out of the hospital, frequently ill and unable to recover from even a common cold for weeks, or sometimes, months. My blood wouldn't clot, which meant that my frequent nosebleeds would require emergency room visits or hospitalization. The effects that have remained to this day include my distinct ability to predict the weather—before rain or snowstorm I experience severe migraines, and at times, seizures. For the longest time, I felt *weak* and *broken*. I often wondered if I would survive into adulthood. I yearned to have superpowers and magical abilities, but had none.

I was 12 when my family and I migrated to United States as refugees. The violence, anti-Semitism and persecution made it unsafe for my family and I to live there and after several years, we were able to escape. Being a new student in seventh grade, one who did not speak English, did not understand American culture, and one who came from a radioactive country, I was an easy target for bullying. I felt like a "freak."

I was afraid to go to school, overthinking my social interactions. I was anxious about my grades, my friendships, my health, and the way others perceived me. I felt as if I had no one to relate to, my anxiety and PTSD symptoms overpowering me.

On most days, I just wanted to die.

Then, a few years later, I saw a movie, which forever changed my life—*The X-Men* (Singer, 2000). The X-Men are Marvel superheroes (or, more specifically, *mutants*), each of whom has a genetic mutation, some of whom have been exposed to radiation, all of whom have been bullied, traumatized and rejected. I felt as if I were watching myself on the screen. Yet, it was not just the X-Men's origin story that held my heart, it was the choice that most of them made—to use their abilities to help others. It was in that moment that I realized that our origin stories do not make us victims, they make us *survivors*. I realized that our origin stories could actually give us the strength, experience and wisdom we need to help others. And that was exactly what I decided to do.

After completing my degree, I focused on incorporating superheroes and other popular culture characters into therapy to help clients to become their own version of a superhero in real life (i.e., *Superhero Therapy*; Scarlet, 2016). As such, this chapter will focus on the clinical and empirical discussion of using superheroes, such as Spider-Man and Storm in therapy to help clients face their greatest fears and anxieties.

Anxiety and Parasocial Relationships

When facing the challenges of anxiety, whether it is a panic attack, social anxiety or a specific phobia, individuals are essentially asked to come face-to- face with their greatest nightmares (Scarlet, 2017). Standard evidence-based protocols for treating anxiety disorders include cognitive behavioral therapy—CBT (Farchione et al., 2012) and acceptance and commitment therapy—ACT (Harris, 2009). In order to help clients face their greatest fears, both CBT and ACT provide techniques to teach clients to expose themselves to their feared situations in a guided, relatively safe and hierarchical way. In a CBT protocol, a client would be asked to write down all of their feared situations and rank order them from least anxiety-provoking to most anxiety-provoking. This list is called *exposure hierarchy*. The client would then learn to gradually face their feared outcomes (exposures) with the assistance of the therapist. For example, someone who struggles with social anxiety may list texting a close friend as the lowest item on their exposure hierarchy, while making a school or work presentation the highest item on their hierarchy (Farchione et at, 2012; Kaczkurkin & Foa, 2015). In an ACT protocol, exposures would be referred to as *committed actions*—steps an individual may engage in because they represent his or her core values. For example, someone who values being a "good student" may be more willing to do a class presentation if they are able to connect the action of the presentation to their core values (Harris, 2009).

Although evidence-based protocols such as CBT and ACT demonstrate significant benefits for assisting clients in managing their anxiety disorders, the dropout rates for these treatments can sometimes be as high as 30% (Clark et al., 2006). One of the best predictors of client retention, as well as the success of evidence-based therapies is the strength of the therapeutic alliance (Bedics, Atkins, Harned, & Linehan, 2015). This means that in order for the client to be able to partake in evidence-based practices shown to be most helpful with anxiety management, therapists have to create a safe and trusting relationship with the client.

Recent studies dealing with parasocial relationships—PSR's (one sided connections with media, such as a person's attachment to a favorite TV show character) have found that these can serve as a surrogate friendship to the individual. Establishing PSRs with fictional characters, such as Spider-Man or Wonder

Woman, for example, can assist people in feeling a sense of belonging and redu-cing feelings of depression and loneliness (Derrick, Gabriel, & Hugenberg, 2009; Hartmann, 2016). In fact, recent studies show that wearing a superhero costume can increase task perseverance (White et al., 2017), as well as increase treatment compliance (Rollins, 2018). These findings could be interpreted to mean that clients who have strong PSRs with certain fictional characters, such as Batman, Harry Potter, or others, would demonstrate better treatment adherence in therapy, stronger alliance with their therapist, and might be less likely to drop out of treatment if their therapist is able and willing to incorporate these characters into therapy.

Although empirical research on directly using superheroes, such as Storm, Spider-Man or Harry Potter, is currently in its infancy stage, there is a promising number of case studies suggesting that these interventions can be useful in helping children and adults alike (Rubin & Livesay, 2006; Scarlet, 2016; Yeo, 2016). There are multiple benefits to incorporating popular culture characters into therapy. For instance, fictional characters can help children learn social skills and perspective-taking (White & Carlson, 2016). Furthermore, connecting to one's favorite heroes can help clients to become more altruistic, compassionate (Hsu, Conrad, & Jacobs, 2014; Huang, Ackerman, & Bargh, 2013; Vezzali et al., 2015) and courageous (Hartmann, 2016). All of these qualities can help clients to better connect with their core values and thus better adhere to treatment (Scarlet, 2016, 2017).

Storm and Specific Phobia

Ororo Munroe (a.k.a. Storm) was born in New York but moved to Egypt with her parents at a young age. When she was approximately five years old, a plane crashed into her house, killing her parents instantly. Little Ororo barely got out of the rubble. It was this experience that later lead to her developing severe claus-trophobia. Years later, when Ororo joins the X-Men, she has to face her anxiety on more than one occasion. Whenever Storm is in a tight space, such as a cellar, closet, or when she is caught in a trap, she experiences severe panic attacks. Her anxiety (as well as other emotions) can lead to her producing weather changes, such as lightning or wind storms, which can injure those around her (Claremont, 1976a; 1976b; Claremont, 1981a; 1981b).

For example, when an evil villain, Dr. Doom, encapsulates Storm in chrome, an ultimate trap, Storm's claustrophobia is triggered. She becomes so distressed that she causes storms and lightning bolts around her, which injure and nearly kill the other X-Men, such as Cyclops (Claremont, 1981a; 1981b). On a different occasion, she is also triggered by a mere mention of the word "tomb." She panics, "Tomb … closed in … rock all around —NO WAY OUT! Rock burying me … CRUSHING me … Can't breathe … Can't think … Mother! Help me" (Claremont, 1976a). Her panic attack prevents her from being able to help her friends, who are being severely hurt by the villain, Juggernaut. As her friends are calling out for her to help them, Storm is devastated, crying and stating, "I'm sorry … so sorry."

Although Storm is initially paralyzed by her panic attack, she eventually finds her courage, "I must ... make ... supreme effort ... conquer my fear." With this determination she fights the Juggernaut, even though her weather powers are weakened due to her anxiety (Claremont, 1976b).

Although her claustrophobia is debilitating during her early years with the X-Men, Storm grows to be able to face her fears over time. For example, when an evil villain and mutant, Masque, kidnaps Storm and locks her into a wooden coffin, he expects that she will be riddled with fear as she has done in the past. Initially, Storm seems to be afraid and pleads with Masque to let her out. However, when he reveals his plans to kill the X-Men, as well as innocent non-mutant civilians, Storm finds the strength to use her powers, causing a massive lightning strike. She breaks out of her confinement, stating, "I may not like confined places ... but it's been a long time since a wooden box could hold me ... so all you've done is make me mad." And with these words, she overpowers him, standing tall, no longer allowing her fear to hold her back from fighting for what she believes in (Brubacker, 2007).

Storm's determination to help her friends, protect innocent civilians, and her sense of compassion even when she is experiencing an intense panic attack, make her an inspirational superhero. I often use Storm in treatment to help my clients with anxiety disorders. The following is a case study with a fictitious client's name in order to protect her confidentiality.

Case Study: "Katrina" Storm

Reason for Referral and Presenting Problem

"Katrina" was referred by her parents and came to see me to help her overcome her driving phobia. Like Storm, Katrina began experiencing her symptoms after a traumatic event—a terrible car accident.

Psychosocial, Developmental and Medical History

Katrina was a 19-year-old woman, who had one older sister. Katrina lived with her sister and her parents. She achieved all developmental milestones as expected and reported to have a close group of friends.

Two years prior to the evaluation, Katrina was in a severe car accident when her car was struck by a drunk driver at an intersection. The car accident resulted in her being unconscious for several hours and developing a concussion. Her car was destroyed and after the accident Katrina reported being unwilling to drive again. There was no other significant medical history in Katrina's life.

During the evaluation session, Katrina was quiet, often looking down. She wringed her hands and smiled uncomfortably. She nodded and shook her head more than she talked. When asked about the car accident, Katrina cried for nearly 15 minutes, unable to speak of it.

Case Conceptualization and Treatment Plan

Katrina's symptoms, presenting problems, and behaviors suggested that she was struggling with posttraumatic stress disorder and specific phobia, situational type. We used cognitive behavioral therapy to challenge her thoughts and explore her emotions during the first part of the therapy and then switched to Superhero Therapy (i.e., incorporating popular culture characters into evidence-based therapy to help the client become their own version of a superhero) for the second part of her treatment (Scarlet, 2016).

Katrina's Treatment

Although not all phobias and anxiety disorders develop after a traumatic event, some do and need to be addressed through focusing on both—the trauma and the anxiety disorder. Katrina believed herself to be "weak" and "broken." She did not believe herself to be capable of driving and believed that certain situations, such as driving, being driven, going through the same location where the accident occurred, being in the same make and model of a car to the one she crashed, and being in a car of the same color as the one she crashed were all dangerous. She avoided any and all reminders of the car accident, being unable to drive herself, unwilling to be driven on the freeway, and unable to attend college or visit with her friends as a result. Katrina's life revolved around avoiding anything that could make her anxious, and as a result, she was anxious all the time.

We began treatment using cognitive behavioral therapy (CBT), analyzing relationships between Katrina's thoughts, feelings and behaviors. Although Katrina was a determined client, who completed all her assigned worksheets, she struggled with willingness to work on exposures related to her fears. She identified thoughts, such as "If I drive, I will have a panic attack and will not be able to handle it," and "If I drive, I will get into another terrible accident," which caused her to feel overwhelmed with anxiety. As a result, Katrina avoided participating in exposures for several weeks.

Katrina did, however, agree to sit in the car with me for a part of the session. Rather than focusing on driving, Katrina and I talked about Storm. She had heard of the X-Men but knew neither of Storm's origin story nor her struggles with claustrophobia. When I talked about Storm's panic attack and her feeling as if she were going to die, too paralyzed by her anxiety to move, Katrina had tears running down her face. She said, "That's me. I'm like Storm. That's how I feel."

We then talked about Storm facing her fears in order to be able to help her friends. Katrina took a deep breath and said, "Okay, I understand." She was scared, her hands were shaking as she started the car. Her breathing was heavy but Katrina agreed to drive around the block. She was gripping the wheel and was visibly tense. She rated her anxiety as 10/10. But she did it. Despite her intense anxiety, Katrina drove around the block with me. When she stopped, she was sobbing, "I did it. I can't believe I did it."

After approximately 10 minutes, Katrina was willing to try again. Again, we went around the block and again she was gripping the wheel, but she was breathing a little slower now, rating her anxiety and 9.5/10. After four times around the block, her anxiety was down to 7/10.

In her next session, Katrina agreed to work on her exposure hierarchy because "that's what Storm would do." During our subsequent driving exposures, Katrina often asked me how Storm handled various exposures to her own fears, stating that learning about Storm was helping her to feel less alone, to better understand her experience, which visibly increased her willingness to work on her exposures. Having Storm as a role model allowed her to design steps to become her own version of a superhero in her own life. Like Storm, Katrina identified that being able to support her friends was "very important" to her and stated that being able to drive to see her friends was a necessary component of this core value.

At the end of our treatment together, we worked on driving past the intersection where the accident occurred—Katrina's highest point on her exposure hierarchy. She anticipated that she would have a severe panic attack. She believed that her anxiety would be "15/10." However, when we drove through the intersection, Katrina was surprised that her anxiety was an 8/10, which she rated as "intense but manageable." After three times of going through the intersection with me in the passenger seat, Katrina's anxiety reduced to 6/10. When I asked her what she thought the next step in her exposure should be, she stated, "I should probably try it alone." I got out of the car and waited as she drove around and through the intersection again. When she was finished, I came toward the car. Katrina was smiling and crying at the same time. "I'm like Storm," she said. She drove through the intersection three more times on her own, reporting that although her anxiety remained high (9/10) for most of it, she found it to be manageable and was "proud" of herself for doing it.

Katrina is now driving herself to and from college, attending events, and is able to drive even while her anxiety is still present. Given her ability to become a super-hero in her own life through her connection with a fictional character, "Katrina" is now a character in "Superhero Therapy" (Scarlet, 2016), whose courage to over-come her driving phobia is now helping others to do the same.

Spidey Senses and Anxiety Management

Because connection with fictional characters can help clients to better understand their mental health condition (Rubin, 2008; Rubin & Livesay, (2006), characters such as Spider-Man are ideally suited to be used in therapy. Spider-Man is relat-able in that he experiences a similar kind of anxiety as many other teens and young adults do. In addition, his origin story is one that many can relate to or understand. Peter Parker (a.k.a. Spider-Man) was born and raised in Queens, New York. Peter is an orphan, who lives with his relatives—Aunt May and Uncle Ben. He is socially shy, academically smart and worries about how others perceive him. He often ruminates about his interactions with others, as well as whether he did something to offend someone else. He is interested in science and attends a science fair, where he is bitten by a radioactive spider, which causes him to have spider-like abilities and mutations. Using his science skills, as well as his new abilities, Peter sews a suit for himself and builds in his webbing abilities to be able to shoot webs from his wrists. He uses the webs to gain motion and momentum. Peter becomes a professional wrestler under his new "Spider-Man" identity, which becomes financially lucrative for him. However, when he apathetically refuses to stop a fleeing mugger, he is devastated to learn that the mugger he failed to stop later robbed and killed Uncle Ben. His uncle's heartfelt message, "with great power comes great responsibility" becomes Peter's own mantra to becoming a superhero. Known as "your friendly neighborhood superhero," Spider-Man focuses on helping others even if it means putting himself in danger (Lee, 1967; Lee & Ditko, 1963).

Similar to people with social anxiety disorder, Peter spends a significant amount of time ruminating about how he is perceived by others. He worries about whether his friends really like him, as well as about his social interactions in general. When Spider-Man is accused of being responsible for a tragedy he worked hard to prevent, Peter worries that he will be judged, rejected and will not be able to use his powers to do good (Lee & Ditko, 1963).

In addition, similar to many people with other anxiety disorders, such as generalized anxiety disorder, Peter ruminates about a number of different topics, including his intentions, his responsibilities and his relationships. For example, when Peter's aunt falls ill and has to go to the hospital, he worries about being a bad nephew, feeling torn between taking care of his family and his self-imposed responsibility to protect other people (Lee, 1965; Lee, 1967). At one point, his anxiety about whether he is helping people for the right reasons becomes so strong, that he throws his Spider-Man costume in the trash. However, later he changes his mind, believing that if he can help others, he should (Lee, 1967).

Case Study: "Jared"

Reason for Referral

"Jared" was 16 years old when he first came to see me. His parents brought him to seek treatment for anxiety, which manifested in Jared overthinking social encounters, obsessively believing that he offended someone.

Psychosocial, Developmental and Medical History

As a result of his anxiety, Jared was struggling with initiating conversations, making eye contact, and asking questions in public. Jared believed that his friends hated him, believed himself to be socially incapable of interactions, stating that if he were to engage in a conversation with someone, he wouldn't know what to say. He sometimes spent hours analyzing his conversations with others, either by writing them down, or by discussing them with his parents. Jared also failed two of his classes due to not showing up to class on the day of his scheduled presentations.

He was unwilling to speak publically and was also unwilling to ask his teachers for an alternate assignment. No medical issues were reported.

Case Conceptualization and Treatment Plan

Jared's presenting symptoms suggested that he was struggling with social anxiety disorder and obsessive-compulsive disorder. We used cognitive behavioral therapy to challenge his thoughts and explore his emotions during the first part of the therapy and then switched to Superhero Therapy for the second part of his treatment (Scarlet, 2016).

Jared's Treatment

When I first met Jared, he made little to no eye contact with me and either shrugged when I asked him a question or responded with a quiet, "I don't know." When asked if he liked any Superheroes or fictional characters, Jared again responded with, "I don't know." I then brought up Spider-Man, stating that he was one of my favorite superheroes because he battled not only external villains but also his own anxiety and insecurities.

> Jared looked up at me.
> "Yeah. I like Spider-Man," he said.

We then spent the session discussing Spider-Man's origin story. Jared revealed to me that his aunt died of cancer a few years prior to him coming in to see me. He said that just like Peter Parker, he also struggled with a painful loss. In the next session, Jared shared with me that like Peter Parker, he often ruminated about his social interactions and worried whether someone would misinterpret his intentions or actions.

As the rapport building continued, I asked Jared what he would do if he could become Spider-Man in real life. Jared said that he would use his superpowers to help other people. When asked to elaborate, he stated that he would save people from danger, protect people who are bullied, and support people who are anxious like him. This session allowed us to connect with Jared's superhero values—helping others.

In order to hone into his Spidey skills, Jared and I then spent a few sessions practicing mindfulness, or guided Spider-Man meditation in this case. Mindfulness practices can be helpful with anxiety management and serve as an important component of numerous evidence-based treatments, such as acceptance and commitment therapy (Harris, 2009; Scarlet, 2016). Here's a sample Spider-Man meditation script.

Bring your attention to your breathing. Notice how your body is moving with each inhale and each exhale (1-minute pause). Notice the sensations of your body, as Spider-Man does, feel connected to your body. Notice the sensations of your feet as they are making contact with the ground (1-minute pause).

Take a moment to notice that at this moment, you are right here, you are not late for anything, you are not in a rush to get anywhere, you are right here in this moment, doing exactly what you should be doing.

And at anytime, if you get distracted or overwhelmed, you can silently ask yourself, "where are my feet?" to gently bring yourself back to the present moment, as if using your spiderweb to bring you back down to the ground. Now, take a few moments to focus on the sounds around you, activating your spidey senses while allowing yourself to gently breathe as you're doing so (1-minute pause). Now, take a few moments to notice the temperature in this room (1-minute pause). Now, take a few moments to notice if there are any smells you can detect in this environment, while continuing to breathe (1-minute pause). Now, take another minute to notice the sensations of your hands and feet in this moment (1-minute pause). And then bringing your awareness back to this room, take a few breaths, and take as much time as you need to open your eyes and come back into the room.

Jared was compliant with the in-office and at-home Spider-Man meditation practices. After several weeks, he reported being able to practice on a daily basis and stated that he felt calmer and less physically anxious. However, Jared still struggled with initiating and engaging in social interactions, and still reported high levels of rumination. Jared and I spent a session designing his exposure hierarchy (Clark et al., 2006), labeling this as his *Spider-Man training*. The first of these included making eye contact with others. After a session of rehearsing and practicing making eye contact with me, Jared and I had a follow-up session at a shopping mall. Jared's task was to embody the "friendly neighborhood Spider-Man" by making eye contact with people around him and saying "hello" to those who would make eye contact with him.

Before we began this exposure, Jared rated his anxiety as 8/10 but stated that he was willing to try it. After he made half a dozen greetings, Jared reported that his anxiety reduced to 4/10. He then decided to help several shoppers by holding the door for them at a busy department store and helped another shopper to pick up a box she had dropped. Jared stated that normally he would not have done either of these actions because he would have been afraid of doing something wrong or making someone angry with him. When asked what prompted him to help other shoppers, he replied, "This is what Spider-Man would do, so I did it."

The top item on Jared's Spider-Man training was initiating conversations with strangers. By this point, Jared was about to begin his junior year in high school. When I asked him how he would like to structure this exposure, Jared replied that he would like to try initiating conversations with freshmen. "I was very nervous when I first started high school. I'm still nervous but at least I have friends. Many freshmen don't know anyone."

For the next two weeks, Jared purposely engaged in conversations with incoming freshmen at his school, particularly those whom he believed to look "lost or nervous." Jared stated that he engaged them in a conversation, asking if they needed help in finding their classroom. He stated that the first time he talked to someone, he was worried that the person would be offended at his attempt to help. However, he stated that everyone he engaged appeared to be grateful and thanked him for helping.

Over the next few months, Jared and I worked on him taking his Spider-Man persona with him everywhere he went. He stated that he would sometimes pretend that he was a secret superhero on a mission to look out for those who may be in need of his help. Although still experiencing anxiety and not always sure about his interactions, Jared now has found a larger circle of friends. He is more consistent with eye contact. He reports being more willing to socially engage with others, and reports that his connection with Spider-Man helped him to find a sense of purpose.

Personal Reflections

Much like "Katrina" and "Jared," I find that many of my clients struggle with verbalizing their experiences. Many of my clients report that they were never taught to label, understand and express their emotions. As a result, the initial focus on these can feel both uncomfortable and unsafe for some. However, most people I have treated, both military service members and civilians, are usually willing to discuss mental health through the lens of fictional characters.

Connecting to another being's experience can create a sense of compassion, as well as common humanity (a sense of connection and commonality in the face of suffering). This type of connection can prompt people to reflect on their own experience, encouraging them to practice a more compassionate attitude toward themselves (Van Dam, 2011). The understanding of the commonality of one's suffering can help validate our experiences and can also show us a way to heal our own wounds.

I have come to realize that much like traditional superheroes, as well as other popular culture characters, including Harry Potter (Rowling, 1997), Luke Skywalker (*Star Wars*; Lucas, 1977), Sam and Dean Winchester (*Supernatural*; Kripke, 2005) and many others, all people have an origin story. An origin story introduces the character's struggle. However, the hero's origin story is merely the beginning. The rest of the journey is up to the hero. And thus, like Storm and Spider-Man, like Harry Potter and Wonder Woman, all heroes' journeys begin with a struggle of some kind.

I have found that the following exercise can be helpful for some people to evaluate their own origin story and find a path to healing. This exercise can be implemented as a written exercise or as a meditative reflection.

Origin Story Exercise

Many people go through numerous losses, excruciating physical or emotional pain, and feelings of loneliness and alienation. Just like our favorite superheroes, or real life heroes, we too have an origin story. An origin story can be a memory of a terrible tragedy, an accident, or a moment when we have decided to make different choices.

Take a few moments to consider your own origin story. Do you remember a defining moment that shaped you? Or perhaps it was numerous moments, trying times, and experiences, which at the time felt unbearable?

Now take a few moments to identify a personal hero. This is someone you see as a figure of ultimate wisdom and compassion. This could be a real person, such as a grandparent, a teacher, a mentor, a star athlete you admire, a creator, or a historical figure you look up to. Or, it can be a fictional character, such as Batman, Dumbledore, Yoda or Wonder Woman.

If you cannot think of a personal hero, that's perfectly okay, see if you can think of a kind of hero you'd like to have to look up to. What kind of qualities would your hero have?

Now, take a few moments to imagine that you have some alone time with your hero. Your hero knows exactly what you have been through, what your origin story is, and how it has shaped you. Your hero is understanding, supportive and encouraging. Your hero knows exactly what to say to you and what you may need to hear.

What would your hero say to you?

If it is too difficult to think of what your hero may say, no problem. It happens to a lot of people. Take a breath. You can always try this exercise at another time.

This exercise is intended to elicit one's connection to their personal struggle while also actively building their sense of resilience. By connecting to their personal hero, people can personalize the kind of message they may need to receive from a role model, and then can practice creating this kind of encouragement for themselves. In my observation, clients not unlike "Katrina" and "Jared" respond well to this exercise and might be able to extrapolate the kinds of actions that they need to take in order to become their own versions of a superhero. These actions can include exposures, such as facing one's fears, as well as alternative core values-based actions, such as helping others, as well as creativity, playfulness and others.

Conclusion

Many people appear to struggle with expressing and identifying their emotional experiences. People who struggle with anxiety disorders, such as specific phobias, social anxiety and other anxiety-related disorders may engage in avoidance behaviors in order to reduce their anxiety. Although in the short term, avoidance strategies may provide a temporary relief, in the long term, people who rely on avoidance typically experience an increase in anxiety and worsening of symptoms overall (Clark et al., 2006; Harris, 2009; Scarlet, 2016).

Although exposure-based therapies have been shown to be helpful with anxiety reduction, as many as 30% of clients might drop out of treatment due to a fear of exposures (Clark, 2006). When people are able to find a person or a character they are able to connect with, they might feel less alone and less ashamed of their experience (Scarlet; 2016). In addition, the ability to discuss fictional heroes with a therapist can possibly help build trust and rapport in the clinical setting, assuring a stronger therapeutic alliance, and a lesser chance of premature termination. Through increased therapeutic alliance, clients may be more likely to adhere to treatment, including exposure therapy (Bedics et al., 2015).

By exploring the parallels in one's own experience and that of a fictional character with a similar experience, clients may be more willing to engage in therapy and be more willing to face their fears. Through exploring their connections with their heroes, clients can learn to take actions to become their own versions of a superhero in real life.

Questions for Clinical Discussion

1. Who are some of the fictional characters that speak to you?
2. What is your origin story?
3. If you were granted superpowers or magical abilities, what would you like to do with them?
4. How can you start taking actions to become your own version of a superhero in real life?
5. If your personal hero could say anything to you, what kind of message would they give you?

References

Bedics, J. D., Atkins, D. C., Harned, M. S., & Linehan, M. M. (2015). The therapeutic alliance as a predictor of outcome in dialectical behavior therapy versus nonbehavioral psychotherapy by experts for borderline personality disorder. *Psychotherapy, 52*(1), 67–77.

Brubacker, E. (2007). Uncanny X-Men: The extremists. *Marvel, 1*(491), 1–44.

Claremont, C. (1976a). The X-Men: Like a phoenix from the ashes. *Marvel, 1*(101), 1–36.

Claremont, C. (1976b). The X-Men: Who will stop the Juggernaut? *Marvel, 1*(102), 1–36.

Claremont, C. (1981a). The Uncanny X-Men: Kidnapped! *Marvel, 1*(145), 1–36.

Claremont, C. (1981b). The Uncanny X-Men: Murderworld. *Marvel, 1*(146), 1–36.

Clark, D. M., Ehlers, A., Hackmann, A., McManus, F., Fennell, M., et al. (2006). Cognitive therapy versus exposure and applied relaxation in social phobia: A randomized controlled trial. *Journal of Consulting and Clinical Psychology, 74*(3), 568–578.

Derrick, J. E., Gabriel, S., & Hugenberg, K. (2009). Social surrogacy: How favored television programs provide the experience of belonging. *Journal of Experimental Social Psychology 45*(2), 352–362.

Farchione, T. J., Fairholme, C. P., Ellard, K. K., Boisseau, C. L., Thompson-Hollands, J., et al. (2012). Unified protocol for transdiagnostic treatment of emotional disorders: A randomized controlled trial. *Behavior Therapy, 43*(3), 666–678.

Harris, R. (2009). *ACT made simple*. Oakland, CA: New Harbinger.

Hartmann, T. (2016). Parasocial interaction, parasocial relationships, and well-being. In: L. Reinecke & M. B. Loiver (Eds.), *The Routledge handbook of media use and well-being: International perspectives on theory and research on positive media effects* (pp. 131–144). New York: Routledge.

Hsu, C. T., Conrad, M., & Jacobs, A. M. (2014). Fiction feelings in Harry Potter: Haemodynamic response in the mid-cingulate cortex correlates with immersive reading experience. *Neuroreport, 25*(17), 1356–1361.

Huang, J. Y., Ackerman, J. M., & Bargh, J. A. (2013). Superman to the rescue: Simulating physical invulnerability attenuates exclusion-related interpersonal biases. *Journal of Experimental Social Psychology, 49*(3), 349–354.

Kaczkurkin, A. N. & Foa, E. B. (2015). Cognitive-behavioral therapy for anxiety disorders: An update on the empirical evidence. *Dialogues in Clinical Neuroscience, 17*(3), 337–346.

Kripke, E. (Creator) (2005). *Supernatural* [TV Show]. Burbank, CA: The WB.

Lee, S. (1965). The amazing Spider-Man: If this be my destiny… *Marvel, 1*(31), 1–36.

Lee, S. (1967). The amazing Spider-Man: Spider-Man no more! *Marvel, 1*(50), 1–36.

Lee, S. & Ditko, S. (1963). The amazing Spider-Man. *Marvel, 1*(1), 1–36.

Lucas, G. (Director) (1977). *Star Wars* [Motion Picture]. Los Angeles, CA: 20th Century Fox.

Rollins, J. A. (2018). Superheroes to the rescue! *Pediatric Nursing, 44*(2), 58–61.

Rowling, J. K. (1997). *Harry Potter and the Philosopher's stone.* New York: Scholastic.

Rubin, L. C. (Ed.) (2008). *Popular culture in counseling, psychotherapy, and play-based interventions.* New York: Springer Publishing Company.

Rubin, L. & Livesay, H. (2006). Look, up in the sky! Using superheroes in play therapy. *International Journal of Play Therapy, 15*(1), 117–133.

Scarlet, J. (2016). *Superhero therapy: A hero's journey through acceptance and commitment therapy.* London: Little Brown Book Group.

Scarlet, J. (2017). *Harry Potter therapy: An unauthorized self-help book from the restricted section.* Seattle, WA: CreateSpace/Amazon.

Singer, B. (2000). *X-Men* [Motion picture]. Los Angeles, CA: 20th Century Fox.

Van Dam, N. T., Sheppard, S. C., Forsyth, J. P., & Earleywine, M. (2011). Self-compassion is a better predictor than mindfulness of symptom severity and quality of life in mixed anxiety and depression. *Journal of Anxiety Disorders, 25*(1), 123–130.

Vezzali, L., Stathi, S., Giovannini, D., Capozza, D., & Trifiletti, E. (2015). The greatest magic of Harry Potter: Reducing prejudice. *Journal of Applied Social Psychology, 45*(2), 105–121.

White, R. E. & Carlson, S. M. (2016). What would Batman do? Self-distancing improves executive function in young children. *Developmental Science, 19*(3), 419–426.

White, R. E., Prager, E. O., Schaefer, C., Kross, E., Duckworth, A. L., & Carlson, S. M. (2017). The "Batman Effect:" Improving perseverance in young children. *Child Development, 88*(5), 1563–1571.

Yeo, B. (2016). Spider-Man: The developmental possibilities of a superhero for a young adopted boy. *Infant Observation, 19*(3), 181–193.

CHAPTER 7

Superhero or Villain? Merging Play Therapy with CBT for Children with Autism

Roz Casey

The Impact of Autism on Play and Development

Not all superheroes are the same. Each has their own unique set of powers. Discovering how Autism impacts one child is similar to learning about a new superhero. Autism is a superpower because it is a differently structured intelligence. Autism is a neuro-developmental and neuro-behavioral disorder affecting an individual's development in a variety of domains. Children with Autism reach developmental milestones later than their neuro-typical peers. How Autism is expressed varies between each individual. Therefore, the best approach to therapy with children with Autism is to tailor therapy to suit each individual's special area of need. Autism is classified as a neuro-developmental disorder that manifests in a child's markedly atypical patterns of social interaction, their communication styles, interests, obsessions, and abilities ranging from below age-related norms to well above age-related norms. It is important to realize that children with Autism use repetitive and rigid behaviors to help them modulate their perceptual and neurobiological deficits and imbalances (March & Schub, 2018).

Social Skill Development

The most typical feature of Autism is a difficulty with social interactions. From an early age and persevering into adulthood, children with Autism appear to others to be living in a world of their own. This is because of atypical neurobiological development children with Autism find it difficult to identify with the internal reality of another. They find it hard to feel what others are feeling. It is as if they cannot "see" what another person is feeling or communicating with them. The Autistic child's difficulties with social skills are also related to their rigid and repetitive behaviors and interests. They may be so caught up in rocking, tapping, whirling, flicking, and playing with toys like small figurines, stones or anything they have obsessively become attached to, that normal social communication is impeded (Zhao & Chen, 2018). It is important to provide children with Autism an opportunity to indulge their repetitive and rigid interests and behaviors, because they provide comfort

116

and reduce sensory overload. Nevertheless, these same obsessions can be great conversation starters with a superhero with Autism.

Child-centered play therapy helps children with Autism develop important social skills by:

- Taking turns
- Problem-solving (Huskens et al., 2015)
- Learning to use imagination and resourcefulness
- Builds social collaborative skills, even if there is one child and one therapist (Daiki, Kyoko, Shiho, & Miyako, 2012)
- Develop fine motor skills
- Playing imaginatively (Rahnama, Hamedi, Sahraei, & Parto, 2014).

Child-centered play therapy can be a valuable therapeutic tool for children with Autism to explore various social situations and conditions in a safe environment and secure relationship with a therapist. If the therapy can focus on developing individual interpersonal skillsets, they can increase self-awareness, and communication skills with others (Ware Balch & Ray, 2015). However, when we are working with a child with Autism, we also need to be very aware and equipped to deal with pathological demand avoidance.

Pathological Demand Avoidance and How to Work With it

Children with Autism can have issues with varying degrees of pathological demand avoidance. Pathological Demand Avoidance (PDA) is an internal and external resistance to what appears to be a demand, by using specific direct and passive behaviors to avoid the demand. What is a demand? Well, it depends on the person. A demand can be a new task, an instruction, a reward, what a child may sense as an expectation to do something or behave in a certain way (Gillberg, 2014). The demand will then be avoided by charming, manipulative behaviors designed to distract the person giving the demand. Or it can be met with varying forms of violence. Children with Autism can begin to engage in play for the purpose of distracting the person giving the demand. Another response is hitting the person giving the demand, or running out of the room to hide. It's important to understand how each child with Autism uses demand avoidance behaviors to avoid therapy if they have determined it is a demand for them. And also, as you get to know a child, the demand avoidance behaviors can change, sometimes weekly, sometimes monthly, sometimes when there has been added trauma or significant environmental change in a child's life.

General strategies which can be used include: rewording the demand to make it sound fun and inviting; avoiding the words "you must," "you will," and "when you" and changing them to "we can," "if we," and "show me how to do this." If a rule must be enforced, blame the government, or the boss! Use statements such as "the government says we can't do that," or "the boss says you can't do that." This works well because blaming a third party will remove you as the demand maker. The main element of PDA awareness is to remove this concept and attitude of having to control the child with Autism. If you think about it, children with Autism have to work hard all day with teachers and parents to get through life and activities. If you are going to enter the session with an expectation of the child having to comply with your requests, they can potentially resist and avoid you. Also, if a child with Autism is having a particularly difficult day, using all the PDA strategies in the world will not usually reap the usual results. If there is significant resistance, it is in the child's best interest to not introduce or contemplate any CBT, as this will be avoided. And if this is avoided over time, then they will associate CBT with their go-to demand avoidance behavior. Don't ever arrive at a safe place with pathological demand avoidance. It's an extra element of Autism which requires us to be on our toes and aware at all times. How can we begin to understand how exactly children with Autism interact with superheroes and villains? By looking through a sociological lens. The theory of symbolic interactionism shows us how to understand how they play with super heroes and villains.

Superhero and Villain Play through the Lens of Symbolic Interactionism

Symbolic Interactionism is a sociological theory which focuses on how people construct meaning in interpersonal relationships. In the creation of symbolic meaning, we consider the relational context of personal attitudes toward someone; societal norms and social rules. Symbols themselves are meanings that we as everyday humans attribute to different interactions. The symbols which are brought forth are also the moral reasoning we use to form values and beliefs about something, someone or a situation. For example, we may label someone as a bad, nasty person if we have had a conflict with them. Or we may decide someone is our best friend, due to our deep, positive interaction we have had and the quality of reciprocal support. In these examples, we have used our previous experiences with someone, the quality of the interaction; and our understanding and perceptions of negative and positive experiences to assign a value to them. These qualities in the relationship then shape our behavior toward the person and the social context (Bernasiewicz, 2017).

Superhero and villain play and engagement for children with Autism, through the lens of symbolic interactionism, would suggest that the meaning of the role of the superhero or villain is shaped through previous engagement through media. Interaction with the superhero or villain through gaming platforms, television and movies gives the child the understanding of the behavior, powers, attitudes and the social role assigned to them. Symbolic interactionism would then suggest that throughout superhero or villain play there can be seen a complex exchange of societies values and how the child sees themselves as the character. Sometimes this may include incorporating some of their own perceived weaknesses or failures. Often the superhero or villain can be seen defeating an enemy with those weaknesses or failures. Sometimes the play may involve acting out of the script that the superhero already has. This is a literal interpretation of the symbolic nature of the character. That is important play at work because the child is experimenting and constantly assessing the symbolic role of the superhero or villain and also doing deep reconciling work subconsciously, to determine how their own values, beliefs and character compare with the superhero. It is through the play of symbolic interactionism that many societal and family rules, assumptions and biases, are processed, reconstructed and deconstructed.

If the play is repetitive and restricted, can there still be a therapeutic benefit? The short answer is yes. Just because it is a slightly different way or lens of engaging with the role of the superhero, the benefit is still the same. Superhero and villain play will incorporate different scenes from games, shows and movies which inevitably lead to an expression of different emotions. This, in turn, increases emotional regulation, thus strengthening executive functioning (Kinard, 2014). Many of my sessions with boys with Autism usually involve some kind of rough and aggressive play with Lego, super heroes and villains, which does lead to a demonstration of emotions such as anger, fear and frustrations displayed in the play. Over long periods of time of play therapy in this way (4 to 12 months at least), the boys learn that it is a safe place to express these emotions. Often times, play as therapy is a chaotic, dramatic expression of emotion, followed by a sense of relief that whatever was the cause of the emotion (and often times, they consciously do not have the language to verbalize). They leave the session feeling as though they have let go entirely of what was upsetting them. Therapy in this way has reduced severe behavioral issues and has increased communication skills (Kinard, 2014). Now the most important question. How can CBT help children with Autism further construct meaning and develop socially, while meeting their developmental needs?

Cognitive Behavioral Therapy for Children with Autism

By using CBT with children with Autism, we are seeking to help them to understand their thoughts which lead to emotions and then behaviors. It's through this purposeful self reflection that they can eventually change negative thoughts to positive. Eventually, those positive thoughts will, in turn, change negative feelings and behaviors to more positive feelings and behaviors (Kuypers, 2011). This kind of socio-emotional training develops vital skill sets in self-management, social awareness, self-awareness, self-esteem, relationship management and cognitive skills (Korinek & deFur, 2016). Consistent CBT for children with Autism has demonstrated reduced Autism symptom severity. Post-CBT treatment data has shown increased social self-efficacy in initiating and maintaining relationships, demonstration of socially acceptable behaviors, and reduced self-imposed social isolation (Wood, Fuiji, Renno, & Dyke, 2014). CBT programs are more successful in group and class settings (Mitchell, 2014). This is because of the social modeling aspect and group discussions which provide important social context for children (Fazio-Griffith & Ballard, 2014).

CBT has its main successes in children who are over 6 or 7 years of age (Mitchell, 2014). For children with Autism, CBT may be more effective when they hit the later ages of 7 to 10 years old. However, again, be aware that each child with Autism is unique and can potentially learn these valuable cognitive skill sets at earlier ages. CBT deals with thoughts first, so how can we help children with Autism to identify and classify thoughts?

Batman: "I Thought We Were friends?" Discovering Thought Processes. Children with Autism can struggle to grasp the very abstract concept of thoughts. We can make this concrete for them, by providing a context of categorizing thoughts into either "good thoughts" or "bad thoughts." Using Socratic questioning here is a great stepping stone to discovering thoughts. This means using open-ended questions such as: What was he thinking when he threw that? Was Batman having bad thoughts or good thoughts at that time? Did that mean that Supergirl was having good thoughts? Socratic questioning and discussions can assist the child with Autism to increase awareness of their own perspective as well as other people's perspectives (Wood, Fuiji, Renno, & Dyke, 2014). It is worth discovering whether a child is ready for a CBT intervention by simply introducing some of these statements or questions. And if they respond, that's a good sign they are ready for more, and if not, that's okay. Keep persisting with these strategies at another time.

It is important that we as therapists listen for the negative talk a child with Autism may say about themselves. Because it is during Superhero and Villain play that it will usually come out. I usually hear statements such as "Superman is brave and smart." Then, later on, I will hear "I am not brave like Superman." Whilst it can be heart-breaking to hear these statements, they are actually tremendous opportunities for introducing cognitive work and cognitive restructuring. Cognitive restructuring means that a possibility of a new thought is introduced and exploring what would happen if we chose that new thought (Mitchell, 2014). The critical part here is the choice of the new thought. For younger children, it would be best for you to suggest a new thought. For older children, it is better practice if you allow them to come up with their own new thought. I often ask the question to older children "What would Superman need to think for this situation to turn out better?"

When Was Superman Feeling sad? Discovering Feelings. Throughout superhero and villain play, it is common for us as play therapists to reflect the emotion being demonstrated in the play (Landreth, 2012). Using emotion stones, pillows and blocks can be great resources which can help to provide valuable concrete examples of feelings. There is a plethora of apps dedicated to emotion recognition in a variety of settings. YouTube is a valuable resource in emotion discovery. Putting on a clip of their favorite superhero and discussing the emotions displayed throughout can enhance developing an understanding of other feelings and when they would feel them.

When exploring feelings, it's important to educate children with Autism that there are no bad feelings. They can often feel guilt, shame and regret when talking about a time where they got very angry. It can take them a few sessions to get comfortable with discussing strong emotions. It is important to normalize strong emotions. We can do this by explaining that even Superman and Batman often felt angry. But in the end, it is what we do that mainly counts.

The B in CBT

Superheroes are superheroes because they do the right thing. Villains are villains because they choose to do the wrong thing. We can help children with Autism to complete the cycle of CBT and most importantly to develop morally if we guide them to do the right thing with their behavior (Wright, Sedlock, West, Saulpaugh, & Hopkins, 2016). Children with Autism, more often than not, do know the right way to behave, or the right decisions to make. They often react in situations because of their executive functioning issues. But with our help, we can help them to look back at a negative social situation and see where they went wrong. And more often than not, they will already know where exactly they went wrong. By again employing Socratic questioning, we can guide them to understand the situation and where their behavior took a turn for the worse. For example: What could you have done better? Was it a good idea to go back and hit that person? When you are angry next time, what can you do? What calms you down?

Sometimes when doing this questioning, we can trigger a nerve in the child. We need to be careful in how long we persist with this questioning. It can sound intimidating and threatening, so proceed with caution. As an alternative to this questioning, we can use a superhero toy to act with. Showing them an alternative positive behavior using the character is demonstrating important social modeling and psychoeducation surrounding developing socially acceptable behaviors. Whether you use the direct or indirect strategy of modeling behavior choices, at the foundation is simply allowing them to dictate the pace of the intervention. That is an important part of delivering person-centered practices (Josephs, 2017).

Great Landing Superman! It's all in the Delivery! The research surrounding CBT as a treatment for children with Autism was implemented with fidelity. This means that if you wish to segue into CBT with a child with Autism, it is best if the program is implemented in its original method (Wood, Fuiji, Renno, & Dyke, 2014). However, if we can use objective reflection of our work to assess the therapeutic benefit of interventions (Rosin, 2015), what do we need to objectively reflect on? Is the child beginning to understand the difference between good and bad thoughts? Is the child beginning to understand when they feel a particular emotion? Can the child identify behaviors which would lead to a positive outcome? Does the child feel comfortable exploring thoughts, emotions and behaviors with me? If the answer is no, to some or all of these questions, then take a step back and focus more on building rapport for a deep therapeutic bond. If the answer is yes to some or all of those questions, then it can be said that they are responding well to CBT as an intervention.

Delivering flexible therapies for children is demonstrating person-centered practice (Joseph, 2017). Flexibility with CBT, using person-centered approaches (Joseph, 2017) entails if a child is struggling with an element of CBT, then reverting to play as their personal therapy; if they have had a bad day (due to tantrums, meltdowns, medication adjustments, family or environment stressors), allow them the time to gain control of emotions and behavior (Gurnett, 2017); acknowledging and building up areas and characteristics of strengths and resilience.

What is great about these CBT programs is that they provide a foundational socio-emotional context. The context here means it is within a set pre-determined curricula utilizing a real-life context via social situations. It is important because they provide engagement with semantic processing at deeper unconscious levels (Brewin, 2006 as cited in Wood, Fuiji, Renno, & Dyke, 2014). Below, I outline and review The Zones of Regulation (Kuypers, 2011); My Fear Zapper (Empowering Innovations LLC, 2018); Trauma- Focused CBT Triangle of Life game (TF-CBT, 2018). and Lego therapy.

The Zones of Regulation

This CBT program can either be done in groups, classes or individually. Children are encouraged to put their feeling into a "Zone." The Zone is a chart which is printed out to display. Each Zone is a representation of all feelings normally felt throughout the day. The Green zone shows all feelings which are attributed to feeling okay. The Blue Zone shows emotions associated with feeling slow, tired and lethargic. The Yellow Zone shows emotions associated with being upset and anxious. The Red Zone shows emotions associated with anger and frustration. The mantra of the Zones program is that there are no bad Zones. Throughout each activity, children are introduced to many social situations where they need to identify their thoughts, feelings and behaviors (Kuypers, 2011). These Zones can be easily incorporated into superhero and villain play. Prompting questions can be used: What zone is Spider-Man in when he hides behind that wall? The Hulk looks mad, is that the Red or Yellow Zone?

My Fear Zapper. My Fear Zapper is a CBT program which helps children to identify their thoughts, feelings and behaviors surrounding a fear they have. This game is played via iPad or computer and is mainly for children between 5 and 10 years. Children identify their fear then are introduced to a solution to overcome the fear. Children enjoy playing and defeating the fear in the games (Empowering Innovations LLC, 2018). We can also normalize fears, by introducing and discussing superhero and villain fears. Superman is afraid of kryptonite. Batman is afraid of being alone. Nova has a fear of rabbits. The Hulk is afraid of his father.

Trauma- Focused CBT Triangle of Life Game

Played on an iPad, children enjoy learning about thoughts, feelings, and behaviors via interaction with African animals. Each level has a social problem, where one

African animal is having a difficulty with another animal. Children need to iden-tify the specific thought which is causing the negative feeling and subsequent negative behavior. By the end of the game, most children become quite proficient at reciting the cognitive behavioral model (TF-CBT, 2018). This knowledge then enables much more in-depth conversation surrounding superheroes and real-life situations.

Incorporating Superhero CBT Play with Lego therapy

Superhero and Villain play involving CBT can be done via using Legos and Lego therapy. But what is Lego therapy? Lego therapy is a relatively new therapeutic modality which involves following instructions in Lego sets, taking turns and problem solving (Huskens et al., 2015). Imaginative play can evolve when certain pieces may be missing from the set. It is not ideal to have a piece of the set missing, and some children with Autism can react strongly to this unexpected event. This reaction stems from executive function weaknesses within cognitive flexibility (Granader et al., 2014).

Whilst there is much literature to suggest that group Lego therapy is the most advantageous,(Huskens et al., 2015), Lego therapy can still be beneficial between one child and one therapist if they work collaboratively. Lego therapy can also increase individual social collaborative skillsets (Daiki, Kyoko, Shiho, & Miyako, 2012). Lego therapy can assist in the development of fine motor skills and can encourage imaginative play (Rahnama, Hamedi, Sahraei, & Parto, 2014).

Children with Autism often have a variety of other interests which support their interest in Lego play. for example Minecraft. And more often than not, these games are usually one of their objects of fixation. This is great because the interest increases motivation and engagement with Lego play. It is through Lego play that children with Autism can discover strengths contained in the small package of a Lego superhero or villain. What does all of this look like put together? Let's dis-cover this in Part III, with case studies and my own personal reflections.

Application of Superhero and Villain Play with CBT

It's easy for me to work with children with Autism because I have a now 22-year-old child with level 1 Autism. Then add to that, my experience as a manager in a disability service setting has also shaped my understanding of the complex comorbidity between disabilities and mental health conditions. My emotional reaction toward Autistic traits themselves is quite low.

But to you reader, who may have not shared my journey, it may be more challen-ging to work with these clients. I do a lot of work with university students I teach, to identify conscious and unconscious bias and stigma toward those with disabilities. Most of these biases are shaped by our cultural understanding of disability and Autism. People can unwittingly project assumptions which lead to discriminatory practice. Non-inclusive beliefs and practices can create a barrier between client and therapist. A way to discover your bias toward those with Autism is to complete a Harvard University Implicit Association Test. Another way is to research the differences between the medical model versus the social model of disability. Seeking professional supervision and guidance surrounding your beliefs, values and practice toward those clients with Autism can also assist in delivering inclusive practices. Perhaps consider spending more time with children with Autism in a group context to get comfortable working with them. Sometimes the therapeutic journey is five steps forward, and seven back with this client group. It requires a therapist who is very patient and flexible. However, if your general attitude is one of inclusivity and respect, then it will keep the doors open for quality work.

There is a lot to remember with CBT. I encourage you to get a taste of CBT as a client working with a therapist who specializes in CBT. The CBT work I have done with my therapist has helped me to understand CBT from the client perspective. My personal favorite CBT program is the Trauma-Focused Triangle of Life game. Generally speaking, I have seen many children grasp CBT very easily using this game.

On the superhero and villain side of things, I make a point of keeping educated on the roles of these characters. I also make a point of watching the Lego superhero movies, which I secretly love. But it's Batman who resonates with me the most. The introvert by day, secret hero by night. I see a lot of myself in Batman. But I am careful not to transfer my perception of Batman onto a child, who may believe differently.

The biggest take away message I have for you, is to not force any therapy onto a child. I have worked with children with Autism, who have been traumatized by other well-meaning therapists, who have pushed CBT to the point of the child getting violent. That way of working does more harm than good, so slow and gentle and steady wins the race. My hope is that the case studies will demonstrate the flexible, person-centered approaches to CBT and super hero play.

Ricky

> My favourite character is Dark Void because he can ruin the world with his powers—Ricky.

Ricky was 7 years old when I first met him. The main issue in the classroom for both Ricky and his teacher was Ricky avoiding work and becoming very confrontational when having to start a new task. This was resulting in a power and control issue between them. At times this would cause Ricky to have either a meltdown or tantrum, and it would take him a long time to calm down and return to work.

I began with play therapy for Ricky, weekly for about six weeks. This worked well for the formation of a solid therapeutic bond. He got straight into his main play theme, which was managing his fears. Every week a toy was chosen to be a fear, and he would spend the session figuring out how to overcome the fear. Some sessions he used the other aliens to defeat the fear in war-based play. Other weeks it would be bashing the fear around the room. Batman was used to round up the fear. The gun was used on occasion to blast the fear. Slime was used to cover the fear and also superheroes. Whilst this play theme had elements of a child dealing with processing elements of trauma, I had no disclosure from his parents regarding any potential trauma he may have experienced. Despite the obvious processing of fear and possibly trauma, Ricky would often diligently return to use Batman as the protector in the situation.

Ricky showed interest in my emotions infinity cube, and also the emotion recognition game on my iPad. Using these tools, we had great conversations about feelings, thoughts and social situations. There were also other times when I brought up the infinity cube or feelings game, that Ricky would avoid this demand by ignoring me and continuing on with other play. One day Ricky had snapped and punched a boy in the face. By using the cube, Ricky was able to tell me what happened and he was able to identify when he got confused in the confrontation.

I recently introduced the CBT program, My Fear Zapper. Ricky showed some interest in it, but lost interest when it got to the point of implementing a solution to overcome the fear. To be continued in that regard. He didn't avoid this task, and that's the main point here.

Lately, the work from Ricky has shifted from aggressive/trauma play themes to basic and simple sensory play. Children with Autism can seek out external stimulation from an object which provides stimulation to either reduce or increase sensory stimulation. For many weeks, we have had intense but consistent play with bubbles. Ricky instructs me to blow the bubbles for him to play with. But I have to blow the bubbles with his rules in mind. This simple sensory play has remarkably reduced anxiety and stress build up and Ricky has gone back to class fresh and refocused. Play in this way has reduced his stress hormone build up.

Ricky is now in Grade 2 and is 8 years old. He has therapy with me every two weeks throughout school terms. While completing academic tasks he does not enjoy is still a struggle, Ricky has become more proficient in managing strong emotions like anger and frustration and managing unexpected events. I've become an important support person in his life, to the point where he will refuse to complete school work until he has seen me (if he knows its therapy day). Ricky recently shared one of his comfort toys with a friend in emotional distress, something that would not have been seen 12 months ago. Ricky will require continued therapy to help him manage his cognitive flexibility, transitions between tasks and strong emotions. Ricky's gradual transformation over the 16 months of working with him has shown me how much Batman can be used as a tool of emotional regulation.

Josh

My favourite superhero is Iron Man because he has cool technology and suits. My favourite villain is Deadpool because he has cool guns and super strength—Josh.

Josh is very interesting. I first met Josh in Grade 3, at 9 years old. The classroom issues Josh was struggling with were transitioning between tasks, participating in specialist classes such as art and music, making friends, and the occasional meltdown which would take him most of the day to recover from. His mother informed me that he saw an external therapist to the school and that they were progressing through the Zones of Regulation program. I agreed to continue this program in our sessions.

One of Josh's fixations was Lego. I attempted to use the Lego as something positive, after completing some Zones of Regulation work. This worked for perhaps two to three sessions and then became this painful and awkward interaction for both of us. It got to the point where he would do the work so that he could leave the session early. I tried presenting the content in different ways, but there was no therapeutic bond there at all. I also knew that I had become a demand for him. I would literally see his face fall when I walked into his room to collect him for our session. I attempted switching CBT programs. We tried the Triangle of Life game. He showed some initial interest in it. However, he again lost interest. I decided to drop CBT as an intervention altogether. Best. Decision. Ever. Just allowing Josh to be present in the room in the way his authentic self-wished, opened the door to a whole new, deep therapeutic relationship and interaction. I spent six whole months, in the non-directive, rapport building stage. I was careful not to bring any form of CBT into the session that had obviously caused so much alienation between us. And like a frightened deer, emerging from the bushes, he approached me ever so carefully and slowly.

Now, he brings me his new favorite library books and we read them together, something I never thought possible 12 months ago. He sits close to me and loves to hear me build him up during his process of play as therapy. Josh doesn't just play with Lego and superheroes. He has to figure out how they work and intersect together in a very scientific way. There is complex, imaginative play surrounding the mechanics of how Lego fits together. He used to spend a lot of time building block for block using the set instructions. He would get upset if instructions were not available or if even one brick was missing. These issues intensified the frustration he felt toward me. Now he is okay if there is a brick missing, or if instructions are missing. Which is a really big deal for him. He now feeds off the strengths-based statements and compliments I give him during his elaborate superhero play, as opposed to forced interaction during CBT. He enjoys showing me how strong he is in his play and how good he is at doing things like aiming to shoot things off the shelf. Strengths-based work using superheroes has saved this therapeutic relationship!

I recently introduced him to My Fear Zapper (Empowering Innovations LLC, 2018). I asked his permission for its usage and he said he would try it. I also gave him the option of not using it again if he did not wish to. The fear we worked on was the monster in the closet. He was interested in the games and the concept of beating the fear, but I have been careful not to bring this in every fortnight, in order to keep that CBT inflicted alienation away. And I will keep persisting with CBT in some form for Josh. But it has to be on his terms, not mine.

My slow work with Josh has probably taught me the most about children with Autism. To not assume what is the best practice. He has challenged my concept of doing therapy with fidelity. Some may look at the work with Josh and think that there has not been much therapeutic benefit here. And I would be quite honest and say that I probably agree with them. But sometimes success is not measured through clinical outcomes. Sometimes the measurement is based on the quality of the therapeutic relationship. And this is a testimony to the fact that a therapeutic bond can be repaired when a particular intervention has not worked.

Stevie

I love Hello Kitty!—Stevie.

Stevie was 8 years old when I first met her, just diagnosed with Level 1 Autism. Stevie struggled at school to make and maintain friendships. Her parents were concerned that she was isolating herself at school. She was, however, performing well academically. Stevie had a keen interest in board games. For many sessions, we had to play her favorite board games for very rigid set periods of time. I was instructed very strongly by Stevie, on my role in the board gameplay, and what my moves were. What was interesting here was that even though we were not doing traditional play therapy, she was using board game play to process how she saw herself. She needed a play that was restricted and repetitive, one where she was in control, to make up for how out of depth and out of control she felt at school. On occasion, if I attempted to question her feelings or thoughts surrounding something that she was not ready to discuss, we then had to play hangman on the blackboard. And not only that, I had to lose. And we could not shift to other work unless I was defeated by the hangman. Note that this was her go to demand avoidance strategy. Notice how I go along with this demand avoidance strategy, to enable her to feel in control.

Occasionally we were able to do some very successful cognitive work using strengths cards and superhero and villain play. She considered herself to be "stupid" because she could not understand social play and interactions. It was through superhero play that I was able to help her identify that she had her own personal strengths and perhaps "stupid" was an unhelpful label. I purposely used the supergirl Lego character with Stevie to help her identify and connect with her individual strengths. Stevie was open to using the Zones of Regulation games. She became quite good at recognizing the socially appropriate answers for difficult social situations. Stevie has over time become less isolating at school. She is now doing better at group work in school, but long-term friendships are still difficult for her to understand and maintain.

Conclusions

Superhero and villain play with children with Autism can be a wonderful journey of self-discovery. Sometimes there are hidden strengths which are discovered within hidden personal labels regarding perceived effort. Sometimes they can surprise you with remarkable insight into their own social development and perceptions of peer's social interactions. It does not matter if they choose to identify as either a superhero or villain, because each character has its own powers and strengths they use to deal with problems. Superhero and villain play used with the medium of Lego figures reflects the nature of current games and interests a child with Autism will most likely have. Having a therapist who is willing to encourage self-exploration through CBT introduces a new world of potential possibilities to encourage tremendous personal growth. Children with Autism are superheroes because of their unique and beautiful way of looking at the world. They show us what is lacking. They show us how to be strong.

Questions for Clinical Discussions

1. How would you address a child being violent at their home, in a therapy session?
2. You have decided that a child requires CBT to address their issues. What do you need to determine first prior to seguing from play therapy to CBT?
3. What do you need to expect for play as therapy for children with Autism?
4. A child with Autism is not responding to CBT as treatment. What are your options?
5. What should you do if you have realized you have become a "demand" to a child with Autism?

Acknowledgments

Thank you to my mentors: Dr. Viviane Golan—Social Worker and Clinical Supervisor and Dr. Christine Gazago—Clinical Psychologist

Thank you to my other helpers: Dr. Mia Gentle, Nee, Stephanie, Mariana and Amber.

Thanks to the following people who have kept me at my best during this journey: Jacob, Monique and Lisa.

References

Bernasiewicz, M. (2017). Working with children at risk in the perspective of symbolic interactionism and situational action theory. *New Educational Review, 48(2),* 167–176.

Daiki, K., Kyoko, H., Shiho, I., & Miyako, M. (2012). Effects of collaborative expression using Lego blocks on social skills and trust. *Social Behaviour & Personality: An International Journal, 40(7),* 1195–1199.

Empowering Innovations LLC (2018). *My fear zapper home page.* Retrieved from www. myfearzapper.com/index.php

Fazio-Griffith, L. & Ballard M. (2014). *Cognitive behavioural play therapy techniques in school-based group counselling: Assisting students in the development of social skills.* Retrieved from www.counseling.org/docs/default-source/vistas/article_18.pdf?sfvrsn=10

Gillberg, C. (2014). Commentary: PDA—public display of affection or pathological demand avoidance? Reflections on O'Nions et al. (2014). *Journal of Child Psychology & Psychiatry, 55*(7), 769–770. doi:10.1111/jcpp.12275

Granader, Y., Wallace, G., Hardy, K, Yerys, B. Y, Lawson, R., et al. (2014). Characterizing the factor structure of parent reported executive function in Autism Spectrum Disorders: The impact of cognitive inflexibility. *Journal of Autism & Developmental Disorders, 44*(12), 3056–3062. doi:10.1007/s10803-014-2169-8

Gurnett, J. (2017). ACT for autism: Enhancing the connection between teachers and autistic pupils. *Good Autism Practice, 18*(2), 51–57.

Huskens, B., Palmen, A., Werff, M., Lourens, T., & Barakova, E. (2015). Improving collaborative play between children with Autism Spectrum Disorders and their siblings: The effectiveness of a robot-mediated intervention based on Lego therapy. *Journal of Autism & Developmental Disorders, 45*(11), 3746–3755. doi:10.1007/s10803-014-2326-0

Joseph, S. (2017). Rethinking human suffering. *Therapy Today, 28*(4), 28–31.

Kinard, T. A. (2014). Flying over the school: Superhero play—friend or foe? *YC: Young Children, 69*(2), 16–23.

Korinek, L. & deFur, S. H. (2016). Supporting student self-regulation to access the general education curriculum. *Teaching Exceptional Children, 48*(5), 232–242

Kuypers, L. (2011). *The zones of regulation: A curriculum designed to foster self-regulation and emotional control.* Social Thinking Publishing.

Landreth, G. (2012). *Play therapy: The art of the relationship.* London: Routledge.

Lo, P. & Chan, S. (2014). Adolescent mental health research in Macau. *Open Journal of Social Sciences, 2014*(2),41–51.

March, P. & Schub, T. (2018). Autism spectrum disorder. *CINAHL Nursing Guide.*

Mitchell, D. (2014). *What really works in special and inclusive education.* New York: Routledge.

Rahnama, F., Hamedi, M., Sahraei, F., & Parto, E. (2014). Effectiveness of play therapy (Lego therapy) on behaviour problems in children. *Indian Journal of Health & Wellbeing, 5*(9), 1084–1086.

Rosin, J. (2015). The necessity of counsellor individuation for fostering reflective practice. *Journal of Counseling & Development, 93*(1), 88–95. doi:10.1002/j.1556-6676.2015.00184.

Sawyer, M. C. & Nunez, D. E. (2014). Cognitive-behavioral therapy for anxious children: From evidence to practice. *Worldviews on Evidence-Based Nursing, 11*(1), 65–71. doi:10.1111/wvn.12024

TF-CBT (2018). TF-CBT Triangle of Life App. Retrieved: https://tfcbt.org/tf-cbt-triangle-of-life/

Ware Balch, J. & Ray, D. C. (2015). Emotional assets of children with Autism Spectrum Disorder: A single-case therapeutic outcome experiment. *Journal of Counselling & Development, 93*(4), 429–439. doi:10.1002/jcad.12041

Wood, J., Fujii, C., Renno, P., & Dyke, M. (2014). Impact of cognitive behavioural therapy on observed Autism symptom severity during school recess: A preliminary randomized, controlled trial. *Journal of Autism & Developmental Disorders, 44*(9), 2264–2276. doi:10.1007/s10803-014-2097-7

Wright, J. C., Sedlock, T., West, J., Saulpaugh, K., & Hopkins, M. (2016). Located in the thin of it: Young children's use of thin moral concepts. *Journal of Moral Education, 45*(3), 308–323.

Zhao, M. & Chen, S. (2018). The effects of structured physical activity program on social interaction and communication for children with Autism. *BioMed Research International, 2018*, 1–13.

CHAPTER 8

Superheroes and Villains in the Treatment of Substance Use Disorder

Michael Smith and Carol Kirby

Introduction

In a dark laboratory, a man in a lab coat lifts an Erlenmeyer flask. Lightning flashes as the scientist puts the flask to his lips and consumes the contents of the vessel. Moments later, he groans and screams as his body transforms into a hideous monster.

Since the days of Robert Louis Stevenson and his famous story "The Strange Case of Dr. Jekyll and Mr. Hyde," scenes like this one have been a staple in popular culture. More modern comic books use versions of this scene for characters like DC Comic's Batman villain The Man-Bat. Dr. Kirk Langstrom injects himself with a serum that transforms him into giant human-bat hybrid. Marvel Comic's Bruce Banner is exposed to gamma radiation and transforms into the Hulk.

These scenes depict a generally good and positive individual internalizing something that completely changes him to the point of physical transformation. The resulting monstrosity tends to be animalistic, elemental and/or amoral. Virtuous, well-respected Dr. Jekyll's diametric opposite, Mr. Hyde, is hideous and depraved. Mr. Hyde is the monstrous manifestation of all of Dr. Jekyll's repressed desires for gambling, sex, and violence. The muscular, almost humanoid, Hulk is a poignant display of backward, meek and withdrawn physicist Dr. Robert Bruce Banner's unchecked anger. Man-Bat represents the base animal instincts of zoologist Kirk Langstrom. Although comics, these stories tell us something about human nature —that we all have within us opposing forces and, when tested, we are all capable of being something we are not. We have within us the best and worst of humanity, but we also have the power to summon the resources to reverse the negative and accentuate the positive. In that way, we possess the inherent ability to transform and overcome.

One of the most powerful literary and cinematic uses of these characters and their transformations can be seen when the "good man" directly confronts the monster in some fashion. Sometimes this happens through a process where separation occurs via "super-science" or some mystical means. Other times, it is a metaphysical confrontation through a dream. Either way, the good man is able to externalize that thing he internalized or see the truth—the monster does not define the man.

This transformative process is the essence of Narrative Therapy and a very crucial part of treating substance use disorder (SUD). SUD has been classified as a disease, but "addiction" to substances is still often seen in modern Western culture as a character flaw or choice. Those people struggling with SUD often internalize the societal view of substance users and develop faulty self-images. In essence, the person learns to associate self with the act—instead of being a person who uses drugs, they become a drug addict.

This chapter explores the utilization of Narrative Therapy concepts and techniques in the treatment of SUD. More specifically, this chapter explores how these approaches can be combined with the concepts of the superhero and villain to help those struggling with SUD to externalize the most detrimental aspects of that disorder. This chapter will include an activity designed to help someone struggling with SUD to develop a concept for a villain that represents their own experiences with SUD. They will also create a superhero who represents the values that person wants to exemplify in order to maintain their future sobriety. In addition, this chapter will include personal reflections on the use of Narrative Approaches.

Narrative Therapy

Narrative Therapy primarily refers to and is associated with the work of Michael White and David Epston, which in the late 1980s and 1990s, reflected an outgrowth of postmodern/poststructural philosophy (Wallis, Burns, & Capdevila, 2011). This treatment modality rejects the modernismistic concept described by Cosgrove (2004, p. 171) as "the belief that truths about human behavior can be found and adherence to the methods of the natural sciences is the best route by which to discover them." Evident in Cosgrove's description, modernism favors truth, reason and objective scientific discovery (Ramey & Grubb, 2009). It is about discovering universal commonalities and causal relationships, then generalizing that knowledge to others. Alternatively, postmodern philosophies in psychology center on the idea that human nature is subjective; and reality is an individual experience that can only be defined by the individual experiencing it. As opposed to modernism's individual-rationalism, postmodernism's emphasis is on relational/communal knowledge, and the uniqueness of individual experiences that are culturally influenced by positions of power and oppression. Significantly, postmodern philosophers also view language as constitutive in that language itself carries with it the power to establish an organized existence (Ramey & Grubb, 2009).

Another philosophy upon which Narrative Therapy is built is that of poststructuralism which, like postmodernism, rejects fixed and deterministic rules and the universality of experience. Linguistically, its adherents assert that language can only be understood in the context of systems and structures of meaning (Olssen, 2003). As opposed to the universal experiences and truths prized by structuralists, poststructuralists focus on contextualized meaning-making (Combs & Freedman, 2012). Poststructuralists espouse that problems are constructed within a cultural context where forces of power invisibly underpin language and discourse (Olssen,

2003). Poststructuralism, like postmodernism, takes a more subjective view and insists that individual experience and perspective changes understanding. Poststructuralism also recognizes that notions of knowledge and truth are formed via conversation. In that way, the things we say to ourselves and others serve to create the truth and knowledge on which we base our lives and decisions (Combs & Freedman, 2012). When combined with the postmodern perspective described above, these conversations serve to organize our sense of self.

Since clients live in a narrative world, White and Epston assert there is power in the act of narration. Therefore, clients should be active participants in narrating their own stories. To that end, White and Epston integrated an array of therapeutic approaches, methods, activities and philosophies to promote the therapeutic process. They first published their ideas in *Narrative Approaches to Therapeutic Ends* (White & Epston, 1990). Their innovative approach revolves primarily around the use of narrative structures to aid clients in understanding the diverse nature of their lives and the multidimensional facets of the issues which confront them. Then, narrative therapists assist clients in contextualizing and reframing their experiences while promoting positive change. In essence, narrative therapists help clients envision their own lives as a story that can be edited or re-written. The power of narration arises from the authorship; and therapeutic assistance with re-authorship helps clients transcend their negative experiences and overcome their negative self-perceptions.

Narrative therapists hold that meaning and purpose arise from life stories. In that way, problem stories are life-limiting; re-authored stories offer renewed focus, purpose, meaning, optimism and hope. Re-authored stories can profoundly become that new perspective around which clients organize or reorganize their sense of self. For that reason, story elements such as important people and events are often highlighted as the therapist helps the client add positive detail to descriptions of people or events (Combs & Freedman, 2012). These edited details and the resultant re-authored life-story help clients to change the thematic emphasis, perceived meaning, or patterns of thoughts and/or behaviors that resulted from the original un-edited pathology-based experience. Narrative therapists understand that it is inspiring and empowering to reframe and rewrite a tragedy into an inspirational guidepost. The re-authored story then becomes the hopeful springboard from which to begin anew.

There are many different Narrative Therapy techniques, but most revolve around the dichotomous notions of internalization and externalization. Lawrence and Valsiner (2003) described the process of internalization as the way that individuals receive and interact with social messages and then construct personal interpretations of those messages. The authors described this as an active process through which an individual learns and grows and whereby social constructs are built and/or influenced when the individual reacts to these messages. Inherent in this process, an internal dialog is created. Alternatively, White and Epson (1990) describe the process of externalization as one that allows individuals to see themselves as separate from their problem. One hallmark of Narrative Therapy involves helping clients understand that they are not the problem; the problem is the problem (White & Epson, 1990).

Consider an adult woman who receives an SUD diagnosis. It is commonly known that individuals with substance use issues are viewed negatively. Labels assigned to these individuals, like "junkie," "crackhead," or even "pothead," have undesirable connotations in American society. As a social creature, this woman receives powerful social messages from those around her. The message is—people with SUD are undesirable and out of control. She then begins to behave consistently with that belief. She may even internalize a set of behaviors associated with one specific negative label to which she attaches. She begins acting in accord with the internalized belief that she is undesirable and has no impulse control. Her behavior then yields predictable negative reactions, which then serve to confirm her conviction in her own undesirability. The negative societal messages she received and internalized are now regularly reinforced. Because of the self-reinforcing nature of these internalized beliefs, they often become entrenched and seemingly inseparable from the client.

Continuing this example, the client enlists in SUD treatment with a behavioral repertoire consistent with her negative internalized self-image. She anticipates rejection, and she expects her negative experiences to continue. However, the narrative therapist responds to this maladaptive internalization through the use of externalization techniques. The premise and purpose of these techniques is to help the client see the problematic internalized concepts as something outside of the individual and acting on them in some way.

Separating the problem from the individual is key. To do so, the clinician might ask the woman to describe "SUD" using concrete descriptors. This helps the woman envision SUD as a monster, or animal, or something else outside of her that is not a part of her. The more detailed the description, the more the woman is able to separate herself from the disease and the associated negative labels. Once separated from the disease, she can work toward establishing impulse control and reducing usage patterns through focusing on meeting or exceeding positive self-values versus struggling with negative self-judgments. She can detest the disease without detesting herself. In essence, when her narrative places her as an addict starring in the story of her life, she will assume that role. Conversely, when her narrative separates her from the problem (addiction), then she can star in her own life in a way that enables her to confront the problem and overcome. She can see the enemy and witness, for herself, that it is not her. The disease does not define her.

Using Narrative Therapy in SUD Counseling

Before a discussion of utilizing superheroes and villains to challenge harmful internalized messages, it is important to consider two significant aspects of Narrative Therapy: language and metaphor. Language is powerful, and altering language used by individuals struggling with SUD can significantly impact treatment. Beyond language and word choice-ability, the symbolic use of metaphors can help reframe perspectives that then generate new meaning and understanding. The polarities of superheroes and villains are particularly useful in Narrative Therapy and their symbolism can become a primary metaphor in the treatment of SUD.

In fact, the good versus evil/superhero versus villain platform lends well in the treatment of a disease often branded by society as a character flaw and the manifestation of wrongdoing.

Most commonly accepted practices in SUD treatment stem from the 12-step model developed for Alcoholics Anonymous (AA) and later adapted for Narcotics Anonymous (NA) and other Anonymous-type self-help groups. Indeed, many treatment facilities and clinicians continue to use a 12-step informed approach to treat SUD, even when they do not adhere strictly to the steps. One hallmark of these approaches is the use of very specific language. In this model, the use of explicit language is about submission and surrender to a higher power. However, the repetitive recitation of negatively charged messages can have broader narrative implications.

One central conflict between Narrative Therapy and the 12-step approach lies in the first step. Twelve-step formats require an individual to accept that they are an addict and, because of their SUD, they no longer have the ability to control aspects of their lives. The common wisdom in AA is that in order to submit—individuals must verbally identify themselves as an addict, each and every time they identify themselves to a group. This adherence to instilled language can be a serious problem in treating SUD. These pronouncements can lead an individual to internalize their disorder, which lies at the heart of the conflict with Narrative Therapy.

Evidence suggests that changing language can increase the effectiveness of treatment while decreasing negative thoughts and feelings. To illustrate this point, Szabó, Tóth, and Pakai, (2014) conducted an experiment with individuals struggling with alcohol-use issues. They had individuals write autobiographical stories, then edited the language in those stories. They tested for hopelessness and means-ends-problem-solving before and after the writing and editing processes. The researchers found a statistically significant decrease in hopelessness and a corresponding increase in means-ends-problem-solving for those who altered their autobiographical language. These results elucidate how changing language can be beneficial in the treatment of SUD.

In addition to language selection, the use of metaphor is essential to Narrative Therapy. Therapeutically speaking, carefully constructing a metaphor with a client pays dividends. Legowski and Brownlee (2001) explicate that metaphor "becomes the means through which the therapist filters and understands the client's experiences and the mode through which the therapist orientates the discussion" (p. 21). In traditional Narrative Therapy, the metaphor is constructed by the client with minimal input from the therapist (Legowski & Brownlee, 2001). After all, the metaphor is about the client—not the therapist. The client is describing their life or the problem in a way that affords them a fuller understanding, while also helping the therapist understand. However, placing the onus of creating the metaphor on the client can be challenging when using Narrative Therapy approaches with people recovering from SUD. Simply put, that difficulty lies in the lack or lag of creativity.

Lack of creativity is common to SUD. The National Institute on Drug Abuse (2018) reports that opioids, and other drugs, increase levels of dopamine, a brain neurotransmitter. In one study, Chermahini and Hommel (2010) confirmed that increased levels of dopamine in the brain correlate with lower creativity. When a person struggling with substance use enters treatment, they stop using substances. Although their dopamine levels should return to pre-use levels, the associated increase in creativity does not appear to be immediate. Few studies have examined the link between creativity and substance use, but it would not be surprising to find evidence for a delay in creative growth following an extended episode of continuous substance use.

Wilson offers one explanation for this delay. Wilson (2013) describes creativity as more of a skill than a trait. This characterization suggests that creativity requires practice. Long periods of continuous substance use would equate to long periods of reduced creativity. As with any skill, it follows that a period of practice is necessary to return to previous levels of functioning.

Reduced levels of creativity can be problematic when attempting to use Narrative Therapy approaches with clients. Because the primary function of the metaphor in Narrative Therapy is the transfer of meaning, the client's creative contribution is a necessary part of the process (Legowski & Brownlee, 2001). Despite the non-directive tenets of Narrative Therapy, when working with SUD clients, especially those in early recovery, it may be necessary and helpful to be more directive. When more directive approaches are employed, it is important to confirm the client's understanding and proceed at the pace at which clients are participative in the process. If the meaning is lost on the client, the therapy will be ineffective.

The Metaphor of the Villain and Hero in Substance Use Treatment

In my personal experience in working with clients struggling with SUD, I have found that one of the more interesting, well received, and effective ways of directing Narrative Therapy metaphors occurs via framing SUD as a comic book-style villain and framing recovery as a superhero. Many clients easily embrace this concept and they have expressed enjoyment in creating the metaphor. More precisely, it was helpful for them to visualize their SUD as a "bad guy." Correspondingly, many participants found it difficult to create a hero.

It is not surprising that crafting the metaphor of a superhero is challenging for these individuals. Factors that may inhibit this process include negative thinking patterns, lack of creativity, hopelessness and shame. It is difficult to think optimistically after an extended period of negative experiences. After all, creating a superhero requires some degree of hopefulness. Many people who have endured SUD are afraid to be hopeful because they fear it will lead to more disappointment. Notably, this process often occurs at a time when clients feel unable to endure even one more disappointment. However, in my experience, there are some individuals in long-term sobriety (5 or more years) who can construct vivid and intricate recovery superheroes. As meaning-making creatures, the restoration of hope inspires positive creativity and that says something telling about the human spirit. To overcome disease, especially one with negative societal implications, we need to repair the broken human spirit. And Narrative Therapy offers an excellent platform for this kind of healing.

I have used a directed metaphor Narrative Therapy exercise with numerous clients. Many times I have been very involved with the client in building every aspect of the metaphorical villains and heroes. I have also used this exercise as a group activity in two different ways: having the group collaborate to create a single villain and hero based on the shared experiences; and having each group member take time to create their own and then share their creations with the group. The format adapts well to individual or group treatment.

I have also seen a wide array of very impressive, dark and unique villains and bright, hopeful and distinctive heroes. No two villains or heroes were exactly the same. One client created a villain who was a vampire who presented as a lurking menace, always in the shadows, watching, following and waiting for a moment of weakness. Another created a horrendous and humongous blob intent on consuming everything in its path. A group of clients created an entire organization of recovery-based heroes (similar to DC comic's Green Lantern Corps) that they dubbed the Recovery Crew. Each crew member had the power to remove a person's inner pain and inspire hope in the hopeless and downtrodden.

As with SUD itself, there are certain themes that repeat. Often villains are shape-shifters or have mind control powers. Beauty, attractiveness or unearthly allure manifest frequently in the villains. One of the most common weapons is "syringe fingers" or gloves that have needles at the ends, similar to Freddy Krueger's gloves. Unearthly power is common to villains, as is their omnipresence and ability to evoke fear.

There are common themes present in recovery heroes as well. They are often plain or regular people in appearance. They tend to have powers that revolve around removing pain or inspiring hope. Often they have a weakness for the villain's powers, but just as often they have a sidekick or a higher power they can turn to for support and strength. What is commonly remarkable about recovery superheroes is their un-remarkability. In that way, art mimics life.

There are universal messages to the stories as well. These messages include that we can prevail over seemingly insurmountable odds and evil things. Life can be restored. Existence can return to some semblance of normal even after incomprehensible pain. Through these stories clients often face the enemy and witness it is not them. The process is transformative.

The instructions for the activity are fairly simple. However, considering the creative limitations of individuals recovering from SUD, it may be helpful to give clarification and examples as well as an outline of the process. An outline of how to introduce the activity follows, it includes guidance to help flesh out the superhero/villain, and a character sheet that can be printed so that the client can write his/her ideas.

SUD Villain and Recovery Superhero Activity

What you will now do is create a villain and hero of your own. You will use your experiences with SUD to craft a villain. This diabolical monster should reflect all of the worst aspects of what you have seen and done during the active phase of SUD. Then, use what you most desire out of your recovery to construct your hero. This shining beacon that is your hero should symbolize all of the best things that you think will come out of living clean and sober.

Consider the following things as you craft your Villain and your Hero.

Basic Information

Think about things like gender, age and race. Is your Villain/Hero male or female? Or possibly neither? How old is your Villain/Hero? When it comes to race, remember this is a fictional character so in addition to ethnic varieties we are familiar with, your characters may be from another planet or dimension, or even be a mystical creature from a magical realm. You are limited only by your imagination.

Physical Appearance

Is your Villain/Hero tall or short? Are they heavy or light? Are they thin, muscular, bulky or average? What color skin do they have? Do they have piercings or tattoos? Are they ugly or attractive? What kinds of clothes/costumes do they wear?

Unique Features

Is there anything about your Villain/Hero that makes them stand out? Perhaps they have eyes that glow, or a visible aura. Do they have horns or a halo? Perhaps they smell good or bad. This can be anything you want it to be.

Weapons, Gadgets, and Vehicles

Does your Villain/Hero have any special tools that they use? Do they have a sword, whip or manacles? Maybe they carry a magic/super-tech phone or have a supply of Nar-can. Do they travel by car/motorcycle or something from extraterrestrial?

Partners, sidekicks, and henchmen

Does your Villain/Hero work alone or do they work with a partner? Maybe they have a sidekick that helps them on occasions. Perhaps they have a group or gang of underlings to do their bidding.

Powers

Even in ancient myths, Villains and Heroes had powers. Strength, flight, mind control, magic, telepathy, and an infinite number of other things. What kinds of extraordinary abilities does your Villain/Hero have?

Weaknesses

Like Superman with Kryptonite, no matter how strong or powerful they are, every Villain/Hero has something that can harm or defeat them. What weakness plagues your Villain/Hero? What threatens to destroy him/her/it?

Motivation

Why does your Villain/Hero do what they do?

Symbol

Heroes and Villains, especially in comic books, tend to have a symbol. Batman wears a bat symbol on his chest, Captain America has his shield, the Joker has his manic smile and Red Skull uses a skull with tentacles coming out of it. Draw a basic symbol that your Villain/Hero uses to represent themselves.

Super Villain/Hero Character Sheet

Basic information

Gender: female   male   neutral

Age: _____

Race (human, alien, magical creature):_____

_____

Physical Appearance

Height:_____

Weight:_____

Body-type:_____

Skin Color:_____

Piercings:_____

Tattoos:_____

Overall looks:_____

Clothes:_____

_____

_____

Unique Features

1._____

2._____

3._____

4._____

Weapons, Gadgets, and Vehicles

1._____

2._____

3._____

4._____

Partners, sidekicks or henchmen

1._____

2._____

Powers

1._____

2._____

3._____

4._____

Weaknesses

1._____

2._____

Motivation

_____

_____

_____

SYMBOL

Case Example

One client I worked with using the above activity meticulously crafted her Addiction villain. This demon assumed a human form. Outwardly her demon could manifest dichotomously as either beautiful or hideous. When the demon was beautiful, it captivated anyone in its presence. It dressed stylishly in fine clothes and typically donned black blazers with button down shirts and slacks. The demon's mesmerizingly bright eyes were a perfect complement to its gleamingly flawless smile. And its well-manicured fingernails were the perfect enthralling accoutrement to its immaculate complexion and youthful glow.

The Addiction demon's tempting desirability deceptively concealed the hideousness of its other form. When it morphed into its more demonic outward appearance, its beautiful skin turned wrinkly and creased, its complexion faded to an austere grey pigmentation, and its skin tone diminished to flaccidity. The perfect nails transformed into talons, the flawless smile mutated into rows of razor-like fangs, and its dancing human-like eyes converted to lizard-like slits. This transformation occurred when the demon became hungry for, and needed to feast on, a human soul.

In its hideous and demonic form, Addiction had a singular motivation: to remain beautiful and human. However, the demon's salvation could only occur by sacrificing and feeding on the human soul of a willing victim. To accomplish this, the demon had a number of powers at its disposal. It could subtly change and shift its form into the intended victim's "type." First, it lured its intended victim with beauty and charm. Then it used its telepathic powers to place thoughts into that person's head until the victim could no longer distinguish their own thoughts from those of the demon. When the demon had complete control over the intended victim's thoughts and resulting actions, it guided the victim into willing submission. Once that happened, the demon fed on the victim's soul and retained its beauty and human-like form. The demon fed through a whip made of human flesh and bones sharpened into needles. The demon wrapped the whip around the victim and systematically syphoned off the person's soul—piece by piece.

The demon has a significant limitation, it can only attach to one person at a time. If that person bolsters their will and denies the demon, when he/she ceases to be a willing participant—the demon cannot feed on that person's soul. Gradually, the hungrier and more voracious the demon became, the more hideous its form as it weakened. When it got weak enough, it could be sent back to Hell. However, even in a weakened state, the demon still had ways of trying to feed. The demon could command shadowy, vaporous, troll-like creatures to invade the victim's body and dreams causing physical pain, sickness and nightmarish dreams. These troll-like creatures were intended to haunt the victim to the point of willingly returning and submitting to the demon.

The client articulately elucidated the conceptual origin of her villain to me. As she explained, she described her Addiction this way because she acknowledged to herself that she was really attracted to the drugs and, for a long time, she was a willing participant. She loved it. Only after she started to get sober did she realize how bad things had gotten in her life. For her, the trolls that her Addiction employed as henchmen represented her acute withdrawal.

This client's hero was more elemental and pure, but it still fit within a dichotomous paradigm. The hero, her recovery, is a Guardian Angel. The Angel had glowing eyes and could project an impenetrable protective force field around potential victims that the demon's whip could not pierce. The Angel breathed truth into the air and when people heard those honest utterances, they unquestionably believed them. However, even heroes have limitations and the demon's whip could temporarily disable the Angel's powers. Nonetheless, the Guardian Angel never let that deter her from her mission of protecting everyone from this deceptive, parasitic, soul-sucking demon.

Many discussions with the client centered on the motifs of honesty and self-direction that are embodied by the Guardian Angel/hero she created. We also discussed how the angel and demon represented her desire for a return of spirituality in her life. There are many ways of interpreting the metaphors she built into her hero and villain and we could have spent much more time than we had unraveling all of them.

As a clinician, my observations are that art often mimics life. That is certainly true about a recovery story even though clients are given broad creative license. Interestingly, in this client's story, the demon steals from its victim the essence of what makes us human for the sake of retaining the ability to appear to be something it is not. For me, it would be difficult to find a more apt description of addiction than that.

Other Ways of Using Superheroes and Villains in SUD Treatment

Another way of incorporating superheroes and villains into SUD treatment is by directly referencing the existing metaphor of certain already extant characters. The beginning of the chapter is an example of how that can be done. Any of those examples can be used in a session to help a client understand the nature of addiction or anger or the power of animal instinct.

There have been many articles written about Robert Louis Stevenson's "The Strange Case of Dr. Jekyll and Mr. Hyde" and how it is a Victorian allegory of addiction. Comitini (2012) wrote such an article interpreting the metaphors and symbols in the story as representing the cycle of addiction. The well-researched allegory can be used in sessions with clients to help them understand and connect with SUD.

However, some younger individuals will only be vaguely familiar with the story through other media, like cartoons or modern movies. The client may not have a working knowledge of Dr. Jekyll and Mr. Hyde. In these situations, it can be advantageous for a therapist to be familiar with more modern metaphors like the Hulk or Man-Bat.

Superheroes and villains can also stand in as metaphors for many other life problems that accompany SUD. Dual identities, masks, traumatic reactions, manipulation, even low self-esteem are all things that can be discussed through the lens of modern comic book heroes and villains. A creative therapist can find numerous ways of connecting SUD related issues to comic book stories and characters.

Some people dealing with SUD, often in the early stages, struggle with hiding their addiction from people in their lives. They try to appear perfect at work and at home, but they opportunistically sneak off to use their substance of choice whenever possible. This sneaking around and hiding can be nerve-wracking and stressful. It could be helpful to relate that to how Peter Parker's personal life is in shambles because he spends so much time as Spider-Man. After all, there is a price paid for a double life, even for superheroes.

Often people with SUD are coping with significant internal pain and feel they are too fragile to allow themselves to be vulnerable around others. In some cases, it can be dangerous or life-threatening to show weakness or emotion. In such cases, people tend to develop a portrayal of themselves as strong, emotionless and/or in charge of everything. In reality they are terrified and in a great deal of pain. Discussing their protective mask through the metaphor of superhero masks can be very helpful.

A large portion of SUD clients are likely to have experienced some sort of trauma. In general, these traumas are either the impetus of their use or came about because of their use as a consequence of the people they are forced to associate with to obtain and use illegal substances. Characters like Batman, Spider-Man, Punisher or Green Arrow can be good metaphors for different types of trauma reactions. Batman can represent the enduring fear-based reaction that accompanies trauma. Spider-Man can represent the overwhelming sense of responsibility akin to survivor's guilt. Punisher can represent hypervigilance and the pathological drive to remain in control of everything, at all times. And Green Arrow can represent the existential drive to find meaning after a trauma.

Villains like Lex Luthor, Joker, Red Skull and the Mandarin are evil geniuses and experts at manipulating others. They are great metaphors for how damaging manipulation can be. This is important for those with SUD because manipulation usually accompanies addiction.

Various superheroes and supervillains can act as metaphors for other mental health disorders as well. A clever therapist can use these characters to connect to depression, anxiety, bipolar disorder, obsessive compulsive disorder, or any of the personality disorders like borderline or antisocial personality disorder.

The key to using superheroes and villains in this way is in making sure the client has a working knowledge of the character. Finding this out may be a matter of simply talking about their favorite superheroes and villains then tapping into those characters. Another good idea may be to keep a collection of a few comic books that have stories that touch on a specific topic. This way, the client can read them and become familiar with the story and the therapist can then use that specific story as metaphor for the issue at hand.

Throughout history, stories have always been able to tap into a deeper meaning. Comic books are a modern medium that often use real life as inspiration to build stories that have depth. These modern allegories are rife with metaphors. A clever therapist can use those metaphors to aide people in recovering from SUD.

Questions for Clinical Discussion

1. When using supervillains as a metaphor for addiction, what are some ways that a clinician might work with a client to conceptualize the remission period? Keeping in mind that comic book villains rarely suffer an ultimate death: might the villain be in jail? Might the villain be victimizing someone else? Might it be attending to oddly ordinary obligations? Or might it be hiding out, gaining power, and planning its next move?
2. What are some ways that Motivational Interviewing (MI) techniques can be incorporated into the story-telling process? For example, might the counselor engage the client in a role play and act out the villain role while the client acts as the recovery hero. Reinforcing change talk is a major tenant of MI. When clients play the recovery hero role and hear themselves defending the recovery message while asserting the recovery position might that serve to reinforce their own change talk?
3. Redemption is a common theme in comic books. What are some ways that a clinician might assist a client in figuring out if (or how) their villain might be redeemed in some way? Possibly the clinician can help the client explore redemption conceptually in that not all redemption is one sweeping singular act: in many ways redemption is one decision at a time, one day at a time. Might that parallel a recovery story through the creation of a mantra that helps the client summon the strength necessary, in the moment?
4. What therapeutic value might come from working with a client to develop an Origin Story for their Villain and Hero? Often the backstory holds the key to understanding present events in our lives. Might that kind of an exploration prove helpful here?
5. Metaphors involving "combat" inherently include an element of "winner" and "loser." The "loser" aspect of a combat metaphor can easily be internalized and negatively impact a client's self-esteem. What are some ways a clinician can work with the struggle between the villain (addiction) and hero (recovery) without making it a battle scenario? What are some ways of keeping the client involved in the struggle between the two?
6. What values, other than ones directly related to recovery, might a clinician work with their client to boost or conceptualize through the metaphor of the Hero? We often focus on large sweeping qualities when small deeds also build character in a way that lends to overall heroic concepts. How might we work to build small acts into larger concepts?

References

Chermahini, S. A. & Hommel, B. (2010). The (b)link between creativity and dopamine: Spontaneous eye blink rates predict and dissociate divergent and convergent thinking. *Cognition, 115*(3), 458–465. doi:10.1016/j.cognition.2010.03.007

Combs, G. & Freedman, J. (2012). Narrative, poststructuralism, and social justice: Current practices in Narrative Therapy. *The Counseling Psychologist, 40*(7), 41033–1060. doi:10.1177/0011000012460662

Comitini, P. (2012). The strange case of addiction in Robert Louis Stevenson's strange case of Dr. Jekyll and Mr. Hyde. *Victorian Review, 38*(1), 113–131. doi:10.1353/vcr.2012.0052

Cosgrove, L. (2004). What is postmodernism and how is it relevant to engaged pedagogy? *Teaching of Psychology,* 31(3), 171–177.

Lawrence, J. & Valsiner, J. (2003). Making personal sense: An account of basic internalization and externalization processes. *Theory & Psychology, 13*(6), 723–752.

Legowski, T. & Brownlee, K. (2001). Working with metaphor in Narrative Therapy. *Journal of Family Psychotherapy, 12*(1), 19–28. doi:10.1300/j085v12n01_02

National Institute on Drug Abuse (2018). Section I: Introduction to the brain. Retrieved September 24, 2018, from www.drugabuse.gov/publications/teaching-packets/neuro biology-drug-SUD/section-i-introduction-to-brain

Olssen, M. (2003). Structuralism, post-structuralism, neo-liberalism: Assessing Foucault's legacy. *Journal of Education Policy, 18*(2), 189–202.

Ramey, H. L. & Grubb, S. (2009). Modernism, postmodernism and (evidence-based) practice. *Contemporary Family Therapy, 31*, 75–86. doi:10.1007/s10591-009-9086-6

Szabó, J., Tóth, S., & Pakai, A. K. (2014). Narrative Group Therapy for alcohol dependent patients. *International Journal of Mental Health and SUD, 12*(4), 470–476. doi:10.1007/s11469-014-9478-1

Wallis, J., Burns, J., & Capdevila, R. (2011). What is narrative therapy and what is it not? The usefulness of Q methodology to explore accounts of White and Epston's (1990) approach to Narrative Therapy. *Clinical Psychology & Psychotherapy, 18*(6), 486–497. doi:10.1002/cpp.723

Wilson, R. E., Jr. (2013, June 30). Surprise: Creativity is a skill not a gift! Retrieved from www.psychologytoday.com/us/blog/the-main-ingredient/201306/surprise-creativity-is-skill-not-gift

White, M. & Epston, D. (1990). *Narrative means to therapeutic ends* (1st edn.). New York: W. W. Norton & Company, Inc.

PART III

Strength in Numbers: Superhero Teams

In this section, we will see how there is clinical power in numbers as we turn to the use of superhero teams in therapy

I Can Be a Super Friend! Using Scripted Story to Promote Social Emotional Skills for Young Children with Problem Behaviors

Judith Lester

Introduction

One of the challenges in providing community mental health services for young children and their families and caregivers is finding simple, effective resources that are free to use, play based, research driven and effective. No small order for the busy play therapist! We need look no further than the Center on the Social and Emotional Foundations for Early Learning at Vanderbilt University for a bona fide Super Hero to come to our rescue. Meet Super Friend, the star of a scripted story *I Can Be a Super Friend!* He leaps tall social skills in a single bound by using his eyes to look, his ears to listen and nice words to tell his friends what he needs. Super Friend can wait his turn and play with his friends nicely. And he holds the single most important Super Hero skill of all—Super Friend can go with the flow! This simple scripted story can be used with early childhood caregivers and parents to teach social skills to young children with difficult behaviors who may have a variety of diagnoses and life experiences. This chapter explores the use of this simple and free resource and is aimed at mental health clinicians who provide early childhood mental health services for young children and their caregivers.

The Challenge

It is no news to anyone who works with young children that early childhood can be fraught with challenges. During 2016, Child Protective Service agencies in the United States received over 4 million reports of possible maltreatment with over 2 million of these reports being screened in for further investigation and response (US Department of Health and Human Services, 2018). This represents about 3.5 million children whose lives are affected by maltreatment of some kind with 676,000 of those children being declared victims of child abuse or neglect and 1750 children losing their lives. Of these victims, 28% are 3 years or younger. These early experiences and the environments in which they happen impact the development of the brain and a person's ability to learn, their behavior and their mental and physical health (Center on Developing Child, 2010). Adverse childhood experiences have strong correlations with poor developmental outcomes that reach into adulthood resulting in physical ailments such as heart disease and cancer, and mental health issues such as depression, suicide and substance abuse and addiction (Center on Developing Child, 2010). Children who experience abuse and neglect are susceptible to a myriad of issues that can impact their ability to learn and relate to others. According to the second National Survey of Child and Adolescent Well-Being, children who experienced severe abuse and exposure to violence were more likely to be behind in their social-emotional, cognitive, language, daily living skills, behavior and social skills development compared to their same-aged counterparts in the general population (Casanueva et al., 2012). They were more likely to be diagnosed with attention-deficit hyperactivity disorder, asthma and emotional problems. They had higher incidents of behavior problems, language delays and other developmental delays indicating the need for clinical interventions. These special needs pose a real challenge to the caregivers in both the child's home and early care and education (ECE) programs. According to Child Trends, a nonprofit research institution dedicated to using research data to promote the well-being of children and youth, children benefit from caregivers who take a trauma informed care (TIC) approach to providing services to young children and their families. They recommend increasing the capacity of ECE providers' ability to deliver trauma informed care, expanding the ability of early care and education providers to make referrals to community resources to benefit children and their families and providing young survivors of trauma a stable early education experience in a supportive and safe environment (Dym et al., 2017. These are key elements for children who often exhibit trauma reactions and utilize coping mechanisms that can be viewed as disruptive behaviors. Symptoms such as temper tantrums, difficulty in self-regulation, withdrawal and dissociation can disrupt the attachment process that is so important in early childhood. Interventions that teach and support a child's ability to self-regulate, attach and interact peacefully with others are critical in promoting healthy social emotional development in young children. Policies and practices that promote the principles of supporting responsive relationships, reducing sources of stress and strengthening core life skills can support healthy development and better educational achievement for children and better lifelong outcomes (Center on Developing Child, 2017).

Nearly 60% of the children from mid-income families experience some sort of peer interaction before they enter kindergarten. Various studies over the past 40 years have shown that early childhood peer groups, such as those found in daycare and preschool settings, have as much influence on a child's social emotional development as does their interactions with parents and families (Peceguina, 2014). Peer interactions can be the basis for friendships even for children of preschool age, and children that do well socially in preschool can be forecasted to do well socially and academically as they develop. In their longitudinal study designed to measure the stability and growth of social competence over the preschool years,

Peceguina et al. found that "Social competence was the central organizing construct of early childhood" (Peceguina et al. 2014, p. 2063). Bringing social emotional skills training to young children in their natural environments can be of great benefit to them and the people who care for them. Thus, reaching children where we find them makes logical sense.

Interventions aimed at teaching appropriate social emotional skills can be very helpful to a variety of children with difficult behaviors. Children diagnosed with Autism Spectrum Disorder displayed an increase in targeted prosocial behaviors after participation in a manualized, multimedia social skills training intervention called Superheroes Social Skills program (Radley et al., 2016, 2017). Concentration on a social communication approach using children's literature can reach children with limited language expression to increase their academic and social functioning (Brinton & Fujiki, 2017). Scripted stories have long had a place in early childhood environments in teaching prosocial skills to young children. The Center on the Social and Emotional Foundations for Early Learning (CSEFEL) at Vanderbilt University is a comprehensive, web-based, free resource available to help caregivers, teachers and professionals teach social emotional skills to infants and children. The website features a variety of practical strategies that include scripted stories aimed at teaching social skills appropriate for early childhood environments. The scripted story that is the focus of this essay, *I Can Be a Super Friend!*, can be used to teach and model developmentally appropriate social skills in the home and early care and education programs. Let's take a look at this inventive and useful scripted story.

Practical Application: Introducing *I Can Be a Super Friend!*

My practice has been in early childhood mental health for many years as a play therapist, providing behavioral health services for children and their families and early childhood mental health consultations for daycares and preschools. I found the scripted story *I Can Be a Super Friend!* in a happenstance encounter with the CSEFEL website. This scripted story can be found at this link to CSEFEL under Practical Strategies, Scripted Stories at http://csefel.vanderbilt.edu/resources/strategies.html. It is a PowerPoint presentation that can be downloaded for use on a computer or printed and put in a binder for use as a book. The hero of the story is a little boy dressed in yellow pajamas, wearing a red cape, ready for action with an engaging smile on his face. Simple line drawings and clip art are used for the illustrations. The narrative of the story follows our hero as he explains that he likes to play with his friends but sometimes he struggles: he wants to play with toys that his friends are playing with and he might use angry words or lose control of his body and hit and kick. He then offers instructions for friendlier ways to interact: he can ask to join in play or ask to play with their toys. The narrative then names specific behaviors that characterize a Super Friend: using nice talking, gentle hands and feet, using eye contact, listening carefully and taking turns with others. There is much repetition as simple social skills are reviewed in this 15-page story. Children are reminded to use their Super Friend skills of deep breathing and going "with the flow" when things don't go as planned. The PowerPoint file includes two slides that extend the experience. Cue cards that can be printed, cut and placed on a ring for children to manipulate and a simple behavior chart to encourage specific social skills are useful in reinforcing the skills presented in the scripted story. This simple free resource holds so much potential in reaching young children who need social skills support.

Practical Application: Early Care and Education Programs

My first use of this resource was in the preschool classroom. In providing early childhood mental health consultations to Head Start classrooms, I was often confronted with students having difficulty with behaviors that were disruptive to the classroom. One teacher with a classroom full of dysregulated first-time 3-year-old children was struggling with how to gain some control over a very chaotic environment. I presented her with *I Can Be a Super Friend!* and we developed a plan. She began by promoting behavioral competence as her basis for classroom rules, a common practice element found in effective classroom interventions (McLeod, 2017). She read the scripted story regularly during circle time. Brinton and Fujiki give us some insight into effective ways to do this (Brinton & Fujiki, 2017). Reading the story slowly, paraphrasing as needed to match the attention of the children, simplifying language structure, and repeating the story regularly are ways to magnify the impact of *I Can Be a Super Friend!*. The teacher donned a Super Friend cape each time she read the story to her students. This teacher was adept at using intonation, expression and gestures to bring the story to life (Brinton & Fujiki, 2017). She led the children in a ritual of reviewing the rules, chanting "Super Friends use nice talking, gentle hands and feet, look with their eyes, listen with their ears, take turns with toys and go with the flow!" She engaged them in the kinetic experience of pointing to their bodies as they named the various parts and mimicked surf boarding as they practiced "go with the flow." The teacher and co-teacher then acted as a team to extend the intervention throughout their day with the children. The use of descriptive commenting, ignoring undesirable behaviors (when appropriate and safe) and proximal praise of other children in order to remind a specific child of desired behaviors are common practice elements in effective classroom interventions (McLeod, 2017). Both teachers watched carefully for any Super Friend behaviors being exhibited throughout their day. When they didn't observe a child demonstrating these prosocial skills, they noticed each other's Super Friends skills, providing an opportunity to model the desired behaviors for all of the children. They intentionally "caught" the students being Super Friends and then shared the cape with them, often facilitating one child sharing the cape with another and then boasting proudly of their collective Super Friend skills. The teachers paid special attention to children with behavior difficulties, sharing the cape with them so they could don their Super Friend skills, and noting even the smallest progress. In just a short time, older children in the classroom were encouraging the younger ones to use gentle hands and feet, listen with their ears, take turns with toys and go with the flow. Disruptive behaviors decreased and children and caregivers reported that they enjoyed the daily ritual of social skills review and use of the cape as a tangible reminder.

Practical Application: Individual and Family

I Can Be a Super Friend! was easily translated to my play therapy work with individual children and their families. Initially, I printed the PowerPoint presentation in color and placed it in transparent sheet protectors to create a book that I shared with clients during sessions. The clear story plot referring to social situations and emotions that are familiar to children is an important first concept in using bibliotherapy to teach social skills (Brinton & Fujiki, 2017). The setting of a preschool classroom and the emotions displayed in *I Can Be a Super Friend!* are relatable concepts for many young children. Most of my young clients were unable to sit attentively through the entire story and so I found myself highlighting concepts of emotional intelligence and prosocial conversational behaviors as we perused selected pages of the book together (Brinton & Fujiki, 2017). The story highlights and normalizes the experience of feeling frustrated in play, using age-appropriate feeling words to describe the child's experience. It also gave easy-to-follow instructions on coping skills and ways to respond to typical social situations experienced in the lives of young children. The script identifies important social concepts of turn taking, using language skills to meet needs, and self-regulation when interacting with others. I used the story as a framework to engage the children and make an emotional connection with them while immersing them in the content of the story. I adapted the story to the needs of the child, connecting to their experience with siblings and peers, helping them to express their feelings and desires. I then began to extend the therapeutic engagement by using props, pretend play and enactments which are other effective, recommended ways to use bibliotherapy (Brinton & Fujiki, 2017). I created a Super Friend cape that I wore while reading to my client. Any simple costume cape would work: I painted the initials "SF" on the cape for further effect. I would then offer to share the cape with my client or caregivers who were present, and comment about sharing as a desirable social skill. Some children were reluctant to wear the cape at first and when this happened I could usually count on the parent to join in the play. If other siblings were present, I would encourage the family to take turns with the cape. We often practiced the skill of "go with flow" by chanting the words together, and moving our bodies as if we were flowing freely through space or surfing on water. This play extends the story into dramatization, supporting the children's imagination and giving them an opportunity to role play the script in ways that offer re-enactment of the concepts being presented (Brinton & Fujiki, 2017). The family was given a copy of the story to take home and encouraged to read it several times a day to reinforce the social skills presented. This accessible narrative and the play it supported became an important educational resource that built on the power of story to enhance language, social and emotional learning in children who had both limited and typical abilities.

I developed other ways to extend the play and reinforce the social skills of being a Super Friend. I printed, cut out and then glued together cue cards with a stop sign on one side and the social skills cue on the other. I put these on craft sticks to be used in role play with dolls, dinosaurs or action figures. As I engaged children in play with the action figures, I would use the stop sign to stop the action and reveal the social skills on the opposite side of the cue card. Using the cue cards we would then practice the social skill: our action figures would "go with the flow," take turns, join friends and play nicely while stopping to think and do as the opportunity presented. These cue cards could also be placed on a ring and used in real time in play with siblings and peers to encourage development of social skills.

Parent and caregiver involvement was an important component to my sessions with children. One hour a week in Ms. Judy's play therapy room was never going to get the job done! I needed to engage parents to bring this intervention to their homes so they could teach and model the skills needed to change their child's behavior. I introduced the caregiver to the concept of child directed play and descriptive commenting. We had filial play therapy sessions with parents present in the playroom or observing from the observation room. Over subsequent sessions we would practice the skills of engaging their child in child-directed play while using descriptive commenting to track the child's activity. I used a chart listing four Super Friend social skills, to concentrate on describing desirable behaviors. If siblings were present, I used sibling play to demonstrate descriptive commenting, noting when the children were playing nicely, taking turns, and going with the flow. When opportunities of conflict arose, I would demonstrate the concepts of stop, think and do, modeling the skills of taking two deep breaths and saying "I can go with the flow," reinforcing concepts from the scripted storyline. A copy of the chart was given to the family for use in the home. In each session, parents were able to practice the art of descriptive commenting while being attentive to their children during play. This type of play strengthened relationships and filled the children with positive attention. I assigned parents the task of using 10 minutes a day to practice the child-directed play and descriptive commenting. I encouraged them to post the Super Friend skills chart somewhere in their home where the family would be reminded to pay attention to the prosocial skills as they saw them emerge in their daily activities.

I used props in my play with the children and expanded concepts that proved to be beneficial in teaching specific skills. The Super Friend cape was used each time I read the scripted story to a child. When a friend's mother made and donated colorful capes to me, I donated them to classrooms and families. Some parents reported that their children solved the need for a cape by simply tying a small blanket around their necks—what a great use of imagination! I heard many reports of children flying through living rooms, capes around their shoulders, declaring, "I can be a Super Friend!" A little bit of fabric went a long way in play! Play with art materials was another way that I extended and expanded the play with children while affording them much needed repetition to reinforce social skills learning. In session, I led the family to create stop signs using the cue cards and craft sticks. As we crafted, I would explain their use and make suggestions for play at home. After practicing and modeling the social skills in play using the cue card stop signs, the family would take the props with them for play at home. Another craft I made with children was aimed at teaching the self-regulation skill of stop, think and do. Using construction paper we created stop lights by gluing red, yellow and green circles on a rectangular piece of paper. Older children would write the words stop, think and do on the red, yellow and green circles, respectively. I would then engage the children in playing a musical game to practice the body skills of self-regulation. I would be "It" and model the game to start. We would play music and dance with great abandon and feeling. When I stopped the music, I would point at the red circle on the stop light, and encourage everyone to stop their bodies. Then, pointing at the yellow circle I proclaimed "Think!" and then modeled deep breathing to calm our bodies. Then, pointing at the green circle, we would "Do" by deciding who had the next turn to be "It." That person was reminded of the rules and then given control of the music and the stop light with prompts to lead the practice of the skills as needed. We would repeat until everyone had a turn or we were exhausted from dancing. This was another game sent home with the family for extended play and practice. The various activities developed from the original scripted story allowed me to repeat the Super Friend concepts over a number of sessions, thus reinforcing the skills through modeling and play.

Personal Reflections

In the midst of companioning young children and their families through the ups and downs of life, Super Friend has been by my side. I hit the play therapy jackpot when I found *I Can Be a Super Friend!*. I am really pleased to have the opportunity to share the free resources available from The Center on the Social Emotional Foundations for Early Learning at Vanderbilt University with other play therapists for several reasons. First of all, it is a free resource from an organization that is steeped in providing research based interventions for providers, parents and caregivers. How generous is that! I've printed and distributed this scripted story to hundreds of children, parents and caregivers. I've sent home Super Friend charts and had them returned by proud children so we could count how many stickers or smiley faces they had earned practicing their skills. One parent reported that they read the story daily to their child and then spent some time in play with their children, watching and commenting on their play, paying attention to them in ways they hadn't experienced before. Sharing her "aha" moment with me, this parent was amazed at how much things had changed in her relationship with this child. She was really enjoying being with her child!

Second, it has been easy to use and versatile. As a busy play therapist I needed something simple and direct that could be used quickly and easily with families. I used it with children one-on-one, in sibling groups and in the classroom. It is written in language that could easily be used by parents and caregivers from diverse backgrounds. I could expand on the concepts and be creative with my presentation of them. Having started my career in early childhood services, I've always looked for interventions that have a sensory piece to them and *I Can Be a Super Friend!* held many possibilities for sensory play. Making the cue cards into stop signs and then practicing the social skills in play was helpful for clients. Wearing and sharing the Super Friend cape was a tangible way for clients to take on the persona of Super Friend. Parents would practice their tracking of their child's skills by putting stickers on the chart I gave them. You just can't use talk therapy with young children—you've got to make it playful to make it effective. *I Can Be a Super Friend!* fit the bill.

Lastly, I've had fun with this: fun with children, fun with teachers and fun with my staff! I've sat in planning meetings with Head Start teachers and watched as they tried on their new Super Friend cape. We laughed as we practiced our best surfing imitation and chanted. "I can go with the flow!" On one particularly playful day, I donned my cape and danced with my staff to a little Rick James ditty in celebration of Super Hero Day. I've found myself filled with joy at the report from a parent that she was actually enjoying being with her child. Now that is success—a child and parent strengthened their relationship by having a little fun while learning some important life skills. My use of *I Can Be a Super Friend!* created relationship—from the Head Start teacher who developed the idea of using Slide 14 as her classroom rules to the friend's mom who made all those Super Friend capes. The positive play allowed light-hearted moments that strengthened children's relationships with their significant adults. That is the power of play.

There are several ideas I would share for your consideration when using this scripted story. In its current version, *I Can Be a Super Friend!* portrays very little cultural diversity. Super Friend is represented as a white male and most of the characters presented in the story are conspicuously white. It would be wonderful to see a female "Super Her" or Super Friends with varying skin tones or features. Maybe a Super Friend in a wheelchair or using crutches or wearing braces. There is only an English language version of the scripted story available on the website, although some other practical strategy resources are available in Spanish. While I have used *I Can Be a Super Friend!* with a diverse clientele, it really is important for children to see heroes who remind them of themselves.

The other cautionary suggestion that I might make relates to the way that adults often interpret and use play. I remember a team meeting where I was reviewing the use of the Super Friend cape in play in a classroom of preschool children. The teacher described the ways she was reading the scripted story daily to the children while wearing the cape. She then would offer the cape to a child for play and facilitate the sharing of the cape with other children. She stated that she did not allow "misbehaving" children to wear the cape—they had to earn that right. I gently examined the benefits of child-directed play, the use of descriptive commenting and proximal praise in increasing desired behaviors and suggested that the "misbehaving" children were the exact people who needed to be wearing the Super

Friend cape. And I did all of this in my best Super Friend manner. These ideas of teaching children social skills, playing with them intentionally and positively encouraging their development can be foreign concepts to adults who are concentrating on discipline in the home and classroom. I have concentrated on creating relationship with each person I meet: one child, one teacher and one parent at a time. By creating relationship, we get a chance to love each other into being, one Super Friend at a time.

Conclusion

Children are faced with a variety of adverse experiences that can impact their brain development, behavior and even their future health and well-being. Offering effective interventions to both children and their significant caregivers early in life can help promote better outcomes for children and their families. One such intervention, a scripted story titled *I can Be a Super Friend!*, is available in the public domain from the Center on Social Emotional Foundations for Early Learning at Vanderbilt University. The scripted story presents clear definitions for desirable behaviors and self-regulation skills for coping, with enough repetition to reinforce the important ideas. This simple story holds much potential for use with individual children, their families and caregivers in early care and education programs. Expanding the concepts through a variety of play therapy techniques and home-based activities make this an especially flexible intervention. This engaging little story promotes fun, better social skills and helps to strengthen relationships between children and their significant adults.

Questions for Clinical Discussion

1. What surprises or intrigues you about use of scripted story as a play therapy intervention?
2. How might a clinician address cultural diversity while using this scripted story?
3. Identify several ways for expanding the use of *I Can Be a Super Friend!* in your setting.
4. How could the interventions mentioned in this chapter be modified and expanded to work with older children or children with developmental delays?
5. What are some other ways this scripted story could be used to strengthen the relationships that children have with their significant adults?
6. What other ways could you imagine using this scripted story in early care and education programs?

References

Brinton, B. & Fujiki, M. (2017). The power of stories: Facilitating social communication in children with limited language abilities. *School Psychology International, 28*(5), 523–540. doi:10.1177/0143034317713348

Casanueva, C., Wilson, E., Smith, K., Dolan, M., Ringeisen, H., & Horne, B. (2012). NSCAW II Wave 2 Report: Child well-being. OPRE Report, No. 2012–38, Washington, DC: Office of Planning, Research and Evaluation, Administration for Children and Families, US Department of Health and Human Services. www.acf.hhs.gov/sites/default/files/opre/nscaw_report_w2_ch_wb_final_june_2014_final_report.pdf

Center on the Developing Child at Harvard University (2010). The foundations of life-long health are built in early childhood. www.developingchild.harvard.edu https://46y5eh11fhgw3ve3ytpwxt9r-wpengine.netdna-ssl.com/wp-content/uploads/2010/05/Foundations-of-Lifelong-Health.pdf

Center on the Developing Child at Harvard University (2017). Three principles to improve outcomes for children and families. www.developingchild.harvard.edu https://46y5eh11fhgw3ve3ytpwxt9r-wpengine.netdna-ssl.com/wp-content/uploads/2017/10/HCDC_3PrinciplesPolicyPractice.pdf

Center on the Social and Emotional Foundations for Early Learning at Vanderbilt University. I can be a super friend. http://csefel.vanderbilt.edu/resources/strategies.html#scriptedstories

Dym Bartlett, J., Smith, S., & Bringewatt, E. (2017) Helping young children who have experienced trauma: Policies and strategies for early care and education. *Child Trends Publication No. 2017–19* www.childtrends.org/wp-content/uploads/2017/04/2017-19ECETrauma.pdf

McLeod, B. D., Sutherland, K. S., Martinez, R. G., Southam-Gerow, M. A., Conroy, M. A., & Snyder, P. A. (2017). Identifying common practice elements to improve social, emotional and behavioral outcomes of young children in early childhood classrooms. *Prevention Science, 18*(2), 204–213. doi:10.1007/s11121-016-0703-y

Peceguina, I., Daniel, J.R., & Shin, N. (2014). Growth of social competence during the pre-school years: A 3-year longitudinal study. *Child Development, 85*(5), 2062–73. Date of Electronic Publication: 2014 April 18. doi:10.1111/cdev.12246

Radley, K. C., Hanglein, J., & Arak, M. (2016). School-based social skills training for preschool-age children with autism spectrum disorder. *Autism, 20*(8), 938–951. doi:10.1177/1362361315617361

Radley, K. C., O'Handley, R. D., Battaglia, A. A., Lum, J. D., Dadakhodjaeva, K., Ford, W. B. & McHugh, M. B. (2017). Effects of a social skills intervention on children with autism spectrum disorder and peers with shared deficits. *Education and Treatment of Children, 40*(2), 233–262. Retrieved from http://bl.opal-libraries.org/login?url=http://search.ebscohost.com/login.aspx?direct=true&db=slh&AN=123675489&site=eds-live

US Department of Health & Human Services, Administration for Children and Families, Administration on Children, Youth and Families, Children's Bureau. (2018). Child mal-treatment 2016. Available from www.acf.hhs.gov/cb/research-data-technology/statistics-research/child-maltreatment.

CHAPTER 10

Stronger Together: The Family as a Super Hero Team

Steve Kuniak

They stand together, tired and worn from the battle. Days ago, they could not get past their own differences to be able to see eye to eye. Now, the conflict at hand has galvanized them. It has shown them that not only can they get along, but together they can excel. They may have their differences, but they have learned that their strengths work together to help them conquer challenges that they would never be able to overcome alone. With a brief look to each other, they stride forward to face their foe.

This scenario could be transposed over any story of a heroic team. The *Avengers* and the *Justice League* are great examples of groups of people that have their own personal strengths and struggles but have to put aside their differences in order to work together. Often a grave danger that is threatening the world helps them to put the needs of the many ahead of their own personal conflicts. If we change the faces, though, we can also transpose this metaphor onto any family. The philosopher Joseph Campbell (1949) explored the phenomenon of every hero sharing a central story. He also proposed that these stories were grand metaphors for how we ought to live our own lives.

All families are made up of individuals that, though connected, experience life from different perspectives. This can cause conflicts which, at their best, are uncomfortable, and at their worst, can be catastrophic. Families, despite the discomfort with these chaotic patterns, will become accustomed to the negative arrangements in which they find themselves. When circumstances become too uncomfortable, or one member's behaviors are finally too unbearable, the family may seek the assistance of a counselor to improve their interactions.

Family counseling presents unique challenges, different from traditional individual counseling. Multiple perspectives and personalities are involved in the process, which can make the clinical challenges as complicated as the number of family members in the room. Practitioners work to come up with new and innovative ways to deal with taxing circumstances that arise in sessions. However, for as many challenges as may be present, there are equally as many opportunities to make real and lasting improvements.

A prevalent theory in family counseling is that the structure of the family develops out of interactions that, even though they are chaotic and damaging, are comfortable in their predictability. The family develops patterns of behavior that, though dysfunctional, are repeated over and over again until they become the norm. They become stuck, and the role of the counselor is to destabilize the system, to break the problematic patterns of interaction. Though this may cause more chaos for a short period of time, the hopeful result is that the family will reorganize around new ways of looking at themselves and new ways of interacting. This often requires the family to see themselves differently in order to make change. Using two traditional theoretical approaches, the family is able to reimagine itself in new and meaningful ways. So in my own practice, I wondered "why not reimagine themselves as something heroic?"

Systems Theory/Family Therapy

I think it is important, before we get to the heroics, to start at the beginning. Family counseling has a long and storied development. Early on, clinical work focused exclusively on the individual. In fact, in some instances prior to the 1940s, the practice of including more than one person at a time in psychological treatment was seen as ineffective and, in some cases, unethical. As a result, much of the work that was done with families in these early days was not much more than advice giving (Gladding, 2015).

The first major catalyst for working with families was brought on by the movement of women enrolling in colleges, which resulted in the development of family life education courses (Gladding, 2015). This allowed for some of the discussion of families that was once taboo because of societal pressures and tradition, to become more a part of the clinical discourse. This began with the work of Ernest Groves, whose courses in parenting and family life experiences enabled practitioners to adopt family minded dialogue. In 1934 he wrote the first textbook on marriage (Groves, 1934). Groves took his work beyond the realm of solely education and developed the American Association of Marriage Counselors (AAMC) in 1942. Individuals like Abraham and Hannah Stone became early practitioners and advocates of marriage counseling in the late 1920s and 1930s, with similar practices cropping up in areas like Philadelphia, led by Emily Mudd.

In the 1940s, theorists such as Bela Mittleman (1948), Ernest Groves (1940), and Ruth and Theodore Lidz (1949), through the documentation of their work, began establishing a new language made up of terms focused on processes that occurred between couples and families. In 1946 Congress passed the National Mental Health Act, which focused on establishing a better understanding of mental health diagnoses and treatment. As a result much of the funding from future research on mental health and families came from this Act and led to better research and techniques.

One of the more prominent figures in the field of family counseling was Nathan Ackerman (1958). He began advocating for seeing a family as a system in the 1930s, but his work gained momentum in the 1950s. He published volumes on family systems dynamic, and his work was so convincing that it gained the attention of individually focused psychiatrists of the time. Similarly influential was Gregory Bateson's (1955) work with his team of researchers on the communication patterns in families and the possible links to his patients' struggles with schizophrenia. This landmark research spawned the careers of prolific family counselors such as Jay Haley, John Weakland and Don Jackson, who worked with Bateson (Gladding, 2015).

Other major figures of the time included Milton Erickson (Haley, 1993), who was initially drawn into the field as a consultant to Bateson's Palo Alto research group. Bateson was highly interested in Erickson's focus on the power of suggestion and subconscious messages. Erickson, through his collaboration with Jay Haley (1993), became famous for his contributions to family counseling. Carl Whitaker (Whitaker & Keith, 1981) laid a foundation of psychotherapeutic practice with couples and families with whom he worked while he was chief of psychiatry at Emory University. It was during this time that he also established the first family counseling conference. And lastly Murray Bowen (1985), who gained fame for his work on exploring multigenerational patterns in families, left his mark on the field. He focused his attention, through the support of the National Institute of Mental Health, on drawing all family members into a room at once to conduct counseling. This practice resulted in Bowen formulating his theory on the influence of previous generations in a family impacting current family generations.

The previously described professionals remained prominent into the 1960s, though three major theorists stood out with new contributions. Virgina Satir (1967) who began her work at Don Jackson's Mental Research Institute, branched off to begin her own studies in Chicago. She was unique as the only woman among the classical family theorists, and was distinctive in focusing on the empathic needs of the family. She emphasized the impact of self-esteem and remaining congruent with one's expression of feelings in the context of the family. Along with Satir, figures like Salvador Minuchin (1974) came to prominence. Minuchin, who set up shop in the Philadelphia Child Guidance Clinic, established a theoretical perspective that aligned with Jay Haley's (1973) practice. The two collaborated together until their theories diverged with Minuchin focusing on what he identified as Structural Family Therapy, and Haley focusing on his school of thought, Strategic Family Therapy. These theories, according to Gladding (2015), formalized the family systems approach and remain very popular in the field of Marriage Couple and Family Counseling today

Structural and Strategic Family Therapy

Family systems theory was a heavy influence in my exploration of the family as a super hero team. The focus on the interconnected nature of the family is central to the idea of a heroic family that works together, despite their differences, to accomplish tasks. Each members' roles influence and are influenced by the other members of the family. Family Systems theory relies heavily on understanding the unique structure and roles of family members, and how they interact based on the patterns they create. Though this can be challenging to navigate, it is vital to the success of the team. As counselors, we can use the systems focus to play out the family interactions we want to see in session.

Jay Haley, through his studies in Bateson's Palo Alto research program and their client's struggling with schizophrenia, discovered a problematic family communication pattern called a double-bind (Bateson, Jackson, Haley, & Weakland, 1956). According to the Palo Alto family counseling research, the double-bind occurs when one member of the family presents contradictory messages to the other members of the family. An example of this might be when a parent tells their child that they love them no matter what, but then is disparaging toward their sexual identity. Though the double-bind is problematic in nature, it is an excellent example of the importance of family communication patterns. Messages within families carry weight, and may significantly impact family members' beliefs about themselves. This influences how family members interact with and see themselves in the world. Haley believed that it was essential as a Family Counselor to be central in the process of rewriting these communication patterns. His work advanced when he joined Salvador Minuchin at the Philadelphia Child Guidance Center.

Minuchin, like Haley, believed that family patterns and dynamics needed to be completely reorganized in order for the family to improve. As a result, he used his understanding of what a healthy family ought to look like to strategize a plan for reorganization of the family structure. This shift in understanding and intervening on patterns within the family system was appropriately named Structural Family Therapy. The role of the Counselor was to challenge the messages and communication patterns within the family system and offer different interpretations of looking at the family as a way of shifting the dynamics. Through helping family members see themselves in different places in the hierarchy and organization of the family, the family would begin to reorganize and develop new behaviors (Colapinto, 2015). Minuchin described the family members as being like pieces on a game board, and through the counseling process the clinician would shake the board. The pieces would be moved into different positions, which may or may not result in an improvement. If there was improvement, then the new patterns were adopted. However, if there was not improvement, then the role of the counselor was to again try and shake up the family dynamic. Any movements in reorganization were seen as an improvement from the family's current state of chaos. The takeaway with Structural Family Therapy was to see the family through the lens of a different organization.

A significant premise of Structural Family therapy is that the family needs to look at itself differently. Salvador Minuchin believed that family dysfunctions arose out of the family developing reactions to stressful life circumstances (Gladding, 2015). These reactions, which Minuchin called dysfunctional sets, were like scripts that were developed under stress, but that the family never modified, and just adopted again and again whenever conflict arose. Minuchin believed that it was the counselor's responsibility to use techniques to interrupt these processes and come up with new and better methods of dealing with conflict. Rewriting a family's script is a central part of my superhero family intervention.

A primary method of seeing the family through a different lens is a technique called reframing (Colapinto, 2015). The Counselor helps the family to reframe their current experiences by presenting a new way of looking at an old set of messages. The goal is for the family to see the same experiences through a different and more manageable light. A metaphor for the reframing intervention that I often share with my students is one of literally taking an old picture in a scuffed and aged frame, removing the picture from the old frame, and placing it in a new one. The picture stays exactly the same. However, having it placed within a new and clean frame, results in the picture looking more pleasant and refreshed. In the same way, we can use reframing to change the way a family views their experiences and their members.

A prime opportunity for reframing can be observed when a family sees one of their children as being a problem. I have often experienced family counseling sessions where on the first session a family presents their child and says something to the tone of "fix my kid." Instead of seeing the child's behaviors as problematic, the Counselor can use reframing to help the family see that the child is actually calling out problems in their home and is searching for help in the only way they know how. The Counselor helps the family to see the child as a noble savior who is simply trying to get help for the family they care deeply about. The goal in this shift of representation is that it becomes much harder for the family to paint the picture of a "bad kid" when they see their child as trying to help. Reframing, and as we will see later reauthoring, are primary in the super hero team intervention. The family needs to, quite literally, rewrite themselves.

Similar to the reframing intervention, another tool a Family Counselor may use is a genogram (McGoldrick, Gerson, & Petry, 2008). This tool, often used for assessment was developed by family physicians as a means of tracking and exploring family patterns and dynamics. Michael Crouch was a prominent figure in the early days of genograms. His writing and organizing of ideas surrounding these clinical family trees (Crouch 1986) began the process of using visual tools to track family dynamics. Crouch (1986), among others, work would influence Murray Bowen's thought around multigenerational patterns that occur within families. Genograms were not originally a centerpiece of Haley and Minuchins exploration of Family Systems theories, as they believed in focusing on the here and now rather than looking into the past. Assessments like genograms, however, have found their way into many family counselors' work as they continue to be useful tools for helping to track family dynamics. Additionally, for the practical purposes of this writing, they help to take the unspoken and externalize it into something tangible.

Genograms display the family in interconnected generational rows where symbols (e.g., males as squares, females as circles, etc.) are used to represent the different family members. After demographic information is organized in the genogram, the counselor also depicts family experiences through interconnected lines, called relationship lines. Though genograms are a form of assessment, they can be used as an intervention by visually depicting family processes and providing an opportunity for the counselor to present these to the family. The counselor can then work with the family to decide how best to rewrite the interactions they would like to change. Visualizing family experiences can help make complex or implicit patterns of behavior become much more clear and explicit. This tool directly lends itself to the organization of the family as a super hero team. Without a method of visually organizing the family, the process of transferring their personas becomes incredibly difficult.

Enactments were another Structural Family Therapy technique that were employed to get the family to begin acting differently. Enactments are a technique in which the counselor invites the family members to play out, in the moment, the patterns of interaction they would otherwise just describe (Colapinto, 2015). In this way, rather than the family just speaking to the counselor about what was going on in the home, the counselor would get the family to act out their behaviors in the moment. Enactments allow the counselor the opportunity to intervene on problematic patterns of behavior as they are occurring and then suggest new interactions that the family can try out in the counseling session. They also allow the counselor the opportunity to get the family trying out new behaviors or personas in the moment where they can be tweaked and modified.

The counselor could also apply sculpting to a family to better visualize the family dynamics and intervene. Sculpting is a process of having the family physically depict a dynamic that they believe most replicates the family (Dallos & Draper, 2015). This intervention appears as the physical representation of a snapshot of the family's patterns of behaviors according to one family member. Quite literally, the family will pose like mannequins in a manner that is representative of the actions being observed in the home. After explaining the intervention and giving examples, the counselor will lead each family member in creating their own family sculpt, which will be followed up by a discussion of what led each family member to position all members where they were positioned. It has also proven important, in my counseling with families, to have a discussion on how each family member felt in the position they were placed. The counselor will then give their feedback and help the family to work through the process of repositioning the family members into a structure that is more in line with how they would like to be positioned. They can then discuss what would be needed to help them actually make moves that would shift them into the better position.

All of the interventions that I have described in this analysis of Structural Family Therapy are designed to help the family understand the patterns of behavior that they engage in and then rewrite those behaviors into something more useful. The focus, as Minuchin imagined it, was on breaking patterns of behavior in order to free families to rewrite themselves into more manageable structures. Each of these interventions focuses on the visualization of the family, and then the reframing of the family into something more desirable. As a counselor, I was brought up on these ideas. They provided me with the frame that would help my families to rewrite themselves into a team of heroes fighting for good. However, I needed a few other ideas which were found in another Family Counseling theory, in order to make this intervention come together.

Narrative Therapy

Narrative Therapy is a theoretical orientation that is based on the idea that our concepts of ourselves, and the way we interact with the world, are very much based on the stories we create about ourselves (White, 2009). Instead of taking a general stance toward a theoretical perspective that might apply to any family or family member, Narrative Therapy chooses to focus on the unique story within every individual. The healing process occurs through the counselor helping the client to express their life story into a narrative. Once the story is made external, the counselor helps the client(s) to rewrite their story in order to change it into a narrative that is more in line with the life they want to lead.

Narrative Therapy began through the work of Michael White, a social worker, who began his career helping families in South Australia (White, 2009). He directed his initial clinical focus toward David Bateson's systems approach. He then adapted his perspective after discovering Edward Bruner's ethnographic research. White began exploring the idea that storytelling was not just a method of recording or describing a situation, but was central to the way we as people contextualize our existence. Michael White met the man who would become his colleague, David Epston, as a result of Epston presenting at the 1981 Australian Family Therapy Conference (White, 2009), of which White was an organizer. They began a collaborative relationship and started shaping their ideas around Narrative Therapy together. White passed away in 2008, but Epston continues their work in collaboration with several of their mutual colleagues.

White and Epston both considered themselves family counselors. They were inspired by prominent theorists of the time such as Bateson and Erickson. Narrative family therapy finds its base in social constructionism and the postmodern approaches to counseling. It does not take into account systems theory in the same way as other family counseling models. Rather, it focuses on the here and now through rewriting and reorganizing the family story and roles within the family that present themselves in session (Aniciete & Soloski, 2011).

Carey and Russell (2003) explored White and Epston's operational definition of stories. White and Epston defined any story as having four main components. According to this definition, every story consists of (1) events, (2) in a sequence, (3) across time and (4) organized according to a plot or theme. By using this formula, any experiences could be adapted into the framework of a story-line. One of the counselor's major focuses is to help the client align their own experiences into this framework.

A primary intervention in Narrative Therapy is to get the family thinking about their problems using narrative reasoning (Mattingly, 1998). This process is characterized by the family identifying their life through stories and substories, and through this process helping themselves to ascribe meaning to their experiences. It is the development of meaning that is most important for a person to be able to lead a more fulfilling and healthy life. We cannot change whether or not a trauma happened in our life, but we can change the meaning attached to it. If we see that trauma as our fault or see it as a sign of our own weakness, then we react accordingly to the trauma. If we see it as a challenge that we are more than capable of conquering, then we also react accordingly, but in a different, more positive, way. We cannot change our immediate thoughts and reactions to the experiences we have in our lives. However, through the help of a counselor practicing Narrative Therapy, we can begin to remove the meanings that were pre-attached to our experiences, and look at these experiences objectively as through the pages of a good book.

Externalization (White & Epston, 1990) is the term used to describe the process of separating our personal reactions from the situations that have arisen in our lives. In seeing the problem as something separate of themselves, clients gain greater personal agency over it. Rather than experiencing resentment, for example, the family could see the experiences that are resulting in a feeling of resentment as an invader in their home, or a toxic chemical that is poisoning their family. In this way, they can focus in on getting rid of the problem, because it is harmful to them or their family, rather than just sticking with the feelings they were experiencing before our intervention. In losing the attachments they have to the problem, they are more capable of seeing the forest for the trees, and are more capable of making objective and impartial decisions about the problem. In this way a counselor could help the family to see any number of roadblocks they are experiencing in new and productive ways. Once the problem is seen as something tangible and separate of themselves, the counselor can help the family to begin to make changes within their lives to write the problem out of their story.

Reauthoring (Carey & Russell, 2003) is the actual process of making change in the family system. The conversations between counselor and clients serve two purposes. They serve to keep the problems externalized, and they create alternative storylines in which the family tries different strategies to remove or defeat the identified problems in their lives. Families are able to test out theories safely by exploring lines of logic and seeing what conclusions at which they may arrive. Counselor and the client family can then anticipate potential problems, and continue to reshape and experiment with different possibilities until they arrive at one that works best. It should be noted that the problems and solutions are not simply made up. They are based on actual experiences, and real changes that are based in reality and that the family can try out and practice. Reauthoring conversations can begin in many ways, but essentially are constructed by the counselor taking up the position of questioning and inquiring to gain information about the story. However, the counselor should point out any inconsistencies that do not seem to fit in with the main story. The exception finding experience lends itself to discovering opportunities to intervene and try out new behaviors.

Blending Therapies into Hero Stories

Narrative and Structural Family Therapy, at first blush, look rather different. However, one of the chief underpinnings of both theories is to get the family to reinvent themselves. Similar theoretical motifs appear as we examine techniques like reframing, genograms, family sculpts, externalization and reauthoring. They involve illustrative concepts that get the family thinking about themselves objectively. When the family is able to depersonalize their interactions, it allows for a more unbiased appraisal of the situation. Some of the emotional charge that might otherwise get in the way of making changes is removed or at least given some space.

I began exploring the concept of helping families to develop into their own super hero teams when I was earning my Master's degree at Duquesne University in Pittsburgh. I had professors who encouraged the use of creative counseling techniques in whatever work we students were doing at the time. I happened to be employed as a Family Based Counselor. Family Based Services are a team-delivered counseling approach that is rooted in Structural Family Therapy techniques. A Family Based Team is made up of two counselors who provide services to families in their homes. The restriction for receiving this particular service model is that a child has to be at risk of removal from the home. Reasons that constitute "at risk" can vary greatly, but for the purpose of providing examples, they could be because the child (or children) have significant behavioral problems, and lower levels of care have been tried. It could also be because there are abuse or neglect issues in the home, or the family is ill equipped to handle the unique needs of a child with a weighty diagnosis. Among other possibilities, the child may also have been hospitalized or placed out of the home because of a critical incident, and Family Based Services are being used to help step the child back into a traditional family setting. Regardless of the reason, the families we served were from all walks of life, socioeconomic levels, and mental health needs. They all had multilayered issues and often required significant restructuring. We were also given only eight months to complete our jobs and get the family into a better place. So, no pressure, right?

The fast pace and short window of opportunity associated with Family Based Services lends itself to a need for innovative treatment methods that can shift a family's patterns in a very short amount of time. Counselors are encouraged to utilize any intervention so long as they filter it through the lens of Structural Family Therapy concepts and language. Additionally, because of the intensity level of the cases, counseling staff were required to receive a significant amount of clinical supervision both at the agency level and through a training institute. It was at one of the training institute supervisions that a facilitator provided a discussion on reframing, and how this could be related to interventions in other theoretical orientations. This discussion resulted in the spark of an idea for a new intervention. The way the clinical trainer was describing reframing made me think of the process of reauthoring in Narrative Therapy, which

I happened to be learning about in a Counseling Theories course. I started to draw connections, but wondered how this would relate to the client families I was serving.

Many of the families I was working with were experiencing a common theme of acting as though they were broken or fragmented. What I mean by that is that everyone was caught up in their own problems, or their own experiences, as they related to the presenting problems in the household. So, the parents would blame one of their children because the child is acting out, but the child would also identify that they were acting out because they were not getting enough love or attention from their parents. Similarly, a sibling would become resentful because everyone was focusing so much on their brother's problems but they were getting ignored. A father could be mourning his opportunity to be the parent he dreamed he could be, because his child was struggling with behavioral problems. Everyone was reacting from their own frame of reference. There was no family cohesion. They were all individuals living their own stories, working against one another, under the same roof.

I had been reading an *Avengers* comic book, trying to decompress from my days work, when I was struck by inspiration. The *Avengers* were a team of super heroes that all had their own unique stories, their own problems, their own strengths, and their own arch nemeses. However, they learned to put aside their differences and accomplish goals that no one of them could achieve alone. Over time they came to depend on one another. Their individual stories, and their new conjoined stories, intertwined until they became impossible to separate. This is exactly what the families I was serving needed to do. They needed to merge as a family and learn to support one another, rather than be so fragmented. My experiences with super hero teams would make a great metaphor for the families I was serving. However, I had arrived at this point after years and years of consuming super hero stories, and I did not know if the families would even speak the same geeky language as I did. How could I get a family to understand this concept within a matter of a few sessions? How could I get them to self-identify as the characters in their own story?

I decided that to start this process, I would need each of the family members to design their own super hero based on themselves. My first hurdle was trying to get the families I was serving familiar with super hero stories in the first place. In the years that have passed since, super hero origin stories have become common. However, when I had begun this project, many families were unfamiliar with how a character develops, how the hero's story relates to the villains in the story, and how the characters experience related to other characters over time. So, I had to pack quite a lot of backstory into a short amount of time. Now, my recommendation is that the counselor assigns the family the task of watching a movie like Marvel's *Avengers* or DC's *Justice League* outside of session, and then being prepared to discuss what they experienced at a follow-up session. However, back when I started this, it took a little more work. I developed a short but detailed psychoeducational talk to present to those I was serving.

Regardless of how you, as the counselor, choose to ensure this, I suggest you just make sure you and the family are all on the same page. After a basic framework of how super heroes develop and interact has been established, the counselor can move on to helping the family in reauthoring themselves. I found the use of a Genogram to be particularly helpful with the start of this process. It provided a frame of all of the family members, and their relationship to one another, as well as their relationship within the greater scope of the family. After family dynamics have been organized into a genogram, the Counselor can begin developing character origin sheets with the family.

I constructed a very basic questionnaire that I would use to help guide the family in the development of their origin story. I began by asking them to identify their own super powers. I directed them to consider what their talents or affinities were in real life, and to see if they could then expand this to arrive at a particular super power. I can recall working with a father who was drawn to fishing, for example. He was able to enhance this area of talent and personal interest into a super power similar to that of DC's *Aquaman*. His character could communicate with aquatic creatures, was particularly good at swimming, and had some control of the water. As another example, I was working with a child who really loved video games. He turned his power into being able to interact with technology and shift odds in his favor (he could manipulate luck). I want to also note that this step was assigned as homework for the family, and then we would review it together at the next family session.

Once the super powers were established, my next task for the family involved working backward to establish how they got their powers. This could be accomplished the other way around, but I found it much easier to develop an origin story once we knew what the powers were. If you consider the scenario I mentioned above, for example, it might have been challenging for the father I was working with to come up with an origin story then try and attach it to something that was meaningful to him, like his affinity toward fishing, afterwards. Instead, after identifying their powers, the family would then come up with anywhere from a few paragraphs to a few pages of notes on how they became a super hero. Each family member could also draw, paint or otherwise create their characters costume. Just as above, this was assigned as homework and then reviewed together at the next family session. Each step of this activity, for many of the families I was working with, became something fun that they looked forward to and enjoyed exploring together. Additionally, an unexpected benefit of doing this as a group, was that they would also occasionally support each other in further developing their origins and powers. The creation process became an exercise in collaboration.

After we established their super powers and back story we then began the process of identifying their weaknesses. I gave examples to the family about this potentially being an object (like Kryptonite for Superman), an experience (like Storm being claustrophobic), or something more complex. When I say "more complex" what I mean is something in line with Spider-Man being a more vulnerable person, or struggling with social experiences. I would even offer to my clients that their weakness could be something that has to do with a physical attribute, like Daredevil's blindness. After this homework was completed we would work collaboratively to see if there were ways to connect their strengths and weaknesses together, or how they would see these attributes as balancing each other out. The question was essentially, "How does your weakness challenge your strength, and/or how does your strength overcome your weakness?" Again, this was a great opportunity for the family members to cooperate with one another. It easily transformed into a rich therapeutic dialogue.

Lastly, we would develop an arch nemesis for each of the characters. I explained to the family that their nemesis would likely somehow relate to their weakness. They would get extra praise if they could connect their nemesis to their origin story somehow as well. When it came time to explore the family nemeses, I paid extra attention. I was watching for common themes, or connections to what the family was really going through. Often times I could draw upon at least one, or several of their created nemeses, to involve in a story that would force all of the characters to have to work together. On odd occasions that these characters and the family's experiences did not link up, I would add an additional step to create the scenario that brought all of their individual super heroes together.

We would then, as a group, take several sessions to tell the story of how the problem scenario/nemesis caused all of the characters to come into conflict. They would have to identify how their powers and focuses got in the way, as their characters were developed to fight villains alone up to this point. Then they had to work out how all of their powers would work together in order to save the Earth. As I was saying, this could take multiple steps and stages. It was not something that easily resolved itself in just one session. Nor did I want it to at this point. The family would have invested a lot of time and effort in this process, and shortchanging the experience would be inappropriate.

After the newly established super hero team had saved the day, resolved the conflict, and were now able to work together we would take several sessions to debrief. I would work with the family to relate this back to their actual day-to-day experiences, and now that the situation had been externalized they would practice ideas on how they could reframe their interactions to better work together. We would create comic book panels of the story they created, as well. This ended in the family having an actual comic book style memento of their adventures to reflect upon. It provided an artifact that the family could go back to and refresh themselves on months and years after they had completed their counseling experience.

Summary/Conclusion

The blending of the therapeutic processes found in Structural Family Therapy and Narrative Therapy provided an excellent framework to be able to help get the families I worked with to think differently. In analyzing the structure of their family dynamic, they were able create meaningful avatars of themselves and place them in a fictional universe of their design. Once the family's story was established and the conflicts they were experiencing were externalized they were able to safely explore options that they could not do prior to this intervention.

An unexpected additional benefit of this Super Hero Family intervention was that the family was able to engage in multiple sessions that did not feel as much like traditional counseling to them. As a result, they had many quality interactions, and were able to practice working together to accomplish common goals. These practice experiences in changing structure are naturally a part of family therapy interventions. Building a heroic story is just a metaphorical way of renegotiating the family's structure.

I found it very powerful to help a family to use their imagination to create a new story for themselves and then enact that change. I take inspiration from the famed Fred Rogers who said that "Imagining something may be the first step in making it happen, but it takes the real time and real efforts of real people to learn things, make things, turn thoughts into deeds or visions into inventions" (Rogers, 2003, p. 99). Just like the super heroes that the family was imagining, they used their own inherent gifts to make the change they needed. It started with imagination but shifted into real work. With the power of the story they created together they were able to reshape their lives.

Since I was very young, the heroes in comic books had inspired me to take every opportunity to be selfless, honorable and just. It felt so deeply personal. I had never imagined that their stories could be used to inspire others, or that I could use them to help people to make important changes in their own lives. I had never considered the power of someone to visualize a different reality, and then through their imagination, will it into existence.

In closing, I am reminded of Aunt May's speech to her nephew Peter Parker in the film Spider-Man 2 (Feige, Lee, Ziskin, Arad, & Raimi, 2004). Peter is doubting himself, and Aunt May, through her reaction to their young neighbor wondering where Spider-Man had gone, shares that she "believes there's a hero in all of us, that keeps us honest, gives us strength, makes us noble, and finally allows us to die with pride, even though sometimes we have to be steady, and give up the thing we want the most." Our fantasy heroes provide us a clear example of how to become better people. In today's world, I believe we could use as many of these inspirations as we can find.

Questions for Clinical Discussion

1. What are ways that you could continue to evolve this intervention if you had more time with a family than just the 8 months I had?
2. What kind of "super villains" are present in the families that you already serve? What are super powers that you have already discovered within the families that you serve?

3. Sometimes the heroes differences rise up and get in the way again and again. How can you help a family to anticipate these needs down the road before they arise?
4. What are other theoretical orientations that might lend themselves to this sort of an intervention? How do their underpinnings relate?
5. What are experiences that you can imagine that might get in the way of your clients attempting to reauthor their lives?

References

Ackerman, N. (1958). *The psychodynamics of family life.* New York: Basic Books.
Aniciete, D. & Soloski, K. (2011). The social construction of marriage and a narrative approach to treatment of intra-relationship diversity. *Journal of Feminist Family Therapy, 23*(2), 103–126.
Bateson, G. (1955). A theory of play and fantasy. *Psychiatric Reports, 2,* 177–193.
Bateson, G., Jackson, D. D., Haley, J., & Weakland, J. (1956). Toward a theory of schizophrenia. *Behavioral Science, 1*(4), 251–264.
Bowen, M. (1985). *Family therapy in clinical practice.* Lantham, MD: Jason Aronson.
Campbell, J. (1949). *The hero with a thousand faces.* Princeton, NJ: Princeton University Press.
Carey, M. & Russell, S. (2003). Re-authoring: Some answers to commonly asked questions. *International Journal of Narrative Therapy & Community Work, 2003*(3), 60.
Colapinto, J. (2015). Structural family therapy. In: *Handbook of family therapy* (pp. 134–147). London: Routledge.
Crouch, M. A. (1986). Working with one's own family: Another path for professional development. *Family Medicine, 18,* 93–98.
Dallos, R. & Draper, R. (2015). *An introduction to family therapy: Systemic theory and practice.* United Kingdom: McGraw-Hill Education.
Feige, K., Lee, S., Ziskin, L., Arad, A. (Producers), & Raimi, S. (Director) (2004). *Spider-Man 2* [Motion Picture]. Culver City, CA: Columbia Studios.
Gladding, S. T. (2015). *Family therapy: History, theory, and practice* (6th edn.). Upper Saddle River, NJ: Pearson.
Groves, E. R. (1934). *The American family.* Chicago, IL: JB Lippincott Company.
Groves, E. R. (1940). *The family and its social functions.* Chicago, IL: JB Lippincott Company.
Haley, J. (1973). Strategic therapy when a child is presented as the problem. *Journal of the American Academy of Child Psychiatry, 12*(4), 641–659.
Haley, J. (1993). *Uncommon therapy: The psychiatric techniques of Milton H. Erickson, M.* New York: W. W. Norton & Company, Inc.
Lidz, R. W. & Lidz, T. (1949). The family environment of schizophrenic patients. *American Journal of Psychiatry, 106*(5), 332–345.
Mattingly, C. (1998). In search of the good: Narrative reasoning in clinical practice. *Medical Anthropology Quarterly, 12*(3), 273–297.
McGoldrick, Gerson, & Petry (2008). *Genograms: Assessment and intervention* (3rd edn.). New York: W. W. Norton & Company, Inc.
Minuchin, S. (1974). *Families and family therapy.* Cambridge, MA: Harvard University Press.
Mittleman, B. (1948). The concurrent analysis of married couples. *Psychoanalytic Quarterly, 17,* 182–197.
Rogers, F. (2003). *The world according to Mister Rogers: Important things to remember.* New York: Hachette Books.

Satir, V. (1967). *Conjoint family therapy: A guide to theory and technique*. Palo Alto. CA: Science and Behavior Books.

Whitaker, C. A. & Keith, D. V. (1981). Symbolic-experiential family therapy. *Handbook of Family Therapy*, *1*, 187–225.

White, C. (2009). Where did it all begin? Reflecting on the collaborative work of Michael White and David Epston. *Context*, *105*, 59–60.

White, M. & Epston, D. (1990). *Narrative means to therapeutic ends*. New York: W. W. Norton & Company, Inc.

CHAPTER 11

El Diablo: What His Role in the Suicide Squad Teaches Children about Emotion Regulation and the Power of Connection

Rachel Hutnick

Super and hero, two words I rarely hear my clients use to describe themselves. Instead, they enter therapy with an understanding of themselves as good or bad based on behaviors labeled by others, and at times, themselves. As a play therapist, the focus is not on whether the child is good or bad, because frankly, we are all both, but rather on being a mirror to reflect the child's experience (Landreth, 1991). Sometimes, in order do to that, I need a little help from super heroes, villains and all the characters in between. Garry Landreth (2015) would encourage play therapists to be the telephone booth for which Clark Kent transforms. I would say be the Alfred, the Robin, the Jimmy Olsen, the Speedy, or in the case of El Diablo, be the Deadshot—be the one to reflect, notice, challenge and ground the child. And while you are at it, take advantage of the sidekicks you are gifted with. Luckily for me, El Diablo was a gift I did not see coming.

El Diablo: From Baby to Brotherhood

Many superhero movies hit the big screen in 2016 such as *X-Men, Batman* and *Deadpool*, and it seemed unlikely that *Suicide Squad* would hold any significance compared to them (Simba63, 2016). In short, the Suicide Squad is a group of supervillains, previously incarcerated for unthinkable wrong doings, selected by a corrupt leader to save the world, and with their own lives on the line, they begin to form bonds with each other (Polo, 2015). For this chapter, understanding El Diablo is most significant, and I will tell his story soon, but it is also important to appreciate Dead Shot, another member of the squad, and one whom I reference throughout the chapter. Dead Shot, painted as a villain and described as an expert marksman motivated by money (Polo, 2015), is a loving father to a young daughter and a friend to El Diablo. Their relationship appears most influential in El Diablo's healing process, as explained later.

Superheroes and villains had been a staple in my play therapy work, and fortunately, characters like Batman and Wolverine were well known, easy to identify with, and celebrated in pop culture. Unfortunately, those popular characters did not often resonate with the children in my office, some of whom were struggling with an internal dialogue shouting "I am bad, something is wrong with me, I am dangerous." Initially, Deadpool appeared to be a worthy sidekick—funny, good, bad, someone dealing with situations outside of his control, but Deadpool was ultimately too vulgar, too inappropriate. El Diablo, on the other hand, surfaced as the ideal recipe for mixing the good with the bad, taking responsibility for one's actions, and allowing oneself to heal with the help of others. As an attachment-based play therapist, I needed him.

Like all great sidekicks, El Diablo's back story is key. El Diablo is a name given to more than one comic character, which allows for creative freedom in the play therapy session, but for this chapter, the focus is on El Diablo from the recent movie *Suicide Squad*. His back story is one of sadness, anger, emotionally driven choices, and guilt. Although we do not meet El Diablo as a child, we can infer from his conversation with his counterparts in the bar that he has struggled his entire life with his power, seen as both a gift and a curse (Roven, Suckle, & Ayer, 2016). His power, the ability to create fire from his body and control the element, is linked directly to his emotions, primarily anger. His avoidant attachment style, as evidenced by his disengagement following the intense remorse after he killed his wife and children (Roven et al., 2016), paired with the assumption that his early development lacked sufficient connection to a caregiver, left him without anyone to help him coregulate.

Attachment theory suggests that patterns of emotional expression and regulation begin in the early stages of life within the dyad of an infant and his or her caregiver. Children with secure attachments tend to have more effective and positive ways of experiencing and expressing negative emotion, such as anger (Guo, Leu, Barnard, Thompson, & Spieker, 2015). Whereas, children with insecure attachment patterns, like El Diablo, have difficulty receiving the safety and security they need during intense emotions, often resulting in exaggerated and unhealthy emotional expression (Guo et al., 2015). Infants need caregivers to survive. Without a caregiver, or with a caregiver who is unresponsive to the infant's needs, the infant becomes emotionally isolated, setting the stage for future challenges in relationships, with daily functioning, and with his or her self-worth (Shi, 2003). Although El Diablo attempted to heal from his wounds and transgressions, specifically the death of his wife and children, through isolation, spending his days inside a secure container—unable to be triggered, unable to be provoked, unable to harm others—his real healing only occurred when he was reunited with a family. Sadly, he was unable to reunite with his family of origin or his family of procreation but the relationship among his peers, the Suicide Squad, provided him with the attachment needs he was unable to meet otherwise.

As mentioned before, we can speculate El Diablo did not receive the connection, nurturing and mirroring, especially during early childhood, required to develop a healthy sense of self and framework for emotion regulation. Mirror neurons, motor cells stimulated by observing others complete tasks, are essential in building empathy and attunement between a caregiver and a child (Hughes & Baylin, 2012). The mirroring process between caregiver and child is reciprocal and occurs more quickly than verbal connection, so even without intention, a negative experience can occur, consequently causing a pattern of distress within the relationship. When the mirroring process is consistent and positive, the relationship fosters empathy and trust (Hughes & Baylin, 2012). El Diablo found the mirror when finally embracing his connection to the other members of the Suicide Squad.

Despite El Diablo's evasive demeanor when entering his new family, he soon learns how his connection with them can foster a new sense of self-acceptance, self-awareness and self-control, using his power to now save others. Attachment based family therapy focuses on strengthening the relationship between parent and child, therefore increasing trust, healing past traumas, meeting attachment needs, and facilitating a healthier internal working model. This approach recognizes but does not emphasize the symptoms and behaviors; instead, it focuses on the quality of the relationship, a "relation reframe" (Diamond, 2014, p.15). The Suicide Squad did just that. Due to his past trauma and self-blame, El Diablo viewed himself as awful and unworthy, a monster, yet his counterparts did not. Harley Quinn normalized his behaviors and Dead Shot pushed him to embrace even the darkest parts of himself. His family did not define him by his behaviors, they saw past them.

The Case of Connor

El Diablo entered my clinical world about a year after meeting Connor, a 6-year-old with intense rigidity and explosive meltdowns he coined as "spark outs"—a "fire" he did not realize he had. He was smart, creative, loving, and he was also defiant, aggressive, and at times, dangerous. His calm and playful curiosity about how his brain worked seemed incongruent with his attempts to control his environment with physical aggression. At the age of six, he could recognize the benefits of anger—getting his way, protecting himself from expressing other emotions, and controlling his environment—and he had enough insight to know it needed to change. Although he began family play therapy with my mentor, he was quickly referred to me for individual play therapy multiple days a week, with the recommendation of continued family sessions and individual sessions for his parents.

Treatment Phase 1: Family Therapy and Assessment

Connor's engagement in family therapy with my mentor was brief, approximately six sessions, but significant. Although Connor's parents reported no overt traumas such as abuse, loss or injury, they expressed concern the family's recent move from the city to the suburbs triggered this new pattern of behaviors, aggressive meltdowns and intense rigidity. They mentioned their older son had similar behaviors at this age and expressed concern that witnessing his brother's distress may have been traumatic for Connor as well. It was my mentor who also realized Connor's need for nutritional and medical attention. Connor was malnourished and deficient in multiple vitamins, relying mainly on a diet of breakfast meats and soft pretzels; he had a prolapsed rectum and continuous gastrointestinal discomfort. To top it off, his meltdowns were making parenting difficult and causing conflict within the home. His parents recognized their inability to maintain parenting values due to a fear of his meltdowns, resulting in accommodations and "giving in."

As is common with aggressive youth, his parents felt compelled to accommodate their child's demands and permit his problematic behavior, causing higher levels of parental distress and helplessness. Children with Obsessive Compulsive Disorder, a diagnosis we later realized Connor was suffering from, can demonstrate intense aggression and therefore are more likely to have parents who accommodate and continue the destructive cycle (Kagan, Frank, & Kendall, 2017). Parental anxiety can increase and intensify this cycle, which became apparent with Connor's mom.

Connor's mom, Joan, was a bright, active and nurturing parent, and she struggled with anxiety. Her fears about judgment from others and being viewed as something other than normal caused her to make choices to prevent any possible disruption in her family image. Unfortunately, Connor's anxious triggers were not easy to identify, and despite Joan's greatest attempts, he still had aggressive meltdowns. Joan also felt a strong sense of guilt about the years spent invested in helping Connor's brother and possibly neglecting Connor's needs, which may have caused an attachment disruption. This fueled her anxiety even more and encouraged her to tolerate more than she was comfortable with to keep Connor happy, something she thought she owed him. Because of all the accommodations, Connor now had meltdowns and complete control over the family structure and lifestyle, and he was far from happy.

The family sessions highlighted the emotions of each family member. Connor's mother and 9-year-old brother were often crying, whereas Connor would enter sessions angry and aggressive and then easily participate. When engaged, Connor was bright, charismatic and even insightful. His parents appeared cohesive and joined; his 2-year-old sister, although rarely in attendance, often needed soothing from their mother. His father, Tom, seemed firm yet frustrated, often expressing concern for each family member and shedding tears appropriately. Connor's mistrust of adults, and his inaccurate, and somewhat grandiose, beliefs about himself were also overt in family sessions. He made statements verbalizing he knew best; for example, he said he would not follow his parents in a fire if he thought his plan was better. His actions matched this; Connor often questioned the choices and judgments of his parents, teachers and other authority figures. Even with the intense emotions, Connor and his family members were perceptive. Connor verbalized his feeling of having no choice but to act out, and his parents recognized the difference between Connor's fear of his new school, manifesting as nervousness and avoidance, and other moments of defiance, such as refusing to wear his seat belt in the car or knocking over tables in a public place. They openly discussed the recent transitions, such as moving, as well as the maternal and paternal family history, both of which included high anxiety, substance use, and trauma.

Treatment Phase 2: Assessment and Rapport Building
Using Play Therapy

Often, children are left out of family therapy due to the treatment modalities' lack of developmental appropriateness for children (Willis, Walters, & Crane, 2014). By incorporating play into the family sessions, and continuing with individual play therapy, Connor was more likely to build a relationship with me and most importantly, his family, which in turn would elicit more change. Play-based activities are the strongest predictor influencing child talk. When families can play together successfully, a new emotional experience is created, and the family becomes more unified (Willis, Walters, & Crane, 2014). This, paired with attachment work with him and both parents, as well as his siblings, was the ideal treatment plan.

Upon meeting Connor, I had several clinical considerations to make. Was he anxious? Was he traumatized? Should I work with him individually or should I include his parents in the session? Should I use child-centered play or directive play? Should I integrate a Theraplay approach? Should I address the behaviors? Should I overlook the behaviors? The answer to all these questions was yes but at the time, the only thing I was certain of was that I needed to use play. Children's emotions are not easily communicated with verbal language, so play creates an opportunity for children to explore their experience in a developmentally appropriate way (Landreth, 1991). Lin Shi said it flawlessly, "Play not only is an intellectual and social activity, it is also children's natural 'language'. It reveals children's observations, state of mind, and emotional status" (Shi 2003, p. 19). So, I started with a new activity I created for Connor—The Super Power Test—now a go-to activity when I first meet a child.

I invited Connor's father into the first session, with the hopes of alleviating any anxiety Connor may have and my own. I was unsure what to expect and had briefly witnessed some of his aggression in the waiting area before his family sessions. The Super Power Test was easy and something I quickly came up with the day before, but little did I know this activity was foreshadowing the supervillain interventions to come. After introducing myself, racing Connor to my office, and briefly giving him an idea of what to expect in session, I proposed a test to show me if he had any super powers. This quickly intrigued him. Connor happily followed my directives, which included closing his eyes and using his senses to guess random items from a brown paper bag. He was surprisingly calm and thoughtful in his guesses; he was descriptive and patient. Connor demonstrated great pride with each of his successful guesses and great self-compassion with each of his errors.

The following sessions were similar. Connor would attend most often with his mother, as his father traveled for business during the week, and the three of us would engage in various directive activities. These activities focused on emotional literacy, body awareness, relaxations, and most importantly, attachment repairs. They were not, however, providing me with the insight I needed to assess symptoms on a deeper level, nor the engagement needed to keep Connor motivated—as a result, he often had his own ideas of how the session should go. I decided to integrate child-centered play. Connor expressed nervousness about transitioning to a playroom. I assured him his mother could attend with us, with the hope of increasing his comfort and then decreasing her participation the following session.

My plan did not work; Connor continued to express nervousness when transitioning to the playroom, and therefore, in my own attempts to prevent a meltdown and with a family structure in mind, I invited Joan with us to the playroom for multiple sessions. This structure worked well, at first, allowing us to complete a family genogram in the sand and allowing me to observe Connor's play and the play interactions with his mom (Higgins-Klein, 2013). Joan was present, engaged and reflective. Then one session, her emotions became very intense. She cried and asked, "What is this?" "Is this normal?" It became clear she was not asking about his play, for Connor was playing calmly in the sand, demonstrating no signs of distress or clinical impairment. Joan's anxieties were in the room; she needed reassurance, she needed answers, she needed me. Connor noticed and inquired about her crying; he was thoughtful and calm, yet uncomfortable and somewhat puzzled. Connor knew his mother was struggling with him. Connor knew "something was wrong"—he could see it and feel it.

A parent session followed, and Joan was able to express and explore her anxieties from the previous session. We collaborated on a plan for her to transition out of the playroom and also receive the support she needed from me in parent sessions. When Connor returned, I proposed an idea at the start of a new session— he would hold on to the end of a string and his mother would wait outside the playroom holding the other end. Connor agreed, and within the first minute, he decided to let go of the string. As was apparent with most of Connor's worries, big and small, it was the anticipation of something going wrong that stopped him, that caused him to explode, not the actual outcome of the feared event. Connor's play was creative and focused; he wanted to master tasks. He made small attempts to connect with me, and each session, he invited me closer, literally. Connor often requested I sit far away and offer minimal reflection, and each session, he asked for more help, more reflection, more connection, and more proximity, similar to El Diablo's gradual process of connecting to the Suicide Squad. Although child-centered play was not the main intervention used, this early work allowed us to form a foundation for which deeper work could occur later, like when Connor used physical force in a session after I set a limit due to time, the first time I saw his "fire" emerge.

Most of Connor's sessions consisted of three parts, the first being a check in with his mom. Joan and Connor would share about positive moments and stressful moments from the week. Then, I would prepare a directive activity to engage Connor and hopefully implement an intervention to help decrease his symptoms and also increase his bond with Joan. Lastly, we would spend the remaining few minutes of session wrapping up, and for Connor, that meant playing a quick hide-'n-seek game in my office. Connor would take an item, usually small and easy to hide, and then direct me to leave the office while he and his mom hid the item. Although many clinical considerations may determine a therapist's choice to follow his directive or set a limit, it felt natural and appropriate for me to follow his lead. One day, Connor broke one of the few rules I set for this game—the closet, drawers, and my bags were off limits for hiding. Connor hid an item in my lunch box, and although he did not mention this when I returned, Joan's anxiety made it clear he had broken a rule. I requested Connor find the item for me and try again, this time following the limit. He questioned the limit, rationalizing that it was just a lunch box; this interaction took the remainder of the session, and even with time prompts, Connor was not able to complete the "do over" I had suggested. Instead, I had to set a time limit and request we try again at the next session. This was not easy for Connor.

When setting a limit, I only do so if needed, and I hope to connect, reflect and offer alternatives, just as instructed by the great Garry Landreth (1991); however, Connor had difficulty accepting this approach. He verbally questioned my limit, over and over again. Connor was sitting on the floor about two feet across from me, with the item in his hand. His face began to look sad and hurt, as if I had rejected him. He grabbed my long, curly hair, and he did not let go—I wasn't just seeing his fire, I was in it. He started to kick and pull; Joan quickly wrapped her arms around him in an attempt to soothe and also restrain. No words or movements were helping; I just had to breathe and hope he would join me—he did not. Joan was successful in removing Connor from my hair, but Connor continued to yell and approach me, stating he had to get back at me. He had to "make it right," an experience I soon learned was consistent with his OCD and strong urges for fairness, something that also seemed connected to early experiences of unfairness at home. Joan escorted Connor out of the office, down the stairs, through the waiting area, and into the driveway. I followed, thinking I could help with my reflections, my professional knowledge. I was wrong, Joan knew how to help him. I removed myself in hopes of decreasing his anger in the moment—I was the trigger, I was the fuel.

Upon returning to my office, I noticed I was 15 minutes late for my next session, there were items all over my office, and I was sweating. I knew something had to change, I had to "do something"—just as Dead Shot shouted to El Diablo in hopes of motivating him to channel his anger, and embrace his fire, to protect his new family (Roven et al., 2016). My approach was only allowing for small gains, and if I did not make a change soon, I feared losing my relationship with him altogether. Much like El Diablo, Connor could "master the calm," a term he later trademarked, in the absence of stressors, and much like El Diablo, the deeper work was yet to come. I wish I could take credit for recruiting El Diablo as my sidekick, but it was Connor who introduced us. I had watched the movie before and felt no connection to the character, but when Connor casually mentioned him, something his mother would share her own anxieties about, I grabbed onto the character. Joan appeared nervous, hesitant—as if I would judge her, when she shared about letting Connor watch the movie as a motivation to complete another task, a common occurrence in their house. Although *Suicide Squad* was rated R and had a list longer than I could count of scenes inappropriate for a young boy in first grade struggling with aggression, it was not judgment I was feeling, it was relief—I now had a way to connect on a deeper level.

Treatment Phase 3: Skill Building and Healing with Play Therapy—El Diablo's Debut

A few weeks had passed between the emersion of Connor's "fire" in my office and his next appointment, most of which his mom explained with scheduling conflicts, and all of which I felt was connected to a deeper issue—an issue El Diablo could help shed light on, an issue entwined with avoidance and shame. At Connor's next session, we entered the playroom. It felt, as described earlier, natural and appropriate to follow his lead, and because of our foundation from earlier in treatment, Connor was able to heal the disconnect between us within 45 minutes. First, directing me to sit far away, verbalizing his disinterest in my reflections and his lack of need for my help. Slowly, he invited me closer, directing me to hold items, watch him create in the sand, and learn from his strategies. By the end of session, he was playing actively and inviting me in, eager to attend the next week—such a relief for me. I had an opening and I was going to take it.

My first goal was to learn everything I could about El Diablo, become the expert, and then adapt his storyline to best match what Connor was experiencing. They had many demographic differences, but the biggest contrast was Connor's strong support, his family. He could heal and recreate emotional experiences within his family of origin; he did not have to wait for a pseudo family to find him. Even with those differences, the similarities were strong. Connor and El Diablo both had intense emotional experiences paired with quick, uncontrollable acts of aggression—their "fire." They both loved deeply and hurt others; showing remorse, shame and withdrawal afterwards. They both wanted and needed to heal within the context of others, their families.

After building my knowledge of El Diablo, I implemented my first activity, a scavenger hunt. Connor often entered session with great excitement, at times even directing me how to help him—like the time he drew a circular shape on my white board, placed a dot in the center, and directed me to teach him about anger in the brain. He was curious and often paced my office, sharing his inner world out loud. I directed Connor to search my office for orange pieces of paper, each with an instruction specific to facts about El Diablo, and then complete each one. He did this enthusiastically—practicing mindfulness like noticing sounds, colors and textures in my office; identifying emotional triggers at home, at school and in relationships; noticing his body through movement and dance; acknowledging his challenges with the help of his mom; and creating his own "Suicide Squad" filled with his family and closest friends.

Connor engaged in all the activities within the scavenger hunt, which created options for future sessions. We practiced relaxations—using our senses, breathing deeply, visualizing calm spaces. We took ownership over our bodies and made choices both in and out of session. For example, in session, Connor would spin in a chair, sometimes knocking over items and kicking others. This became something he started to notice, apologize for, and change. At home, Connor would melt-down, sometimes causing property damage and harming others. These became actions he could also soon predict, control and then repair—either through cleaning up a mess or reconnecting with a family member. Play interventions in session included the use of movement and impulse control activities, such as "Red Light, Green Light," "Simon Says," and "Mother May I." With time, Joan reported Connor's ability to stop aggressive acts even though his anger was intense and at times, acceptable. Connor took pride in being able to keep his hands tense like a fist, instead of throwing or hitting. The introduction of El Diablo provided a language, a common ground for Connor's family to use at home. The connection with the character gave Connor permission to look inward, recognize the danger of his behaviors, and change to save himself and his family.

Treatment Phase 4: Implementation of Other Interventions

Once Connor's aggression subsided, it became clearer that his anger outbursts were more than learned behavioral patterns and anxiety about new situations. Connor was struggling with Obsessive Compulsive Disorder. El Diablo had done his job; he normalized Connor's experience, and he engaged Connor in a way I could not. He provided me with an opening, and for that, I am thankful. El Diablo was no longer needed during our sessions—Connor was engaged and motivated on his own. Through collaboration with his parents and multiple psycho education sessions, Connor agreed to try Exposure and Response Prevention (ERP), a type of Cognitive Behavioral Therapy used to treat OCD (Foa, Yadin, & Lichner, 2012). In addition to Connor's ERP, we also implemented more family work, focusing on his relationship with his siblings and both parents—most of the initial work was with his mom, repairing any other attachment injuries and strengthening the bonds between all members of the "squad."

Treatment Phase 5: Parental Role and Maintenance Planning

Connor's entire treatment lasted almost two years, and it ended due to a combination of significant progress and my maternity leave. Although recommended, due to continued patterns of rigidity and challenging family dynamics resulting from years of intense emotional expression by multiple family members, his parents decided not to transfer to another therapist. His parents attended multiple sessions to understand Connor's needs and treatment, and they agreed to continue implementing interventions at home. Eight months after Connor's last session and five months after I returned from maternity leave, his parents came in to see me. They reported remarkable progress for all family members, especially Connor. This time, they wanted help encouraging Connor to embrace more parts of himself—and so I did just that. We focused on his strengths, encouraged him to leave his comfort zone, and created opportunities for growth through art classes, social connections and community involvement. Connor attended a few sessions, sharing passionate stories about his friends, his family, and his inventions, a hobby which often became stressful due to his OCD. We reviewed strategies for managing his OCD and focused on flexibility. My sidekick returned one last time.

Connor expressed frustration with school, describing his teachers as misunderstanding and the math strategies as senseless; he wanted to do it his way. After multiple attempts to explain and reframe the need for learning multiple strategies, El Diablo popped into my head. I mentioned how El Diablo was a strategy I used to teach Connor, not because it was how I learned, but because it was how he learned—emphasizing the benefit of being flexible and open throughout life. Connor understood; he smiled, he giggled, and he agreed to use the base ten method in math from now on because one day, he explained, he may teach others.

Personal Reflections

Throughout this chapter, I compare a struggling young boy and a violent villain, and often give credit for the therapeutic effectiveness to a character who does not exist in real life, nor is developmentally appropriate for a child of such a young age. El Diablo did not heal Connor. El Diablo offered me a window to utilize evidence-based interventions such as play therapy, attachment-based family therapy, and Exposure and Response Prevention. The real healing came from Connor, Joan, Tom, and their willingness to lean into the fire instead of away from it. At the beginning of the chapter, I share my own doubts from the start of treatment. While reflecting back on Connor's story, I realize my own anxieties did not consume me as his fire once did, but they warmed me—I became vulnerable and curious; I was willing to see myself and in turn see Connor more authentically; I was able to adjust treatment as needed; I was able to seek support. I leaned into the fire and, with the help of a sidekick, discovered a profound connection with a child.

Questions for Clinical Discussion

1. In the case of Connor, developmentally advanced and inappropriate content was used during session. What ethical guidelines may shape your decision about the appropriateness of this intervention?
2. Imagine yourself in a client's fire—what strategies can you use to regulate your own emotions?
3. What possible counter transference may occur witnessing an act of aggression in session?
4. What challenges may arise when balancing the needs of multiple family members in session?
5. When working with a similar case, what limits may you decide to set with the client throughout treatment? How will you decide which limits you are most comfortable with?

6.   Who are the members of your Suicide Squad? What role does each of them have in helping you as a clinician?

References

Diamond, G. (2014). Attachment-based family therapy interventions. *Psychotherapy,* *5*, 15–19.

Foa, E. B., Yadin, E., & Lichner, T. K. (2012). *Exposure and response (ritual) prevention for obsessive-compulsive disorder* (2nd edn.). New York: Oxford University Press.

Guo, Y., Leu, S., Barnard, K. E., Thompson, E. A., & Spieker, S .J. (2015). An examination of changes in emotion co-regulation among mother and child dyads during the strange situation. *Infant and Child Development, 24,* 256–273.

Higgins-Klein, H. (2013). *Mindfulness-based play-family therapy: Theory and practice.* New York: W. W. Norton & Company, Inc.

Hughes, D.A. & Baylin, J. (2012). *Brain-based parenting: The neuroscience of caregiving for healthy attachment.* New York: W. W. Norton & Company, Inc.

Kagan, E. R., Frank, H. E., & Kendall, P. C. (2017). Accommodation in youth with OCD and anxiety. *Clinical psychology: Science and Practice, 24,* 78–98.

Landreth, G. L. (1991). *Play therapy: The art of the relationship.* Florence, KY: Accelerated Development.

Landreth, G. L. (2015). The art of the relationship in play therapy: Deeper issues (I). In: R. Gaskill (Chair), *32nd Annual Association for Play Therapy international conference.* Symposium conducted at the meeting of the Association for Play Therapy, Atlanta, GA.

Polo, S. (2015). The Suicide Squad, explained [Web log post]. Retrieved from www.polygon. com/2015/7/16/8974897/suicide-squad-explainer

Roven, C., Suckle, R. (Producers), & Ayer, D. (Director) (2016). *Suicide Squad.* Burbank: CA: Warner Bros. Pictures.

Shi, L. (2003). Facilitating constructive parent-child play: Family therapy with young children. *Journal of Family Psychotherapy, 14 (3),* 19–27.

Simba63 (2016). Poll: 2016 Comic Book Movies [Web log post]. Retrieved from www.imdb. com/poll/XmdDDwU811w/

Willis, A. B., Walters, L. H., & Crane, D. R. (2014). Assessing play-based activities, child talk, and single session outcome in family therapy with young children. *Journal of Marital & Family Therapy, 40,* 287–301.

CHAPTER 12

Using the Avengers to Influence the Self-Actualization Process for Children

Brenna Hicks

Avengers Assemble! This rally cry is one of the most widely recognized phrases in the world of the Marvel Cinematic Universe (MCU). And in the coming together of six unlikely teammates, with both their gifts and their shortcomings, it becomes evident that the existence of both is what makes them special. As they each bring their own flaws and abilities to the assembly, they become something greater than they were as individuals. This transpires through their efforts to push past their failings and celebrate their capabilities.

This battle of opposites, though hard to quantify, is extremely powerful when present in a story. Nick Fury of S.H.I.E.L.D. might have put it best:

> There was an idea ... called the Avengers Initiative. The idea was to bring together a group of remarkable people, see if they become something more. See if they could work together when we needed them to. To fight the battles that we never could.
>
> (Feige & Whedon, 2012)

Fury knew that imperfect as they are, they are capable of incredible things. And by seeing the greatness within them, despite their baggage and weaknesses, they are given the opportunity to rise to meet the greatest of expectations. Even if sometimes they aren't quite ready to believe yet that they can. These dichotomies observed in the Avengers—greatness and weakness, confidence and fear, victories and failings—are also observed in children in the playroom. And like Nick Fury, all the while believing that they are greater than the sum of their individual and oft flawed parts, the child-centered play therapist knows that kids have the capacity to self-actualize into their best selves, too.

The similarities abound. The Avengers, brought together unaware of what is about to transpire, parallels a child entering the playroom for the first time. The Avengers resent and resist the process, just like kids during the resistance phase in play therapy. The Avengers are not convinced that they want the responsibility and the burden of the task, mirroring children questioning why they come to play every week. And the Avengers certainly aren't ready to face their pasts and their traumas in order to accomplish their mission, exactly like kids who try to avoid the painful and difficult parts of their lives. But, in the midst of S.H.I.E.L.D. and the playroom, one witnesses personal transformations. One observes incredible moments of insight and growth. One is privy to the development of self-awareness and self-concept. One is aware of the acceptance of flaws as part of the human existence. One marvels at self-actualization as it occurs.

Because of these likenesses, it makes sense that kids would identify with the Avengers in a meaningful way through their play. Because if a superhero can save the world while secretly struggling with their demons, children begin to explore the possibility that they can be in equal parts confident and flawed. And through this paradigm shift, kids can embrace the best parts of themselves while still making changes in the areas that need tweaking.

The Superhero Narrative

Film has consistently conveyed current cultural conditions through cinematic characters, more specifically with heroes. A brief look at the inclusion of bandits, cowboys and superheroes in movies and television reveals significant ideological beliefs throughout American history. However, these characters can be traced back to ancient storylines as well, as they are often found in mythology and English folklore. It is only recently that the hero has expanded to comics and the MCU.

One of the original hero stories that Americans embraced was Robin Hood. Predating the formation of the United States, the bandit known as "The Noble Robber" became popular and lauded because he worked tirelessly to make life more fair and equitable for the poor. The earliest Americans understood the inequality in England before they rebelled against the feudalist system and formed a new government, making Robin Hood a natural hero in their eyes. Veronica Williamson (2016) said:

> Robin Hood was able to create the fantasy of the world that people needed— one that was more equal—he was, however, not powerful enough to transcend different societal structures to remain relevant and applicable. Thus, a new hero was born out of a specific political and cultural climate.
>
> (p. 2)

When Robin Hood's noble pursuits were no longer applicable to the culture of the United States, a shift in the perception of a hero occurred.

Early American settlers began to see the same heroic tendencies in the cowboys of the west, thereby replacing the bandit narrative. For many years, iconic heroes in the Wild West were rugged individualists fighting for honor, justice and battling to remain unbridled in the midst of growing society (Folsom, 1967). Once the west was settled and it became less wild, the concept of the cowboy as the American hero faded away in favor of something more relevant.

Noah Gittell noted the shift away from an idyllic view of the west, stating, "the cowboy has been replaced by the superhero as the most common expression of American values" (Gittell, 2014, p. 1). With origins in comics, and initially on the periphery of cultural acceptance until popularized by Hollywood, superheroes are the newest figures to represent American idealism. However, it is worth noting that all three of these heroic figures in American history share meaningful similarities: they all are characterized by "independence, resourcefulness, and solitude," demanding the "social marginality of the principle figure" because they are "authority figures rebelling against authority" (Sparks, 1996, p. 351).

Since superheroes have emerged as a replacement for long-standing accounts of idealism that express humanity's search for a sense of the world and a person's role within it, it is not surprising that the hero narrative remains. Recently an author posited:

> Just as ancient man used stories of gods and monsters to explain the world, modern man uses stories of godlike heroes and monstrous villains to do the same. Comic books are modern mythology, in that they are modern man's method of explaining the world around them through the fantastical.
>
> (Modern mythology, 2016)

And similar to the stories of old, comics and superheroes allow for self-exploration in deep and meaningful ways.

Stan Lee's Superhero Creation

Stan Lee, creator of many of the Marvel characters, had very specific intentions during the development of the Avengers. He deeply believed that comics and superheroes can teach—specifically children—lessons about humanity and the world. He stated in reference to writing superhero stories:

> One of the options is to make the good guy the one that the reader would want to emulate, rather than the bad guy. The more the young reader likes the hero and admires the hero, and the more the hero does good things, subliminally the kid absorbs these things.
>
> (Lee, 2013, May 22)

His intention was to inspire kids to see the good qualities in the superhero and want to become more like him or her, just like Errol Flynn, Franklin Roosevelt and Winston Churchill inspired Lee as a child (Lee, 2018). Additionally, even Lee's villains were never meant to stay that way. Prior to Lee's characters, villains were presented as bad guys to the core, and his intention was to write into the villainy narrative characters who were actually good deep down so that the reader could see the inherent goodness masked by the bad decisions (Stevens, 2017).

Another desired outcome was that he could create a character to whom the reader would feel deeply connected. Lee said:

> To me, the human aspect of superheroes has always been, perhaps, the most important part. We assume your superhero might be extra strong, or might be able to fly, or run as fast as a comet. But, unless you care about the superhero's personal life, you're just reading a shallow story. Just because a person has a superpower, doesn't mean he might not have the same personal problems that you or I might have.
>
> (Lee, 2013, December 27)

His purpose in creating his Marvel superheroes was to ensure that the characters were relatable. He wanted the reader to see a connection between himself and the superhero. He purposed that the character "lives and breathes and worries and experiences things just the way you and I do, except for the fact that he or she has a superpower" (Lee; 2013, December 27).

One additional understanding also influenced Lee's superhero schemata; the superhero had to have flaws. When Lee was a teenager in the 1930s, Superman was the only comic book superhero around. But Lee was troubled by his perfection. He felt there needed to be a strong sense of realism in the lives of superheroes, which included shortcomings, failures, unfavorable traits, traumatic experiences and flaws (Lee, 2006). Early in his career, Lee was expected to write mostly fight scenes without dialog in his comics. He complied but wasn't particularly satisfied with the results. Armed with a challenge from his wife to write the kind of stories he really wanted to, regardless of whether they would be published, Lee began to introduce good guys who were real, relatable and flawed; an era known as the Marvel Age, which includes the creation of The Avengers. This decision "revolutionized the medium by focusing attention as much on the dysfunctional lives of its characters as on the super battles they fought" (Lewis, 2016, p. 3).

Appreciating the Hero

Research indicates that in typical hero narratives, people are more likely to enjoy the story when there are measures of attractiveness, morality and sympathy related to the hero (Shafer & Raney, 2012). This has been termed Affective Disposition Theory (ADT), and this predicts the likelihood of readers to connect with the hero because of their positive motives and behaviors. Interestingly, this is exactly what Lee desired for his readers when he created comic book superheroes who were good at their core, even when they did bad things.

This concept has also been expanded to the viewer's value system, in that he compares his own values to that of fictional superheroes (Zillmann, 1996). As the reader assesses the moral judgments that the heroes make, he finds a parallel in his own life's decisions. This also carries over to the idea that during these moral conundrums, the superhero is also battling internally with their own flaws. Hohle

(2016) said that he believes "no story would be compelling without some doubt in the hero's efficacy in overcoming their own shortcomings. All heroes' flaws must be recognized, measured, and compared as they are encountered in stories" (p. 53).

Identification with the Superhero

It is important to note that as superheroes became more flawed, they became more real to the reader. Lee wanted people to see that the superhero was not only tasked with defeating the villain, but they also had to fight against their own insecurities and hang-ups. Jon Favreau, the director of *Iron Man,* believes that when characters face the same problems that humans have, they become a proxy (Associated Press, 2008; Favreau, 2008).

Further, there is a significant and meaningful association with the humanity of the flawed superhero, as it is a reminder that perfection is unnecessary. There is freedom for the reader in realizing that brokenness and personal failures are companions to the incredible acts and accomplishments of the superhero. They coincide and coexist, sharing the same space. Akiva Goldsman, another producer of *Iron Man,* stated, "We identify more with people who are broken, people who are damaged. Those are the heroes who stick with us, the ones who are imperfect despite all their gifts, because everyone feels imperfect" (Associated Press, 2008).

The extensive literature on the hero storyline, inclusive of a psychological component, provides the reader with a hope that it is possible to conquer any foe and win any battle—internal or external. Not surprisingly, there is a pervasive belief that a catharsis is offered in the hero myth (Campbell, 1949), long appreciated by cultural critics and replicated by authors and producers. However, Gibbon (2002) believes that the modern definition of a hero is insufficient. He says:

> The greatest burden the word *hero* carries today is the expectation that a hero be perfect. In Greek mythology, even the gods have flaws. They are not perfect but rather hot-tempered, jealous, and fickle, taking sides in human events and feuding among themselves.
>
> (p. 28)

So, as the reader experiences the renewal that comes from relating to the hero, he also understands, possibly at a deeper level, that said relation is partially due to the commonality of insecurity and failures.

Comic book superheroes have offered a glimpse into the lives of the beautifully broken, which "speak to us as we go about making sense of our world" (Hohle, 2016, p. 49). As we seek to better understand ourselves, we can peer through our heroes' lenses. We witness their experiences and interactions, thereby informing our own. Much of what we relate to and understand in our heroes' stories is that their past plays a large role in their current circumstances.

Often these past experiences lead them down the path on which they find themselves where we meet them; caught in some moral dilemma, driven by their past, afraid of their future, and not convinced that they can do a thing about any of it. This is known as the origin story. "It tells you how the protagonist became who they are, sketching in the traumas that ultimately define what kind of hero they would be" (Ross, 2015, p. 1).

What makes even more of an impact on the reader is that the conventional fantasy script has been turned upside down, so that these superheroes are now living in "a mythological universe grounded in a world brimming with humor and heartache that the readers recognized as close to their own" (Ross, 2015, p. 4). It gives way for the imagination to put oneself in the superheroes' places and decide if the same decision of valor, courage, selflessness or sacrifice would be made.

Historical literature reveals a plethora of commentary regarding the definition of a hero, the criticism of heroes, and the emulation and affirmation of the heroic pursuit. However, the thread that weaves much of the varying opinions together is that heroes are in equal parts inspiring and flawed. Gibbon (2002) states that "19th-century idealists knew their heroes were not perfect. Even so, they believed that heroes instruct us in greatness, that heroes remind us of our better selves, and that heroes strengthen the ordinary citizen trying to live decently" (p. 28).

Gavaler (2014) termed this dichotomy a "dual-identity hero" who has become "one of the most enduring staples of American comic books" (p. 49). Interestingly, even though the personal struggles were made famous by superheroes in comics and the MCU, the hybrid figure "originates decades earlier and encompasses a multi-generic, transatlantic array of texts unified by the central trope of controlled, individual transformation employed for social good" (Gavaler, 2014, p. 49). This transformation is central to the experience and necessary for the reader's catharsis. Yet, even so, often the superhero does not fully conquer his or her failings, unwilling or unable to overcome them.

Therefore, armed with an understanding that heroes are not and have never been perfect, there is an embracing of both the positive and negative aspects of superhero characters. There is also a desire to become more like a hero in the positive sense, while realizing that shortcomings do not disqualify the superhero from his or her capabilities. And through this acceptance of polarity, there emerges a self-actualization process where one can become a better person without completely eliminating his flaws.

Self-Actualization

Abraham Maslow (1954) popularized the term self-actualization in the 1950s, but it has its origins in the late 1930s and early 1940s when Kurt Goldstein (1939; 1940) introduced the concept. It was later embraced and adopted by Carl Rogers in the person-centered theoretical model (Roger, 1961).

Maslow (1954) connected self-actualization with reality-centered and problem-centered individuals who had senses of humor and accepted themselves and others. He also considered them humble and respectful to others. Ironically, the majority of those familiar with Maslow's theory (1954) understood that self-actualization was the pinnacle of success in life; "the end of the line" (Greene & Burke, 2007, p. 118). Interestingly, in his later publication, Maslow (1971) further explained that the process of self-actualizing actually goes beyond the self, and manifests itself in "such terms as selfless, devoted, working at a calling, and being-values" (p. 128).

With this greater awareness of Maslow's intention, there is a distinct differentiation between an inner focus, i.e., attaining a certain personal potential, and the goal of bettering the self by moving from self to others. Without dispute, Maslow (1971), Erikson (1994), and Rogers (1961) each "affirm in their research the concept of selflessness or the ability to look outside oneself as a critical characteristic of the highest level of human development" (Greene & Burke, 2007, p. 124).

Gibbon (2002) writes extensively about what defines a hero, and that the self-actualization process is an integral part of the development of heroic tendencies. He not only believes that every human is capable of being a hero, but that heroism is observed and modeled. He states:

> Human beings are deeply divided, eternally torn between apathy and activity, nihilism and belief. We wage a daily battle between a higher and lower self. The hero stands for our higher self. To get through life and permit the higher self to prevail, we depend on public models of excellence, bravery, and goodness.
>
> (p.1)

As the superhero, both in comics and the MCU, has emerged as the face of sacrifice for the greater good, it provides an example to Americans in need of an ideal to emulate. The higher self wins out, against all odds and in spite of the lower self clinging on for dear life, thereby inspiring the process in others.

Similarly, play therapists provide children with a safe and neutral environment in the playroom to connect with the flawed hero narrative, test their capability for goodness, conquer their fears, overcome their failures, and trust themselves to become better. But this takes place on the child's terms, in the child's time, and in the child's manner. Because like every superhero, one can only provide them with the opportunity to rise to the occasion; it cannot be forced.

Child-Centered Therapy

Child-centered play therapy is rooted in the Rogerian principles of congruence, empathy and unconditional positive regard (Rogers, 1959) and was utilized by Virginia Axline (1947) specifically for work with children and their unique needs and developmental levels. The child-centered play therapist creates an environment free from judgment and allows the child to self-direct his or her actions, responsibility and psychological insight. Through this dynamic relationship, children are given the freedom to "solve their own problems and make self-enhancing choices" (Ray et al., 2013, p. 45).

This is especially important in the context of self-actualization because children process their struggles and shortcomings through playing, essentially overcoming their previous failures or flaws through the self-discovery process. However, it is not prescribed nor dictated how and when they will work toward self-acceptance and self-actualization. First, they learn to trust the therapist; then they learn that they can trust themselves to face their deepest fears and become better for it.

Similar to The Avengers struggling with their labels of "heroes" while simultaneously feeling inadequate and flawed, kids in the playroom try to resolve the conflict between their ideal selves and their actual selves, too. Many times they have been made to believe they are bad, or at the very least they realize that they are maladaptively coping. Often, their past experiences influence their self-concept and understanding of the world as well, leaving them believing that they are flawed or broken. So, the playroom is where all of these confusing, conflicting and contradictory pieces of who they believe themselves to be converge. This allows children to break down the parts that they want to discard and build up the parts that they want to keep.

The Avengers' Flaws

Weaknesses are at the center of the self-actualization struggle because they have to be overcome to grow. Therefore, the significance of weaknesses in the greatest superheroes should not be ignored or discounted. Steve Kamb (2017) notes that the best characters are the superheroes who "have critical flaws and tons of baggage that often sabotage their own efforts. Although they are superhuman, they are … human. And that's what makes them interesting" (p. 4). As such, the Avengers are relatable, especially if one has awareness of their histories, past, and backstory.

Iron Man

Tony Stark, known as Iron Man in the MCU, was an orphaned child adopted by Howard and Maria Stark. While Maria loved him unconditionally, Howard was an alcoholic who was verbally abusive to Tony and their relationship was strained, likely due to the conflict of Tony's emotional and sensitive personality with Howard's desire for physical accomplishment and mood swings ("Anthony Stark," n.d.). As early as five, Tony began to cope by pursuing electronics, since he could predict how they would react and they were reliable, unlike people. At seven, he was sent to boarding school by his father, to toughen him up. This occurred, but he also spent a great deal of time reading books alone, which introduced him to the concept of causes "greater than oneself, of chivalry, honor, and armored heroes" ("Anthony Stark," n.d., p. 8).

Tony excelled in school and easily succeeded in college. However, at 21 years old, his parents were killed in a car crash as a result of a faulty brake system. His solution, and arguably his coping strategy, was to purchase the company that manufactured the car and to redesign the brakes in all future models. It was also during this time that he began to run Stark Industries, but the pressure of owning a company led him down the same path as his father into alcoholism ("Anthony Stark," n.d.). Tony continued to make decisions based on an inherent need to please his deceased father since he was never accepted as a child. Then, once he realizes that his company was responsible for the deaths of people around the world, he makes the decision to take the company that his father built in a completely new direction, essentially tearing it apart ("Marvel Cinematic Universe," 2015).

Connection for children in play therapy. It is easy to see how children would connect with Iron Man on several levels. First, children who are adopted or have lost their parents in a tragic way can inherently understand what Tony went through and relate to his grief. Further, his withdrawal from others and his interest in predictability and structure is another point of connection. A child who has an alcoholic or abusive parent also resonates with Tony's experience. Finally, a child who is constantly trying to get approval or make amends for the past deeply connects with Iron Man.

Captain America

Steve Rogers, known as Captain America in the MCU, was born in 1918 but grew up in the 1930s facing The Great Depression. This meant much of his childhood was spent waiting in breadlines and going to soup kitchens to survive. Further, his father was a soldier who died in World War I when he was a young child, and his mother was a nurse who later died of tuberculosis when he was a teenager ("Steven Rogers," n.d.). As a result of the death of both of his parents, he spent time in an orphanage and a boys' home, and struggled with paying his bills and putting himself through art school. He was required to work to make ends meet, but because of his small stature was often bullied (Coker, 2013).

When he and his best friend learned that the United States had entered the war, Steve wanted to enlist. He was immediately rejected because of his health and condition, and went to other cities to try to enlist there. He was continually rejected and told that he was not cut out to be a soldier, even though his sense of duty and honor was stronger than anyone who was immediately accepted ("Steven Rogers," n.d.). Steve was eventually chosen for a special experimental serum and trained to fight the Nazis in Germany. He is the "idealistic, honest, righteous, and extremely patriotic soldier" who is compelled to those traits because his mother made him promise on her death bed that he would never lose his good and kind heart even when things were difficult (Lal, 2016, p. 6).

Connection for children in play therapy. Children can relate to Captain America in several ways as a result of his experiences. Children who have experienced the loss of a parent relates to the grief and tragedy of Steve. Additionally, children who grow up in families who struggle to pay the bills or do not always have enough to eat understand Steve's plight. Children who have been bullied or ridiculed by their peers also connect with Steve's feelings of inadequacy. As a result, they also feel compelled to prove themselves and seek justice for the underdog, just like Captain America.

Hulk

Bruce Banner, known as Hulk in the MCU, grew up with a physicist father who hated him for several reasons. One was that he did not want children and another was that he resented that Rebecca, Bruce's mother, loved him so affectionately. His father was an extremely angry man who was physically abusive to Bruce, and he believed that Bruce was a mutant son ("Bruce Banner," 2018). A significant turning point in Bruce's young life was when his father murdered his mother, and Bruce was placed in a mental hospital. After he was released, he went to live with his Aunt who was aware of his extreme rage and hurt due to his childhood traumas and sufferings ("Bruce Banner," 2018).

After escaping from the negative influence of his father, he became a scientist and wished to pursue philanthropic pursuits with his knowledge. However, in an attempt to save a civilian from a bombing, he was exposed to gamma radiation. This transformed him into a monstrous, green beast with healing capabilities and super-human strength. However, this is in sharp contrast to the weak and socially withdrawn personality of Bruce who values his intelligence and control. This makes him embarrassed about what he becomes, thereby making him hide and become reclusive so that no one knows about Hulk. Due to his fear and emotional distance, he is "blind to his heroic potential. The creature in him, if used properly, could be a hero. Bruce takes a while to see that. That's a flaw when you undermine your potential" (Associated Press, 2008, p. 14).

Bruce is possibly the most dichotomous character in the MCU because he is daily fighting the battle within himself of ideal versus actual self. "His human intelligence, reason, and empathy are constantly juxtaposed with the unbridled anger of the beast that lies within him" (Hagley & Harrison, 2014, p. 121). When he is Bruce, he is almost awkward in his mild-mannered nature and is constantly fearful that Hulk might emerge; Hulk destroys anything without rational thought and is afraid of nothing. He says to Tony Stark, "I don't get a suit of armor; I'm exposed, like a nerve. It's a nightmare" (Feige & Whedon, 2012).

Connection for children in play therapy. There are several connections that children can make with Hulk. First, children whose lives become chaotic and out of their control harbor a great deal of anger; these kids can connect with the aggression and power that Hulk displays because they feel the same. Children who have been physically abused understand how deeply that impacts trust and safety and relate to Bruce. Children can also relate to being hospitalized as Bruce was, as involuntary commission to hospitals of minors is on the rise. Kids are also able to connect with the embarrassment and shame associated with losing control and hurting others due to their angry behavior, which can make them withdraw like Bruce does. Hulk is easily relatable because kids see the internal warring between the man who is reclusive wanting control and the beast who is destructive and unmanageable.

Thor

Thor, based on the mythical demi-god, is also incorporated into the MCU. Thor was the son of Odin, ruler of Asgard. Thor was raised alongside his adopted brother, Loki, who resented and competed with him to the point that he tried to kill him out of hatred. Thor was groomed from birth to be a future ruler, and Loki's jealousy of his brother consumed him ("Thor Odinson," 2018). When Thor was eight, he was sent on a journey to the Land of the Dwarves, to have three treasures created for Asgard's ruler. One of these treasures was the hammer, which Odin enchanted so that the only person who could wield it was truly worthy. Later, Odin declared that it would be for Thor when his selfless deeds proved him worthy of it. This put Thor on an insatiable quest to become physically strong enough to lift it, all the while accomplishing many good deeds ("Thor Odinson," 2018).

When Thor was 16 years old, Odin finally sent him on a quest to learn that the only things he needed to become worthy of the hammer were a pure heart and humility. Ironically, in Thor's attempts to become righteous and worthy, he became obsessed with the might-over-right mentality, lending himself to dangerous attempts at ruling and victory without morality and compassion. Odin's response was to cast his hammer to Earth and remove Thor's power to wield it in an effort to teach him a lesson (Hagley & Harrison, 2014). Thor, always feeling the pressure of a brother who has nothing but enmity for him and a father who expects him to become the ruler he is destined to be, lives with a great deal of both external and self-imposed pressures. This can cloud his judgment at times and drives him to prove himself by his strength rather than his intrinsic worth.

Connection for children in play therapy. Kids relate to Thor in a unique way, as he has never been human and therefore did not have a physical transformation or evolution. Instead, he dealt with family struggles and the natural outcome of striving too hard, rather than just accepting who he is without unrealistic expectations. Any child who tends to have a perfectionistic or over-achieving bent also connects with Thor. Additionally, children in families with contentious sibling relationships relate to the dysfunction amongst Thor and Loki. Finally, once kids are able to develop a self-worth rooted within an internal locus of control, they are also able to appreciate the journey that Thor took to realize that he had what he needed inside of himself all along.

Hawkeye

Clint Barton, also known as Hawkeye in the MCU, grew up in a rural Iowan town working in his father's butcher shop. His father was an abusive alcoholic and Clint's brother taught him to fight and develop his aim to defend himself against the abuse. His father and his mother were both killed in an alcohol-related car accident during childhood, and he was placed in many foster homes after being orphaned ("Clint Barton," 2018). Clint eventually ran away from one of the foster homes and discovered a traveling circus where he began to work. He apprenticed under excellent marksmen in the circus, and honed his archery skills to become a star carnival attraction known as "Hawkeye: The World's Greatest Marksman." After watching the swordsman embezzle money from the carnival, Hawkeye was beaten and left to die before he could report it to authorities. It was at this point that he met Black Widow, and became a reluctant villain ("Clint Barton," 2018).

After pursuing Black Widow on missions in Russia and Europe, he became an assassin for hire with pinpoint accuracy. He remained in the shadows and distant from others, with a deep connection and devotion to Black Widow and no one else to speak of. However, on one of their missions, Black Widow was severely injured and Clint fled the battle to save her life. That marked a turning point where he decided he no longer wished to fight criminally ("Clint Barton," 2018).

After missions all over the world that required a lack of conscience to accomplish, Clint struggles to relate to others and preserve relationships. In one of his missions, he lost his hearing and struggled with becoming deaf, leaving him as the only superhero in The Avengers without superpowers and with a disability (Stevens, 2017). He also has tried to redeem his past by doing good and becoming a family man, but does not naturally fit into the others in The Avengers because he is just a human with a bow and arrow. Hawkeye said it himself, "The city is flying, we're fighting an army of robots, and I have a bow and arrow. None of this makes any sense" (Feige & Whedon, 2012).

Connection for children in play therapy. Children are provided with several points of connection with Hawkeye. First, he is the only superhero in The Avengers who has a physical disability. Children who have limitations due to a disorder or disability can relate on a deep level. Further, when kids have, often regretfully, pursued a path of destruction, disobedience or rebellion, they are often very remorseful and try to make amends with being "good." This is mirrored in Hawkeye's attempts at redemption as well.

Black Widow

Natasha Romanoff, better known as Black Widow in the MCU, possesses one of the more tragic back stories with which children can connect. During the Battle of Stalingrad, her dying mother gave Natasha to a friend to raise her. He eventually took her to Department X with other very young orphaned girls, and she was raised from a very young age in combat and espionage in the secret Red Room facility ("Black Widow (Natasha Romanova)," 2018).

During this training, she was brainwashed and made to believe things about her past that were never true, as well as having her memories wiped before every new mission to ensure that she would remain loyal. After becoming a Russian double agent, she was known for her stealth killing and became a femme fatale secret agent with the KGB ("Black Widow," 2018).

As part of her education and indoctrination training in the Red Room, her graduation ceremony included a sterilization process that would prohibit personal distractions from getting in the way of her missions. This is something that she regrets throughout her life (Clark, 2015). She relates to Bruce Banner in this capacity, as he is also unable to have children because of his exposure to gamma radiation. Natasha also is aware of her past, and knows that with her missions and training comes a great deal of killing, death and pain. After joining S.H.I.E.L.D., she feels the weight of her past and spends time trying to atone for it (Kamb, 2017). She mentions the "red" in her ledger and that it haunts her, a constant reminder of everything she wishes were different about her past (Hagley & Harrison, 2014).

Connection for children in play therapy. Black Widow presents as a character who masks her emotions and pain extremely well but still gives glimpses of the effects of her past. Kids who have been through traumatic experiences, especially physical procedures, connect with Natasha. Further, kids who have had to endure difficult situations, especially those over which they had no control, relate to her feelings of desperation and regret. Also, children who wish that they could go back and handle things differently inherently understand the impossibility of that desire but the draw of it all the same.

Case Study of Elliott*

(*Pseudonym to protect confidentiality and identity)
Elliott, a 5-year-old boy in VPK, began play therapy after his mother presented concerns of unmanageable anxiety and dysregulation in multiple environments. Even from an early age, he was extremely fearful of situations over which he felt he had no control. When he began swimming lessons as a toddler, he screamed until he vomited. When he started VPK, he had diarrhea every day at school and at home. He would sit by himself in the classroom rocking back and forth as a coping mechanism until he was able to calm down after his mother left for work. As the school year went on, he would improve in his anxiety, but it always remained a concern in new environments.

When his mother and grandmother, who were both primary caregivers during his early childhood, left simultaneously for trips out of state this year, he remained home with his father. He was completely overwhelmed with fear, asking every day when they were coming home and concerned that they would die. Once they returned, he began to run into other parts of the house to make sure that they were still alive.

When his mother would leave on the weekends, he would cry and "fly into a fit of rage." He became completely inconsolable and it would often take hours before he would regulate his emotions again. His parents were at a loss of how to help him handle the simplest of things, like needing to run errands or go to work. When he was not expecting a change in the schedule or routine, it caused such an upheaval that they began not telling him what was happening. This only made his fear and anxiety worsen. When school began this year, he began to have diarrhea everyday again. This also occurred every time he went to karate practice. He had such digestive and intestinal dysregulation, he lost ten pounds in five weeks. At this point, his pediatrician urged his parents to pursue mental health treatment to help him develop coping skills to handle his world and its unpredictability.

Before the first session, Elliott's mother contacted me concerned about what to tell Elliott about his first visit. She indicated that he was so inquisitive and insistent upon knowing all of the details before doing something, she feared he would not comply with coming. This insatiable need for control and knowledge of what to expect is highly correlated with anxiety and power needs in children.

Upon meeting Elliott in the lobby on the first visit, he was extremely nervous and worried. He did not know me, and did not feel comfortable with a new place and a new person. When I spoke to him about walking back to see the playrooms, he stared at the ceiling and spun his torso back and forth as I talked, clearly in an attempt to disengage and self-soothe. He barely spoke and resisted eye contact of any kind. Eventually, Elliott came into the playroom and immediately began growling and breathing hard. It became evident after watching his mannerisms that he was acting as if he were Hulk. He specifically asked for only green things (markers, paper, toys) and referred to himself as Hulk in the third person. When he presented himself as Hulk, he cussed in almost every sentence. He used the Bobo doll as his inferior opponent and kicked, punched, hit and body slammed it while making guttural grunting noises. He called everything stupid, dumb, idiotic, and aggressively threw toys around the room. He took the large exercise ball and used it as a tool to throw around, destroying the doll house, castle, puppet theater, grocery cart and tree house. Eventually, he began swiping shelves of all of their toys, leaving them in his wake as he made his way around the playroom. He used the entire room as the target of his wrecking ball, creating destruction and devastation.

This play theme continued and Elliott continued to relate to Hulk in a personal way early in treatment. When he would act like Hulk, angry and aggressive, I would respond, "Hulk is showing everyone how strong he is" or "Hulk likes to smash everything." He would reply, "That's because Hulk is stronger than everybody" or "Hulk smashes because he hates being told what to do." Elliott was able to speak about his ideal self rather than his actual self, and process his difficulty listening to rules because of his need for power and control.

The process of reflecting his feelings and tracking his behavior allowed Elliott to speak about his experiences and emotions in the third person as Hulk rather than himself. Interestingly, when Elliott was not acting as Hulk, he was very quiet and reserved, and internalized most of his thoughts. It was only when he became the big, green guy that he could talk about and act out his frustrations, wishes, desires, anger and needs. In the second session, he actually told me, "I remember when puny Elliott was here last week—but not today."

Later in treatment, he began to have some objectivity about his behavior in the playroom, whether he was Hulk or not. At one point in a session, he looked around the room and said, "Hulk made a huge mess. Do I have to clean all of this up? Or do you?" Suddenly, he was aware of the impact that his behavior and actions had on others around him. This perspective allowed him to move toward more balanced attitudes and behaviors with a broader worldview. Additionally, he began to work through his fears and anxiety, with the commonality of Hulk still present. Just as Hulk is perpetually scared he is going to lose control, Elliott was constantly worried of having no power. So, to process this he created unpredictable scenarios that forced him to overcome the worry and build his confidence that he could handle anything that came his way.

He also began to temper his aggression and anger in the playroom and allowed me to have a measure of power again. The giving up of unbridled power, which he had as Hulk, required vulnerability and resilience. He had to test himself against his fear, proving that complete power is just as unhealthy as the lack of it. And, more importantly, allowing others to see your weaknesses is the only way to effectively address them. Once he realized that I was trustworthy, and that the playroom was safe, he was able to become Hulk less and remain as Elliott more. He no longer needed the alter ego to face his demons because he knew that he could on his own.

Eventually, Elliot's teachers and parents noticed that he was more regulated in other environments as well. His shy and reserved personality were a part of his character once again, rather than the counterpart to the angry, aggressive Hulk. When he got upset, he was able to tell others about his feelings; this required vulnerability, but he felt self-assured enough to do so. He no longer was consumed with fear and worry, and his weight loss and digestive issues ceased.

By giving himself the voice of Hulk, he was able to find his own. Through overcoming his own fears, regulating his anger and emotions, and developing a healthy self-confidence, he brought himself closer to his ideal. And as he trusted himself to face his past, his present, and his future, he was able to integrate the best and worst parts of himself into a healthy and happy boy equipped to navigate life effectively.

Conclusion

The lives of The Avengers are complicated and messy, as are the lives of children in therapy. Superheroes are flawed and fall short often, just like the kids who admire them. Therefore, when play therapy allows for the former to influence the latter in a context that promotes growth and self-actualization, it is no wonder that kids find deep connections in the narrative of overcoming obstacles on the path to achievement.

As such, there is power to be found for kids in the child-centered play therapy model. They can use any toys that they choose. They can grow and heal with puppets, cars, animals or costumes. But, many times, they choose superheroes because there is an innate awareness of the goodness of a hero. However, digging deeper, there is also a recognition of their shortcomings. Gibbon says, "Heroes encourage us to search for our better selves. But heroes are not perfect. We should search for greatness but not be surprised by flaws" (Gibbon, 2002, p. 128).

Superheroes provide an example of how to overcome and persevere despite their flaws. They have dealt with difficulties, both physical and personal, and they have battled them successfully. They encourage kids to believe in their inherent worth and possibilities, while reminding them that there is no such thing as perfection.

They model problem solving and determination, even when the odds are stacked against them. This resonates with children because it gives them hope that it is possible to conquer their struggles as well.

Interestingly, more often than not kids are facing circumstances or environments over which they have no say or control. Divorce, abuse, addiction, diagnoses, or dysfunction are present without the child's consent or choice. In these scenarios, kids typically feel resentful and powerless. Kamb (2017) stated:

> Like Bruce [Banner] we are raised in a certain way and don't get to pick our parents or our upbringing or the tragedies that have befallen us. We're products of our environment and upbringing and genetics, and it all mixes together in a really weird way. These things can cause us to feel shame about our place in life, retreating inward, lashing outward, and feeling like a victim or martyr who is doomed to stay stuck because "my problem is unique and unsolvable."
>
> (p. 15)

One of the greatest outcomes of child-centered play therapy is that kids are the masters of their own growth. Their self-actualization process is dictated only by their courage, willingness, and desire. And on the other side of treatment, they are completely different than when they began. The journey itself changed them, as well as the personal changes that they discovered and adopted. This is true of superheroes as well, as Hagley and Harrison (2014) note about the final scene in *The Avengers: Age of Ultron* (Feige & Whedon, 2012):

> The clear "boxes" in which each character could easily be placed no longer sufficiently define them. In the penultimate scene, each hero returns to his or her previous world. But because of the crucible they have all just survived, they return as changed men and women, who no longer fit so easily in the categories they, or society, have defined for them.
>
> (p. 123)

The same could also be said for the child returning to his school and family after play therapy, where anxious, bad, angry or controlling are insufficient adjectives to describe who the child now is.

Superheroes have survived for decades as a representation of who we want to be because they "are like fairy tales for older people. All those things you imagined— if I could only fly or be the strongest—are about wish fulfillment" (Cavna, 2011, p. 5). And as such, when we wish to be greater than we are but can also accept that with greatness comes inadequacies, we open ourselves up to the healing process of self-actualization. Morrison said:

> We love our superheroes because they refuse to give up on us. We can analyze them out of existence, kill them, ban them, mock them, and still they return, patiently reminding us of who we are and what we wish we could be.
>
> (Morrison, 2012, p. 398)

Kids seem to always know what they wish for and who they would like to be. Play therapy helps them to make sense of what is feasible and encourages them to make their wishes a reality.

Watching The Avengers struggle with their destinies, especially after coming to understand their past experiences, can be frustrating and difficult. Often the reader or viewer sees their potential before they do, despite their lack of self-confidence. Similarly, the play therapist possesses the same belief of the children who enter the playroom. Regardless of the intended outcome of treatment, the process is usually challenging and difficult. It requires kids to examine their pasts, their circumstances, their ideal selves, and most importantly their acceptance of failures. Brené Brown (2010) says, "The ability to hold something we've done, or failed to do, up against who we want to be is incredibly adaptive. It's uncomfortable, but it's adaptive." When both The Avengers and children participating in play therapy are able to do that simple task, their self-actualization journey begins.

Questions for Clinical Discussion

1. How do personal flaws either hinder or help in the therapy process?
2. Which of The Avengers goes through the most difficult self-actualization process and why? Which one changes the most?
3. What role does a play therapist have in helping a client to overcome weaknesses or hindrances?
4. Why are superheroes so relevant for kids now, after decades of similar storylines?
5. How did the inclusion of superheroes' traumas and background change comics and the MCU?
6. What parallels can be drawn between The Avengers and children in therapy?

References

Anthony Stark (Earth-616) (2018, October 22). Retrieved from http://marvel.wikia.com/wiki/Anthony_Stark_(Earth-616)

Associated Press (2008, April 30). Human flaws plague summer's superheroes. Retrieved from www.today.com/id/24389322#.W6kTBtMvzVo

Axline, V. M. (1947). *Play therapy: The inner dynamics of childhood*. Cambridge, MA: Houghton Mifflin.

Black Widow (2018, October 27). Retrieved from http://marvelcinematicuniverse.wikia.com/wiki/Black_Widow

Black Widow (Natasha Romanova) (2018, October 27). Retrieved from https://en.wikipedia.org/wiki/Black_Widow_(Natasha_Romanova)

Brown, B. [TedxHouston] (2010, December 23). *The power of vulnerability* [Video file]. Retrieved from www.ted.com/talks/brene_brown_on_vulnerability?language=en

Bruce Banner (Earth-616) (2018, October 24). Retrieved from http://marvel.wikia.com/wiki/Bruce_Banner_(Earth-616)

Campbell, J. (1949). *The hero with a thousand faces*. New York: Bollingen.

Clark, N. (2015, May 5). *Joss Whedon talks Black Widow's painful past, romantic relationships and more.* Retrieved from http://herocomplex.latimes.com/movies/joss-whedon-talks-black-widows-painful-past-romantic-relationships-and-more

Cavna, M. (2011, May 11). *Stan Lee: As 'Thor' scores, creator considers why the superhero film endures.* Retrieved from www.washingtonpost.com/blogs/comic-riffs/post/stan-lee-as-thor-scores-creator-reveals-why-the-superhero-film-endures/2011/05/10/AF6rSpqG_blog.html?utm_term=.3e9f12907d86

Coker, C. (2013). Earth-616, Earth 1610, Earth 3490—Wait, what universe is this again? The creation and evolution of The Avengers and Captain America/Iron Man fandom. In: M. J. Costello (Ed.), *Transformative works and cultures, no. 13.* http://doi.org/10.3983/twc.2013.0439

Erikson, E. (1994- rev.). *Identity and the life cycle.* New York: W. W. Norton & Company, Inc.

Favreau, J. (2008). *Iron Man* [Motion Picture]. Burbank, CA: Marvel Studios.

Feige, K. (Producer) & Whedon, J. (Director) (2012). *The Avengers: Age of Ultron* [Motion Picture]. Burbank, CA: Marvel Studios.

Folsom, J. K. (1967). "Western" themes and western films. *Western American Literature,* 2(3), 195–203.

Gavaler, C. (2014). The well-born superhero. *The Journal of American Culture, 37*(2), 182–197. doi:10.1111/jacc.12162

Gibbon, P. H. (2002). *A call to heroism: Renewing America's vision of greatness.* New York: Atlantic Monthly Press.

Gittell, N. (2014, June 17). What the western means now. Retrieved from www.theatlantic.com/entertainment/archive/2014/06/the-return-of-the-western/372871/

Goldstein, K. (1940). *Human nature in the light of psychopathology.* Cambridge, MA: Harvard University Press.

Goldstein, K. (1939). *The organism: A holistic approach to biology derived from pathological data in man.* New York: American Book Company.

Greene, L. & Burke, G. (2007). Beyond self-actualization. *Journal of Health and Human Services Administration, 1*(1), 116–128.

Hagley, A. & Harrison, M. (2014). Fighting the battles we never could: *The Avengers* and post-September 11 American political identities. *American Political Science Association, 47*(1), 120–124. doi:10.1017/S1049096513001650

Hohle, P. J. (2016). How viewers respond to transgressive protagonist-heroes in film. *Projections, 10*(2), 49–74. doi:10:3167/proj.2016.100204

Kamb, S. (2017, January 24). *You are flawed. And so are your heroes.* Retrieved from www.nerdfitness.com/blog/you-are-flawed-and-so-are-your-heroes/

Lal, A. (2016, May 8). *The flawed superhero: What the evolution of Chris Evans' Captain America points out.* Retrieved from www.firstpost.com/entertainment/the-flawed-superhero-what-the-evolution-of-chris-evans-captain-america-reveals-2769580.html

Lee, S. (2006, December 27). Stan Lee on realism in the world of comic heroes: Interview by R. Montagne. *The Long View: NPR* [Video file]. Retrieved from www.npr.org/templates/story/story.php?storyId=6684820

Lee, S. (2013, May 22). Interview by M. Ray. *Take Part TV* [Video file]. Retrieved from www.youtube.com/watch?v=QM9pVbwMBqc

Lee, S. [TEDx Talks] (2013, December 27). *What makes a superhero?* [Video file]. Retrieved from www.youtube.com/watch?v=DSGf6is3U2w

Lewis, A. (2016, July 21). *Stan Lee reflects on his successes and regrets: "I should have been greedier."* Retrieved from www.hollywoodreporter.com/features/stan-lee-reflects-his-successes-912577

Marvel Cinematic Universe and Daddy Issues (2015, July 23). Retrieved from https://observationdeck.kinja.com/marvel-cinematic-universe-and-daddy-issues-1719675914

Maslow, A. H. (1954). *Motivation and personality.* New York: Harper & Row.

Maslow, A. H. (1971). *The farther reaches of human nature.* New York: Arkana/Penguin Books.

Modern mythology: What superheroes can show us about humanity (2016, October 8). Retrieved from https://owlcation.com/social-sciences/Modern-Mythology-What-Comic-Books-Can-Tell-Us-About-Humanity

Morrison, G. (2012). *Supergods: What masked vigilantes, miraculous mutants, and a Sun god from Smallville can teach us about being human.* New York: Spiegel & Grau.

Ray, D. C., Lee, K. R., Meany-Walen, K. K., Carlson, S. E., Carnes-Holt, K. L., & Ware, J. N. (2013). Use of toys in child-centered play therapy. *International Journal of Play Therapy, 22*(1), 43–57. doi:10.1037/a0031430

Rogers, C. R. (1959). A theory of therapy, personality, and interpersonal relationships as developed in the client-centered framework. In: S. Koch (Ed.), *Psychology: A study of a science: Vol. III. Formulations of the person and the social context* (pp. 184–256). New York: McGraw-Hill.

Rogers, C. R. (1961). *On becoming a person: A psychotherapist's view of psychotherapy.* Boston, MA: Houghton Mifflin.

Ross, J. (2015, March 23). *How Marvel's universe of strange, flawed, streetwise superheroes conquered our own.* Retrieved from www.newstatesman.com/culture/2015/03/how-marvel-s-universe-strange-flawed-streetwise-superheroes-conquered-our-own

Shafer, D. M. & Raney, A. A. (2012). Exploring how we enjoy antihero narratives. *Journal of Communication, 62,* 1028–1046. doi:10.1111/j.1460-2466.2012.01682.x

Sparks, R. (1996). Masculinity and heroism in the Hollywood "blockbuster:" The culture and industry images of crime and law enforcement. *The British Journal of Criminology, 36*(3), 348–360.

Stan Lee (2018, August 28). Retrieved from https://myhero.com/stan_lee

Steven Rogers (2018, October 22). Retrieved from http://marvel-movies.wikia.com/wiki/Steven_Rogers

Stevens, M. (2017, April 3). *Stan Lee's 15 most iconic superhero creations.* Retrieved from www.cbr.com/stan-lees-15-best-superhero-creations/

Thor Odinson (Earth-616) (2018, October 25). Retrieved from http://marvel.wikia.com/wiki/Thor_Odinson_(Earth-616)

Williamson, V. (2016, July 26). *American heroism: A discussion of bandits, superheroes, and more.* Retrieved from https://journeys.dartmouth.edu/edge/2016/07/26/american-heroism-a-discussion-of-bandits-cowboys-super-heroes-and-more

Zillmann, D. (1996). The psychology of suspense in dramatic exposition. In: P. Vorderer, H. J. Wulff & M. Friedrichsen (Eds.), *LEA's Communication series. Suspense: Conceptualizations, theoretical analyses, and empirical explorations* (pp. 199–231). Hillsdale, NJ: Lawrence Erlbaum Associates, Inc.

PART **IV**

Villains Rise to the Challenge of Helping

In this section, we will see how, in their own way, villains can provide heroic support to therapists.

CHAPTER 13

No Joking Matter—Villains are People, Too: Working with the School Bully

Meridith Nealy Starling

Children who get into fights at recess and break school rules typically do not enter a counselor's or principal's office on their own accord, but instead are escorted by a concerned and often frustrated adult who wants them "fixed." Other issues such as excessive whining, fighting at recess, rougher-than-normal play, lying, stealing and lack of respect for authority figures are all hallmarks of a child who is struggling and often deemed a bully. These children are angry and frustrated and may internalize negative beliefs that they are bad or weird. They are often sad, embarrassed and confused because the fight on the playground wasn't even started by them. They are frustrated because they wanted to play kickball with the others, but no one would let them play. As they are escorted into the principal or counselor's office for the umpteenth time they hope and wish that maybe this time their story will be believed. Maybe this time the principal or counselor will really see them for something other than their behaviors. Perhaps someone will finally peek behind the masks they wear to guard and hide underling issues with which they are struggling.

This chapter discusses the necessity of using both play therapy theories and crime themed comics to help children who have been labeled as school bullies before they fester and grow into mega-villains. Play therapists can help transform the therapeutic process and quickly engage children in counseling by looking at the dichotomy of the superhero/villain stories that comics provide. Speaking the children's language in this way can provide a level of fun that these children are missing. Utilizing these movies and comics that the child finds interesting also builds the therapeutic relationship over shared interests. Therapists can provide a way of talking about situations metaphorically by substituting in the characters as a representation of the child's own self and struggles. These children have their own backstories that explain their current behavioral issues just like most super-hero/villain movies have prequels. These potential at-risk children can rewrite their own futures if they can tell their own story within a supportive and thera-peutic relationship.

Villains are People Too

Comic books and movies often feature a villain who doesn't fit in, lacks social supports, and is misunderstood. The villain is often unpopular and envies the popular hero who has amazing powers the villain wishes he had. The frustrated villain begins to act out for attention and revenge. The villain plots a scheme to gain attention and maybe even some popularity. This is what The Joker in *The LEGO® Batman Movie* (Lin et al., 2015) was seeking, and this is depicted in the dialogue below:

> Joker—Save the city or catch your greatest enemy. You can't do both.
> Batman—What did you say? … You think *you're* my greatest enemy?
> Joker—Yes! You're <u>obsessed</u> with me.
> Batman—No, I'm not.
> Joker—Yes, you are.
> Batman—No, I'm not.
> Joker—Yes, you are.
> *{Minutes of banter continue as The Joker hopes that Batman will admit that he matters to him, even if this means Batman thinking of him as an enemy.}*
> Joker—Are you seriously saying there is nothing, nothing special about our relationship?
> Batman—There *is* no us. Batman and Joker are not a thing. I don't need you. I don't need anyone. *You mean nothing to me.* No one does.

After Batman delivers his gut-punching last words of this scene, The Joker appears distraught and heartbroken. He may be labeled as the villain of this tale, but he wants what most people want—to fit in, have friends, and be thought of as interesting and worth being around. Robertie, Weidenbenner, Barret, and Poole (2007) relate that villainy is essentially a solitary undertaking, and Maslow's hierarchy of needs further explains why The Joker wanted Batman to validate and acknowledge him even as an enemy. Friendships and being connected to others are greatly needed to be happy and healthy, the lack of which eventually leads to loneliness and despair (Maslow,1987). The Joker in this film was lonely just like many children who are struggling socially or have been deemed a school bully. Some children look up to superheroes but struggling kids may identify with the less popular characters since they share common issues.

The LEGO® Batman Movie (2017) is rich in opportunities to discuss the following concepts: human feelings and behaviors, villains are people too, and superheroes can act villainous. This movie provides a powerful message that both superheroes and villains cope with the same issues with which children cope. Superheroes and villains have common feelings and behaviors. This cartoon movie provides a child-friendly approach to normalize struggles that children often face in social situations. The school bully and prized-student may have more in common than once thought. The Joker and Batman share both positive and negative characteristics, just as other archrivals do. The positive traits that Batman and The Joker share include the following: intelligence, cleverness, resourcefulness, often likeability within their circle of friends, persuasiveness, pride, ambition, kindness, and determination. Their negative attributes include vengefulness, aggression, and arrogance.

The LEGO® Batman Movie (2017) is an example of how to work from both a strength-based and humanistic basis with children who are receiving therapy because of bully-like, villainous behaviors. This pairs perfectly with play therapy principles.

Bullying: What It Is and What It's Not

Bullying has become a buzzword in our society that teachers, students and parents often use to describe fights on the playground or gossip in the halls. Often adults assume that children instinctively can self-regulate, follow rules and make friends. However, for some children this is not the case. These children require extra time and attention. Behaviors such as difficulty sharing, playing too roughly, refusing to complete school work, name-calling, irritability, moodiness, poor social skills and defiance toward teachers are just a few examples of issues that children may be struggling with at school. Bullying is a set of behaviors that has myriad manifestations that depend on the child involved, the setting in which these behaviors occur and cultural differences. According to the American Psychological Association, bullying behaviors are intentional and repeated with the purpose of causing harm or distress to others (American Psychological Association 2018). Girls tend to use gossip, relational bullying and social exclusion. Boys tend to act out more physically. Cyberbullying is another form of aggressive behavior for both genders. Platforms like Snapchat, Facebook, Twitter and Instagram allow immediate displays of malicious comments, rumors and unflattering moments that can exist indefinitely in cyberspace. Children with aggressive behaviors unfortunately can start building a negative reputation both with the teachers and their peers early on and may be labeled as a bully before fall break.

The term bullying only describes the negative actions of a child. This term masks and disguises the other aspects of that child who may often struggle to make friends and fit in. However, these children can learn positive feelings toward peers, the ability to feel empathy, and feelings of personal responsibility (Espelage et al., 2014). In this context, Abraham Maslow noted, "the thing to do seems to be to find out what one is really like inside; deep down, as a member of the human species and as a particular individual" (Maslow, 1987, p. 6). The word bully distorts the whole picture of who the child is, and can have detrimental effects on her educational, psychosocial and emotional growth which in turn may contribute to a self-image akin to being a villain. According to Robertie et al. (2007, p. 146) "the universe tends to provide positive consequences for positive behaviors and negative consequences for negative behavior." Children with aggressive behaviors know this all too well. In some cases, unless the child/family moves to a different school system, this label follows them like a perpetually dark cloud. It is crucial that more information is gathered before the word bully is used to describe a child. It is the clinician's responsibility to gather a full history and consult the DSM prior to giving a diagnosis.

Definition of Bullying

According to the organization *Stopbullying.gov*, the clinical definition of bullying is "unwanted, aggressive behavior among school-aged children that involves a real or perceived power imbalance. The behavior is repeated, or has the potential to be repeated, over time" (StopBullying.Gov, 2018). Aggressive behaviors are concerning, but not all aggressive behavior is bullying. Recent research from the University of Buffalo states that while bullying is a subtype of aggression it must meet the clinical definition of repetition and power imbalance (Gambini, 2018). Prior to labeling a child as a bully, one must assess if this is an ongoing behavior directed at gaining power and control versus a solitary act. Counseling is warranted regardless of the answer.

Brief Facts and Statistics

- Six out of ten high school students have witnessed bullying, and 64% of students who were bullied did not report it (Anti-Bullying Institute, 2018).
- The *Stop Bullying Now Foundation* in Florida suggests that a child who is identified as a bully is six times more likely to become incarcerated by the age of 24. This same child is five times more likely to have a criminal record by adulthood (The Stop Bullying Now Foundation, 2018).
- The National organization for anti-bullying StopBullying.Gov suggests that zero tolerance and expelling the school bully does not prevent further acts of aggression.

When adults respond quickly and consistently to bullying behavior they send the message that it is not acceptable. Research shows this can stop bullying behavior over time (StopBullying.Gov 2018).

These facts and statistics show that schools and community therapists need to pay more attention to the child who has been identified as a school bully as early as possible (elementary school years) to help change the dangerous path on which these kids walk by providing support and rehabilitative services.

Common Themes

Most children do not wake up one day to decide, "Today is the day I become the school bully!" It is instead a process that develops over time based on many factors. When these children enter counseling due to behavioral concerns, they already feel poorly about themselves. They often have a history of multiple time-outs, trips to the principal's office and poor results on behavioral charts created by concerned parents and/or teachers. These behavioral concerns typically arise when the child begins school for the first time or at the start of a new school year. School can be a stressful and overwhelming experience for children, and sometimes the school rules and their family rules differ. At school children are faced with many new experiences each year including adjustment to new teachers, new rules, new classmates and sometimes an entirely new building/school. For some children, this can be a difficult transition. There are some reasons children act out in socially inappropriate and aggressive ways at school and in other social settings.

Labeling and the Self-Fulfilling Prophecy

Quite often humans are quick to judge and place labels. Students and teachers begin sizing one another up as early as the start of a new school year. Who is liked or disliked? Who is helpful and who has problematic behaviors? Negative behaviors quickly receive more attention compared to positive behaviors. The fight at recess or pushing in the lunch-line is quickly noticed, but the same child holding the door for a classmate or sharing his/her markers goes unnoticed. If this child begins only to receive attention for negative events, then over time this can lead to a self-fulfilling prophecy. The child will begin to identify with how others see them and relate to them.

Learned Behaviors

Children are constantly learning. They absorb socially acceptable behaviors, but they also mimic their parents, characters on TV, and others in their lives. Children who live in a household where domestic violence occurs may learn that yelling and physical aggression is normal. Children who were previously picked on or bullied themselves may begin to pick on a smaller child to feel power and control. The picked-on child may reach their boiling point to finally target their aggressor and could even become a bully themselves.

Psychosocial and Emotional Factors

Mental health problems and developmental delays may also be an indicator as to whether a child may act out and have behavioral issues. Children diagnosed with ADHD are often labeled as a "bully" because of their behaviors associated with this diagnosis such as impulsivity, blurting out, inability to sit still and take turns, and clowning around (Williams, n.d.). These children have difficulty with impulse control and social cues. They often take longer to learn from their mistakes. They often have trouble making friends, and this can cause depression and anxiety. The executive functioning center of the brain that regulates self-awareness, self-control and emotional regulation is often not as developed in children with ADHD, and as a result they have a harder time remembering the school rules or learning from past mistakes as quickly as other children (Barkley, n.d.).

Children who experience their parents' divorce(s), death of a parent/sibling or a move to a new community may experience adjustment disorders. Their behaviors may appear unregulated, moody and angry. In *Making a Place for the Angry Hero on the Team*, Harry Livesay (2007) suggests that angry heroes are frustrated due to a grievous injustice that has occurred in their life. This can be applied to villains as well. Batman is an orphan, and The Joker experienced facial trauma leaving him disfigured. Children who have limited or poor adult and peer support may feel isolated, and this can lead to several maladaptive traits.

Anger is a way to let off steam and to cope with feelings when other coping mechanisms are absent. Issues such as divorce, death of a parent, death of a pet, not getting picked for kickball at recess, are all reasons why a child would feel angry and act upon their anger.

Supportive Interventions

The lack of positive relationships is an overarching theme in children who have been identified as bullies from clinical experience. While the popular/ super-hero classmates tend to have multiple friends, the villain/bully does not because of their often-alienating behaviors (Robertie et al., 2007). Positive relationships are an integral part to life. It is within these supportive relationships that humans learn and grow. These same relationships help humans feel important, admired, nurtured and included (Maslow, 1987). Play Therapy therefore is a perfect match-up to counteract the negative impact of being labeled a bully.

Adlerian and child-centered play therapy (CCPT) both share concepts that pair nicely and provide relationship-based counseling. In both Adlerian and CCPT the therapist maintains respect and acceptance of the child to create a positive relationship with them and does not place expectations onto the child in therapy (Schaefer, 2011). CCPT is a non-directive approach to play therapy, but Adlerian interventions are more directive. Combining these two approaches allows for sessions to be time-limited, goal-oriented and meaningful without sacrificing the needs of the child. These two approaches can be implemented not only by school play therapists but community therapists despite time constraints.

Adlerian Play Therapy

Adlerian play therapy utilizes concepts from Alfred Adler's Individual Psychology as the basic concepts suggest that the client should be looked at from a holistic and ecological approach. "All behavior has a purpose" (Kottman 2011). Children who are struggling are no different than any other children. However, these children's experiences have shaped them into their current self. People are socially rooted, goal-oriented and creative beings and social interests are primary in this theory (Ray 2011).

Adlerian play therapists develop an egalitarian relationship with all who are involved in the counseling process (teachers, parents, child). They explore thoughts, feelings and attitudes while exploring the child's self-thoughts and perceptions and those they have of others in their life. They develop ideas of what constitutes both the interpersonal and intrapersonal dynamics of a child's life. This includes dynamics with parents, teachers and peers. Supporting the child is paramount in gaining insight into these issues while assisting the child to learn ways of operating in their world (Schaefer, 2011). In Adlerian theory, there is a balance between changes in the mind/brain and with relationships. Therapists want to help their child client learn different ways of coping and understanding issues such as self-esteem, difficulty with peers, or relationship difficulties. Believing that all behaviors, both positive and negative have a purpose or goal, Dreikurs and Soltz (1964) proposed that there were four main reasons for a child's misbehavior: attention, power, revenge and proof of inadequacy. These all contribute to a self-fulfilling prophecy (Kottman, 2011). The Adlerian therapist can identify which goal or goals the child is attempting to meet with their behaviors, and then can shape interventions around those goals. One method of helping children alter the negative means of reaching the above four main reasons is "The Crucial C's" created by Lew and Bettner (2000). The "Crucial C's" are feeling connected with others, feeling capable, feeling that they "count" or matter to others in their lives, and having courage/being courageous-the ability to take risks and try new things (Lew and Bettner (2000).

Adding the Crucial C's to a child's history/intake forms and their treatment plan (see Appendix A) is an effective way to counteract negative behavioral concerns and poor self-concepts. It also provides a reference with which the therapist may track goals and progress, share with a child's parents and/or teachers to engage them in the process as well. The Crucial C's also provide qualitative data of a child's strengths and weakness from which one can build upon in counseling. Taking this concept outside of the confines of the counseling session provides parents and teachers with information of where the child needs help. It also identifies the areas in which the child is finding success.

Child-Centered Play Therapy

In child-centered play therapy (CCPT) the therapist provides the child with the freedom to be themselves and play at their pace in a manner that is comfortable to them. CCPT is a way of being with the child rather than a procedure or technique; meaning that instead of prescribing and directing, the play therapist remains in constant relationship with the child (Schaefer, 2011). CCPT's main premise is that children can grow and heal when a growth-producing climate is provided for them, free from agenda and construction. (Schaefer, 2011). While it may look like just playing to onlookers, this may be the only time in a child's day that he/she is

able to make his/her own choices which is very powerful. Outside of the therapeutic playroom children are being told what to do and how to act, but in the playroom, they are allowed space to just be themselves. The therapist sits with the child
in their session restating the child's verbalizations, and reflects possible meanings
and feelings observed on their face or in their body language. Often the therapist
uses "I wonder" statements to let the child know that the therapist is present with
them and interested in the child. Virginia Axline held the belief that when children were provided unconditional acceptance and safety then they would be able
to make positive changes on their own accord (Landreth, 2001). The predictability
the therapist creates in the playroom provides the child with emotional security
needed to support growth and change (Landreth, 2001). CCPT is not a technique
the therapist applies or prescribes to a child, but rather a way of being in relationship with the child (Kottman, 2011).

Allowing the child to lead the session does not indicate the absence of rules
and structure. The child-centered play therapist allows the child to be him/her-
self while providing consistency in each and every session, and maintains positive
regard for the child regardless of how the child plays. This includes when the child
becomes aggressive or begins to test the limits. Limit setting communicates to the
child that the playroom and their sessions will be safe, secure and consistent to
reduce anxiety and maintain a positive, accepting relationship. Garry Landreth's
ACT method provides a simple and clear method on setting limits in a caring
manner. <u>A</u>cknowledge the child's feelings, desires and wants. <u>C</u>ommunicate the
limit or rule. <u>T</u>arget an acceptable alternative that allows the child to express him/
herself in a way that is allowed in the playroom (Sweeney & Landreth, 2011).

Blending Adlerian and Child-Centered Play Therapy Methods

Child-centered play therapists remain non-directive in their approach, as described
in the previous section. However, Adlerian therapists are typically more directive.
By blending these two play therapy methods, one can formulate a treatment plan
that provides parents/caregivers with a roadmap of how their child's sessions will
unfold. This can be incredibly valuable when sessions are time-limited due to
insurance company restraints, school-based time constraints, or when a family
has concerns about what they can afford to pay for services.

The principles of these two methods can even be included in the psychosocial
history forms and initial intake session. Forms can be worded to elicit positive
answers. These forms are also child-focused and strength-based rather than
diagnostic. Consider this example. After asking about problematic behaviors
and concerns, the clinician can follow with, "What are some things you admire
about your child?" Adding in strength-based questions to the history forms forces
parents and caregivers to think of their child in a more positive manner. This also
provides the therapist with more information about dynamics in the family. Other
child-centered and positive questions that are valuable at intake and on the history
form include: What does your child like to do? Where does your child feel most

successful? What hobbies does your child have? How many friends does your child have?

Utilizing a pure form of child-centered play therapy during the first few sessions seems to work best for several reasons, and one example is that it allows the child to warm-up to the therapist and the playroom. It also allows the therapist to gage what the child prefers to play with, their style of play, if the child will push limits, and if the child asks the therapist to engage in play or prefers to play alone.

After a few sessions, the treatment plan can now be developed because the therapist has identified the child's style of play and personality, and the therapist will be better suited to suggest different methods that will help the child reach their goals. (See Appendix B for a sample game plan). As sessions progress and the therapist senses they have a solid rapport, adding in more directive play helps meet the goals of counseling.

Case Study

Mike

At age 8, Mike's mother had him evaluated at an outside counseling agency due to behavioral concerns that had been building over the years. He was given the diagnosis of ADHD with possible Oppositional Defiant Disorder (ODD), prescribed medication, and referred to one of their counselors. Mike is now 9 years old and his mother contacted my office interested in play therapy. She shared hesitation because nothing had seemed to work thus far. Mike's mother explained that she was afraid he would be expelled from school. I validated her concerns and educated her about my play therapy techniques, and I arranged his initial intake.

I met alone with Mike's mother for the initial intake to gather the needed information and discuss her concerns prior to meeting with Mike. Mike's mother reported daily disciplinary issues at school, impulsivity, blurting out in the class room, roughhousing at recess, difficulty with peers at school, sibling rivalry with his younger brother and defiance toward teachers and parents. The most recent incident at school involved playing with sticks at recess in a "sword fight" and Mike took things too far and injured another child with the stick.

Mike's bio-psycho-social history noted that he was born prematurely at 36 weeks gestation but with normal birth weight. All developmental milestones were met within normal limits, and the family history was absent for traumas and other mental health issues. Academically, Mike's grades were average except for math and reading, in which he was considered advanced. Of note, he did not have a current IEP or 504 Plan for behavioral support. Socially, his mother reported he only had one real friend and that classmates seemed to be either afraid of and/or annoyed by him. He and his younger brother would either play nicely or fight intensely. She further remarked that Mike would tell jokes or prank classmates to engage them but would often go too far and hurt other's feelings. She also shared that Mike was a very bright and caring child, and that she did not think he purposely misbehaved.

Mike's First Session

Like all first sessions, I began by introducing Mike to the playroom and reviewed the few rules I have to ensure both safety and a positive relationship. Mike was not hesitant to enter the playroom without his mom and seemed slightly excited. He remarked that he had never seen such a fun looking place and thought counseling was going to be boring. Without hesitation, he ran over to my bin that held the dart gun and stress balls. He then shot me with the dart gun followed by throwing a few stress balls at me with a grin on his face. Knowing that he was testing my limits, I enlisted the ACT method. I acknowledged his desire to gain my attention, communicated the limits of the playroom, and targeted/identified other suitable options to meet those needs. He grinned and went over to the punching bag and verbalized that most grown-ups would have sent him to the office. After a few minutes of playing with the punch-bag, he began asking me questions about things I like to do, and our relationship began. When I would restate his questions using the CCPT methods, he point-blank asked why I was talking like that. I could tell that strictly adhering to child-centered play methods would not be in Mike's best interests as he was very inquisitive and was seeking a relationship with me.

Sessions 2 to 3

In Mike's next two sessions, he repeated the themes from our first session together of shooting the dart gun, and aggressively punching the punch bag for about the first 10 minutes. Reflecting feelings and tracking his play set the scene for building rapport with him and he seemed to respond well to non-directive CCPT. I often voiced phrases including, "You are hitting that so hard" and "Boy, I can tell you feel frustrated." He added complaints about school and classmates as he punched the punching bag. He pretended that the punch bag was a teacher at school when he shot it with a dart gun. Using ACT methods and tracking his behavior, he was able to self-regulate without damaging the toys. Mike then asked if he could draw as he was out of breath and lower on physical energy. He drew dragons with fire and villainous looking characters with swords. He then asked if I would hang them on my wall, and I allowed this. Over the course of these sessions the themes of anger, frustration, power/control, the desire for attention even if negative (testing limits) and a low self-concept emerged. Utilizing the Four C's from Adlerian theory I was able to begin to formulate and structure interventions to blend into his sessions.

Mike's Game Plan

After his three sessions, I had a clear idea of what interventions would work with Mike. The plan would include a blend of child-centered play therapy mixed in with Adlerian principles, especially the Crucial C's. Taking the information I had gathered from both his psychosocial history and my interview with his mother,

I now devised a plan to work on his self-regulation, relationship building and self-esteem. At the top of his treatment plan (the Game Plan) I listed the Crucial C's. *Mike's C's included the following: Courage*: It did not appear he struggled with this area as he tested my limits well; *Connected*: he seemed to have limitations from parent/teacher/self-reports making meaningful connections with other children, and *Capable*: he was very bright and capable with imagination and math/reading, but he does not see that he is, *Count*: he currently did not feel that he mattered at school and home as he was always in trouble for his impulsive behaviors. I used this information about Mike to tailor his sessions by alternating CCPT and Adlerian techniques. This allowed him to be himself in his play, but also helped me focus to lead on the behavioral goals. His sessions were structured to allow for Mike to have time to get out his pent-up anger and frustration. I chose activities that helped bolster self-concept, model start-stop behaviors, and build on connections by modeling positive relationship with him. Several sessions also involved his brother and his parents.

I shared the Game Plan with his parents and suggested that we engage the school guidance counselor and his teacher with this plan. After all, most of his struggles occurred at school. His parents agreed, and we eventually set up a meeting with his school.

Session 4

Mike came in ready to play and began with the punching bag. He then transitioned to swinging and throwing around the beanbags. He asked if I had seen a recent superhero-villain movie and he shared with me about how "epic" the fight scenes were. He reenacted some of the scenes as he moved around the room, asking me to join in this play. On this visit, he also showed interest in my sand tray and asked if he could play with it. I provided him with the objects that were allowed in the tray, and gently suggested that he create his own movie scene in the tray. He gravitated toward the pirates, snakes, and weapons, and played out battles often. On one side he had the army men lined up and on the other side he lined up the dogs. He divided them with trenches and mounds of sand (I use kinetic sand, so it forms and holds shapes), and another side held the pirates, snakes and spiders. While he placed the figures, he spoke through the army men and pirates and the dialogue was one of banter of who was better/stronger. In this scene the army men took out the pirates.

Following Sessions

Each session almost always began with his desire for physical activity. He seemed to need the outlet of being able to hit, punch and move after being in school all day. I was able to determine if he had had a rough day at school based on the intensity of his play. He continued to create scenes in the sand tray. On one visit as he set up the scene he paused, looked up, and said, "Today, the bad guys are going to win." He took several pirates and had them bury the army men, and the pirates celebrated. He seemed quite satisfied. Using "I wonder" statements, I took this opportunity to ask who decided that the army men were good, and the pirates are bad. I stated they each had weapons, each had their own group of friends, and each seemed to "fight" for valid reasons. While neither of us had answers for this, I hoped that this planted the seed that he was not a bad child.

Introducing Super Heroes and Villains into the Playroom

Several sessions later after I had recently seen *The LEGO® Batman Movie (2017)*, I had a realization; The Joker's struggles in this movie reminded me of Mike's who wanted to fit in and was not purposely misbehaving at school out of malice. At his next session I introduced *Batman* vs. *The Joker* and he shared he too had seen the movie. Using this movie allowed us to work through his issues at school and he was able to understand that everyone was capable of both good choices and bad choices. I took the list of characters and had him identify who in his life was Batman, The Joker, Robin and The Mayor. He waffled between picking The Joker or Batman for himself, Robin was his little brother, and the Mayor his mom. We also listed out the common attributes of the characters in a pro/con fashion to normalize that people are not "just" bad or good; that we as humans have many qualities. At the end of this session, I brought Mike's mother into the playroom to show her our list of pros and cons related to *The LEGO® Batman Movie's* list of characters with the hopes of providing her with insight, as well as to validate her own feelings that her son was not "all bad." I suggested that this could be shared with his guidance counselor at school as another way to support Mike outside of our sessions.

In following sessions with Mike, I brought in mini-figure Joker and Batman Legos to add to my collection. Mike would swap the heads of the characters to see what they each would look like in "different" bodies as well as played out movie scenes. He played out Batman being quite mean to The Joker and The Joker "retreating" into a cave he made in the sand tray. He used the other mini-figure Legos to join sides, most being on Batman's side, and the theme of loneliness was played out. In one session he buried Batman in the sand. Often, he would transition his play to the punching bag when his stories were finished. While he had been the identified "bully" at school, his stories were telling a different story; he felt isolated and picked on by his classmates who were often pointing out his mistakes to the teacher, and in a sense was feeling bullied himself.

In one of our sessions I suggested that he make up his own comic book about himself, and taking off my CCPT hat, put on my Adlerian hat to work on his goals of feeling capable and he counted. We got out construction paper, markers and a stapler and he quickly began drawing/coloring. On his cover page he wrote, "SUPER MIKE." He would draw out fight scenes like one would find in store-bought comics and would write words like "WHAM, BAM, POW!" This project took a few sessions to complete. While I kept the book in my office, he would bring in new pages to add to it. This project was another method of bridging the gap between home-school-counseling, and he seemed to really enjoy it, or otherwise he wouldn't have worked on it outside of session. While most of his book was drawings of him with swords, capes, and laser beam powers, I suggested he write down words that described him. He came up with this list: awesome, funny, clever, strong, smart, to name a few. While this book was not a real comic book with dialog and a natural progression of a story, it was a symbol to him that he was a super cool kid. Inside of the playroom his identity was revealed to not just me, but to himself.

Summary of Mike's Sessions

I worked with Mike for over two years, but I knew we were making progress the moment he verbalized that the pirates could win. In the sand tray, he was able to finally feel vindicated and win for once. Contrast to this, being one of the only kids in his class that was always being sent to time out at recess. After a few sessions, his parents reported improvements at school and at home. He began making more friends and was getting in less trouble at school. His desire to belong and fit in was hindered by his impulsive nature and under-developed social skills, but in play therapy he was able to practice self-regulation and social skills.

Utilizing child-centered and Adlerian methods helped me shape counseling sessions that worked for Mike. Mike was constantly being told what to do at school and home, and he heard the words "no" or "stop" frequently. It was important for him to have the freedom to be himself in the playroom. There were times I thought maybe my punching bag would be destroyed, but by using the ACT method consistently he was able to self-regulate and redirect his play.

Activities Involved Throughout Mike's Sessions

1. Creating his own deck of "power cards." Think of these like baseball collector cards. His cards included phrases like "I'm Smart, I'm an Inventor, and I'm good at math."
2. Making up new jokes and pranks that would get him positive attention at home/school and not in trouble.
3. Sword fights with foam swimming noodles (cut in half) that provided an outlet for his frustrations. To maintain safety, limit setting and boundaries were in place which included: no hitting above the neck or too hard (demonstrated on the punch bag a hard hit vs. soft hit), the rule that this play was <u>only</u> allowed in the playroom and he would need permission from his parents to do this at home, limiting swordplay to the use of pool noodles and terminating the session if his play became too aggressive. *(While some therapists and even parents do not endorse rough-house and aggressive play,*

please note that it can have positive effects in boys when limits are set as aforementioned.)

4. Creating his own comic book. As described above, over a few sessions, Mike created his own comic book and he often would come in to session with new pages to add to his book. His book was titled, "Super Mike" and he would draw fight scenes with the typical "POW," "BAM," "WHAM" captions one would find in a comic.
5. Taking turns hitting the punching bag while shouting out things that bothered us.
6. Created a two-sided *Joker* mask: One side is how he felt he was viewed by others, and the other side of how he viewed himself.

Refer to Appendix B for more activity ideas.

Conclusion

My work with Mike incorporated both child-centered and Adlerian play therapy methods while enlisting the help of Superhero films. Mike was able to be his own agent of change. Throughout my journey with Mike and his family, I developed a deeper understanding of the complex needs of children who are deemed the school bully. By utilizing CCPT and Adlerian principles, I was able to connect with Mike on his terms. He could evolve from the shadows of his internal self-concept of a villain to a regular child who has the same concerns as others—just like The Joker and Batman.

The dichotomy of using super hero and villain stories helped transform this therapeutic process into a memorable one, and it was action packed at times! Each child has the capacity for change and growth and utilizing the popular theme of superheroes and villains within the Play Therapy process. Children can learn ways to lasso more super powers into their "tool boxes" while squelching maniacal thoughts and actions.

Therapists working with this type of child can replicate this process using movies and characters that each child likes. Being able to normalize feelings of anger, frustration, revenge, and the need for power by using movies such as *The LEGO® Batman Movie* (2017), can be very powerful. Understanding that there is a yin/yang in all of us can greatly impact a child's life. This understanding can help the child wipe off the façade of their own Joker mask to reveal what truly lies beneath the surface—another child wanting to belong and matter.

Questions for Clinical Discussion

1. When working with a client who plays aggressively, if the ACT method does not work, what would you do to regain control and safety of the room/session?
2. If parents object to having their child play with aggressive play items in the playroom such as the Bop-Bag, toy guns and toy knives, how would you handle this?

3.   When a child perceives himself negatively, what techniques would you implement to counter his negative self-concept?
4.   How would you respond if a child-client hit you while in session?
5.   In what ways are you able to identify with The Joker?
6.   It can be challenging to work with aggressive children. What are ways you can support your own self-care?

References

Anti-Bullying Institute (2018). *Bullying facts and the challenges to be met.* Retrieved September 24, 2018 from http://antibullyinginstitute.org/facts#.W3L2sq2ZMfN.

American Psychological Association (2018). *Bullying.* Retrieved October 4, 2018 from www.apa.org/topics/bullying/.

Barkley, R. (n.d.). *7 Executive function deficits tied to ADHD.* Retrieved October 8, 2018 from www.additudemag.com/7-executive-function-deficits-linked-to-adhd/.

Dreikurs, R. & Soltz, V. (1964). *Children, the challenge.* Howthorn Books.

Espelage, D. L, Polanin, J. R., & Low, S. K. (2014). Teacher perception of school predictors of student aggression, victimization, and willingness to intervene in bullying situations. *School of Psychology Quarterly*, 29(3), 287–305. doi:10.1037/ispq0000072.

Gambini, B. (2018, July 5). *An aggressor is not necessarily a bully—and the distinction matters* [Press release]. Retrieved from www.buffalo.edu/news/releases/2018/07/002.html.

Kottman, T. (2011). *Play therapy basics and beyond* (2nd edn.). Alexandria, VA: American Counseling Association.

Landreth, G. (Ed.). (2001). *Innovations in play therapy: Issues, process, and special populations.* New York: Routledge.

Lew, A. & Bettner, B. L. (2000). *A parent's guide to understanding and motivating children* (Revised edn.). Newton Center, MA: Connexions.

Lin, D., Lord, P., Miller, C., Lee, R. (Producers), & McKay, C. (Director) (2017). *The LEGO Batman Movie* [Motion Picture]. Burbank, CA: Warner Bros. Pictures.

Livesay, H. (2007). Making a place for the angry hero on the team. In: L. Rubin (Ed.), *Using superheroes in counseling and play therapy* (pp. 121–138). New York: Springer.

Maslow, A. H. (1987). *Motivation and personality* (3rd edn.). Delhi, India: Pearson Education.

Ray, D. (2011). *Advanced play therapy: Essential conditions, knowledge, and skills for child practice.* New York: Taylor & Francis, LLC.

Robertie, K., Weidenbenner, R., Barret, L., & Poole, R. (2007). A super milieu: Using superheroes in the residential treatment of adolescents with sexual behavior problems. In: L. Rubin (Ed.), *Using superheroes in counseling and play therapy* (pp. 143–166). New York. Springer.

Schaefer, C. E. (2011). *Foundations of play therapy* (2nd edn.). Hoboken, NJ. John Wiley & Sons, Inc.

Sweeney, D. S. & Landreth, G. L. (2011). Child-centered play therapy. In: C. E. Schaefer (Ed.), *Foundations of Play Therapy* (pp. 129–149), (2nd edn.). Hoboken, NJ. John Wiley & Sons, Inc.

StopBullying.Gov (2018). What is bullying. Retrieved July 20, 2018 from www.stopbullying.gov/what-is-bullying/index.html.

StopBullying.Gov (2018). Stop bullying on the spot. Retrieved July 20, 2018 from www.stopbullying.gov.

The Stop Bullying Now Foundation (2018). School bullying affects us all. Retrieved July 20, 2018 from www.stopbullyingnowfoundation.org/main/.

Williams, P. (n.d.). ADHD in children: Symptoms, evaluations, treatments. Retrieved October 8, 2018 from www.additudemag.com/adhd-in-children-symptoms-diagnosis-treatment/.

Appendix A: Play Therapy Game Plan

Therapist: _____

Child's Name: Age: DOB: Date:

Presenting Concerns:

_____

_____

The 4 C's	Information
Connect	
Capable	
Count	
Courage	

Targeted Areas	Goals/Objectives	Play Therapy Activities
Connections		
Capabilities		
Counting		
Courage		

Appendix B: Super Powered Play Therapy Ideas

1. Create your own "Would You Rather" game with a villain and super hero theme

Example of Questions

Would you rather be The Joker or Lex Luther?
Would you rather live in the Bat Cave or in "The Phantom Zone?"
Would you rather fly like Super Man or Iron Man?

Have the child help you come up with examples for each card and then have them play this in session with their parent/sibling/caregiver.

2. Paper Plate Mask

On one side of the paper plate draw the face you "paint" for how others see you at school. On the other side, draw how you want them to see you. You may use words too if you like. Then discuss.

3. Comic Collage

Collect DVD/Movie covers or inserts, magazines, comic books, Lego® directions, and anything that has super heroes and villains depicted on them. Many of these items can be found in thrift stores, or in your own basement! Have a box of these comic book themed graphics for the child to make his/her own collage. Other materials needed would include poster board, scissors and glue.

4. LEGO® Comics

Use Legos to create a comic strip to tell a story. Many of the Legos today are from various movies, including Batman and The Joker.

Materials Needed

Legos and mini-figures: figures that have a variety of faces and expressions, as well as weapons, hand-cuffs, etc., blank sheets of white paper, black magic marker, digital camera or Polaroid if possible, and the ability to print each photo of each scene, poster board or construction paper.

Instruct the child to create their own comic strip using Lego mini-figures. Show an example if you have one. Have the child create at least three still-frames by placing their scenes flat on white paper and then writing phrases or words to tell their story.

Take a photo of each scene, print them out, then have the child glue them to poster board/construction paper. This may take a few sessions.

CHAPTER 14

Brain Food: Integrating IPNB and Zombies with Diverse Populations

Robyn Joy Park

Introduction

As with superheroes, there is a fascination with zombies. Cross-culturally, zombie enthusiasts consume these characters through comics, graphic novels such as *The Walking Dead* (2010), radio and music with zombie infused lyrics, television, video games and films like *Zombieland* (2009), *Shaun of the Dead* (2004), *World War Z* (2013) and books such as Max Brooks' *How to Survive the Zombie Apocalypse* (2003). While our human brains eat up these various shows, songs and series for their entertainment value, it is also important to note the symbolism and timelessness of zombies. This chapter will explore the symbolic link between zombies and mental health, for just like zombies mental health issues can ruthlessly attack and cause destruction to both individuals and communities. This chapter will also provide therapeutic approaches and interventions that can be used to combat mental health zombies. One such approach is Interpersonal Neurobiology (IPNB) which, like a zombie, is also interested in the human brain, but rather than destroy it, this relational-based approach seeks integration between the brain, mind and relationships in order to create a powerful force that can protect and shield anyone from their "attacking zombies." Zombies are not just imaginary supervillains; they very much represent our fears and anxieties on both an individual and collective social level. We both love and hate them and by accepting the existence of zombies in our lives, we can become better equipped to identify, fight and coexist with them. Adapting from zombie historian Max Brooks' perspective on zombies as a metaphor for mental health, this chapter will explore how we can therapeutically combat our own internal and external zombies and equip ourselves with the tools, support and resources to prepare for an apocalypse and survive anything that might come our way.

Theoretical Discussion

In an interview with *The New York Times*, author Max Brooks discussed the ways in which zombies can be anything that enters your life without invitation or prejudice and destroys it (Brodesser-Akner, 2013). For many of the clients and families with whom I have worked, zombies have been a part of their lives and ruthlessly attack their brains. For example, many families, particularly those who have experienced relational traumas, the zombies are the separations and losses— the unknowns. For many children and adolescents that I work with, "life is not fair" becomes a point of argument and tension with caregivers, parents, and other figures of authority. Zombies are real.

Across the lifespan, it is clinically significant to note the ways in which the human brain responds to threat and vulnerability, such as the flight/fight/freeze response. The autonomic nervous system is at the core of our daily functioning, shaping our experiences of safety and influencing our capacity for connection. According to Stephen Porges (2011), the Polyvagal Theory helps us better under-stand in response to traumatic experiences, how our autonomic pathways of connection are replaced with patterns of protection. One of our brain's main functions is safety, and when it is confronted with situations that are perceived as unsafe, it will go into a reactive or receptive state. Therefore, if we think of this in terms of how we might respond to any zombies that are trying to attack our brains, we will either go into fight, flight or freeze mode. Being able to bring awareness to this is important and can help one understand the ways in which we might respond when we are feeling vulnerable or threatened. Through recognizing this, when we think about zombies in terms of anxiety or even trauma, our capacity to feel safe is functionally disrupted and undermines our abilities to co-regulate with others, which then impacts our mental and physical health and well-being. Our interpersonal relationships, or connections with others, play a vital role in cre-ating safety when there have been such traumatic attacks. Therefore, our ability to connect with others will help create a deeper sense of awareness, transformation and growth.

Neuroscience has become the focus of much attention within therapy and con-tinues to reveal the ways in which, from an IPNB perspective, we need to experi-ence a triangle of well-being that integrates the mind, body and relationships (Siegel, 2012). Our role as clinicians is therefore to help awaken the mind for humans to survive and thrive. In the *YES Brain* (2018), Dan Siegel and Tina Payne Bryson write much about the ways in which we can expand our window of tolerance-meaning we all have an optimal state of arousal level from which we function. These levels can shift when we are faced with challenges or adverse experiences that can cause one to feel anxious, hurt, anger or pain (Siegel and Bryson, 2018).

When working with children and adolescents, it is always important to be mindful of the ways in which the brain is still developing and their window of tolerance is expanding. During the teen years, our minds change in the way we remember, think, reason, focus attention, make decisions and relate to others. From around age 12 to age 24, there is a burst of growth and maturation taking place (Siegel & Bryson, 2014). Understanding the brain and how it creates linkages and becomes integrated with development helps us to more optimally perform and function, thus working with teens to help cultivate and develop the life skills they need to face any adverse situation.

As metaphors, zombies can assist clients in facing their own unconscious fears and anxieties, and therapists can help them expand their stress and distress tolerance. We have the power to find regulation when often we are in a state of dysregulation. It is from these various theoretical understandings that we can begin to acknowledge the ways in which our client's behaviors or defense mechanisms have served a purpose with the hopes of finding new more integrated ways of conquering past or current stressors.

While a zombie apocalypse is a disastrous process that is both ugly and frightening, if one can tap into their inner strengths and resiliency, positive emergence of strength and courage may arise. I propose that like superheroes, zombies or supervillains that we love, hate and fear, can help individuals face the real dangers of the world. When our brains are integrated and connected, we can make connections with ourselves and with others, which provides the abilities for us to form healthy relationships.

Superheroes represent the face of significant adversity and exhibit phenomenal strength and courage. They are typically characterized as altruistic, caring, clever and attractive. While they promote resiliency, on the contrary, we often overlook the ways in which villains can also cultivate this and create empowerment and transformation. When we think of a classic villain, they are typically in conflict with the superhero and are the face of evil. They threaten the welfare and independent existence of the social group (Klapp, 1962). Villains evoke a visceral, instinctive fear response and often are characterized opposite of the hero being selfish, lacking empathy and unattractive or deformed. Their appearance elicits us to have a response that often carries a negative association.

Zombies certainly fit these criteria while also representing society's collective anxieties. They are not just imaginary monsters created from nothing; they very much represent our fears and anxieties on both an individual and social level. By accepting the existence of zombies in our lives and minds, we can become better equipped to identify and fight them. The discussion will be followed by personal reflections and different settings where the zombies have been applied clinically.

Case Discussion: Clinical Vignette

It has been a unique personal and professional journey to discover the reasons why I have become fascinated with superhero/supervillain play. As I broaden my work with clients who feel inadequate, isolated and anxious, zombies provide a tool through which I can and have creatively explored counseling. As I have dedicated my practice to working with diverse populations, particularly children and adolescence touched by foster care and/or adoption, my other areas of focus include addressing dysregulation, particularly around anxiety and depression. It has been my personal and professional experiences that have inspired my curiosities and creativity to create therapeutic support and interventions that address individual and collective community's zombies.

In this next section, I present two clinical experiences that highlight the ways in which I have creatively integrated zombies into various settings, both outpatient, in-home and school based. The first case focuses on the course of individual treatment and the second reflects on a therapeutic application for groups within a school-based setting.

Mine Up

For many tweens and teens, video role-playing games are a place to escape and explore a fantasy world. As a clinician inspired by popular culture and the ways in which this influences children and adolescents, I am drawn to the ways in which the client's fascination surrounding different role-playing games can be a tool and a way to explore their inner worlds; a window into that client's life. In the gaming world, the hero or superhero is not necessarily the one who has a superpower but one who must overcome the odds and remain true to their beliefs and values (Enfield, 2006).

Therapeutically, I integrate video games as an opportunity to connect and build rapport. Within sessions with various clients who are particularly drawn to video games, I share curiosity in the ways in which the video games, which often revolve around superheroes and supervillains, impact the client's life and can be utilized as a tool to dig deeper into their inner world. Minecraft, a popular video game that was released in 2011, allows players to control an agent and build structures, craft tools and destroy zombies. Playing the game involves surviving by using blocks to build shelters and using various materials to destroy the game's many supervillains (zombies, creepers and skeletons).

While working in post-adoption services within a community-based organization, I met Jose who was experiencing intense daily temper tantrums that could range from one to many hours—exhausting everyone in its wake. Often exasperated by Jose's challenges to cope and manage his big emotions when he became dysregulated caused much concern, frustration and stress to his parents. While Jose was adopted alongside his siblings, there was a sense of sadness and anger in his interactions with his family and with the therapist when first starting treatment. During the first sessions, as I was building rapport and forming a therapeutic relationship with Jose, he was barely able to tolerate being in the room. On multiple occasions, he would become extremely dysregulated, express his displeasure and storm off exploding in another room, projecting his anger toward his parent. Eventually, therapeutic sessions were moved to the home and I was able to meet with Jose in the comfort of his environment where he was able to feel safe, seen, soothed and secure (Siegel & Bryson, 2018). In time, I was able to introduce Minecraft, through which I was able to get a deeper glimpse of Jose's inner world that appeared to bring not only joy, but also assist him with co-regulation and working through various interpersonal relational issues. Jose's abilities to stay regulated continued to grow and I observed his window of tolerance continue to expand. During these moments, I seized the opportunity to get a deeper glimpse into his thoughts and feelings. I observed his abilities to be more receptive to discuss more sensitive past experiences. As our time together progressed, we were able to transition from the tablet into activities that touched on his adoption journey. In subsequent sessions we created a time-line that highlighted the various faces and places he had experienced. Jose was able to identify the different zombies that would trigger him and cause much fear and anxiety. Jose's creative abilities became evident in his animated and expressive arts activities with zombies; and like the zombies he was running from in the game who wanted to eat his brain, I was seeking his brain with the hopes of helping re-wire different pathways toward integration.

For Jose, many core adoption themes and issues were present in his everyday life, and while he may not have been consciously aware of this, as an adoption informed therapist I would gently try to heighten his awareness around these issues. Rejection and control were primary focuses and it was clear during our play when these themes would come out. In order to address this, it was important to cultivate a therapeutic framework that was safe and consistent. For many children who have experienced disruption or traumatic histories, chaos and inconsistency become the norm from which they operate. The lack of con-trol can often create a sense of powerlessness, and in order to regain this sense of control, parents often become the target for this projected anger and pain. Play is children's way of working out balance and control in their lives, for, as children play, they are in control of the happenings in play, although it may not be possible to actually be in control of the life experience represented in the play (Landreth, 2012).

It is the sense or feeling in control in play therapy that is essential to children's emotional development and sense of safety (Landreth, 2012). Utilizing the zombies in the virtual Minecraft game as well as in Minecraft Lego, we built alongside one another. We were able to incorporate storylines around the relationship between the zombie and the Minecraft character, Matt. As we would go back and forth between online and offline play, Jose appeared to enjoy teaching me how to play and learn the ins and outs of Minecraft.

During our termination period, we processed the ways in which his zombies may continue to chase him, emphasizing that no matter where he goes, he has the tools in his mental Minecraft toolbox to conquer his zombies. During our last session together, he gave me a note that to this day reminds me of the importance of creating a world that explores zombies and stated, "Dear Robyn, I hope you have a good life. Use your mind to get out of that cave. Remember in Minecraft to mine up not down. In Minecraft worlds you are now a Master Builder."

Zombies Are Real: Teens and Group Setting

While in graduate school I had the opportunity, alongside my Child Studies and Community Psychology specializations, to create and pilot a program within an adolescent group therapy setting at my clinical training site. Alongside my fascination with zombies and another zombie enthusiast Davis Jung, I decided to create a unique curriculum tailored for the adolescent brain in order to address the challenges (zombies) many teens are facing these days (D. Jung, personal communication, 2012). Within a school-based setting and understanding the challenges of launching a support group, it was important to creatively inspire and mobilize participants who were not only other fellow zombie enthusiasts, but also willing to explore the idea of a zombie metaphor that addresses mental health issues within a group context.

Group Format

The goals of the therapy group included:

- To better equip ourselves with the tools, support and resources to prepare for an apocalypse and survive anything that might come our way
- To identify, enhance and strengthen the innate skill sets we already have
- Learning more adaptive coping skills and strategies including:
  - Identifying and expressing feelings
  - Promoting understanding of the stress response and personal stressors and red flags (triggers)
  - Managing anxiety and stress
  - Learning social skills
  - Building positive interpersonal relationships
  - Learning how to live and coexist with inner zombies.

I was able to pilot the zombie curriculum over the course of 10 sessions within a Los Angeles area public high school. What made this support group particularly unique was that it was comprised of teacher and self-referrals. In terms of facilitation and other logistics, flyers were distributed throughout the school and teachers and other counselors were notified about the support group. In order to find the most optimal time during the school day to meet without creating more anxiety by missing class, we met during the lunch hour. This way, we could refuel and re-energize together. Prior to the initial start date, screenings were conducted to ensure the best fit for participants.

A unique aspect of bringing such a group together was that the group members all had similar conditions, issues, concerns and experiences. This group created a space where one's interest in zombies and similar struggles with anxiety helped reduce isolation, promoted cohesion and provided emotional support. With the group powers combined, there was a hope to unite and conquer. As a result, natural social skills could develop which enhanced their abilities to produce better interpersonal relationships and promote self-confidence.

After creating a safe and affirmative place we were off and running as a new pack becoming comfortable and building trust amongst each other. During the first group sessions, we focused on what traditional zombies represent and are defined from macro, meso and micro levels. The common definition of zombie entailed a deceased human being, only partially alive with gross motor functions but without emotion or the sensation of pain.

Drawing from alternative definitions including the ways in which Max Brooks has re-defined zombies, I provided a prompt for the group to explore and address what past, present and future zombies of our world look like. Each participant was given a post-it note and could identify these however they wanted, whether through words, drawings and/or symbols. Discussion questions included: What defines a "zombie?" How do you see them operating in our society both locally and globally? What makes our communities vulnerable to them? What are some ways in which our society has tried to combat them? What do you think our future zombies represent? How could we prevent zombies in the future?

In order to promote understanding of the stress response, personal stressors and red flags, it was important to use different case examples to assist participants with increasing their own awareness of their own intrinsic personality traits, strengths and assets they can foster in order to be a leader in their own survival. In order to do this, the group explored different characters/heroes/superheroes such as Rick Grimes, Hermione Granger and Superman.

Superman for example, is a fascinating superhero and in terms of exploring his possible zombies we first must better understand his context. Knowing that Superman is one of the last Kryptonians who must live in exile on Earth after his home world is destroyed, raises many questions and curiosities around his identity and isolation. Not to mention he even lives in a place called the Fortress of Solitude. Additionally, it is important to acknowledge his trials and tribulations as an adoptee. Given his history, we can begin to imagine what kinds of zombies Clark Kent/Superman might be battling. While he is from another planet, he can fly and shoot laser beams from his eyes, he also struggles like the rest of us.

While his Superman persona includes obvious strengths such as superhuman powers like flight, X-ray vision and invulnerability, his Clark Kent persona could arguably give him the greatest strength. By being Clark Kent, he learns humanity, love and compassion, giving him the drive to be a protector of Earth. The unwavering sense of justice was instilled in him by his adoptive parents. Although this sense of justice can make him more rigid in personality, it is what drives many of his actions.

Another popular character who struggled with anxious thoughts and feelings around academics, and with whom many of the students were able to identify with was Hermione Granger. While brave and courageous, she has high expectations of being "smart" and one of her greatest fears, as represented by the encounter with a boggart, is her fear of failure. A common trait among high achievers is the fear of doing something wrong or disappointing others. Her pursuit of knowledge and academic strength saves her friends numerous times. Often it is her rigorous educational pursuits that help solve riddles and mysteries. In addition to being bullied for her big teeth and frizzy hair, she is also ridiculed for being Muggle-born. Being an outsider in the wizarding world has led Hermione to have great compassion, especially for minorities and outcasts and her leadership skills naturally lead her to create the Society for the Promotion of Elfish Welfare (S.P.E.W.). Despite her intelligence, Hermione was put into Gryffindor for a reason. She displays great courage, even in times of great danger.

After being able to identify with other's experiences, explore their zombies and identify various innate leadership qualities, it was important to have each participant identify and externalize the zombies and their own strengths and superpowers. An activity that helped do this included creating a zombie profile. Participants were asked to identify those areas in their lives where zombies existed, and if there were times when they were dormant and when they would reanimate. Together we created a list of zombies that included and was not limited to: parents, homework, teachers, anxiety, anger, friendships, the unknown, the known, school, people, expectations, consistency, the future and rudeness. When digging deeper and exploring some of these zombies in more detail, participants shared that zombies particularly around the issues of high school included things such as: being tired, it being a difficult time in their life, feelings of being uncomfortable, hopelessness, confinement, stress, being misunderstood, having point reduction systems, disgusting smells, fear of failing, struggles with time management and frustration with teachers and parents.

I was struck by the various zombies they identified around the pressure and expectations of high school and being an adolescent. In many ways, the school year becomes a battleground and a hot bed full of zombies. During adolescence, there is both a thrill and fear of the unfamiliar. However, never knowing what zombies are lurking and waiting to attack outside of the safety of one's home can be frightening and incredibly anxiety provoking.

Providing reflection questions to assist with group member's abilities to recognize their own innate strengths, helped create a dialogue around the overlap between people's zombies and strengths. We posed several questions—food for zombie thought so to speak. How do these characters turn their zombies into the greatest strengths? If you could have a superpower what would it be? What inner strengths do you possess that help make you resilient during difficult or challenging times?

Interactive Interventions

After the group was able to explore and identify their own zombies, it was important to integrate different interactive activities that provided opportunities to more deeply discuss the impact these zombies had on our brains and relationships. This included providing psychoeducation on our fight, flight and freeze responses, exploring the ways in which each individual's defense mechanisms were activated in various situations and looking at relational issues that can come up particularly with friends and peers.

Just as when preparing for a zombie apocalypse, group members created an emergency kit and safety plan including important survival resources such as food and water, health supplies, personal care items and documents. Integrating this same concept and applying it clinically, creating Bug Out Bags (B.O.B.) for each participant became a way to explore what each person needs during a time of an emergency when their zombie(s) attack. Identifying items that uniquely accommodated their needs was a unique way to address self-care and tailor this to their individualized care. Thinking about the importance of items they could not live without, each group member created a list including items that would help when feeling dysregulated or anxious and stressed.

Music can be a healing tool and songs and artists often reflect our feelings that we may not verbally communicate to others. Many of the participants chose songs that tapped into strengths and resources needed when they became dysregulated and needed to self-soothe. Each participant was encouraged to create their own "Zombie Survival Playlist." Together participants shared their favorite songs and we listened collectively to them exploring the deeper meaning to each individual behind the music and the words, sharing curiosity in the feelings and memories that were evoked when they listened to these songs.

Cultivating connections and relationships is another important aspect of IPNB and an important element to address within the content and process of the group. When faced with a zombie apocalypse, creating a support system is critical. As we see in *The Walking Dead*, the different relational dynamics can mean life or death. Conflict is inevitable and therefore if we can prepare for this within various social situations, relationships can survive and thrive. Learning and practicing various conflict resolution skills assisted the group with addressing relational communication issues. In order to facilitate a discussion around this, we watched a scene from a movie in which a group of friends argued over the last candy bar as they are on the verge of the world coming to an end. Each friend states why they should have the candy as the conflict escalated. Highlighting this interaction at an apocalyptic moment when conflict is inevitable, we discussed the significance of navigating challenging group dynamics and situations. Additional psychoeducation around promoting the understanding of other individual's personal stressors and their stress responses when feeling threatened or vulnerable was also important to discuss in order to help continue to build healthy relationships. Each group member was able to identify their own fight, flight or freeze response and discuss when they feel threatened.

Outcome

At the end of the sessions and as the group moved toward termination, it was rewarding to see how the group had created new relationships and how members felt more equipped and empowered to face any zombies that might come their way. The group was able to address their fears, enhance their social skills, and expand their window of tolerance in cooperation with one another. While there were two group members who knew each other initially, the rest of the group members were different grade levels. With the wide spectrum of ages and grade levels, it provided a unique opportunity for these students to connect when they might not otherwise have had the opportunity to cross paths.

While we often look to other superheroes and identify with them, it was a unique experience to help the group realize how they are in fact their own superheroes and already have the inner strength and resiliency to combat any zombie or supervillains that they might encounter. We came, we conquered.

Personal Reflections

As I evolve as a therapist, I continue to deepen my practice and expand upon the integration of supervillains with superheroes. Behind every superhero's mask or cape is a tender soul that has, despite trials and tribulations, faced all obstacles. Superhero's stories inspire us to unite and conquer our own personal challenges. Similarly, supervillains challenge us to face our fears and bring out aspects of ourselves we might not have otherwise known had we not encountered their existence. While working alongside vulnerable children and youth, I find that these are the new heroes of our future that deserve much attention and credit. They are the ones who are being their own superheroes and courageously facing their supervillains. I always emphasize the ways in which each individual can utilize their superpowers toward being helpful or hurtful in this universe. We all have the capabilities of going to the dark side, using our magic for dark purposes or becoming a supervillain or zombie. Being mindful and aware of this is an important aspect to staying on a course that is often filled with challenges of both love and hate but can be inspired by hope and joy.

I am forever humbled and appreciative of the adventures I get to experience and the journey alongside the individuals and families with whom I work. The amount of strength and courage it takes for everyone to acknowledge and face their own zombies never ceases to amaze me. Together with our powers combined we will continue to survive and thrive.

Questions for Clinical Discussion

1. How do zombies come up in your clinical work?
2. What clinical utility do you find in the zombie metaphor?
3. Can you think of any particular clients where zombies could be utilized to explore their inner world?
4. In what ways might you be able to integrate the use of supervillains or zombies with the populations that you serve?
5. How might you address the violent aspects of zombies while working with younger children and their caregivers/parents?
6. What tools and resources do you need as a clinician in your Bug Out Bag (B.O.B.)?

References

Brodesser-Akner, T. (2013, June 21). Max Brooks is not kidding about the Zombie apocalypse. *The New York Times*. Retrieved from www.nytimes.com/2013/06/23/magazine/max-brooks-is-not-kidding-about-the-zombie-apocalypse.html?pagewanted=all&_r=0

Enfield, G. (2006). Becoming the hero: The use of role-playing games in psychotherapy. In: L. Rubin (Ed.), *Using superheroes in counseling and play therapy* (pp. 227–241). New York: Springer Publishing Co.

IGN (2013, June 3). This is the end: "Can I have the Milky Way" [Video file]. Retrieved from http://youtu.be/cubI6GyvjbI

Kjeldgaard-Christiansen, J. (2016). Evil origins: A Darwinian genealogy of the pop cultural villain. *Evolutionary Behavioral Sciences, 10*(2), 109–122.

Klapp, O. E. (1962). *Heroes, villains, and fools: The changing American character*. Englewood Cliffs, NJ: Prentice-Hall, Inc.

Landreth, G. (1991). *Play therapy: The art of the relationship*. New York: Bruner Routledge.

Landreth, G. (2012). *Play therapy: The art of the relationship*. London, UK: Routledge.

Porges, S. (2011). *The polyvagal theory: Neurophysiological foundations of emotions, attachment communication and self-regulation*. New York: W. W. Norton & Company, Inc.

Rubin, L. C. (2006). *Using superheroes in counseling and play therapy*. Springer Publishing Company, Kindle Edition.

Siegel, D. J. (2013). *Brainstorm: The power and purpose of the teenage brain*. New York: Penguin Putnam.

Siegel, D. J. (2012). *The Norton series on interpersonal neurobiology. Pocket guide to interpersonal neurobiology: An integrative handbook of the mind*. New York: W. W. Norton & Company, Inc.

Siegel, D. J. & Payne-Bryson, T. (2014). *The whole-brain child: 12 revolutionary strategies to nurture your child's developing mind*. New York: Bantam.

Siegel, D. J. and Bryson, T. P. (2018). *The yes brain: How to cultivate courage, curiosity, and resilience in your child*. New York: Bantam.

CHAPTER 15

How Secrets Influenced Relationships for Harry Potter Heroes and Villains: Parallels in Contextual Family Therapy

Sarah D. Stauffer and April D. Pachuta

The Harry Potter series, penned by J. K. Rowling, has entertained millions of readers, young and old, by interweaving classic threads of friendship and belonging into intricate tapestries of magic, mystery and secrets. A secret is something that is meant to be unknown or unseen. It is characterized by discretion. Rowling carefully crafted the ways of the Wizarding world in which Harry Potter, the main protagonist of the story, suddenly found himself invited to (re-)join as a student at Hogwarts School of Witchcraft and Wizardry upon his eleventh birthday.

From the beginning of the series, this world was shrouded with intrigue for readers and for Harry, who had lived the better part of his life with his (non-magical) Muggle relatives. The meaning and significance of the magical world's various layers were revealed to readers through Harry's own discoveries and interactions with his protectors, friends and enemies in equal measure. An analysis of the secrets held about and around Harry Potter will serve the reader to better understand the significance of secrets in systemic relationships and the dynamics they create. These dynamics have parallels in and implications for contextual family therapy.

Contextual Therapy and the Ethics in Relationships

Contextual therapy combined premises from individual and family therapies, positioning itself "to reintroduce the truth of personal uniqueness into systemic therapy, and to bridge with individual therapy through relational linkages and balances" (Boszormenyi-Nagy & Krasner, 1986, p. 7). Four dimensions of "relational realities" and their intertwinement compose the contextual therapy framework: individual and family history, psychology, transactional patterns and power, and relational fairness (Boszormenyi-Nagy & Krasner, 1986; Goldenthal, 1993). Boszormenyi-Nagy and Krasner (1986) were clear that transactional patterns and relational responsibilities could be significant at different levels, for example, from person to person or across generations, influencing how "specific *consequences* evolve and, in their flow from one life to another, impinge on the futures of people who are still unborn" (p. 8, italics in original). With these tenets in mind, Harry

Potter's story clearly illustrates how his birthright as a wizard and the protections provided by his parents' deaths (individual and family history), his capacity to belong, to love, and to help others (psychology and relational fairness), and the transactions that passed between generations both older and younger than he, produced relational responsibilities and consequences around Harry that evolved throughout his life and touched future generations in the Wizarding world in meaningful ways by the end of the saga.

The contextual approach, which is more empirical than theoretical, is employed in family therapy to help people act based on the fair consideration of others' needs (Goldenthal, 1993). In contextual therapy terms, by way of his suffering at the death of his parents and his treatment by the Dursleys, Professor Snape, and Minister of Magic Cornelius Fudge, Harry had earned an "ethical accumulation" of entitlement (Boszormenyi-Nagy, 1993, para. 5). Accumulated entitlement can manifest constructively or destructively. Several villains in the Harry Potter series acted out of destructive entitlement motives, namely Severus Snape and Tom Riddle/Lord Voldemort. Used destructively, entitlement can harm relationships when it is wielded "against an innocent person, taking the past out on the future … [creating] a new injustice and perpetuating the cycle" (Boszormenyi-Nagy, 1993, para. 7). However, Harry's surplus of entitlement constructively galvanized what his friends referred to as his "acting the hero" (Ronald Weasley, *Goblet of Fire,* Rowling, 2000, p. 437) as part of his "saving-people thing" (Hermione Granger, *Order of the Phoenix,* Rowling, 2003, p. 646), wherein he would put himself (and sometimes others) in harm's way to help people in peril. Lucius Malfoy admitted to his sister-in-law, Bellatrix Lestrange, that "the Dark Lord understands this about him," and used Harry's "great weakness for heroics" to lure him to a fight to procure the prophecy linking Harry to Voldemort (*Order of the Phoenix,* Rowling, 2003, p. 690), a fight in which members of the Order of the Phoenix, indeed, died. By and large, though, Harry benefitted from earning this constructive entitlement, experiencing a sense of justice and merit in giving to others, and others, like Dobby the house-elf, Peter Pettigrew and Fleur Delacour, often felt indebted to him in return for his honorable actions toward them or their family members (e.g., Goldenthal, 1993).

Notwithstanding all the obstacles and the brushes with others' and his own death he faced throughout the story, Harry's presence, attitude and capacity to thrive provoked the jealousy of some of his classmates (friend and foe) and the ire and vengeance of several of the series' villains, notably Professor Severus Snape, Slytherin classmate Draco Malfoy, and the Dark Lord Voldemort himself. Many truths about the interconnectedness of the characters were cloaked in secrets that rendered their significance invisible throughout large passages of the story. Upon learning these truths, the reader could develop greater understanding for some of the characters' motives, despite their monstrous past behaviors.

The "relational linkages and [im]balances" (Boszormenyi-Nagy & Krasner, 1986, p. 7) that are interwoven throughout the Harry Potter series give great importance and meaning to the keeping of secrets and their influence on relationships, the consequences of which are interesting to consider for the milieu of contextual family therapy. A therapist can adopt a posture of multidirected partiality, holding himself or herself accountable to all who may be affected by his or her interventions, whether they are physically present or not, sequentially "siding *with* (and eventually *against*)" every member of a family (Boszormenyi-Nagy & Krasner, 1986, p. 419, italics in original) and focusing on the humanity of each client, even the family's "monster member" (p. 418). In so doing, empathy and credit are accorded to family members when credit is merited. When a therapist cannot credit a person's current stance, because it is abusive or abhorrent towards another, for instance, then the therapist can at least recognize and "credit a person in terms of past, childhood victimization" (Boszormenyi-Nagy & Krasner, 1986, p. 419).

In the case of the three aforementioned villains, past victimization figured into Severus Snape's story somewhat prominently, Rowling's revelation of which unfolded slowly and methodically across the series; though outright victimization played a less prominent or even non-existent role for Draco Malfoy and Voldemort, respectively. However, Tom Riddle's ethical accumulation in youth stemmed from also having a mother who died early in his life and being fostered in a group home. What he learned about his family of origin fueled his desire to enact revenge on others as Lord Voldemort throughout the story, including Harry Potter and Lucius Malfoy.

As Boszormenyi-Nagy and Krasner (1986) explained, employing contextual intervention implies understanding two main convictions:

> (1) That the *consequences* of one person's decision and actions can affect the lives of all the people who are significantly related to him, and (2) that *satisfactory relating* for one person is inseparable from the responsible consideration of consequences for all of the people [with] whom he or she is in significant relationship … The term "context" … convey[s] a highly specific meaning: the dynamic and ethical interconnectedness—past, present and future—that exists among people whose very being has significance for each other.
>
> (p. 8, italics in original)

The Harry Potter series is rife with examples of the interconnectedness that makes Harry's *being* significant in the lives of his protectors, friends and arch rivals in the past, present and future across the saga. Although we begin with The Boy Who Lived, himself, Rowling revealed much more about the secrets and truths of Harry's story through his interactions with his family, friends, professors and rivals throughout the main septilogy. Those relationships, and the revelation of the secrets held within them, are instructive from a contextual therapy perspective. In this vein, the following character analyses and interaction schemes may provide parallels to real dynamics that clients present in counseling.

Harry Potter: The Boy Who Lived (Through Multiple Traumas)

Harry Potter's parents, James and Lily, were members of the Order of the Phoenix, a group of witches and wizards who fought against the Dark Lord Voldemort's injustices and his Death-Eater minions' crimes to try to restore peace and order to the magical world. They each died protecting Harry from Lord Voldemort's killing curse, the only time in known magical history that such a curse marked someone (Dumbledore, *Half-Blood Prince*, Rowling, 2005, p. 343), leaving Harry with the characteristic lightning-shaped scar across his forehead. These events represent Harry's earliest traumas, of which he had only spotty memories as a child, but which would resurface in the form of partial flashbacks (e.g., hearing his father and mother's cries and deaths, having nightmares during his school years, and seeing the flashes of green light associated with the *Avada Kedavra* killing curse), including hearing "a high, cold, cruel laugh" (*Philosopher's Stone*, Rowling, 1997, p. 46).

The first big secret revealed in the series was that Harry Potter, a boy who could do extraordinary things without even trying, was, in fact, a wizard. Before learning about his true identity, Harry was fostered by his maternal aunt and her husband, Petunia and Vernon Dursley. They begrudgingly kept Harry upon his parents' deaths as a promise to protect him made to Albus Dumbledore, the Headmaster of Hogwarts School. As the last living blood relative to Harry's mother, who made a blood sacrifice for him, Petunia Dursley's agreement to board Harry once a year sealed the charm Dumbledore placed upon him to shield him from Voldemort's harm (*Order of the Phoenix*, Rowling, 2003, p. 737). However, the Dursleys never allowed Harry to ask questions about his wizarding relatives and maintained their lie to him that his parents were killed in a car crash, the same they said gave him the lightning-shaped scar on his forehead. In counseling, people often keep secrets for their own reasons, some of which may never be known and others for which hypotheses may be more easily drawn and employed therapeutically based on what people are willing to share.

Petunia Dursley's reasons for not sharing the secret of Harry's identity with him became more evident when Rubeus Hagrid, the Keeper of Keys at Hogwarts, informed Harry that he was a wizard on his eleventh birthday and presented him with an invitation to attend Hogwarts School. Harry questioned the Dursley's secret keeping with anger and odium. His aunt Petunia replied with her own anger and disdain. She had always known that Harry was a wizard, and had foreshadowed for the reader her own jealousy of not being a witch herself, and garnering more attention and affection from her family of origin for it, something she had been waiting to say for many years:

> *Knew!* Of course we knew! How could you not be, my dratted sister being what she was? ... I was the only one who saw her for what she was—a freak! But for my mother and father, oh no, it was Lily this and Lily that, they were proud of having a witch in the family! ... Then she met that Potter at school

and they left and got married and had you, and of course I knew you'd be just the same, just as strange, just as—as—*abnormal*—and then, if you please, she went and got herself blown up and we got landed with you!

(*Philosopher's Stone*, Rowling, 1997, p. 44; italics in original)

In this last part of her rant, Petunia Dursley also unwittingly admitted to Harry that she had kept secret the true means by which his parents had met their demise, in effect, disavowing any connection she may have had with the Wizarding world. She may have done this out of her own fear, though fear and misunderstanding of something does not make it retreat or dissolve. As Dumbledore explained to Harry, "the Dementor attack [on her son Dudley and Harry] may have awoken her to the dangers of having you as a surrogate son" (*Order of the Phoenix*, Rowling, 2003, p. 737), to which Harry largely agreed.

To assuage Harry's need for truth about his past and his parents' deaths, Hagrid told what he could to Harry, acknowledging that some parts of his story remained a mystery to everyone in the Wizarding world. Further in this exchange, Hagrid learned the secret of Harry's upbringing and the ambiance of maltreatment that surrounded him. Hagrid was the first person in the Wizarding world to know that Harry was not only devalued, but unreservedly detested by his aunt, uncle and cousin. The Dursleys, as Harry's first "protectors," his physical guardians, were not protective in nearly any sense of the term, in fact. They psychologically abused and physically neglected Harry. The Dursleys "behaved in ways that *violate[d] social norms*," employing "elements of malevolence, betrayal, injustice, and immorality" in their relationship with Harry that are characteristic of interpersonal victimization (Finkelhor, 2008, p. 23, italics in original). As an example, Vernon Dursley snarled at Harry:

Now, you listen here, boy … I accept there's something strange about you, probably nothing a good beating wouldn't have cured—and as for all this about your parents, well, they were weirdos, no denying it, and the world's better off without them in my opinion—asked for all they got, getting mixed up with these wizarding types—just what I expected, always knew they'd come to a sticky end.

(*Philosopher's Stone*, Rowling, 1997, p. 46)

Despite those harsh words, for the first time in his memory Harry experienced being defended and protected, as Hagrid rose to Vernon Dursley and continued to give Harry the details of his parents' deaths and the mystery surrounding how Harry had survived.

These raw and unfettered truths piqued Harry's curiosity about having any special or magical abilities at all. However, Hagrid helped him understand that he probably made things happen without really trying to when he was scared or angry, for example. Harry considered, "every odd thing that had ever made his aunt and uncle furious with him had happened when he, Harry, had been upset or angry ... hadn't he got his revenge, without even realising he was doing it?" (Rowling, *Philosopher's Stone*, Rowling, 1997, p. 47). Afraid of Harry's potential power, the Dursleys "kept him as downtrodden as possible," determined to "squash the magic out of him" (*Prisoner of Azkaban*, Rowling, 1999, p. 8), not allowing him access to his books, his broom, or his owl, Hedwig, for his first few summers home from school.

Harry's treatment stood in stark contrast to that provided to the Dursley's son Dudley. They allowed Harry only a bedroom in the cupboard under the stairs for many years, while their son had two bedrooms, one in which to sleep and one in which to store his toys and games. For the Dursleys, "having a wizard in the family was a matter of deepest shame" (*Chamber of Secrets*, Rowling, 1998, p. 9). Upon leaving Harry with them, Dumbledore admitted, "I knew I was condemning you to ten dark and difficult years ... to keep you alive" (*Order of the Phoenix*, Rowling, 2003, p. 736). "You arrived at Hogwarts neither as happy nor as well-nourished as I would have liked, perhaps, yet alive and healthy. You were not a pampered little prince, but as normal a boy as I could have hoped under the circumstances" (Dumbledore, *Order of the Phoenix*, Rowling, 2003, p. 737).

In addition to the sudden and horrific losses Harry experienced in his parents' deaths and in his place in the Wizarding world, he also faced ongoing developmental trauma and formed an insecure attachment to the Dursleys. This pattern of repeated childhood trauma and the development of an insecure attachment to one's caregivers renders relying on others and self-regulating one's emotions difficult, in addition to provoking excessive anxiety and the deep desire to be taken care of (van der Kolk, 2005), all of which Harry manifested at different times and in different ways throughout the saga. "What he really wanted (and it felt almost shameful to admit it to himself) was someone like—someone like a *parent*: an adult wizard whose advice he could ask without feeling stupid, someone who cared about him" (*Goblet of Fire*, Rowling, 2000 p. 25, italics in original).

Like other childhood maltreatment victims, Harry was susceptible to other forms of victimization, from interpersonal to institutional, that likely affected the externalizing problems he presented (Finkelhor, Ormrod, & Turner, 2007a, 2007b; Horn, Roos, Beauchamp, Flannery, & Fisher, 2018). Although some of his enemies unerringly perceived Harry's air of entitlement, they misjudged its origins, attributing his attitude to his (undesired) fame and to the attention that being The Boy Who Lived or The Chosen One garnered. For example, Professor Severus Snape often humiliated him in front of his classmates, placing emphasis on his "celebrity" status: "Potter has to keep up with his press cuttings" (*Goblet of Fire*, Rowling, 2000, p. 446). Professor Snape also privately chastised Harry. Rowling revealed the depth of Snape's loathing for him in this typical exchange:

> Snape followed, sat down at his desk and watched Harry unload his cauldron. Determined not to look at Snape, Harry resumed the mashing of his scarab beetles, imagining each one to have Snape's face. "All this press attention seems

to have inflated your already overlarge head, Potter," said Snape quietly, once the rest of the class had settled down again. Harry didn't answer. He knew Snape was trying to provoke him; he had done this before … "You might be laboring under the delusion that the entire Wizarding world is impressed with you," Snape went on, so quietly that no one else could hear him … "but I don't care how many times your picture appears in the papers. To me, Potter, you are nothing but a nasty little boy who considers rules to be beneath him."
(*Goblet of Fire*, Rowling, 2000, p. 447)

As hurtful and vexing as Professor Snape's treatment was, Snape seized on what he perceived was Harry's arrogance, rather than attacking his personal credibility outright. However, when Harry told the truth far and wide about Voldemort's second rise to power, Minister of Magic Cornelius Fudge institutionally disreputed Harry through the public newspaper, casting doubt on his veracity and credibility, and adding a systemic layer of bullying to Harry's unwanted fame.

They're writing about you as though you're this deluded, attention-seeking person who thinks he's a great tragic hero or something … They keep slipping in snide comments about you. If some far-fetched story appears, they say something like, "A tale worthy of Harry Potter," and if anyone has a funny accident or anything, it's "Let's hope he hasn't got a scar on his forehead or we'll be asked to worship him next" … They're trying to turn you into someone nobody will believe. Fudge is behind it, I'll bet anything.
(Hermione Granger, *Order of the Phoenix*, Rowling, 2003, p. 71)

Harry's spluttered response clearly positioned him as the censored victim in this example of institutional oppression: "I didn't ask—I didn't—*Voldemort killed my parents!* … I got famous because he murdered my family but couldn't kill me! Who wants to be famous for that? Don't they think I'd rather it'd never—" (*Order of the Phoenix*, Rowling, 2003, p. 71, italics in original). From all these instances of felt discrimination, Harry legitimately *earned* a sense of entitlement from a contextual point of view. Each of his main rivals are considered below to illustrate the dynamics of Harry's relationships with them in the order in which he met them across the saga.

Ambition and Jealousy: Draco Malfoy's Achilles' Heels

After their first Head of House, Salazar Slytherin, who was "shrewd," "power-hungry," and "loved those of great ambition" (The Sorting Hat, *Goblet of Fire*, Rowling, 2000, p. 157), true Slytherins would "use any means to achieve their ends" (The Sorting Hat, *Philosopher's Stone*, Rowling, 1997, p. 90). Draco Malfoy, born to a rich, powerful and pure-blooded family, offered his friendship to Harry Potter on their first voyage on the Hogwarts Express, the train that took them from Platform 9¾ at King's Cross Station in London directly to the school. This often-overlooked fact highlighted Draco's first instinct to pursue ambition and attempt to garner favor with Harry.

In fact, the Malfoys, like many other Death-Eater families, believed the "many stories circulating about [Harry Potter], rumors that he himself was a great Dark wizard, which is how he survived the Dark Lord's attack" (Severus Snape, *Half-Blood Prince*, Rowling, 2005, pp. 35–36). They did not want to be on the wrong side of a powerful wizard, believing that "Potter might be a standard around which [the Dark Lord's followers] could all rally once more" (Severus Snape, *Half-Blood Prince*, Rowling, 2005, p. 36).

The fame and recognition that Harry received for being The Boy Who Lived, coupled with his rejection of Draco's ideals and offered friendship, galvanized Draco's jealousy of and stoked his malevolence toward Harry from the beginning of the series. Draco had learned to despise Muggle-born witches and wizards and looked down on all Muggles as being inferior to pure-blood wizards, telling Harry "You'll soon find out some wizarding families are much better than others, Potter. You don't want to go making friends with the wrong sort. I can help you there" (*Philosopher's Stone*, Rowling. 1997, p. 81). However, Harry's fierce loyalty to his best friends, Hermione Granger, a witch born to Muggle parents, and Ronald Weasley, a pure-blood wizard born to Muggle sympathizers, both of whom Draco found unacceptable and beneath his pure-blood status, caused rancor and rivalry to flourish between the two schoolboys.

When Harry wouldn't join Draco as his friend, Draco used his money and connections to try to beat him at anything and everything he could, from Quidditch to the annual House points competition, producing near-death conditions for them both several times across the series. Although Malfoy's attempts were often foiled by Potter and his friends, the acridity of their rivalry deepened across the saga. For example, Draco's father bought Draco's way onto the Quidditch team by offering the newest state-of-the-art brooms to all of the Slytherin House players. Draco often recruited two of his "large and thuggish cronies" (*Chamber of Secrets*, Rowling, 1998, p. 75), Vincent Crabbe and Gregory Goyle, to attempt to thwart Harry and his friends in their endeavors.

The three Slytherin classmates once stood on the Quidditch pitch dressed in tall, black hoods as Dementors, creatures that "suck the happiness out of a place" (George Weasley, *Prisoner of Azkaban*, Rowling, 1999, p. 76), playing on Harry's susceptibility to them to distract him in a match against Ravenclaw; their plan backfired when Harry cast a strong stag Patronus Charm, driving the three of them away in fright and embarrassment. In their fourth year, Draco made and distributed "Potter stinks" badges in support of the other Hogwarts entrant into the Triwizard tournament, Hufflepuff Cedric Diggory. In their fifth year, Draco punished Harry and his friends by removing points from Gryffindor House in a demerit-like way in the House competition, first as a Hogwarts Prefect, then as a member of Professor Dolores Umbridge's autocratically imposed Inquisitorial Squad. And, during the Battle of Hogwarts in their last year, when Harry captured Rowena Ravenclaw's diadem, which had been imbued with a part of Voldemort's soul, Crabbe cast a Fiendfyre spell upon them to try to impede their escape (*Deathly Hallows*, Rowling, 2007a, pp. 510–511); his use of cursed fire resulted in Crabbe's own death, and in Harry saving both Malfoy and Goyle in their escape from the Room of Requirement.

Despite Draco's defeats in facing Harry and his friends, the Malfoys instilled in Draco that anything and everything he wanted could be obtained either through money or influence. He was privileged and pampered in his well-to-do family. His mother lavished him with love and praise. His father's love was conditional, a prize to be earned, and was never fully awarded, as evidenced by his cold and detached demeanor with Draco. Lucius was a distant and controlling figure while Narcissa rarely denied her son anything he requested. Draco felt he was legitimately entitled to having the world handed to him, an attitude that he mimicked from his own father's modeling.

Lucius Malfoy exploited his riches to ingratiate himself with powerful political figures and businessmen alike, demanding obsequious subjugation and favors in return. Once arrogant, brazen and proud, his spirit was broken after losing social standing as a consequence of his repeated failures to fulfill the Dark Lord's orders. He was captured and imprisoned, first in Azkaban for crimes against the Wizarding world, and later in his own home for failing to help Voldemort achieve his objectives in capturing the lost prophecy tying the Dark Lord to Harry Potter. This lessening of himself was not something he dealt with easily.

As a prime example of his inveterate stratagem and self-import, Lucius only reluctantly gave his wand when Voldemort demanded one to use to kill Harry Potter. Once given, and after Voldemort drew his own wand for comparison, "Lucius Malfoy made an involuntary movement; for a fraction of a second, it seemed he expected to receive Voldemort's wand in exchange for his own. The gesture was not missed by Voldemort, whose eyes widened maliciously" (*Deathly Hallows*, Rowling, 2007a, pp. 14–15). Subsequently, the Dark Lord subjected Lucius to taunts, ridicule and accusations of lying in front of the other Death Eaters present in the Malfoy home, which had been usurped as their headquarters.

Voldemort questioned Lucius and his behavior, casting aspersions about the Malfoy family's loyalty to him. "Why do the Malfoys look so unhappy with their lot? Is my return, my rise to power, not the very thing they professed to desire for so many years" (Voldemort, *Deathly Hallows*, Rowling, 2007a, p. 15)? Each of them appeared too weary to address the accusation made in a soft hissing voice. Confronted with this perceived crisis of faith, Lucius's "skin appeared yellowish and waxy in the firelight and his eyes were sunken and shadowed" (*Deathly Hallows*, Rowling, 2007a, p. 14). While his wife nodded oddly and stiffly at Lucius's assertion that they did desire Voldemort's reign, Draco avoided Voldemort's gaze, "terrified to make eye contact" (*Deathly Hallows*, Rowling, 2007a, p. 15).

Narcissa began to break loyalty with and faithfulness in the Death Eaters when Draco was commanded to kill Dumbledore as punishment for Lucius's failings in the Hall of Prophecy. Through a movement Boszormenyi-Nagy and Krasner (1986) described as a revolving slate, the relational debt accrued by one person (i.e., Lucius, at Voldemort's hand) is passed on unjustly to another person (i.e., Draco), much like making someone else pay one's tab at a restaurant. Lucius Malfoy failed to obtain the prophecy that tied Voldemort to Harry Potter in the Ministry of Magic's Department of Mysteries, preventing him from ever being able to hear it for himself.

Narcissa realized that Voldemort had "chosen Draco [to kill Dumbledore] in revenge" to punish the Malfoy family, stating to Severus Snape that "it doesn't matter to [Voldemort] if Draco is killed" (Narcissa Malfoy, *Half-Blood Prince*, Rowling, 2005, p. 39). Her decision to confide in Snape and break Voldemort's trust was something that was unthinkable and almost unheard of in the Death Eaters' circle. Her sister, Bellatrix Lestrange, and Snape tried to convince Narcissa that she shouldn't break Voldemort's confidence at her and the responsibilities placed upon her family by talking about it. Revealing secrets in this way could change several relationship dynamics permanently.

This represented the first of two major signs of her break in faith and loyalty to Voldemort, both motivated by her loyalty to her own family. The second was when Voldemort performed the killing curse on Harry in the Battle of Hogwarts, and she was sent to confirm his death. She surreptitiously questioned Harry about whether Draco was still alive, then duplicitously reported Harry to be dead to Voldemort and the other Death Eaters. Beyond sparing Harry Potter from further torture, Narcissa's motive demonstrated that loyalty to her own family had become far more important to her than subscribing to her family's formerly pledged loyalty to Voldemort. She knew that by confirming Harry's death, she "would be permitted to enter Hogwarts, and find her son ... as part of the conquering army," further proof that "she no longer cared whether Voldemort won" (*Deathly Hallows*, Rowling, 2007a, p. 582).

Righteousness and Revenge: The Redemption of Severus Snape

Professor Severus Snape served as a Potions and Defense Against the Dark Arts teacher at Hogwarts for 16 years under Headmaster Albus Dumbledore before he was Headmaster of the School, himself. His marked allegiance to the Death Eaters allowed him to become a double spy, ultimately serving the interests of the Order of the Phoenix in their attempts to defeat Voldemort after the Dark Lord's second rise to power. The courage Snape displayed in acting as a double spy and his reasons for doing so were only revealed at the very end of the series, when he gave Harry his memories before taking his last breath, killed by Voldemort's snake, Nagini, on the Dark Lord's orders.

Severus Snape's nefarious persona and iniquitous treatment of Harry Potter gives the reader the distinct impression that he loathes Harry's mere presence at Hogwarts from their first meeting. His multiple attempts to have Harry expelled were a direct reaction to Snape's belief that Harry was "mediocre, arrogant as his father, a determined rule-breaker, delighted to find himself famous, attention-seeking and impertinent" (Severus Snape, *Deathly Hallows*, Rowling, 2007a,

p. 545), though "other teachers report that the boy is modest, likable and reasonably talented … an engaging child" (Dumbledore, *Deathly Hallows*, Rowling, 2007a, p. 545). The odium that Snape directed at Harry was due partially to his exasperation at Harry breaking school rules with his friends, but the rancor behind it stemmed from the fact that Harry closely physically and behaviorally resembled his father, James, with whom Snape had fought when they were schoolmates.

Through his own accumulated destructive entitlement, Severus Snape often made Harry pay the sins of his father through the revolving slate dynamic Boszormenyi-Nagy and Krasner (1986) described. In this triad, Snape accrued relational debt at James's hand from James's bullying of him and passed it on gratuitously to Harry. Although this type of debt and payment may not be secret, it may not be explicitly named, either, leaving the person who pays with the distinct feeling of injustice in the interaction. However, Professor Snape also was capable of acting responsibly on his entitlement (Goldenthal, 1993) to pay forward to Harry a life debt that he owed James Potter from their school days. In Harry's first year at Hogwarts, Professor Snape protected Harry from spells cast upon him during a Quidditch match by Professor Quirrell, who was being controlled by Voldemort at the time. Dumbledore explained Severus and James's relationship dynamic and his hypothesis about Snape's reasons for protecting Harry.

> Well, they did rather detest each other. Not unlike yourself and Mr. Malfoy. And then, your father did something Snape could never forgive … He saved his life … Funny, the way people's minds work, isn't it? Professor Snape couldn't bear being in your father's debt … I do believe he worked so hard to protect you this year because he felt that would make him and your father quits. Then he could go back to hating your father's memory in peace.
>
> (*Philosopher's Stone*, Rowling, 1997, p. 217)

At the end of the series, the reader eventually learns that Professor Snape, though filled with righteousness and revenge, could also act in ways that eventually redeemed him in Harry Potter's and the readers' eyes.

In fact, Severus Snape had acted as a double spy to stop Voldemort and the Death Eaters' plans to rule both the Wizarding and Muggle worlds by dark magic. To further this endeavor, Dumbledore trusted Snape, as a reactivated Death Eater, "to give Voldemort what appears to be valuable information while withholding the essentials" (Dumbledore, *Deathly Hallows*, Rowling, 2007a, p. 549). As a double spy, he reported Voldemort's intentions and maneuvers back to the Order of the Phoenix, where his true loyalty lay. He was so skilled in maintaining both covers, that even Harry, who knew he was part of the Order, did not know if Snape understood or was going to act on the coded warning about Voldemort's actions that Harry surreptitiously passed him in front of Professor Umbridge in his fifth year of school. However, as Dumbledore explained to Harry, Professor Snape had understood the message, had acted upon it, and had alerted members of the Order of the Phoenix to his need for help at the Ministry in the Hall of Prophecy.

However, Snape's raison d'être and the true source of the secrets he maintained to sustain his cover as a double spy, certainly to protect his own skin, served primarily to protect his unrequited love's only son, Harry Potter, from Voldemort's reprisal. Snape's ostensible hatred for Harry masked the secret pain he carried from his affection not being returned by Harry's mother, Lily. Lily and Severus entered Hogwarts as best friends, and remained so for several years thereafter, until Snape showed greater interest in the Dark Arts and surrounded himself with friends whose sense of humor was "just evil" (Lily Evans, *Deathly Hallows,* Rowling, 2007a, p. 531).

At school, James Potter and his friends often bullied Severus, and Lily often came to his defense, oblivious to the fact that Snape was also a "provocative victim" or "victim-bully," displaying both anxious and aggressive reaction patterns (Olweus, 1993, 2010) to his taunts. Researchers recently have detailed the characteristics of provocative victims that Severus Snape also displayed, notably, making a few, but not many, friends; being prone to internalizing issues, such as fear, sadness and rejection; exhibiting risk behaviors (e.g., engaging in the Dark Arts, inventing dangerous spells, such as *Sectumsempra!*); and getting into fights with others (e.g., Carvalho, Branquinho, & Gaspar de Matos, 2017; Olweus & Breivik, 2014). One particularly painful example of his bully-victim position paved the way for Severus Snape to learn a powerful lesson about how others deserve to be treated. After having been bullied by James Potter and his friends and defended by Lily Evans, Severus punctured his friendship with Lily by shouting the hurtful wizarding profanity "Mudblood" at her as an insult to her Muggle parentage. The loss of this cherished friendship likely would have driven Severus Snape further into feelings of sadness, perhaps, even into depression.

It became clear in later years that the great loss of his best friend and secret love proved to be an even greater lesson learned for Severus Snape as Headmaster of Hogwarts. From a contextual perspective, "although insight into oneself and one's relationships can be very helpful, direct action that brings relationships closer to a balance of fairness is always necessary" (Goldenthal, 1993, p. 7) to produce corrective experiences. As proof that he truly had integrated this lesson, and perhaps in homage to Lily, Snape corrected Phineas Nigellus, former Headmaster of Hogwarts and Head of Slytherin House, when he called Hermione Granger by the same slur, sharply cutting him off to say, "Do not use that word!" (*Deathly Hallows,* Rowling, 2007a, p. 553). This gesture showed a more sensitive side of Severus Snape to the saga's readers and may have partially redeemed him in their eyes for his advocacy.

Snape lived a life of shifting loyalty, based on where and by whom he felt acceptance and appreciation for his talents, like many clients who present for counseling. His friendship with Lily Evans Potter shaped his childhood, and his love for her later guided his actions in adulthood. His fascination with the Dark Arts and subsequent loyalty to Voldemort as a Death Eater characterized his young adulthood. In the years preceding his death, the hidden themes of both his lost and unrequited love for Lily Potter and his broken trust in the Dark Lord underlay his loyalty to Dumbledore. In fact, Dumbledore trusted Severus Snape because love was at the root of Snape's motives for helping him and the Order of the Phoenix. As Dumbledore explained several times to Harry throughout the saga, "You are protected, in short, by your ability to love! ... The only protection that can work against the lure of power like Voldemort's" (*Half-Blood Prince*, Rowling, 2005, p. 477).

In turn, Severus Snape's ability to love Lily Potter, even—and perhaps especially—beyond her untimely demise, is how Dumbledore knew he could place his trust in Severus Snape's actions and stock in Snape's loyalty to the Order of the Phoenix's mission to defeat Lord Voldemort. Snape protected Harry upon Dumbledore's request so that Lily Potter did not die in vain (Dumbledore, *Deathly Hallows*, Rowling, 2007a, p. 544). Then, he swore Dumbledore to secrecy as to his true motives, though Snape offered his memories to Harry to view in the Pensieve as a dying wish that he would see them and know this truth.

> Very well. Very well. But never—never tell, Dumbledore! This must be between us! Swear it! I cannot bear ... especially Potter's son ... I want your word!
>
> "My word, Severus, that I shall never reveal the best of you?" Dumbledore sighed, looking down into Snape's ferocious, anguished face. "If you insist ..."
>
> (*Deathly Hallows*, Rowling, 2007a, p. 545)

Interestingly, an often overlooked dynamic around this secrecy and the Snape-Dumbledore relationship is that Dumbledore exploited the best of Severus Snape to achieve his own goals in defeating Voldemort. As he was with Harry, Dumbledore was kind to and protective of Severus Snape, and also grateful for his loyalty and kindness in return. Dumbledore offered him safe haven in the wake of Voldemort's fall from power, and often recognized Snape's extraordinary magical abilities, expressing his gratitude after Snape contained a curse in Dumbledore's hand: "You have done very well, Severus ... I am fortunate, extremely fortunate, that I have you, Severus" (Dumbledore, *Deathly Hallows*, Rowling, 2007a, p. 546). To which, Snape affirmed his loyalty in return, "If you had only summoned me a little earlier, I might have been able to do more, buy you more time!" (*Deathly Hallows*, Rowling, 2007a, p. 546).

Part of Dumbledore's plan was to use Snape to set into motion several events to help defeat Voldemort that would allow Snape to continue to conceal his true loyalties. This plan included Severus killing Dumbledore as an act of mercy to relieve the pain his cursed hand caused, instead of allowing Draco Malfoy to do it to settle his father's accounts with the Dark Lord, as Voldemort had planned; taking over as Headmaster at Hogwarts, to ensure that all Hogwarts students would be safe once Voldemort had seized control of the school; and telling Harry what he must do in the end to deliver the final coup de grâce to Voldemort, effectively ending the Dark Lord's immortal life and reign.

As Snape discovered, Harry Potter was just as much a pawn in Dumbledore's plans as he had been. The secret message Dumbledore entrusted Professor Snape to pass to Harry after his death was that the night Voldemort tried to kill Harry as a baby, he imparted a piece of his soul within Harry. "And while that fragment of soul, unmissed by Voldemort, remains attached to and protected by Harry, Lord Voldemort cannot die" (Dumbledore, *Deathly Hallows*, Rowling, 2007a, p. 551). Dumbledore specified that Harry must die, and Voldemort must be the one to kill him. Snape communicated his shock and horror to Dumbledore, "I thought … all these years … that we were protecting him for her. For Lily … You have kept him alive so that he can die at the right moment?" (*Deathly Hallows*, Rowling, 2007a, p. 551). Snape unfurled the full breadth of Dumbledore's exploitation for readers to see, as well as the betrayal he felt in having his feelings for Lily manipulated to this end.

> I have spied for you and lied for you, put myself in mortal danger for you. Everything was supposed to be to keep Lily Potter's son safe. Now you tell me you have been raising him like a pig for slaughter.
> (*Deathly Hallows*, Rowling, 2007a, p. 551)

Severus Snape was clear with Dumbledore that he agreed to protect Harry only to honor Lily's memory, releasing a doe Patronus, the same form that hers had taken, as proof of his continued love for her, "Always" (Severus Snape, *Deathly Hallows*, Rowling, 2007a, p. 552).

Seeing Snape's memories in the Pensieve from a first-hand perspective, Harry finally understood Severus Snape's anguish from being bullied by James Potter and his friends, as well as the unrequited love he felt for Harry's mother. The dissonance Harry felt in seeing his father bullying Snape, coupled with Harry's knowledge of Professor Snape's protection of Harry at several turns, led Snape to redeem himself in Harry's eyes. Although Harry was never able to credit Severus Snape in life for the balanced restored in their relationship by revealing his secrets to Harry (e.g., Boszormenyi-Nagy & Krasner, 1986; Goldenthal, 1993), Harry named his second-born son Albus Severus Potter after the two Headmasters of Hogwarts that most influenced him, describing to his namesake that Severus Snape was "probably the bravest man I ever knew" (Harry Potter, *Deathly Hallows*, Rowling, 2007a, p. 607).

The Killing Curse and the Curse of Killing: Voldemort's Rise and Undoing

The first glimpses of Tom Riddle, later known as Lord Voldemort, show a bright and handsome boy, one who is engaging and, on the surface, a well-liked individual. Through the part of himself he imparted into his diary, Riddle appeared charming and like a good listener to both Ginny Weasley and Harry Potter, then in his second year of school. However, it was later in the series, looking back through the memories of others, that the cracks in Riddle's smooth veneer began to appear.

Tom Marvolo Riddle was the last progeny of the Gaunt family, and descendant from Salazar Slytherin, a Hogwarts founder. He was born to a Muggle father also named Tom Riddle and to a witch mother, Merope Gaunt Riddle, who enchanted the senior Riddle using a love potion. The Gaunt family was "a very ancient wizarding family noted for a vein of instability and violence that flourished through the generations due to their habit of marrying their own cousins. Lack of sense coupled with a great liking for grandeur" (Dumbledore, *Half-Blood Prince*, Rowling, 2005, pp. 200–201) left the family poor at the time of Tom's birth, with Slytherin's ring and locket being the only possessions of any worth left to their name. Merope pawned the latter of the two for money after her husband left her but before her son Tom was born. Pregnant and penniless, she left for London, and had Tom on a bitter cold and snowy New Year's Eve night; within an hour of her arrival, she named him after his father and her father, then died shortly thereafter (Mrs Cole, *Half-Blood Prince*, Rowling, 2005, p. 249).

The younger Tom's conception under the influence of a love potion, symbolic of having come from "a loveless union" and a product of coercion, rendered him incapable of understanding love or empathy, as "there can't be many more prejudicial ways to enter the world than as a result of such a union" (Rowling, 2007b, para. 89–90). As a child, he terrorized other children at the orphanage where he was born and had resided his entire life until his scholarship at Hogwarts began. Mrs Cole, the matron at the orphanage, explained to Albus Dumbledore that she thought Tom must be a bully, "but it's very hard to catch him at it. There have been incidents … nasty things" (*Half-Blood Prince*, Rowling, 2005, p. 250) that were done to both animals and other children. She shared that two children "were never quite right" after having explored a cave with Tom on a school outing, though they never explained what had happened (*Half-Blood Prince*, Rowling, 2005, p. 251).

Through Dumbledore's memories of this orphanage visit, Tom was not surprised to be told he was "special." Dumbledore revealed that Tom frequently stole from other children, keeping "trophies" of his exploits. The final and most disturbing of Dumbledore's impressions was that Tom was capable of using and already controlling his magic somewhat consciously. Riddle excitedly relayed to Dumbledore his personal discoveries, reveling in his power to control others.

> I can make things move without touching them. I can make animals do what I want them to do, without training them. I can make bad things happen to people who annoy me. I can make them hurt if I want to.
>
> (Tom Riddle, *Half-Blood Prince*, Rowling, 2005, p. 254)

Among his special abilities, "his ability to speak to serpents did not make me nearly as uneasy as his obvious instincts for cruelty, secrecy and domination" (Dumbledore, *Half-Blood Prince*, Rowling, 2005, p. 259). Once at Hogwarts,

Dumbledore, "did not take it for granted that he was trustworthy" and he "resolved to keep a close eye on [Tom]" (*Half-Blood Prince*, Rowling, 2005, p. 338).

Dumbledore described to Harry how Tom was surrounded by followers at Hogwarts who became the forerunners of and some of the first official Death Eaters he recruited thereafter, but that "Riddle undoubtedly felt no affection for any of them" (*Half-Blood Prince*, Rowling, 2005, p. 259). Dumbledore characterized their composition as "a motley collection; a mixture of the weak seeking protection, the ambitious seeking some shared glory, and the thuggish, gravitating towards a leader who could show them more refined forms of cruelty" (*Half-Blood Prince*, Rowling, 2005, p. 259). Importantly, the homogeneity of this group (i.e., being pure-blooded, a trait prized by his ancestor Salazar Slytherin; The Sorting Hat, *Order of the Phoenix*, Rowling, 2003, p. 185) was not as much a concern for Voldemort as the loyalty they professed to him. Voldemort set his plans by the faithfulness of his Death-Eater servants carrying out his every capricious demand.

Voldemort's cruelty and capacity for irascibility and revenge knew no bounds, and he shredded his soul into pieces with the atrocities he committed in the name of absolute power. By killing others, Voldemort willingly relinquished his humanity and split his soul into seven different pieces to try to thwart Death. The heinous acts he encouraged amongst his followers and executed himself changed him both physically and fundamentally. The creation and concealment of Horcruxes, or objects possessed by the removal of pieces of his soul, became Voldemort's obsession and the source of his arrogant confidence that he would never be able to be defeated again. What neither he nor the reader realized until the end of the saga was that Harry Potter was, in fact, an unintentional Horcrux that Voldemort created when he tried to kill him as a baby. Voldemort never fully appreciated or understood the power of the magic that saved Harry's life, and resented the idea that Harry thwarted his plans for power and prestige simply by continuing to exist that fateful day.

Harry's *being*, in and of itself, represented a failure to circumvent an old prophecy for Lord Voldemort: "born to those who have thrice defied him, born as the seventh month dies … the Dark Lord will mark him as his equal … and either must die at the hand of the other for neither can live while the other survives" (Sybil Trelawney, *Order of the Phoenix*, Rowling, 2003, p. 741, italics in original). In his attempt to cheat Death and achieve immortality, the Dark Lord was unable to kill Harry Potter as he had intended, both at the beginning of the story, when Harry was a baby, and at the end; all in all, Harry Potter thwarted Voldemort four full times.

Earlier in the saga, Tom Riddle had remarked that "there are strange likenesses between us, Harry Potter … Both half-bloods, orphans, raised by Muggles. Probably the only two [snake-speaking] Parselmouths to come to Hogwarts since the great Slytherin himself. We even look something alike" (*Chamber of Secrets*, Rowling, 1998, p. 233). Voldemort did not count on how differences in their souls and Harry's willingness "to greet Death as an old friend" (The Tales of

Beedle the Bard, *Deathly Hallows,* Rowling, 2007a, p. 332), like Harry's ancestor, Ignotus Peverell, had, would lead to the Dark Lord's undoing. Harry's capacity to love and to set aside his own needs, desires, and even his life for the greater good of humanity was a manifestation of constructive entitlement in its noblest form. Harry's decision to do so allowed him to face the death proffered by Voldemort with courage and the understanding that "walking into the arena with your head held high ... that there was all the difference in the world" (*Half-Blood Prince,* Rowling, 2005, p. 479).

During the Battle of Hogwarts, Harry Potter did just that: faced Voldemort and allowed him to perform the *Avada Kedavra* killing curse without defending himself. This had the secret effect of eradicating only the Horcrux that Voldemort did not know existed within Harry, and spared Harry's life. It also equipped Harry with the necessary courage and fortitude to deliver the final death blow to the Dark Lord, effectively ending his reign of terror for good.

Tom Riddle was cold, callous, capricious, friendless and incapable of love. As Lord Voldemort, he used people for his own needs and discarded them when finished with them. He was incapable of empathy or of understanding the basic fundamentals of love and belonging. He was concerned only with power and with what power could do for him. Voldemort's fear of death was his undoing, as it ultimately gave others the ability to destroy him, as knowing and exploiting anyone's fears can.

Applications in Counseling

When using metaphors drawn from the Harry Potter septilogy in counseling and contextual family therapy, it is important to note that the heroes and villains of the story were all flawed characters. "Harry is not, and never has been, a saint. Like Snape, he is flawed and mortal. Harry's faults are primarily anger and occasional arrogance" (Rowling, 2007b, para. 139–140). Although rightly considered a villain in the series, Snape partially redeemed himself through a few specific acts. Rowling (2007b) once wrote that Severus Snape could be considered a hero:

> though a very flawed hero. An anti-hero, perhaps. He is not a particularly likeable man in many ways. He remains rather cruel, a bully, riddled with bitterness and insecurity—and yet he loved, and showed loyalty in that love—and ultimately laid down his life because of it. That's pretty heroic!
>
> (para. 92–93)

Each client who presents in counseling, like each Harry Potter character, is capable of using the ethical accumulation of entitlement that every person accrues (Goldenthal, 1993) in constructive or destructive ways. What counts, and what should be emphasized in counseling, is how people use what they were given (for better or worse) in their individual and family histories and their own consideration of relational fairness in their transactions with others to restore balance in relationships in ethical ways. Actions speak louder than words, and actions are necessary for righting relational wrongs. Putting a better foot forward in the present may not heal injustices committed in the past, but it could help produce corrective experiences for relationships in the future.

Conclusions

The keeping of secrets permeates and dictates the dynamics of many people's relationships, as readers could perceive and appreciate throughout the Harry Potter saga. There are many reasons why some therapy clients remain discreet or keep secrets about their personal experiences. Notably, accruing ethical entitlement may facilitate the presentation of internalizing issues that push some people to avoid thinking about and processing the traumatic events or memories that led to this accumulation, as Harry Potter, Severus Snape and Tom Riddle all experienced. For others, this entitlement may manifest in the externalization and destructive passing of their problems from one person to another in a movement similar to the revolving slate (Boszormenyi-Nagy & Krasner, 1986) that Draco experienced at Voldemort's will and that Harry experienced at Snape's will. In systemic therapy contexts, clients' secret-keeping behavior usually serves as a means of maintaining relational equilibrium (Dale, 1981), or "not rocking the boat" in their various environments and relationships. Improving systemic functioning may decrease the need for such behavior.

However, employing multidirected partiality (Boszomenyi-Nagy & Krasner, 1986) may assuage both clients and therapists in these circumstances. From this therapeutic viewpoint, the therapist empathizes with different family members at different times, siding with them when their behavior merits recognition and against them when it does not. Dumbledore best represented this trait throughout the series, though he was a flawed hero, himself. His capacity to see—and utilize— the best in people, allowed Dumbledore to teach them to soar to great heights, as well as to delve into great depths of unyielding understanding of what it means to be and to feel fragilely human. After all, Harry Potter, Severus Snape and Tom Riddle, "the abandoned boys, had all found home" at Hogwarts under Albus Dumbledore's watchful eye and gentle guidance—"the first and best home [Harry—and, arguably, Severus and Tom] had known" (*Deathly Hallows*, Rowling, 2007a, p. 558).

Questions for Clinical Discussion

1. With which character from Harry Potter do you most identify and why?
2. How might keeping secrets affect clients' relationships?
3. How might jealousy affect clients' relationships and their interactions with significant others?
4. What are some of the dynamics that living through developmental trauma could create in relationships?

5. If one must consider a "monster member" in counseling (in the client's family or the client himself or herself), how could s/he be "credited" for past injustices or childhood victimization?
6. What kinds of actions may lead clients to have corrective experiences in their relationships?

References

Boszormenyi-Nagy, I. (1993, March). From here to eternity. *Psychology Today*. Retrieved from www.psychologytoday.com/us/articles/199303/here-eternity

Boszormenyi-Nagy, I. & Krasner, B. R. (1986). *Between give and take: A clinical guide to contextual therapy*. New York: Bruner/Mazel.

Carvalho, M., Branquinho, C., & Gaspar de Matos, M. (2017). Bullies, victims and provocative victims in context: Discriminant factors in a Portuguese adolescent sample. *European Scientific Journal, 13*, 23–36. doi:10.19044/esj.2017.v13n20p23

Dale, P. (1981). Family therapy and incomplete families. *Journal of Family Therapy, 3*, 3–19. doi:10.1046/j.1981.00542.x

Finkelhor, D. (2008). *Childhood victimization*. New York: Oxford University Press.

Finkelhor, D., Ormrod, R. K., & Turner, H. A. (2007a). Poly-victimization: A neglected component in childhood victimization. *Child Abuse and Neglect, 31*, 7–26. doi:10.1016/j.chiabu.2006.06.008

Finkelhor, D., Ormrod, R. K., & Turner, H. A. (2007b). Polyvictimization and trauma in a national longitudinal cohort. *Development and Psychopathology, 19*, 149–166. doi:10.1017/S0954579407070083

Goldenthal, P. (1993). *Contextual family therapy: Assessment and intervention procedures*. Sarasota, FL: Professional Resources Press.

Horn, S. R., Roos, L. E., Beauchamp, K. G., Flannery, J. E., & Fisher, P. A. (2018). Polyvictimization and externalizing problems in foster care children: The moderating role of executive function. *Journal of Trauma and Dissociation, 19*, 307–324. doi:10.1080/15299732.2018.1441353

Olweus, D. (1993). *Bullying at school: What we know and what we can do*. Malden, MA: Blackwell.

Olweus, D. (2010). Understanding and researching bullying: Some critical issues. In: S. R. Jimerson, S. M. Swearer, & D. L. Espelage (Eds.), *The handbook of bullying in schools: An international perspective* (pp. 9–33). New York: Routledge.

Olweus, D. & Breivik, K. (2014). Plight of victims of school bullying: The opposite of well-being. In: A. Ben-Arieh, F. Casas, I. Frønes, & J. E. Korbin (Eds.), *Handbook of child well-being: Theories, methods and policies in global perspective* (pp. 2593–2616). Dordrecht, The Netherlands: Springer. doi:10.1007/978-90-481-9063-8_100

Rowling, J. K. (1997). *Harry Potter and the Philosopher's Stone*. London: Bloomsbury.

Rowling, J. K. (1998). *Harry Potter and the Chamber of Secrets*. London: Bloomsbury.

Rowling, J. K. (1999). *Harry Potter and the Prisoner of Azkaban*. London: Bloomsbury.

Rowling, J. K. (2000). *Harry Potter and the Goblet of Fire*. London: Bloomsbury.

Rowling, J. K. (2003). *Harry Potter and the Order of the Phoenix*. London: Bloomsbury.

Rowling, J. K. (2005). *Harry Potter and the Half-Blood Prince*. London: Bloomsbury.

Rowling, J. K. (2007a). *Harry Potter and the Deathly Hallows*. London: Bloomsbury.

Rowling, J. K. (2007b, July 30). J. K. Rowling web chat transcript [Web log post]. Retrieved from www.the-leaky-cauldron.org/2007/7/30/j-k-rowling-web-chat-transcript

van der Kolk, B. A. (2005). Developmental trauma disorder: Toward a rational diagnosis for children with complex trauma histories. *Psychiatric Annals, 35,* 401–408. Retrieved from www.traumacenter.org/products/Developmental_Trauma_Disorder.pdf

PART V

Superheroes at the Intersection

And finally, we will see how superheroes and villains of diverse origins and identities come to the clinical rescue.

CHAPTER 16

Female Superheroes: Raising a New Generation of Girls and Boys

Lara Taylor Kester

By the age of 2 years most children are aware of gender roles and have already identified themselves as one of the two main categories: male or female (Murnen, Greenfield, Younger, & Boyd, 2016). With those identifications and roles comes a large amount of baggage, so to speak, about behaviors, attitudes, activities, values and interests that are expected of a member of either group. As these children grow up, the media they engage with can influence their views, either by supporting, challenging or enhancing them. For the most part, boys learn that they can be strong, powerful leaders, who are capable of anything. Girls usually find themselves with role models that take a more passive part, letting the male figure take the lead or rescue them. Female superheroes flip those roles and allow us to see that something different is possible. As clinicians, it is important for us to recognize the benefits of challenging harmful beliefs in a safe way, which engaging clients surrounding strong female characters, such as superheroes, can do.

Disempowered Women

The fairer sex. Like a girl. Wearing the pants in the relationship. All of these common phrases imply that women are weaker than, less than, and not as competent as men. That men are inherently smarter, stronger, more important and better able to handle any task that comes before them. This is an image that society has clung to for much of recorded history. Women have been seen as property that belonged to their father until it was time to marry them off for a dowry, at which time they belonged to their husband. They have been seen as fragile, incapable and unintelligent, needing to have men make decisions for them. As society has moved forward, giving women rights to vote, accepting that women can work outside the home, allowing them to own property, and giving them agency over their own lives, women are still locked out of positions of power and asked if their husbands would be okay with their decisions.

The mental health impact of being part of the disenfranchised group is extensive. Women are more likely to report lower self-esteem, as well as higher rates of depression and suicide (Collins, 2011). Eating disorders and body dysmorphia are more common, due to a focus on the importance of being thin and looking good to attract a romantic partner and look good for them. Advertisements and other depictions of women on television are typically aimed at making women look sexy, feel sexy, or turning them into submissive, sexual objects (Rubie-Davies, Liu, & Lee, 2013).

Media representation of women has increased over the years, but it still is not where it should be. Women's presence in the workforce has expanded to almost equal rates as men (1.2 to 1, males to females); however, in the media, women still only represent around 33–38% of the characters in varying media formats (Collins, 2011). Of the representation available, much of it shows women in subordinate or sexualized roles, perpetuating the stereotypes and gender roles that have been in existence since the beginning of electronic media. One genre that is starting to take hold and is pushing back against those stereotypes is that of female superheroes.

Power of Positive Representation

One of the great things about being a fan of fiction is the ability to become fully immersed in the story and ignore the surrounding world for a period of time. Fictional narratives allow us to explore novel or challenging experiences in a safe way, without fear of rejection by those around us (Shedlosky-Shoemaker, Costabile, & Arkin, 2014). When we watch superheroes such as Captain Marvel or Wonder Woman fly through the air, we imagine what it would be like. Or, more realistically, when we watch Wonder Woman stand up to all of the men around her and question their actions, motives and beliefs, we can picture ourselves or other women doing the same. The capability to look at a character's situation and make connections to your own is part of the process of identification (Krause, 2010).

Identification is the ability of an individual to apply the behaviors, feelings and characteristics of another individual onto one's own identity (Schrier, 1953). When we watch Scarlet Witch accidentally injure civilians in Captain America: Civil War, we might be moved to think about a time in which we tried to do our best, but still hurt others and were blamed for it. In that moment, we would be able to identify with Scarlet Witch and feel empathy for her situation. Characters which fans identify with can also be seen as extensions of themselves. In this way, people can safely explore difficult emotions (grief, anger or shame) or frightening events (a combat zone) from a safe distance (our couches).

Fans can then use their favorite characters' experiences to learn how to behave or not to behave in given situations or how they might feel if such situations arise. While the average person will not land in an alien invasion or the middle of a battlefield, it is likely that they will find themselves having to stand up for someone or confront someone in the wrong. This becomes even more important for women, who have historically seen themselves depicted in demure, submissive or weak roles. If all you can see around you are women who stay at home, take care of children, and yield their voices to men, it is difficult to see yourself as capable of anything other than that. Strong female characters, such as superheroes, not only break that mold, they destroy it.

When female superheroes are on our screens and in our comic books, women can more easily compare themselves to the characters. Similar appearance and experiences increase identification with characters, which makes it easier to explore our feelings about experiences those characters have. Teenage girls reported increased self-esteem and hope for their future after watching these strong, relatable characters in action (Women's Media Center, 2018). Valiant Entertainment's superhero Faith brings body positivity into comics, showing young girls that not all bodies need to be thin or muscular in order to be important. Faith is overweight, confident and ready to battle whatever comes her way.

By exhibiting various strengths and virtues, strong female superheroes, such as Wonder Woman, Supergirl, Batwoman, Captain Marvel, Scarlet Witch, Black Widow, Ms. Marvel, Shuri, Gamora, Valkyrie, and so many others, give an expanded range of possibilities of what a woman can be and do. Even 10 years ago many of those names would have been unrecognizable to most. Now they are household names with many of them on the big screen, and on our small screens at home.

Effects of Strong Female Representation on Boys

When a young girl sees Shuri from Black Panther building technology and fighting alongside her brother as an equal, or an army of Amazons standing up to men, she can imagine herself doing these same things. A boy who sees those same qualities depicted in female characters is also able to see those qualities in the women in their lives. Research has shown that poor media representation can cause lowered self and in-group opinions, and also showed that the portrayals of under-privileged groups can have an influence on how outsiders view the group (Mok and Driscoll, 1998), and that media representation can influence behavior toward and beliefs regarding other groups (Rubie-Davies, Liu, & Lee, 2013).

If the only media boys are exposed to depict women in submissive or inactive roles, they may gain the impression that women are only allowed to have those roles and should be treated in a way that leads them to act in those ways toward women (domineering, aggressive, overlooking). As stated earlier, most boys have already identified with their gender roles before preschool. Boys who are exposed to media typically geared towards girls are more likely than their peers to exhibit feminine characteristics (Coyne, Linder, Rasmussen, Nelson, & Birkbeck, 2016). In other words, they have been influenced by the media they consume. Engaging with media in which women are depicted as strong, confident, smart and brave heroes allows boys to see a world in which women are capable of having those traits. As members of the dominant group of the culture, it is important that they envision a world that is different, and one in which having strong females does not make them feel as though they are lesser.

Case Studies

While the majority of this chapter has focused on girls and how female super-heroes can improve their self-esteem and confidence, as a clinician the majority of my work has been with adolescent males. My work is behavioral based, meaning I target specific problematic behaviors and use behavioral techniques to teach clients more adaptive ways of coping with their triggers. For some background, both of the young men that will be discussed were living at a high level group home at the time I saw them, meaning that they were severely emotionally disturbed and unable to live in a foster home due to violence and aggression. These two clients in particular left an impression on me, and are some of the most interesting geeks I have come to know.

Wayne

Wayne was 13 when I started working with him. He was referred to me for his aggressive behaviors. He had been in the foster care system for several years, moving from placement to placement due to his difficulties with authority figures and a lack of anger management skills. Wayne was removed from his mother's home due to Wayne's inappropriate sexual contact with his younger brother, and his stepsister. Later it was discovered he was acting out his own molestation by his stepmother. He was diagnosed with ADHD and Mood Disorder NOS, as well as Oppositional Defiance Disorder before I began work with him.

By the time I met Wayne, he had a reputation for being a "bad kid." He was the only Caucasian boy in the group home, the rest of his peers being of African or Latin American descent. His father was from the Deep South, and as such, Wayne would make some inappropriate racial remarks toward his peers that would get him into trouble. He was very disrespectful toward staff, particularly those who were people of color and women. Most days I met with Wayne, staff would complain about the racial or sexual comments he would make, or his constant refusal to comply with their directions or program rules. His file had report after report of assault, profanity, property destruction, and inappropriate sexual contact with his male peers.

My first impression of Wayne was that of a young man who was trying to exhibit behavior that would make him look like less of a target in a group home. He was pretty large for his age, but still came off as someone of his age or younger. His peers were interested in girls, sports, music, drugs, and looking toward becoming an adult. Wayne was into music and sports much like his peers, but he also watched cartoons, played Magic: the Gathering, and read comics, which would sometimes gain him negative attention from his peers. Wayne was polite to me, insightful, and wanted to be helpful when he felt he was not being ordered around.

I did however see some of the behaviors that staff were complaining about first hand (which is not typically the case in my position). He would go on tirades using every derogatory word he could think of to describe female staff members, male staff who challenged him, and his peers. A few times he had to be talked down from assaulting staff, including female staff. For the most part he was respectful toward me, although there would be times he would say "I should slap you in the face" or some other form of that phrase, with some profanity added in. Usually he would apologize later, although I am not sure if he really understood the impact his words and actions had on others. When his peers would assault female staff or become disrespectful toward them, he would come to their defense immediately, saying that they should not treat women that way.

Once I caught him watching 50 Shades of Grey, a controversial movie that glorifies the abuse and dominance of women, as well as stalking behavior. This led to a conversation with him about his views about women. For the most part he said what he thought I wanted to hear, and told me he was just curious about what the older boys at school were talking about. It was around this time that his treatment team and I decided that while my main focus was on his aggressive outbursts and developing anger management skills, that working with him on his relationships with women might help curb some of the aggressiveness as well.

Wayne and I had a lot of common interests, which made it easy for us to build rapport. One thing we really had in common though, was our love for superhero movies and comics. We were both avid video gamers and would talk video games during most of our sessions. Sometimes it would be easier to get him to open up about what was causing him to act out when we were playing together. Something about not looking me in the face, but being able to still engage with me helped him feel less intensely and like I would judge him less.

One particular session sticks in my mind in my work with Wayne, as far as helping him gain insight into his feelings toward women. Wayne asked me if we could play DC's Injustice video game, a fighting game in which you can play many of the DC Comics' heroes and villains. Usually when we would play board or card games together, he would beat me, or cheat if he thought I would win. His self-esteem was so low that he could not handle it if I were to beat him at something he was good at. With Injustice, he could not cheat.

We played several rounds that day, and he only won once. I had been waiting for an opportunity to show him was it was like to be a good winner (since he liked to gloat), and see what his reaction to losing was. His interaction with me over the game yielded a few insights. He commented that the only time he beat me was when he played as Wonder Woman, and that I had beaten him several times as Wonder Woman. He said it was because she was the strongest, and "unbeatable!" The other take away he had was that a woman could be better than him at a video game.

We talked for a while about how he felt about not being able to win, and what it felt like to finally be able to win when he played as Wonder Woman. I commended his ability to accept his disappointment without acting out aggressively, which was a significant accomplishment for him. We also talked about why it was that Wonder Woman was so much stronger than the other characters. Eventually the conversation evolved into talking about her role in the comics, and what made her different from other heroes. His answer was that she was compassionate, but also that she knew when it was time to fight, and when it was time to talk things out. He also came to the conclusion that he could learn some things from her.

Over the course of treatment, we had many more discussions about Wonder Woman, as well as other superheroes (both male and female), as examples of how to handle (or not to handle) conflict, anger and disappointment. After we began our discussions on Wonder Woman, Wayne's derogatory talk about women began to lessen, without him having to be prompted or reminded to rephrase what he was trying to communicate. Wayne still has some very real and significant issues and reasons to distrust and feel angry toward women. His stepmother broke his trust when she abused him, and his mother broke his trust by having him removed from his home and not putting in an effort to see him after he was put in foster care. Those are issues that he will continue to struggle with for a long time. Through his interactions with Wonder Woman, and with me, he was able to see that there are other possibilities for what women can be.

Jason

Jason was 15 when I met him and 17 when I started working with him. His referral was different than what I was used to, in that his target behaviors were less about aggressive behaviors toward others, and more about his avoidance of wanting to learn independent living skills and work toward his transition out of the foster care system. He, like most of the other youth I have worked with, had a history of trauma and abuse. Jason also held resentment toward women, mostly stemming from his mother not defending him when his father would hit him. Much like Wayne, he would disrespect authority figures, but used more derogatory language toward women.

Jason's anxiety about aging out of the foster care often caused him to shut down, refusing to leave his room, or skipping class when he would go to school. Any direct attempt I made to address the concerns of the treatment team and help Jason face his future was met with his withdrawal and refusal to talk to me. One way I found to get around that was to talk to him about superheroes.

To my surprise, he disclosed that his favorite television show was the CW's Supergirl. We would start our sessions talking about the most recent episodes he had seen, and what those episodes might have brought up for him. During one particular session, he made a comment about Supergirl's sister, Alex Danvers, always trying to protect children. His comment led to a short but deep discussion about protecting children being important to him, and his feelings surrounding women and the protection of children. He was also better able to discuss his stress and self-doubt about his future after we spent time discussing characters and stories he enjoyed.

Jason often struggled with understanding and accepting the boundaries of the women around him, particularly women in authority. Sexually inappropriate jokes were something he would consistently engage in, especially with older women who held some power over him. He would often take female staff member's assertion of their boundaries as rejection and disrespect, which would lead to him acting out. When we would debrief incidents that had been reported to me, part of the conversation would usually surround how the characters of Supergirl would react to what he said, and how the situation might have gone differently. Jason continued to be disrespectful toward female authority figures after our sessions, but it began to lessen.

Personal Reflections

One of the most difficult things about working with these two young men was being a woman, and having to listen to them speak so disrespectfully about women. I suppose that was also part of what made seeing their progress especially rewarding. I was able to give them a positive relationship with a woman, and help break their perceptions even before starting work with them around female superheroes. As a more masculine presenting woman, I already broke some of the mold of what they thought about women. It may have been a little easier for them after their interactions with me to accept examples of women who were feminine, yet strong.

In particular, I had difficulty dealing with Wayne. Any time a session was rescheduled due to vacation, illness, or meeting with his treatment team, he would regress and threaten that he should slap me. Each time was like a betrayal for him, another example of a woman in his life not showing up when he needed her. Each time was a struggle to gain his trust back, but I was successful. He was able to accept that it was not his fault, or mine, but circumstances that neither of us had control over. I spent several sessions with my clinical supervisor, talking about blaming myself and him reframing it as good boundaries. Sometimes I wish I was still working with Wayne, because after the end of our work together, I've found several examples of miscommunication or unfortunate circumstance in some of the comics he enjoys, which could be helpful to him now.

Because I've known Jason for so long, we already had a relationship built, but surrounding his interactions with me and whichever client I was working with at the time. I found it difficult to shift that relationship to a more working therapeutic one. In order to do that, I had to slowly shift the amount of time we focused on similar interests, to more on him and what he felt he needed to work on. Each time we met it was a little bit less of the former, and a little more of the latter. It would have probably been an appropriate approach even without our prior relationship, due to his difficulties focusing on himself.

Jason also tested my boundaries several times when he would make sexual comments about other women who work in my office. I think at first he felt that I would be his buddy, and agree with him. When I first told him it was not appropriate and that those were people I respected and I thought he respected, he looked confused. Holding boundaries with Jason was difficult, as he was a funny young man, and I have to admit that if I were in a room with friends in a different context,

I would laugh. Being with Jason in this context, though, I had to make it clear that teasing or sexual comments about people I respect was not something I was okay with. After that, he continued, but as with his other behaviors, it lessened.

These two young men were success stories for me. Of course they are out there, still in treatment somewhere, but I was able to make a connection with each of them and observe some real improvement in being able to function outside of their group home milieu. It is always exciting for me when I am able to connect with a client over shared interests, and I believe it to be exciting for them as well. However, with these two, it did not feel like I was talking about the same subject over and over again (even though often we were working on the same issue we had talked about in previous sessions) because they were excited each time I brought up a new episode of a show, or a new comic that had come out, or the latest movie trailer release. Each event provided me with an opportunity to help them make a connection between something they loved, and the real world. If that is not the best example of client buy in, I do not know what is.

Conclusion

It can be argued that we still do not have enough representation of strong female characters for children (and adults) to look up to. In the Women's Media Center's 2018 study with the BBC, the majority of teenage boys and girls interviewed stated that there were not enough strong, relatable female characters in television and film. However, it can also be said that representation is getting better. In recent years we've seen Wonder Woman lead her own movie and begin building a franchise, as Marvel is following suit with Captain Marvel and Black Widow movies. Comics publishers are also seeing the benefits of leading female heroes, with DC putting Batwoman at the head of the Detective Comics series, traditionally led by Batman, and Marvel giving us Ms. Marvel, Ironheart, Shuri, and promoting Kitty Pryde to the leader of the X-Men.

These companies are not making these decisions out of a sense of moral obligation. They are doing it because they feel like it will help bring money in for their companies. Girls make up half of the population, and if they want to tap into that, there needs to be a focus on narratives that will appeal to them. Whatever their reasons are, the young people (and adults) that are now able to see these positive, relatable, powerful female superheroes are able to imagine a world in which women can be more than what people expect of them now. They can be leaders. They can be confident. They can be strong and compassionate at the same time. Women can have and hold boundaries which are respected. Men can be comfortable following a woman's lead. Men can work alongside women without necessarily thinking about romantic relationships. Women can save themselves.

These images open up the possibilities for us as clinicians and for our clients. These portrayals and rich narratives can help young girls improve their self-esteem, self-confidence and outlook on life. Girls are able to envision themselves in a situation other than what is causing them distress. Boys, like the two clients presented in this chapter, are able to think differently about women, what their relationships with women are like, and how they could be different. Envisioning that one's own situation could be different is the first step to change. If we can help them change, we can help give them power … or superpower.

Questions for Clinical Discussion

1. What role has media played in you forming your identity?
2. Who are your role models? What role does gender play?
3. What impact do female superheroes have on girls' perceptions of themselves and their abilities?
4. How are female superheroes perceived in comparison to male superheroes?
5. How might your client's self-perception change if introduced to female superheroes?

References

Collins, R. L. (2011). Content analysis of gender roles in media: where are we now and where should we go? *Sex Roles, 64*(3), 290–298. http://doi.org/10.1007/s11199-010-9929-5

Coyne, S. M., Linder, J. R., Rasmussen, E. E., Nelson, D. A., & Birkbeck, V. (2016). Pretty as a princess: Longitudinal effects of engagement with Disney princesses on gender stereotypes, body esteem, and prosocial behavior in children. *Child Development, 87*(6), 1909–1925. http://doi.org/10.1111/cdev.12569

Krause, R. (2010). An update on primary identification, introjection, and empathy. *International Forum on Psychoanalysis,* 19, 138–143.

Mok, T. A. & Driscoll, D. (1998). Getting the message: Media images and stereotypes and their effect on Asian Americans. *Cultural Diversity and Mental Health, 4*(3), 185–202.

Murnen, S. K., Greenfield, C., Younger, A., & Boyd, H. (2016). Boys act and girls appear: A content analysis of gender stereotypes associated with characters in children's popular culture. *Sex Roles, 74*(1–2), 78–91. http://doi.org/10.1007/s11199-015-0558-x

Rubie-Davies, C. M., Liu, S., & Lee, K. C. K. (2013). Watching each other: Portrayals of gender and ethnicity in television advertisements. *Journal of Social Psychology, 153*(2), 175–195. http://doi.org/10.1080/00224545.2012.717974

Schrier, H. (1953). The significance of identification in therapy. *American Journal of Orthopsychiatry, 23*(3), 585–604.

Shedlosky-Shoemaker, R., Costabile, K. A., & Arkin, R. M. (2014). Self-expansion through fictional characters. *Self and Identity, 13*(5), 556–578.

Women's Media Center (October 2018). Superpowering girls: Female representation in the sci-fi/superhero genre. *Women's Media Center.* Retrieved from www.womensmediacenter.com/reports/bbca-wmc-superpowering-girls

CHAPTER 17

Beyond Canon: Therapeutic Fanfiction and the Queer Hero's Journey

Larisa A. Garski and Justine Mastin

"Really? I'm a hero?" In our current age of storytelling where superheroes and villains seem to be storming off the comic book page and into the cineplexes every other month, the modern viewer regularly witnesses the trials of their favorite heroes writ large across the silver screen. When not watching or reading the exploits of their fandom heroes, fans can write about them on blog posts—changing those parts with which they disagree, adding dramatic interludes they felt were missing, imagining themselves within the story—and with the click of a button sharing these fanfiction adaptations with the world—or at least with the internet. But how do we bring the hero off the screen and into the therapeutic space, thereby enabling our clients to see the truth that is obfuscated by many of our modern myths—that the real hero lies within?

While fanfiction and the hero's journey may initially feel like disparate concepts for clinical work, this chapter will lay out the ways in which these concepts are not only congruous but incredibly healing in a therapeutic setting. The narrative therapy techniques of externalization and reauthoring narratives are powerful tools for both working with and enriching the lives of queer clients (Steelman, 2016). Though the hero's journey wasn't written for them, queer clients can re-author their lives to be the hero that they deserve by using key concepts of narrative therapy.

Enter the Queerdom

In our experience working with clients who identify as being in the LGBTQIA+ community, the term "queer" is being reclaimed as the preferred nomenclature with which to self-identify. In this chapter we continue to follow this practice, using the word "queer" instead of repeating LGBTQIA+. This is not done to diminish or exclude any individual identity or to take away from anyone's autonomy to identify, but rather to take a stance of "resistance to fixed identity categories" (Tilsen, 2013, p. xxvi).

Queer clients are still widely underserved and misunderstood (Blackmore, 2015). Those who are able to find quality care may still find resources lacking that are easily available for their heterosexual counterparts, as the societal norms in western culture are still written for a predominantly cisgender heterosexual audience (Boulware, 2017). In order to see themselves in the media that they consume, queer people harnessed the power of writing fanfiction to place their own experiences into the stories that they loved (Willis, 2006). What many of these fanfiction writers do not realize is that the use of this skill can transfer into the real world; the stories in real life that do not serve them can be rewritten (Kannengieber & Kubitschko, 2017).

Mapping the Story

"Narrative therapy" is a psychotherapeutic practice created by Michael White and David Epston (1990). Founded on the Foucauldian concept of social constructionism and feminist theory's critique of heteronormative cultural hierarchies, narrative therapy is a postmodern therapy with an emphasis on bringing social justice work into the therapeutic space (Chavez-Korell & Johnson, 2010). It empowers clients by putting them at the center of their own personal story. Utilizing a number of techniques, chief among them externalization and re-authoring, narrative therapists help their clients break free of problem saturated mainstream narratives to create an expanded story that recognizes the unique gifts and attributes of the client (White, 2007).

"Externalizing the problem" places the source of distress outside of the client themselves. In sum, the person is not the problem, the problem is the problem (White, 2007). This allows the person to look at the problem with more objectivity and feel as though they have increased control. While there are as many ways to externalize problems as there are clients who are struggling with them—co-creator of narrative therapy Michael White was partial to maps. In this chapter, we explore the use of hero narratives as tools for externalization (White, 2007). When a client and therapist co-create language using heroes, it offers the opportunity to speak of the problem not just in external terms but in a manner that harnesses the power of the monomyth and moves the client into the role of hero.

"Re-authoring" is another powerful technique in narrative therapy and the cornerstone of this therapeutic approach. It combines other ancillary skills such as unique outcomes—events challenging the status quo of the problem saturated story—and re-membering—helping clients to reorganize or change the members of their identity support team—with externalizing to help clients craft new identities that allow for both growth and change (White, 2007). Clients often come to psychotherapy with a limited view of themselves and their place in the world. Re-authoring helps clients break free from these limiting paradigms, enabling them to expand both their perception of themselves and the environment in which they live (Elderton et al., 2013).

Narrative therapy acknowledges the power that story plays in both societal and individual growth, echoing the work done by psychoanalyst Carl Jung (1963) on both the collective unconscious and archetypes as well as the work of mythologist Joseph Campbell into the monomyth or "the hero's journey" (Campbell, 1949/2008). In this chapter, "the hero's journey" or "monomyth" are used interchangeably in reference to the coming-of-age or coming-to-identity story that is found in all cultures (Blackmore, 2015). Though the monomyth contains the same raw architecture—an unknown hero leaves their ordinary life to descend into the supernatural world to return both gifted and changed—it is inherently malleable. This enables both client and therapist to use the basic architecture of the monomyth to tell the story of the client's own hero's journey. In previous centuries, the tropes, characters and symbols that individuals used as inspiration for crafting their own story came from the myths and legends of their age (Campbell, 1949/2008). But as Campbell observed, the mythologies of ancient times no longer speak to the modern human experience (Campbell, 1988).

Modern Mythologies

Enter the modern mythology of fanfiction. "Fanfiction" refers to creating one's own stories based on beloved characters from pop culture (Yin et al., 2017). Fanfiction writers fix stories that they believe the authors got wrong, making character choices that they believe are more in line with what they feel to be the character's genuine motivations (Boulware, 2017). It is also a common practice for fanfic writers to insert themselves, or an idealized projection of themselves, into their stories (Coppa, 2017). We argue that through the reading and creation of fanfiction, these alternate narratives can be taken out of the realm of pop culture and placed squarely in the real world. If a writer can create *Supernatural* fanfiction—in which Dean Winchester embraces his sub-textual bisexuality and is still loved by his brother—then can they not also write a real world where they are open about their own bisexuality and still accepted by their family (Boulware, 2017)?

While there are a number of reasons why a person might choose to write fanfiction, the reason that many fanfiction writers will cite is that they write in order to fix what the canon is missing or to fix what has happened in canon (Lee, 2011). While fanfiction has gotten bad press for many years, the reality is that fanfiction, just like the monomyth, is ancient (Yin et al., 2017). Human beings have been telling and retelling stories, adding in what we like best and omitting what does not serve us since the time of Virgil (who riffed off Homer) and Shakespeare (who riffed off everyone). Fanfiction can be both oral or written, as any attendee of a comic convention can attest. It is common to see groups of fans huddled together sharing stories from their own fanfiction universe or headcanon with one another. The community aspect is a vital part of the fanfiction experience and bears strong resemblance to the co-construction of reality experienced between client and narrative therapist as they begin to re-author a client's story.

Fanfiction enables client and therapist to rewrite the hero's journey using narrative techniques.

Fandom Attachment Heals

Fanfiction speaks directly to the concept of "fandom attachment," a term that we use to describe the relationship between individual fans and pop culture characters. Fandom attachment describes the real emotional connections that a fan develops over time with beloved fandom characters who they experience via reading, watching, listening and/or imaginative world building (Cole & Leets, 1999). Historically, the terms "parasocial relationship" and "parasocial interaction" have been used interchangeably to describe this phenomenon (Horton & Wohl, 1956). We have chosen to use the term fandom attachment for two reasons. First, this term is more in line with the way geeks, nerds and fans refer to themselves and, second, it is our hope that using this term will dispel some of the negative judgments and mischaracterizations that continue to plague this idea, which was first popularized in the 1950s.

Fandom attachments offer clients the opportunity to practice burgeoning social skills in an environment where there is less risk of social rejection and emotional misunderstanding. Within the therapeutic context, fandom attachment can be discussed, normalized and expanded to help clients gain new insight into their past and build hope for the future. Narrative therapy is in many ways the ideal space for this kind of work where concepts such as externalizing the problem, re-membering the client's social groups, and re-writing identity provide psychotherapists with the tools they need to use both fandom attachment and fanfiction in a clinical context. "Fanfiction reminds us that storytelling isn't a professional activity, but a human one in which publishability is rarely the point" (Coppa, 2017).

A Unified Field Theory of Geek Narrative Therapy

Using fanfiction to both rewrite and remake the monomyth is where the therapeutic work begins. In order to equip clients with the language of modern myths, we display fandom art and introduce fandom-based symbols and analogies into the therapeutic space. Once clients understand that play is welcome, they eagerly engage in meaning-making activities first via fandom avatars and then via their own experiences, re-casting themselves into their own personal hero's journey. By de-gendering the monomyth, we allow our clients to expand this cycle, challenging such heteronormative stereotypes as "growing up means getting monogamously partnered" or "being successful means sacrificing fun."

The tools and skills inherent to queer clients—to read subtext in order to see themselves represented—provides therapists with a unique opportunity to use this process of fanfiction to guide the re-processing and re-writing of painful internal narratives. As we have discussed, fanfiction is the art of transforming an existing work in some way, using an existing universe and/or characters to tell a different story or the same story in a new way (Yin et al, 2017). Since fanfiction is most often character-driven; getting inside the head of a character and asking "what if," we are able to do the same with our clients—to focus on one character, namely, themselves. For many clients, seeing themselves as the hero feels unfamiliar and here is where fandom attachment can be uniquely helpful. Clients can use their emotional connection with fandom characters to create therapeutic fandom avatars and craft a fanfiction story that mirrors their own lives. With therapeutic support, they can begin to see their own heroism from the perspective of these beloved characters.

Case Study: Heroic Self-Acceptance

While canonical fandom is slowly embracing more diverse storytelling with such character iterations as an African-American Spider-Man a.k.a. Miles Morales, Muslim Ms. Marvel, bisexual Wonder Woman and pansexual Deadpool, it still has much work to do when it comes to diversifying and expanding its representations. This is where fanfiction and a client's personal headcanon are key. As our case study makes apparent, a character need not be a canonical match for a client to engage them as an avatar on their queer hero's journey.

The following case study is an amalgam of several clients with whom we have worked over the years. Key information has been changed to protect the identity of these clients. All of the clients were either adults or emerging adults and each of them struggled with anxiety at least partially related to complicated feelings related to their sexuality, gender identity and biological gender.

At the time of treatment, Cas was a 25-year-old gender non-binary individual (biological gender female) of Ashkenazi Jewish descent. Cas used they/them pronouns and referred to themselves as queer, explaining that they were "technically bisexual" but preferred the term "queer." Cas presented for treatment initially due to low frustration tolerance often leading to outbursts of anger toward friends, chosen family, and their romantic partners. They expressed growing concern that such angry outbursts would bleed into their professional life: "It hasn't happened yet, but I'm starting to feel like a ticking time bomb." During the intake session, Cas showed symptoms of both ruminating and obsessive thoughts centered around fears of being "queer enough" and "good enough," as well as parental enmeshment with both mother and father. They also reported sleep disturbances—intermittent insomnia—that had lasted for approximately five months.

Midway through the first session with Cas, they verbally noted our *Adventure Time* BMO tea mug, commenting that they had never seen a tea mug that was "quite so square." We took this as an invitation to begin therapeutic fanfiction early in our work. We shared that BMO, the gender nonbinary robot and video game console, was one of our favorite characters in *Adventure Time* and asked Cas if they, too, enjoyed this cartoon? Cas eagerly explained that they loved this cartoon show and that BMO, in particular, resonated with them because BMO is on a journey to be "both a little living boy and girl who drinks tea." This is an excellent example of the ways that fandom art and figurines can be used to not only initiate conversation but to deepen the therapeutic bond quickly. We noted that after this fandom disclosure, Cas' posture relaxed, they made eye contact more frequently, and they began using hand gestures and vocal modulations when speaking.

During our second session with Cas, we introduced the concept of the genogram—a modified version of the family tree diagram that helps clinicians and clients articulate and understand family dynamics in a visual form (Brown, 1999). Cas was eager to engage in this activity, asking us for the sketch pad and pencil once we had explained the general topic. Cas drew a genogram that included themselves, their parents, and only one set of (maternal) grandparents, explaining that their paternal grandparents died shortly after the end of World War II, long before they were born. Cas explained that during childhood and early adolescence, they were very close to their parents. Cas was an active member of their temple and underwent the traditional rite of passage of Bat Mitzvah to become an adult member of the faith. Cas attempted to be as female-presenting as possible in order to be close to their mother, though even at the time, they did not feel as though this gender identity was authentic. The two bonded particularly during Cas' preparation for Bat Mitzvah. As this event approached, Cas shared that they struggled more with anger. "My dad said it was just nerves but my mother was worried about what it meant. I don't think I was really that angry." Once the genogram was fully rendered, we engaged Cas in a narrative discussion exploring the roles, values and rules in their family of origin. It became clear that Cas had struggled with mild-moderate "angry outbursts" since approximately 6 years of age and that they actively worked to hide their anger from the age of 13 onward. Though their outbursts seemed developmentally appropriate, it was evident that recalling their history with anger caused them both shame and pain. As the second session drew to a close, Cas shared that they felt less angry after coming out and moving to a large midwestern city for college: "Away from my parents, I guess I just felt able to be me ... or maybe just a different kind of me. Whatever it was, it felt better. And easier." They expressed sadness and regret that anger was resurfacing for them. They felt sure that leaving home was the answer to all of their problems and expressed frustration that this was not, in fact, the case.

Upon meeting with Cas for our third session, we fully introduced the narrative tool of externalizing the problem via everyone's favorite green superhero, The Incredible Hulk. This conversation was again initiated by Cas who remarked on the SuperEmoFriends (Salvador, 2016) Hulk painting displayed on the wall: "Ha! That's really true: mad does make sad." We engaged Cas in a narrative therapy discussion around Bruce Banner (a.k.a. The Incredible Hulk), explaining to Cas that just as Bruce was not The Hulk, they, i.e., Cas, were not their anger. We explained that understanding themselves as both connected to, but distinctly different from, their anger might help them start to understand anger's presence and reason for being in their lives. We then used the language of The Hulk comics to process Cas' recent angry outburst with them. In subsequent sessions, we used the increased insight that Cas was gaining around both anger and the events that trigger anger to help them create a fanfiction action plan using Bruce Banner/The Hulk as a stand-in for Cas. As part of this work, Cas was to pay mindful attention to their mood state and when they noticed that they were beginning to feel angry, to place themselves into an *Avengers* fanfiction story in the role of Bruce Banner. They were to imagine that the team was working on a case and to ask themselves who was needed most; Bruce Banner or The Hulk, playing out both scenarios to determine who would be best equipped to resolve the situation at hand. If the answer was The Hulk, then they were to give themselves permission to feel anger without shame. If the answer was Bruce, then Cas was to engage in deep breathing and call upon their inner Black Widow to say soothing words to calm the inner Hulk. This was effective not only because this type of verbal play added a feeling of fun and whimsy to therapy, it also helped Cas maintain enough distance from anger so that shame was not triggered.

In the following session, we went over the hero's journey structure and asked where Cas felt they were at this time. Cas said they felt as though they had just crossed the threshold, meaning they were beginning their descent into the unknown. Over the next three months of weekly sessions, Cas was able to continue the use of therapeutic fanfiction to both develop and implement strategies to de-escalate feelings of anger and to increase their frustration tolerance. They gained renewed insight into the heart of their anger, explaining in one particularly moving session: "I'm angry because the world wasn't built for people like me. I don't fit into a [gender or sexuality] box and it's exhausting to have to explain myself and my pronouns and my-my *thing* to everyone I come into contact with." As sessions progressed, they brought in fandom themes that felt particularly resonate for them. Inspired by their use of The Hulk narratives, Cas re-watched *The Avengers* film in which Bruce Banner explains that he is "angry all the time." Cas expressed the insight that they, too, could radically accept anger's presence rather than trying to shove it down or away: "I think trying to ignore it was part of what made the Hulk come out."

As our sessions neared the halfway mark, Cas exhibited an increase in anxiety symptoms including sleep disturbances. Bruce Banner/The Hulk fanfiction became less helpful during this period as Cas explored in session their feelings of sadness and worry connected to their family of origin. We explored with Cas again where they felt they were on the hero's journey. Cas said that they felt as though they were in the abyss. We reflected that the abyss feels like a terrible place to be, but that it shows how far Cas had come and once they are able to cross the abyss there would be a metaphorical re-birth. Cas found this notion hopeful, reflecting on other times when they had found themselves in the abyss and been able to move through it and "get out on the other side." As we reflected to Cas the heroic nature of this journey, they referenced the *Legend of Zelda* video game series, likening their current journey to that of Link. Like Link, they fought many battles, each time leveling up and "becoming stronger in the end." During this session, Cas expressed the desire to tell their new chosen family more about themselves and their past experiences: "I'd like them to know more about who I was back then … but I've changed so much. Nobody wants to hear about how girlie I was." We validated these fears, while offering the reframe that the act of sharing the hero's journey is often the penultimate step to completing the cycle of growth. By sharing the story of our journey, we give our trusted friends and family the opportunity to see ourselves as truly heroic. Cas responded by asking: "Really? I'm a hero?"

The idea that their chosen family might see the story of their identity transformation as heroic rather than pathetic marked a turning point for Cas' treatment. In subsequent sessions, they recommitted to regular self-care and began to make progress in not only identifying trusted community supports but in reaching out to them for help in times of stress. Though they continued to keep their family of origin at a physical distance, their negative feelings toward them began to decrease in both intensity and frequency. As they expressed near the end of treatment: "My friends accept me for who I am. And so do I. It will always hurt that my family doesn't but it's just not as important to me anymore." By using therapeutic fanfiction, Cas was able to successfully rewrite their hero's journey of coming out into one of coming into self-acceptance.

Personal Reflections

In our professional and personal lives, fandoms have been integral to the ways that we both understand and engage with change. My (JM) early fandom attachment to *Twin Peaks*' Special Agent Dale Cooper helped me to view my own strangeness as something wonderful—a potential source of community rather than alienation. For me (LG), growing up in a small town meant being surrounded by football and little else. My connection to both fanfiction and fandom helped me to believe in a future in which supportive community IRL could be possible. Within a clinical context, we have found the power of story and fandom to be crucial tools for sustainable change. As meaning-making creatures, human beings are both defined by and understood through the stories they tell. If clients can find the tools to rewrite their own personal stories—the internal monologue that narrates our internal daily existence—then they unlock the power of internal change.

Conclusion

We hope that this chapter shed light on the ways that fanfiction and the hero's journey can be used therapeutically with queer clients. We invite future clinicians considering using these techniques to keep the following in mind: allow the stories to develop organically. Using both visual aids—such as fandom art, action figures and fandom-inspired mindful coloring books—and therapeutic fandom disclosure, the psychotherapist both invites the client to share their own resonant fandoms as well as creating a safe space for therapeutic fanfiction to take shape. We can introduce a character which we think will resonate, but therapy will be more successful if the client introduces the fandom from which we can then draw. As clinicians, it is our job to meet the client where they are at, which includes not forcing an ill-fitting story upon them. In a similar vein, it is vital to engage the client in processing where they feel they are on the hero's journey. We may have an idea of where we believe they are, but, again, their feeling is going to be more meaningful and resonant. These dialogues allow the clinician to get curious with the client about what might help them move from where they are on their journey into the next phase. This opens the door for the opportunity to re-write narratives or apply fanfiction and question the narrative in which they are currently residing. Because of the marginalization of the queer community these conversations are all the more important, as there are fewer pop culture narratives made specifically for this population.

Questions for Clinical Discussion

These questions are meant as both prompts and invitations for further clinical discussion. They are not directives, how to's, or value judgments.

1. What might be the benefit of displaying popular fandom paraphernalia—figurines, action figures, plushies, posters, paintings etc.—that is either personal to you or potentially personal to your client demographic in your office?
2. How do you encourage clients to bring their fandom attachments into the therapeutic space?
3. What fandoms and narratives have helped you rewrite your story to create your personal journey of growth and development?
4. How might you use this knowledge to create space for a similar act of fanfiction by your client?
5. What might be behavioral indicators or paraverbal signs that the client is using fanfiction to distance rather than integrate painful experiences either past or present?
6. When is therapeutic fanfiction contraindicated in treatment with a client?

References

Blackmore, C. K. O. (2015). Queer archetypal lifespan development theory and the new myth: Re-visioning the hero's journey through the practice of terrapsychological inquiry. *The Journal of the International Association of Transdisciplinary Psychology*, 4(1), 1–13.

Boulware, T. (2017). *Fascination/frustration: Slash fandom, genre, and queer uptake* (unpublished doctoral dissertation). Seattle, WA: University of Washington.

Brown, J. (1999). Bowen family systems theory and practice: Illustration and critique. *Australian & New Zealand Journal of Family Therapy*, 20(2), 94–103.

Campbell, J. (1949/2008). *The hero with a thousand faces* (3rd edn.). Novato, CA: New World Library.

Campbell, J. (Writer) & Moyers, B. (Director) (June 21–26, 1988). The power of myth [Television series]. In: C. Tatge (Producer). Arlington, VA: Public Broadcasting Service.

Chavez-Korell, S. & Johnson, L. T. (2010). Informing counselor training and competent counseling services through transgender narratives and the transgender community. *Journal of LGBT Issues in Counseling, 4*, 202–213.

Cole, T. & Leets, L. (1999). Attachment styles and intimate television viewing: Insecurely forming relationships in a parasocial way. *Journal of Social and Personal Relationships, 16*(4), 495–511.

Coppa, F. (2017). *The fanfiction reader: Folktales for a digital age.* Ann Arbor, MI: University of Michigan Press.

Elderton, A., Clarke, S., Jones, C., & Stacey, J. (2013). Telling our story: A narrative therapy approach to helping lesbian, gay, bisexual and transgender people with a learning disability identify and strengthen positive self-identity stories *British Journal of Learning Disabilities, 42*, 301–307.

Horton, D. & Wohl, R. R. (1956). Mass communication and para-social interaction. *Psychiatry, 19*, 215–299.

Jung, C. G. (1963). *Memories, dreams, and reflections.* A. Jaffe (Ed.). (C. Winston & R. Winston, Trans.), New York: Random House.

Kannengieber, S. & Kubitschko, S. (2017). Acting on media: Influencing, shaping, and (rupee) configuring the fabric of everyday life. *Media & Communication, 5*(3), 1–4.

Lee, A. (2011). Time travelling with fanfic writers: Understanding fan culture through repeated online interviews. *Journal of Audience & Reception Studies,* 8(1), 246–269.

Salvador, J. (2016). *SuperEmo Hulk* [paint on canvas], private collection], Chicago, IL.

Steelman, S. M. (2016). Externalizing identities: An integration of narrative therapy and queer theory. *The Journal of Family Psychotherapy, 27*(1), 79–84.

Tilsen, J. (2013). *Therapeutic conversations with queer youth: Transcending homonormativity and constructing preferred identities.* Lanham: Jason Aronson.

White, M. (2007). *Maps of narrative practice.* New York: W. W. Norton & Company, Inc.

White, M. & Epston, D. (1990). *Narrative means to therapeutic ends.* New York: W. W. Norton & Company, Inc.

Willis, I. (2006). Keeping promises to queer children: Making space (for Mary Sue) at Hogwarts. In: K. Hellekson & K. Busse (Eds.), *Fanfiction and fan communities in the age of the internet: New essays* (pp. 153–170). Jefferson, NC: McFarland and Co.

Yin, K., Aragon, C., Evans, S., & Davis, K. (2017). Where no one has gone before: A meta-dataset of the world's largest fanfiction repository. *Proceedings of the ACM Conference on Human Factors in Computing Systems (CHI '17),* 6106–6110. New York: ACM Press.

CHAPTER 18

The Black Panther Lives: Marveling at the Internal Working Models of Self in Young Black Children Through Play

LaTrice L. Dowtin and Mawule A. Sevon

Introduction

The development of the self occurs in the first years of life through mirrored interpersonal experiences and the rehearsing of familiar roles during play. Since young children begin to conceptualize culture, race and gender roles during their preschool years, opportunities for meaningful play experiences become an essential aspect of childhood. For example, it is common to observe children in preschool classrooms engaging in play activities. These observations often reveal young girls cooking, cleaning and caring for baby dolls; while young boys are found engineering structures with blocks, conducting science experiments, and engaging in play fighting. While these activities assist children in developing their understanding of appropriate gender roles as determined by their culture, children of color, particularly African-American/Black children, develop their gender identity while also adding the complex layer of racial identity development. In today's technologically-based society, mass media exerts a significant influence on the development of race and gender roles. The 2018 portrayal of the Black Panther and related characters provided high-quality examples that challenge stereotypical culture, race and gender roles in Black males and females. This chapter addresses how clinicians can use play to interpret internal working models of self in the children they serve. Specifically, psychodynamically oriented play therapy (also referred to as psychoanalytic play therapy and is used interchangeably) can be used to explore how children make sense of their expected roles in society, which are based on images constructed by people outside of their communities.

An important discussion of race and terminology is unpeeled in this chapter. Therefore, we believe that it is vital that the reader start here with an understanding of how we use the terms Black and African-American within this context. Crenshaw (1988) suggested using an uppercase "B" when referring to Black people to be respectful of individuals belonging to this specific cultural group, making it a proper noun. Using a capital letter for culture is also common practice when referring to other cultural minorities such as people who identify as culturally Deaf

(Padden & Humphries, 2005). Therefore, while frequently argued in grammatical English (Tharps, 2014), *Black* and *Black American* are used throughout this chapter to respectfully and inclusively discuss Black and African-American people, except when making specific distinctions regarding Black Panther characters. As a final point, in this chapter the term Black generally includes all cultural groups of people from the African diaspora, while Black American refers more specifically to Black people with American nationality.

Psychodynamically Oriented Play Therapy

Young children gradually show growth as verbal communicators. That is because they are still developing their receptive and expressive language skills and learning that they have a wide range of emotional states (Yanof, 2013). Ideally, young children first discover that they have emotions. Then, usually with guidance from adults and older peers, they learn to label and identify the associated feelings. Eventually, the goal is for young children to be able to regulate their own emotions. Through co-regulation with their caregivers and their budding self-regulation skills, young children begin to develop empathy and form healthy social and emotional relationships with others. Between the ages of 2 and 5 years old, play becomes one of the most effective methods for young children to express themselves, explore their environment, and rehearse new identities and emotional states. However, this developmental trajectory can be stunted or completely derailed when a child experiences a traumatic event, or a trauma, "a deeply distressing or disturbing experience" ("Trauma," 2018). Child psychotherapy is helpful in alleviating stress and assisting young children process their thoughts and feelings regarding their experience. However, for preschoolers, traditional talk therapy might not provide the space for them to express their conscious or subconscious feelings adequately. Psychodynamically oriented play therapy is supportive of typically developing preschoolers who have the capacity for symbolic play.

Hermine von Hug-Hellmuth (1920) is credited with being the first to use play in the context of psychotherapy for children; however, researchers most often cite Anna Freud with the specific development and application of psychodynamic play therapy theory (Schaefer, 2011). In the seminal work of Anna Freud (1974), psychoanalytic play therapy was thought to help children unveil their innermost thoughts and feelings and understand their behaviors, which would, in turn, bring about healthy individual change. Not unlike her father, Sigmund Freud, Anna Freud's understanding of the human psyche explored internal struggles or anxieties and their defenses that develop to manage traumas and significant life events. However, Anna Freud tailored her knowledge of humans to a focus on children and child psychotherapy. It was through the lens of children that Anna Freud conceptualized play as a window into the child psyche. Thus, psychodynamically oriented play therapy began to develop.

Psychodynamically oriented play therapy allows the child a safe space to openly express and explore both inner thoughts and worldly experiences. This approach to child psychotherapy is inherent in the belief that the combination of three crit- ical situations can lead to healing: (1) the expression of life from the child's per- spective; (2) the therapist's ability to create a *holding space* for the child; and (3) the therapist's capacity to interpret and verbally frame the child's experience without judgment. Winnicott (1991), discussed the details of therapeutic holding within the context of young children without an emphasis on interpreting the child's experience. This holding space or *therapeutic hold* is figurative and refers to the way that a caregiver holds a vulnerable infant (Winnicott, 1991). The caregiver, often a mother, holds a young infant and cradles the infant protecting her from a variety of harsh happenings in the world. This space grows in complexity as mother and infant interact or play together, opening the pair's inner world and bringing it within visibility of the external world. The holding space remains safe and protected due to the mother's acceptance of the relationship. In the thera- peutic relationship, the therapist *holds* the child and protects her from bearing the weight of her psychological stress alone. The therapist remains available for the child but avoids being intrusive in the child's play (Winnicott, 1991). Through this experience, the child learns that the therapist will accept the child as a whole person regardless of what troubling situations the child may bring to sessions.

In many ways, the therapist is a mode of change when approaching cases from a psychodynamically oriented framework. That is, the therapist works to create a relationship with the child that provides empathic understanding, freedom and acceptance so that the child can let down her troublesome defenses and adapt healthy emotional regulation strategies. This is the pin- nacle of psychodynamically oriented play therapy. The therapist refrains from punishing or providing unnatural consequences for the child's play unless the child is in danger of harming herself, the therapist, or a difficult to replace item. In instances where the child's play seems to suggest underlying internal conflicts, the therapist speaks to those feelings and may occasionally provide interpret- ations for their meaning; therapist interpretations remain neutral. Therefore, the child is free to deepen her journey into her psychological struggle. With depth comes healthy ego strength, enlightenment, self-acceptance and poten- tial for change.

Imaginary play is the way children communicate their internal states, thoughts and fantasies. The age of the child impacts their unconscious content of their play (Yanof, 2013). Typically, children under the age of 5 do not have the cogni- tive recognition that their play and their internal thoughts are related. However, older children are more aware that play is their understanding of their own mind and intention; with this understanding, older children often use play defensively to keep themselves from experiencing the consequences of their reality (Yanof, 2013). Equipped with this knowledge, therapists decide when and whether to ver- bally interpret the child's play. Psychodynamically oriented play therapists also recognize the importance of first understanding the internal working model of the child, or the child's unspoken view of the self, because it is the foundation of iden- tity development. The child's identity impacts their perception of external world experiences and provides the play therapist with information regarding how the child may process challenging life events.

The Developing Self

There are many different theories that conceptualize how the *self* develops from infancy through early childhood. It is believed that the self grows from one's interaction with the world first through our basic senses and exists from an egocentric view (Piaget, 1951/2013), and that the self develops as a result of interpersonal relationships with others (Winnicott, 1977). These different, yet common threads suggest two versions of the self: "I" and "Me." The self as "I" is the full world of the infant and toddler, who believes that objects and others exist to meet the needs and desires of the self. The self as "Me" introduces the ability to take on the perspective of others. This is the beginning stage of empathy development.

Initial signs that an infant has a measurable and developing sense of self has been studied through observing infants' reactions to their videotaped, mirrored, and photographed images (Lewis & Brooks-Gunn, 1979). As infants grow in the first 12 months of life, so does their capacity for understanding that they are distinct beings separate from the parts of the world that come in contact with them. They first learn by experiencing much of the world through their senses (Piaget, 1951/2013; Zeanah,2009). Around the second year of life, typically developing children experience a language explosion that allows them the verbal skills to express their differentiation of *self* versus other (Zeanah, 2009). Then, close to age 3, young children emerge with a budding *self-concept* (Zeanah, 2009), "an idea of the self constructed from the beliefs one holds about oneself and the responses of others" (Self-concept, 2018).

The young child's self-concept is fragile, yet robust in material for the play therapist to understand the child's therapeutic needs. Self-concept is put on display when children engage in play therapy. To the watchful and observant play therapist, the child dances, fights, creates and generally exudes who they are and how they think about themselves. This display of self-concept may be specially illuminated in young children who engage in superhero play because superheroes allow children to take on a variety of roles between victim and savior. Children identifying with a specific superhero may demonstrate to the clinician how strong or wary, or how brave or shy, they perceive themselves during play therapy session. Likewise, their play may reveal their wishes. Superheroes from the Black Panther provide children with intricate characters to express their versions of self.

Character Analyses

The Black Panther

The Marvel Comics' Black Panther is a revolutionary character that was first created in 1966 as a comic book hero. He was unique in that he introduced fans to the strength and fury of African characters during the rise of the Black Panther party in America. This was a time in American history when Black people in America were fiercely fighting for their due rights as disenfranchised, abused and hunted citizens. Likely, it is no coincidence that the Black Panther comic series was created in the same year that the Black Panther Party was founded (Staff, History.com, 2017) in Oakland, California. The most recent movie portrayal of the Black Panther is as critical now as it was important for Black children from the 1960s to the early 2000s who may have never even known that he existed. That is because Black children are unique when compared to other minority groups in the United States, largely due to the historical race-based human slave trade practices embedded in the foundation of this country. Many, if not most, Black Americans do not know their full ancestral heritage (Lo Wang/NPR, 2018; Routheni, 2017). While it is commonly believed that Black Americans are generally from the same race, rarely can Black Americans trace their roots to specific continents, countries or cultures. While many Black Americans either equally or alternatively identify as African-American, some do not know if, from where, and from how long ago their African genes began. This experience is different from that of other cultural and racial groups that voluntarily migrated or even fled to this country for refuge or pleasure. There is an inherent sense of lost or missing identity when one does not know from where their ancestors originated. Furthermore, Africa is a large continent full of richly diverse cultures, beliefs, religions and languages; to say one is African means something, but to say one is Togolese or Ethiopian or "Wakandan" can mean something uniquely different. Therefore, while Black people share many racial features including skin color, there are differences in expressions of culture that shape our views of ourselves, our communities, and of the outside world.

Exploring Black Identity

It is important to consider that race is a social construct which is used to define the physical characteristics of group membership, while culture is the expression of the shared values of a group of people (Boykin, 1986; Sellers, Smith, Shelton, Rowley, & Chavous, 1998). Black identity is considered dynamic due to balancing being of African descent with living in the United States and developing within the mainstream culture (Boykin, 1986). This dynamic property of Black racial development differs from the development of racial identity of other groups and has led to extensive research on the Black experience. The differences are related to African people's arrival to this nation and the systems of oppression which were built into the constitution during the subsequent centuries. Systems of oppression previously did not allow for maintaining of indigenous culture which resulted in the merging of African and European/American culture creating an original cultural experience (Sellers et al., 1998). The Black cultural expression includes three experiences: (1) being of the Black racial group; (2) acculturating to the mainstream culture; and (3) being considered a minority (Boykin, 1986). The Multidimensional Model of Racial Identity (MMRI), developed by

Sellers and colleagues (1998), defines four dimensions of racial identity for Black people as a significance in the perception of self (i.e., salience, centrality, regard, and ideology). Sellers and colleagues (1998) suggested that the *salience* (the significance) of race for an individual changes across their lifespan, resulting in the individual holding a different dimension (Sellers et al., 1998). Racial *centrality* refers to how one defines themselves by their race and it is stable across situations. *Salience* and *centrality*, both refer to race and perception of self. Differing from racial *regard,* which is the judgment of one's racial group as a positive or negative view, and *ideology*, referring to the belief of how the group should behave in the larger society. *Regard* and *ideology* both refer to the complexity of being Black and formulating an understanding of how other groups perceive Black people. The MMRI allows us to see how racial identity development merges in tandem with the development of self. Children gain understanding of who they are and who their racial group is from the world around them.

For decades, this character and storyline has had the potential to inspire thousands of Black children. However, it can be argued that until recently, the Black Panther superhero primarily reached comic book readers and perhaps only a small number of other populations (Jao, 2018). The 2018 release of the *Black Panther* major motion picture (Grant et al., 2018) finally exposed this character to a worldwide audience and thus, jump-started a global conversation about positive representations of Black people in mass media. The characters in the movie provide children, teens, adults and mental health clinicians with deeply moving and complex experiences to explore identity development through play therapy. Moreover, the movie showed liberation, intelligence, gentleness and strength in African female characters that have been rarely portrayed on a grand scale, challenging both stereotypical racial and gender roles. This movie provided our young Black girls with opportunities to not only see themselves, but also gave them a glimpse of who they could become.

T'Challa: Growth of a King
In the silver screen version of the *Black Panther,* audiences were propelled into diverse depictions of Black men. We were introduced to T'Challa as a confident and strong adult male, the newly presumed King of Wakanda. However, those who saw his debut in *Captain America: Civil War* (Russo et al., 2016), witnessed his early identity struggles with being the prince of Wakanda and wanting to rule differently than his father, T'Chaka. This strife exposed him to be slightly at odds with T'Chaka right up until the moment when his father is killed and T'Challa eventually emerges as the Black Panther. T'Chaka's death abruptly begins T'Challa's journey as King.

Seminal theorist, Erik Erikson (1968), discussed identity development to be a "process of simultaneous reflection and observation … by which the individual judges himself in light of what he perceives to be the way in which others judge him" (p. 22). T'Challa's developing identity worked to gain equilibrium as he considered how he believed others defined kingship. He questioned whether he could be as strong and as respected of a leader as was his father. While the importance of family and cultural tradition were common themes in their storyline, T'Challa also grappled with what it meant to be the son of the most revered man in the kingdom. His love and admiration for his father caused T'Challa to feel the pressure to lead as his father led. That was until he realized that when given a variety of potential outcomes, T'Chaka chose to kill his brother, Prince N'Jobu, and abandon N'Jobu's son in the United States without any Wakandan support. This realization jolted T'Challa into a harsh reality that his father was not a perfect man and may not have always acted as such.

T'Challa led with his heart as much as he led with his head. He fell in love with a woman, Nakia, who did not fit the traditional status of a queen. She was not from wealthy lineage, she was an activist and a skilled fighter (Grant et al., 2018). T'Challa's expression of love was initially masked in more traditional views of masculinity. Later, T'Challa was able to express his love for Nakia and also his feelings about his father's shortcomings. His sense of love and pride on a large scale, perhaps, makes it okay for Black boys to not only have feelings, but to also express them. Expression of emotion is often a challenge for Black boys who are socialized to be emotionally inexpressive or to prioritize expression of hypermasculinity such as aggression (Wade & Rochlen, 2013), not unlike the concept of machismo among other men of color (Griffith, Gunter, & Watkins, 2012).

T'Challa's struggle to become a man both respectful of his father, yet still independent in his own right, is a growing pain to which other boys may be able to relate. Culturally, he challenges many of the social norms that exist in his community. For example, he questions meanings of manhood, the definition of kingship, and works through his beliefs about his roles as a future husband.

T'Challa eventually becomes flexible in his conceptualization of gender roles within a heterosexual marriage. Understanding the complexities of T'Challa's male identity development allows for clinicians to help young boys unpack, explore and create their definitions of self.

Killmonger: Finding home—Wakanda Forever

Erik "Killmonger" Stephens is introduced to the audience looking over African artifacts on display in a British Museum (Grant et al., 2018). When discussing the artifacts with the museum curator, Killmonger's comments reveal his distaste for Europe's colonization of the African continents, by suggesting the items were stolen from their original home. He continues to correct the misnomers and inaccuracies in the information recalled by the curator. Killmonger ends his conversation with the curator by labeling an item as vibranium and stating he will be returning the item to Wakanda; this leads to a battle in the museum and Killmonger leaves with the artifact. After the introduction to this character, the film continues to unpeel the layers of Killmonger and his current perception of self and his relationship with a country he feels a close tie to but has never visited. This scene also unpacks Killmonger's battle with the dominate culture he has lived with his entire life, and the harm it has done to his native culture with which he identifies.

The identity and learning history of Killmonger is unknown when he first appears, but as the film continues we begin to understand how his identity has developed and how it proceeds to impact his actions. Killmonger, born in Oakland, California, is the son of the N'Jabu, T'Chaka's younger brother, and an unidentified Black woman. King T'Chaka murdered N'Jabu in 1992 for arranging to steal vibranium to distribute to the global Black community to rise against oppression (Grant et al., 2018). Killmonger was a child when his father was murdered. While he did not witness the death of his father, he found his father's lifeless body. This event appeared to be a transformational point for Killmonger. He was fully aware of his Wakandan heritage and was taught to be prideful of this component of himself. However, his father's death led him to blame Wakanda for the destruction of his family. He vowed to avenge his father's death by taking the throne in Wakanda. Killmonger appears to feel displaced and angry. He spends the remainder of his life training physically and mentally to complete a coup in Wakanda.

In the *Black Panther* film, Killmonger is the only representation of the Black American experience. His exemplification of *self* explores a unique differentiation of race and culture. Racially, most of the main characters are Black, meaning of African origin; however, they do not all have the same cultural identity. Culturally, he is Black American and throughout the film his attire, body language and comments reveal a differentiating value system from the Wakanda natives because he has never lived in Wakanda. Using Black racial identity theories allows for analysis of Killmonger's attitudes toward his race and his resulting behaviors. While having a particular identity attitude does not predict all actions, there are stable properties which influence behaviors at specific events (Sellers et al., 1998).

When talking to his father during a vision he tells him, "Everyone dies, that's just life around here" (Grant et al., 2018, 1:27:41) representing the historical devaluing of Black lives in the United States. Unlike the other characters, Killmonger has lived in a colonized nation as a minority. Characters from Wakanda, however, reside in a country that is uncolonized and racially homogenous. Killmonger is different from his Wakandan family because his personality, decision making and expression of self are directly related to where and how he was raised. Race is salient and central to his identity. His presence in the film ends with the quote, "Bury me in the ocean with my ancestors that jumped from ships because they knew death was better than bondage" (Grant et al., 2018, 1:58:07), bondage in which he believed Black people around the world are currently held. As a man who has fought to end the oppression of his people, living without having accomplished his goal would be bondage.

Killmonger's character sheds light on the difference between race and culture. The visibility of his race and culture can be used by play therapists to unpeel the wrinkled folds of the complex racial and cultural composition of their child clients. Play therapists can use their recognition of Killmonger to distinguish differences between themselves and their clients to reduce incorrect assumptions and mediate implicit bias. It is true that while their child clients and client's families may share the same race, they could have very different cultures. These differences in culture do not cancel their membership from their shared racial group. Rather, the differences add an example that the complexities of race and racial identity can differ for each client. Like many child clients, Killmonger's history and identity are interlaced with his experiences and emotions, thus supporting the need for play therapists to continually engage in education and discussion regarding cultural awareness and responsiveness.

Gender Identity Development

The impact of media and its representation of gender expression are largely based on the theory of social cognitive gender development (Ruble, Martin, & Berenbaum, 2006). Children learn their gender roles and identity through modeling and practice during early childhood. Research suggests that children between the ages of 17 and 21 months are already starting to make accurate identifications of the gender of themselves and others (Zosuls et al., 2009). Gender labels and the application of labels to oneself increases as children are socialized and encouraged toward gender-specific toys and activities. Moreover, gender-specific emotion expression is based on socialization variances. For example, there are recognizable differences in emotion expression as early as preschool age, such that girls are more likely to show submissive emotions than boys (Chaplin, Cole, & Zahn-Waxler, 2005). During middle childhood, socialization by parents later impacts one's selection or rejection of gender-typed occupations (Lawson, Crouter, & McHale, 2015). Studies show that girls identify gender labels earlier than boys (Zosuls et al., 2009), while boy's understanding of gender expression appears to be moderated by paternal attention towards masculine attributes (Chaplin et al., 2005). Therefore, girls may be more susceptible to gendered representations in media regardless of parental involvement.

Okoye: Warrior, Woman and Wife

Okoye is the leader of the Dora Milaje, *adored ones*, or a military organization formed of selected women from Wakanda (Coleman, 2018). She carries herself with pride and appears to be a fearless and loyal warrior. Okoye serves the throne, rather than the person who holds the title of king. In the movie, she is a female leader who holds one of the highest positions in the country as her job is to protect Wakanda. While perhaps subtle to some (Truitt, 2018), she is married to W'Kabi, a respected tribe leader. There are times in the movie when Okoye and W'Kabi express their love for one another, yet later in the film, they are at odds on opposite sides of the war. In many ways, Okoye opens the door for a different representation of what a Black woman, a Black woman in love and what a Black wife can look like. Okoye provides girls with a portrayal of a woman who is proud of her beauty, stands strong in her beliefs, and is not confined by European influences on beauty, or American patriarchal expressions of gender roles in heterosexual married couples. Media images suggest that dark skinned Black women with natural or short hair are less likely to get married and less likely to be viewed as potential love interests (Hunter, 2005; Uzogara & Jackson, 2016). Therefore, Okoye demonstrated a contradiction to common portrayals of Black women. Also, she pays homage to the historical West African all-female military forces referred to as "Dahomey Amazons" in French literature from Dahomey (currently the Republic of Benin; Coleman, 2018).

Play therapists can use their knowledge of Okoye's character to invite her into the play therapy room. Her toy figurine may serve beneficial to some young Black girls as well as Black women who engage in psychodynamically oriented play therapy or even those who engage in sandtray play therapy with the use of miniatures. In psychodynamically oriented play therapy, the child is the story teller of her experience. She uses the toys to express the intricate details of her life, while the therapist follows the journey sometimes narrating what transpires. A child who selects Okoye may not be able to put her unyielding strength into words. She may stand as a warrior fighting against injustice. She may signify a child's struggle with gender, racial and cultural identities. She may represent a child's struggle to understand or define femininity and beauty.

Shuri: Princess, Scientist and Activist

Shuri is the younger sister of T'Challa and the teenage Princess of Wakanda. She is best known for her advanced intelligence in the area of science, technology, engineering and mathematics (STEM), a field which is current predominately male in the United States (US). In 2017, Women made up only 24% of all STEM jobs despite being 47% of the US workforce; therefore 76% of STEM employment is occupied by men (United States Department of Commerce Economics and Statistics Administration, 2017). Of graduates with STEM degrees, women are the least likely to work in a STEM occupation (United States Department of Commerce Economics and Statistics Administration, 2017).

Shuri also presents a different image of a princess. In the United States, the Disney princesses are popular and seen as the aspiration of young girls (Coyne, Linder, Rasmussen, Nelson, & Birkbeck, 2016). Traditionally, Disney princesses have been portrayed as damsels in distress, unable to solve their problems without a male hero (Golden & Jacoby, 2017). Shuri presents a different type of princess as she actively engages in the solution for the problem, rather than as a bystander or victim in need of saving. Her storyline provides therapists material to examine gender identity development and intersectionality between media and social acceptability.

Traditionally, media has depicted the experiences of women similarly to Disney princesses, as being solely images of beauty. Beauty is considered the greatest attribute while material objects have the ability to improve women's status (Golden & Jacoby, 2017). History has provided an alternative image of women, including princesses. Across several cultural groups there have been historical images of women who, like Shuri, used their skills to fight against injustice. The comparison between Disney princesses and historical images of women reveal the gaps in the representation of women in various roles presented to young children. The image is often based on beauty and materialization and carried forth by a princess. Therefore, when determining the definition of "girl" for children, their answer is of a princess (Coyne et al., 2016). When the question asks what it means to be a "Black girl," the response is often missing from media altogether. However, with the induction of Black Panther into cinematic history, the answer could be Shuri, a highly intelligent princess who uses her intelligence to fight for her people.

Shuri is smart and fiercely ingenious in her fight for her family and community. She is a representation of a fighter and a scientist that has rarely been shared with young children. Psychodynamically oriented play therapists are well skilled in understanding the value of play in revealing the feelings and ideas of young children. A child who selects Shuri may replicate the examples of strong family networks by including relatives past and present during play therapy. Play therapists may experience children displaying the exceptionality of their gender group as observed in their environment. Children will also demonstrate the limitations of their gender or racial group that they believe to be true, as such play therapists may observe children avoiding or hesitating to play with items which are perceived as inappropriate for their gender or racial group. Shuri may be a glimpse into those experiences and internal struggles with gender identity and roles. During these times, it is important for play therapists to consider the child's hesitation and create a *holding* space for them to explore and practice accepting or challenging those roles.

Case Application

DeShaun (a Pseudonym)

Intake
DeShaun was a 7-year-old Black male referred for psychotherapy due to severe physical outbursts and confirmed physical abuse. He was the oldest of four children; however, his behaviors were noted to be the most severe and he was the only child for which child abuse was confirmed. At the time of referral, DeShaun was living in foster care with two of his biological siblings, while his infant sibling was living in a separate foster home. He had recently been placed in a classroom specifically designed for children with emotional disabilities. Although it was unclear how he gained enrollment in such a program when there were no records indicating data collection to support his placement. He was referred by his foster care social worker and accompanied by his foster mother, a Black woman in her late 60s, to the intake appointment. His foster mother expressed her fears for his behaviors as they related to him being a Black child. She worried that he would one day be arrested and misunderstood because he is Black. Viewing his caregiver through an MMRI lens, the clinician believed that his caregiver was expressing that race was salient and central to her identity and understanding of her foster

child. Her concern told the therapist that her ideology of Black children is that they are perceived as violent and maybe more likely to get arrested than children from other racial and cultural groups. Furthermore, his caregiver commented on the fact that she was thankful that DeShaun would have a Black therapist; this implied that at least in this instance, his caregiver may have a positive racial regard and view a Black therapist as someone who could be more helpful to her foster child than a therapist from another racial group.

Assessment
Clinical assessment of DeShaun took place over four sessions. In the first session with DeShaun, he presented as reserved and yet curious. He explored the room and abruptly told the clinician that he never plays with toys, while eyeballing the many toys that were meticulously placed in the room. DeShaun cooperated when asked to draw a picture of his family engaged in an activity, a house, a tree, and a person. DeShaun happily talked about his family and then drifted into his thoughts of missing his father. He spoke mostly of his father and almost never discussed his mother. He described himself, not as a boy, but as a man with responsibilities to take care of others, particularly his family. It became clear that for DeShaun, his father may as well have hung the Moon, placed the stars, and lit the Sun. This was initially an endearing quality, but quickly became problematic when DeShaun revealed some of the rules and mantras that he learned from his father. By the end of the assessment phase, DeShaun had expressed his identity struggle to be like his father while also trying to experience his childhood as a Black boy.

Psychological records reported that DeShaun's father had below average intellectual functioning and a substance use disorder. During his times of sobriety, his father held steady employment as a construction worker, reported to work on time, and seemed to be a present father to his children and a loving partner to DeShaun's mother. However, when his father was using and/or going through withdrawals, he presented with dangerous behaviors, had a short temper, and would often skip work. DeShaun seemed to know details about his father's substance use that suggested he had either seen his father actively using drugs or had been told such information. According to DeShaun, his father believed that men have to always be ready to fight for what is theirs, never take no for an answer, love their family but never let others think you are weak, and boys are just short men. This knowledge caused DeShaun to create a complex definition of manhood that said that being a man also means doing dangerous things. DeShaun believed the following: Men primarily show when they are angry, usually no other feelings are appropriate; men fight with their fists to protect what they believe in; men never let anyone tell them no; men do not play with toys, only babies and children can do that.

Psychodynamically Oriented Play Therapy
DeShaun loved superheroes. Both his parents and foster parents allowed him to have comic books, which they read to him as bedtime stories. Initially, DeShaun reported that he was like Killmonger because Killmonger was "a real man." The

clinician wondered aloud if sometimes DeShaun felt that real men were always angry. DeShaun reported that real men are not always angry, but that they have to show that they are strong and showing anything besides anger means they are weak. He drew pictures of his father and Killmonger and selected miniatures that had muscles and primarily solved their problems in major battles. DeShaun would comment during his play that he was strong and scary like his father. He would re-enact scenes of his fights in school and comment how he handled it just like his father would have wanted him to, just like Killmonger, too.

More than halfway through his time with this clinician, DeShaun finally replayed his major trauma scene with him playing the role of his father and the clinician in the role of DeShaun, which was the catalyst that involved child protective services and resulted in him and his siblings' placement in foster care. During a discipline session after DeShaun received a call from school, DeShaun's father injured DeShaun resulting in a broken bone and hospitalization. DeShaun instructed the clinician to feel sad and hurt, but to initially refrain from crying. He studied the clinician's face intensely. The clinician interpreted DeShaun's resistance in allowing the clinician to express pain, fear and sadness. The clinician spoke as injured DeShaun, *But I am your son. I am a little boy. I am scared, and my body really hurts. I need to cry. It has to be okay for me to cry.* DeShaun then instructed the clinician to scream and cry in pain. At the end of this session, DeShaun was able to talk about how scared he was when his father hurt him and how he tried hard not to cry, but he was so badly hurt that he could not help himself. Over time, however, DeShaun more closely resembled T'Challa. DeShaun used psychodynamically oriented play therapy to explore his internal working model of his identity of being a Black male child trying to live in his father's image. Like T'Challa, DeShaun began to integrate his view of his father. He started to play out the kind, possibly sober, versions of his father in session. He began to use language that expressed that sometimes his father was loving and safe, while other times his father was scary and dangerous.

Outcome

DeShaun attended weekly psychotherapy sessions with the same clinician for one full school year until the case was transferred due to parental reunification. By the end of treatment with the clinician, DeShaun presented with an integrated view of himself as a Black male child and as a son. He continued to identify his younger siblings as his responsibility and was mindful of who he could show childlike vulnerabilities, but he was better able to openly express feelings outside of anger. DeShaun had an infectious laugh, that he sometimes shared with others. And, toys—DeShaun went from thinking he was too grown up to play with toys, to wanting to play with toys in sessions and with his siblings.

Personal Reflections

I feel honored to have been allowed the opportunity to share in DeShaun's life story. For such a young child, he had already endured experiences that many adults cannot fathom, and yet he managed to enter each day with hope. He exposed me to his fears, desires, and to his complex developing identities.

Working with DeShaun was to work with his foster mother, and that meant that I had to confront some norms that exist within my own culture. For example, DeShaun explored traditional attitudes of Black male identity, notions of being strong and the belief that boys and men are not allowed to cry. He also played with a different child-like and playful side that I imagine few ever saw. I had never seen DeShaun light up with exuberant joy the way that I saw the first time he found a mirror and put on a pink sparkly tutu. First, he twirled with excitement. Then, he turned to me and asked if we could find a mirror. Once in front of a mirror, he marveled at himself and released squeals. His eyes sparkled, and his smile was so wide that I imagined the balls of his cheeks may start to hurt. As his therapist, I allowed him to have the freedom to express himself in ways that made him feel comfortable and accepted. However, I knew that in my community, the Black community, typically young boys are not allowed to even so much as look at toys and articles of clothing that are deemed to be feminine.

During initial glances at traditionally feminine items, DeShaun asked for permission for each action that is usually forbidden in the Black community. He asked before touching the tutu. He asked before putting it on. He even asked before engaging in his first twirl. As a play therapist, each time I expressed the play therapy statement, "In this room, you can do just about anything that you like. If there is something that you cannot do, I will let you know." I must admit that I was worried about what his foster mother or even his father would think, say or do if they learned of DeShaun's play in the play therapy room. I also had feelings of confusion as I wondered how I would feel if a male child in my family engaged in this play. In theory, I would be accepting and allow him to explore all safe things. Intellectually, I understood that with DeShaun's suppression of select emotions and identification with adult male behaviors, he was likely experiencing psychological benefits from stepping outside of the "tough guy" exterior that he wore in his everyday life. On the other hand, a part of me felt the pull of my cultural upbringing that suggested something different. However, I worked to remain present with DeShaun. I wanted to ensure that I was holding his feelings, rather than projecting my worries onto him.

Upon entering the play therapy room, the session after DeShaun played with the tutu, he informed me, with sadness in eyes and despair dripping in his voice, that he was not allowed to play with "girl things." He told me that tutus were for "sissies." I fought my anger and frustration. I labeled and reflected his feelings based on what he told me. I wondered with him to explore how he came to the notion that he was not allowed to play the way that he played the previous week. He told me that when he got in the car with his foster mother the previous week, he was excited to tell her about how much better he felt after therapy. She asked him what he did in therapy, and he told her about his play with action figures, labeling feelings, and eventually about his play in the dress-up area. At that point, I realized that my fear had come true and I thought about how to repair the relationship with his foster mother.

In my view, I felt that I had lost her trust or respect because she had specifically discussed being happy that I was a Black clinician. Her designation of me being a Black clinician inherently meant that she assumed that I shared in her beliefs and would use that lens while helping DeShaun process his traumas. I believed that as a result of DeShaun's dress-up play and the fact that I did not discourage it, meant that she categorized me as *less Black* or not accepting of Black culture.

I am not confident that I ever completely regained her trust as a Black clinician, but we did discuss her feelings and views. I scheduled a caregiver-only session with her instead of avoiding the proverbial elephant in the room. I approached her from a place of honest reflection and asked if she wanted to talk about what DeShaun had shared with her. She spoke of her fears regarding his sexual orientation and how children in the Black community would treat him. She illuminated the point that she was uncomfortable with him engaging in activities that could lead to him later having an even more difficult life than what he was facing as a Black American; she noted that his life would be difficult enough because he was Black. What I heard in her voice, saw in her face, and read in her body language was love. In many ways, I understood her fears, and I worked with her to meet on common ground.

At times, I saw my mother, aunts and even myself in her. I felt the trepidation that she had for DeShaun's future. I did not want to dismiss that; I wanted to acknowledge it. So, we openly discussed those anxieties. We worked together to unpack the top layers of a multifaceted history of what it means to be Black in America. Then, and only then, was I able to introduce the possibility that DeShaun needed one space in his life where he could feel vulnerable. I thought with her to see if DeShaun might, at least temporarily, need to detour away from his superhero persona. I wondered with her to see if the play therapy room could be that place. I would like to think that she continued to bring DeShaun to therapy because she saw that it was helping him and that she felt safe with me.

Conclusion

The first years of development are a crucial time of learning, exploration and play. Young children gain an understanding of themselves and rehearse this understanding through play. As they continue to develop, children are continuously exposed to images from mass media revealing how they are perceived by the world. Psychodynamically oriented play therapy unpacks the internal thoughts and beliefs of children during their play, while also giving a window to their view of their *self* and their role within society. While the interpretation of Black people in media has often been negative, the Black Panther character's inception during the 1960s was a look at the Black person's role in their community, as change agents to a system of oppression. Building on the original comic, the 2018 movie portrayal of the Black Panther characters provide a fresh expression of being Black for developing children and adults alike. The movie uncovers the racial and cultural complexities of the Black racial group while simultaneously challenging gender stereotypes.

T'Challa and Killmonger are both Black men with fathers from Wakanda, yet their cultures are distinctly different. Distinctions between T'Challa and Killmonger contribute to differences throughout the film and our discussion of each character. In fact, analysis of Killmonger and T'Challa take us on a journey through a deepened examination of the differences between race, culture and nationality. Throughout this chapter, we referenced communities based on carefully selected components of each character's layered identities. However, we are forthcoming in the awareness that space did not allow us to unpack all layers of these characters.

Inspecting the development of the self, race, culture and nationality we uncovered how they influence the way young children see themselves and how this influence continues throughout life. Furthermore, we consider gender identity, which undoubtedly adds an additional layer for acknowledgment. Shuri and Okoye present non-stereotypical images of Black women. Both characters exhibit complex identities distinct and separate from the identities of the male characters in the film, which is unique when compared to many other movies marketed to children. Okoye and Shuri show us that there is no one way to be a Black woman.

Finally, as play therapists, it is essential to recognize the developing identity of child clients who enter our play therapy rooms. Play therapists are already equipped with the understanding of play in a child's life, especially in the context of a child who has faced trauma or toxic stress. Psychodynamically oriented play therapists understand subconscious thoughts and know how to facilitate a psychologically and physically safe environment that allows the child's unspoken experience to surface. Understanding characters such as T'Challa, Killmonger, Okoye and Shuri may be a vital step toward conceptualizing some Black child clients and their family members. The next step toward helping the child client is considering the play therapist's identities and exploring how they influence children engaged in play therapy sessions.

Questions for Clinical Discussion

1. Why is exploring a child's multiple identities significant in understanding their play in the play therapy room?
2. How do intersecting identities (e.g., racial and gender) impact child clients' development and readiness for therapeutic change?
3. As a clinician, how does your understanding of your own multiple identities impact the therapeutic relationship when using play therapy with child clients?
4. How would you begin to unpack how your identity group is perceived by society and how that impacts your perception of children from other identity groups?
5. How would you use the information you have obtained in this chapter to start the conversation about childhood identity development with other clinicians?
6. What do you think about the parent's role in identity development and its clinical implications?

References

Boykin, A. W. (1986). The triple quandary and the schooling of Afro-American children. In: U. Neisser (Ed.), *The School Achievement of Minority Children: New perspectives.* Hillsdale, NJ: Erlbaum.

Chaplin, T. M., Cole, P. M., & Zahn-Waxler, C. (2005). Parental socialization of emotion expression: Gender differences and relations to child adjustment. *Emotion, 5*(1), 80–88.

Coleman, A. L. (2018, February 22). There's a true story behind *Black Panther's* strong women. Here's why that matters. *Time.* Retrieved from http://time.com/5171219/black-panther-women-true-history/

Coyne, S. M., Linder, J., Rasmussen, E. E., Nelson, D. A., & Birkbeck, V. (2016). Pretty as a princess: Longitudinal effects of engagement with Disney princesses on gender stereotypes, body esteem, and prosocial behavior in children. *Child Development, 87*(6), 1909–1925.

Crenshaw, K. W. (1988). Race, reform, and retrenchment: Transformation and legitimation in antidiscrimination law. *Harvard Law Review, 101*(7), 13–1–1387.

Erikson, E. H. (1968). *Identity, Youth, and Crisis.* New York: W. W. Norton & Company, Inc.

Freud, A. (1974). *The Writings of Anna Freud.* New York: International Universities Press. (Originally published 1927).

Golden, J. C. & Jacoby, J. W. (2017). Playing princess: Preschool girls' interpretations of gender stereotypes in Disney princess media. *Sex Roles,* doi:10.1007/s11199-017-0773-8

Grant, D. J., Feige, K. (Producers), & Coogler, R. (Director) (2018, February 16). *Black Panther* [Motion picture]. Burbank, CA: Marvel Studios and Walt Disney Pictures.

Griffith, D. M., Gunter, K., & Watkins, D. C. (2012). Measuring masculinity in research on men of color: Findings and future directions. *American Journal of Public Health, 102*(Suppl 2), S187–S194. http://doi.org/10.2105/AJPH.2012.300715

Hug-Hellmuth, Hermine von (1920). On the technique of child-analysis. *International Journal of Psycho-Analysis, 2,* 287–305.

Hunter, M. (2005). *Race, Gender, and the Politics of Skin Tone.* New York: Routledge.

Jao, A. (2018, March 20). Before "Black Panther" movie, black comic creators spent years breaking down barriers. *NBC News.* Retrieved from www.nbcnews.com/news/nbcblk/black-panther-black-comic-creators-spent-years-breaking-down-barriers-n848461.

Lawson, K. M., Crouter, A. C., & McHale, S. M. (2015). Links between family gender socialization experiences in childhood and gendered occupational attainment in young adulthood. *Journal of Vocational Behavior, 90,* 26–35.

Lo Wang, H. (2018). 2020 Census will ask Black people about their exact origins. Retrieved from www.npr.org/2018/03/13/593272215/for-the-first-time-2020-census-will-ask-black-americans-about-their-exact-origin.

Lewis, M. & Brooks-Gunn, J. (1979). *Social and the Acquisition Of Self.* New York: Plenum.

Padden, C. & Humphries, T. (2005). Introduction: The lens of culture. In: C. Padden & T. Humphries (Eds.), *Inside Deaf Culture* (pp. 1–10). Harvard University Press, London, UK.

Piaget, J. (1951/2013). *Play, Dreams and imitation in childhood* (Vol. 25). London: Routledge. (Originally published 1951.)

Routheni, M. (2017, February). *The Hunt for Black Family History.* Institute for Policy Studies. Retrieved from https://ips-dc.org/the-hunt-for-black-family-history.

Ruble, D. N., Martin, C. L., & Berenbaum, S. A. (2006). Gender development. In N. Eisenberg, W. Damon, & R. M. Lerner (Eds.), *Handbook of Child Psychology: Social, emotional, and personality development* (pp. 858–932). Hoboken, NJ: John Wiley & Sons, Inc.

Russo, A., Russo, J., Markus, C., McFeely, S., Feige, K., Evans, C., Downey, R., … Buena Vista Home Entertainment (Firm), (2016). *Captain America: Civil war.*

Self-concept. (2018). In: *English Oxford Dictionaries online.* Retrieved from https://en.oxforddictionaries.com/definition/us/self-concept

Sellers, R. M., Smith, M. A., Shelton, N., Rowley, S. A. J., Chavous, T. M. (1998). Multidimensional model of racial identity: A reconceptualization of African American racial identity. *Personality and Social Psychology Review, 2*(1), 18–39.

Schaefer, C. (2011). *Foundations of play therapy* (2nd ed.) Hoboken, NJ: John Wiley and Sons, Inc.

Staff, History.com. (2017). *Black Panthers.* A+E Networks. Retrieved from www.history.com/topics/black-panthers

Tharps, L. L. (2014, November 18). The case for Black with a capital B. *New York Times.* Retrieved from www.nytimes.com/2014/11/19/opinion/the-case-for-black-with-a-capital-b.html.

Trauma. (2018). In *English Oxford Dictionaries online.* Retrieved from https://en.oxforddictionaries.com/definition/trauma.

Truitt, B. (2018, May 1). Exclusive 'Black Panther' deleted scene shows Okoye and W'Kabi having a marital tiff. *USA Today.* Retrieved from www.usatoday.com/story/life/entertainthis/2018/05/01/danai-gurira-daniel-kaluuya-fight-exclusive-black-panther-deleted-scene/568040002.

United States Department of Commerce Economics and Statistics Administration (2017). *Women in STEM: 2017 Update.* Retrieved from www.esa.gov/reports/women-stem-2017-update.

Uzogara, E. E. & Jackson, J. S. (2016). Perceived skin tone discrimination across contexts: African American women's reports. *Race and Social Problems, 8*(2), 147–159.

Wade, J. C. & Rochlen, A. B. (2013). Introduction: Masculinity, identity, and the health and well-being of African American men. *Psychology of Men & Masculinity, 14*(1), 1–6.

Winnicott, D. W. (1991). *Play and reality.* London: Routledge. (Originally published 1971.)

Winnicott, D. W. (1977). *The Piggle: An account of the psychoanalytical treatment of a little girl,* New York. IUP.

Yanof, J. A. (2013). Play technique in psychodynamic psychotherapy. *Child and Adolescent Psychiatric Clinics of North America, 22*(2), 261–282.

Zeanah, C. H., Jr. (Ed.). (2009). *Handbook of Infant Mental Health* (3rd edn.). New York: Guilford Press.

Zosuls, K. M., Ruble, D. N., Tamis-LeMonda, C. S., Shrout, P. E., Bornstein, M. H., & Greulich, F. K. (2009). The acquisition of gender labels in infancy: Implications for sex-typed play. *Developmental Psychology, 45*(3), 688–701. http://doi.org/10.1037/a0014053

CHAPTER 19

Un-Masking the Alter Ego: Fear and Freedom in the Affirmation of the Inner Hero

Kory Martin

The Shining Knight and the Schoolyard Vigilante

This chapter will explore the construction of identity that occurs for clients by way of narrative storytelling. However, this will not be a chapter solely focused on the theory of narrative family therapy or identity development. As the title of this book promises, this chapter will examine individual narratives through the lens of superheroes and comic book mythos. I will detail my work with clients of color and share their heroic journeys to uncover their inner most hero. I will also detail the evolution of this approach and how, through culturally reflective clinical practice, I began to experience significant barriers to the deconstruction of these negatively saturated stories due to deeply rooted discrimination, white privilege, and institutionalized racism that perpetually impacted my clients' capacity for hope of change. Their biographical accounts stemmed from oppressive external narratives and stereotypes that tore at their resiliency, created dissonance, buried their inner hero, and on a long enough timeline for some, created a villainous identity.

In this chapter I will explore the commonalty of a created alter ego for these clients and will explore how, though it is unique to the individual, for clients of color there are common themes including motivating forces that propel the creation of a second self to fit the white racial frame and in some respects, keep the client(s) safe in an often unsafe society. I found that the creation of my clients' alter egos served common functions and were largely shaped: (1) by a response to the systemic differences and stigma cross culturally surrounding how clients of color are talked about, written about and related to in academic and clinical settings: and (2) out of both conscious and unconscious necessity to fit what structures the majority, or dominant group in a society allows them to safely be. The underlying motivations began to narrow and repeat, and I was able to consistently identify what I call "the three P's."

The Three P's

The three P's—preservation, placation and protection will be defined through case studies and I will detail how they manifested as an alter ego for my clients.

Preservation was a consistently reported goal for my clients. It ranged from keeping a job or maintaining the surface perception of a healthy family to one client describing the need to preserve the guise of the passive black man despite a well of anger resultant from recurrent experiences of racialization. Placation was similar in some respects in that it was meant to pacify others, most times those in a majority position of privilege and power. Many clients I have worked with using this notion of an alter ego, reported that their second self is a necessary projection they felt compelled to maintain in order to skirt fear, suspicion or subjugation at the hands of the other. Protection is, as it sounds, a need to protect oneself and one's family from the threats of racism and discrimination that are still very real, even in this post-civil rights era society.

Throughout this chapter, I will touch on limitations to this approach including, but not limited to, the importance of self of the therapist to challenge and acknowledge layers of privilege that are therapist-specific and if not named and cross-validated, will subvert trust and derail the essential element that makes this approach effective: the therapeutic relationship. The cases I will present are real cases and the insight gleaned is anecdotal. The shared experiences I had with these individuals are dear to me and I am dedicated to honoring the stories that they so bravely shared with me. A second limitation to acknowledge at the onset is in the fact that though the age range of these clients varies, I have primarily utilized this approach and experienced the greatest amount of momentum in working with African-American males.

Additionally, by virtue of the anecdotal nature of these case conceptualizations, it was not my intent to employ qualitative measures or tracking and thus, there is a distinct lack of intentionality to create bracketing. Gearing (2004) asserts that "the researcher's orientation and theoretical approach influence the entire research protocols, method, and analysis of any investigation" (p. 1433). This initial phase of bracketing establishes the entrance of the researcher into his or her study and requires clear methodological forethought (Gearing, 2004). I didn't do that. What that means for my findings is that my results and assertions about the efficacy of this approach are inherently biased by who I am, the scope of learning that occurred along the way, and my proficiency and affinity for specific theoretical orientations and modalities. I will use these cases to introduce the notion that superheroes can be used therapeutically to address and combat deeply insidious concepts including systemic racism, oppression and historical trauma.

The Alter Ego: A Hero's Second Self

I began to think critically about alter ego and superhero identify formation after watching the Quentin Tarantino (2004) directed action extravaganza, *Kill Bill: Volume 2*. The moment that held the most impact for me came at the end of the second of the two-film series; during the final showdown between the titular villain and the movie's heroine, Beatrix Kiddo. Bill delivers a monologue of why he has done, and does not regret doing, the life destroying things he did to Beatrix. Bill begins, "As you know, I am quite keen on comic books, especially the ones about superheroes" (Bender & Tarantino, 2004). As a powerful paralytic takes hold over our protagonist of the film, Bill details his fondness for a particularly intriguing element of superhero mythos, the alter ego. "There is the superhero and then there is the alter ego. Batman is actually Bruce Wayne; Spider-Man is actually Peter Parker. Now, when that character wakes up in the morning, he IS Peter Parker. He has to put on a costume to become Spider-Man" (Bender & Tarantino, 2004).

Then Bill makes delineation between the likes of Batman or Spider-Man as compared to Superman, in that Superman is Superman. Kal-El, his given name, is the same person as Superman and when he takes off his super suit, he is still a being from a different world. Bill explores the stark difference of Superman's alter ego. It was necessary for Kal-El to create a persona that served the function of off-setting his true power; that of his true self (Bender & Tarantino, 2004). Out of that necessity, he creates Clark Kent, an unassuming persona characterized by passivity, projected cowardice and self-doubt.

Though this distinction was one I had been aware of prior to this movie, I began to consider this creation of an alter ego in the context of how it served the respective characters' needs. The Batman identity was canonically born out of trauma resultant from the loss of his parents and a need to take action; one might even call it vengeance in its earliest manifestation (Beatty, Greenberger, Jiminez, & Wallace, 2008). Bruce Wayne created an alter ego that elevated his identity to that which was more than a man; a dark entity that fights evil and wrong-doing using fear, violence and intimidation. Superman, on the other hand, created an alter ego that represents a dialed down version of his true self, Kal-El of Krypton. He shaped his alter ego to be less than he was: to blend in. He sought to incorporate traits that he considered to be "average" or below to hide in plain sight, protect his alien lineage, and set others more at ease to avoid potential persecution.

Now, one could argue that Batman, over time, became the dominant identity and far more a "true self" for Bruce Wayne than the aforementioned monologue would have us believe. However, Bruce Wayne is still just Bruce Wayne. Batman is who he has decided to be and in that, he demonstrates the power of identity formation through an individual personal narrative. He repeated the narrative of Batman to himself, absorbed the external narrative of Batman as a symbol, vigilante and hero, and that narrative slowly overpowered and replaced the less dominant narrative of Bruce Wayne. Both heroes shaped the narrative of their identities to fit the function they needed to achieve, and it was further reinforced by the delicate dance of internal and external storytelling.

Theoretical Origins

Narrative Therapy

There is a notion that history is influenced largely by the lens through which it is recounted. Foeman (2009) cites Walter R. Fisher in his assertion that people are story-telling animals; a good story holds to standards of both probability, the possibility that it could have happened, and fidelity, the extent to which it resonates (p. 15). One can concede that history is rife with events; historical battles for example, that involve multiple perspectives and participants. Though it can be agreed by all involved that those events objectively occurred, the details of the events would subjectively vary largely based on the perspective of each side and furthermore, a master narrative that supplanted all others (Foeman, 2009). Looking back to my middle school history textbooks, I understand now that the content was presented and laid out from a decidedly white perspective and often, the more dominant perspective of what was deemed more socio-normative. Even before the days of textbooks tailored for forced perspective, narration has been used by individuals, families and societies to pass down history, expectations and important cultural connectivity. As I detailed for the initial example of myself in my aforementioned story, it is (and was) an essential component in both in the initial cultivation and further evolution of a powerful identity.

Nichols (2010) asserts that, "the truth of one's experience is not discovered; rather it is created" (p. 349). A narrative approach to therapy seeks to understand how the client makes meaning of their problems by how they think and speak about their problems. I initially gravitated toward this modality because its strength-based and non-pathologizing approach seemed to offer an important commodity in therapy; it offered hope. I began to use narrative tenets to empower clients to explore the possibility that they are not defined by their symptoms, unless they continue to define themselves by their symptoms (Hart, 1995). In doing so, clients are encouraged to additionally see problems as rooted in dominant cultural narratives that influence people to think of themselves as inadequate (Nichols, 2010). Deconstruction occurs in therapy when the therapist supports the client in peeling back the layers of destructive and problem maintaining internal and external narrative; giving way to a reconstruction of new and more empowering narratives of self that introduce more optimistic and hopeful accounts of their experiences.

Strategic Therapy

Whereas narrative therapy is largely focused on creating an experience of allowing the client space to explore and re-create their story, strategic therapy is more contained. In its original incarnations, namely MRI Strategic, Milan Systemic and Jay Hayley's Strategic modality, it was conceptualized as a fast-moving approach which asserted that the need for the therapist to take a more active and at times, highly directive approach to the therapeutic work (Klajs, 2016). Strategic therapy focuses on the family system and tenets of the model seek to achieve two directives being: (1) Highlight and interrupt pathological sequences; and (2) Change hierarchy and determine the boundaries so they are more functional for the system (Klajs, 2016). It is a prescriptive approach at times that relies heavily on the therapist's ability to build a strategic plan for therapy and engaging the family in such a way that the clinician, over time, can predict client responses and individualize systemic interventions. Nichols (2010) noted that strategic family therapy is, "more concerned with getting individuals and families to see things differently than they were with getting them to behave differently" (p. 149).

The use of the superhero metaphor lends itself well to creating the kind of shift in thinking that is the objective of strategic theory because like externalization, it creates an alternative way of thinking about themselves individually and collectively that can root the presenting issues in something other than blame and scapegoating. There are many worthwhile interventions and therapeutic skills to be gleaned from understanding strategic theory; however, in my work, I primarily employ three major tenets: Reframing, Positive Connotation, and the Function of the Symptom. All three of these interventions are geared toward changing the interpretation of presenting issues, symptoms and behavior to reduce pathologizing of the identified patient and allows the therapist to position in such a way that affords them the opportunity to take a non-blaming and empower stance when joining the family system.

Reframing and positive connotation were terms that were coined by the MRI and Milan Systemic schools respectively and are tools to create new interpretations of why problematic dynamics occur in families and maintained by individuals (Nichols, 2010). Positive connotation moves one step further than reframing in that it seeks to "attach a more positive function for a behavior or 'problem'" (Nichols, 2010, p. 149). Positive connotation, when paired with superheroes, becomes a powerful tool in a therapeutic setting because it allows the clinician to frame what is identified as a problem or behavior and elevates it to something more akin to "an ability," a superpower that has yet to be harnessed to its full effectiveness.

The third of my default strategic tools is the function of the symptom; a somewhat controversial element of strategic theory that Klajs (2016) explains is the notion that, "the symptom has a systemic function; it serves the family, stabilizes it. Its [the symptom's] aim is to support the family, not an individual, in keeping relative balance" (p. 21). This concept of balance is known in systemic thinking as homeostasis, or family homeostasis, and is comprised of patterns, family rules and various mechanisms that bring families back to equilibrium and serve to resist change, regardless of the level of dysfunction being experienced within that system. When used appropriately, this technique can result in a wealth of new possibilities to interpret how a family or individual therein conduct themselves. By exploring the function of a presenting symptom and how it serves a purpose to preserve the functionality of the family, a clinician can frame, for example, self-sacrifice into a truly heroic expression of love by the individual for their family.

Critical Race Theory

Awareness and inclusion of critical race theory is an essential component of my work with the clients I will present in this chapter. It is paramount, when seeking to cultivate a culturally reflective practice of therapy, to understand the assertion of CRT theorists that racism is ordinary, not aberrational (Delgado & Stefancic, 2017). It is rooted in the very functionality of our society and is an essential mechanism for maintaining invisible and unacknowledged patterns of power and privilege that elevate and advance white ascendancy. For much of our history as a nation, more than "85%, the United States of America has been grounded in, and shaped by, extreme racial oppression in the form of slavery and legal segregation as a foundational reality" (Feagin, 2010, p. 1). Understanding that this is a real and very much operational systemic dynamic impacting clients of color in this country is vital for a (Caucasian, heteronormative, cis-gender male) clinician such as myself working cross-culturally in that it allows me to accept and subsequently challenge my power and privilege and then create and promote openness for courageous conversations with clients and colleagues.

Delgado and Stefancic (2017) posited that "if racism is as deeply embedded in our thought processes and social structures as CRT theorists believe, then routines, practices and institutions that we regularly rely on will function to keep minorities in subordinate positions" (p. 27). This creates real barriers in therapy, in so far as actions and interventions, even if well intentioned, if done from a place of ignorance to the systemic nature of racism, power and privilege, can result in the posturing of the clinician's privilege to prescribe interventions that may not be realistic given the intersectionality of circumstances for a client. As a result, the intervention in and of itself would serve as a reminder of the gap that exists between individuals, with respect to those that are elevated and those that are subjugated.

Another important assertion of critical race theory is that of interest convergence. Delgado and Stefancic (2017) describe interest convergence as the tendency for people to believe what benefits them (p. 48). A common example of this idea can be frequently seen in politics in the propensity for majority individuals supporting the causes or movement of minority members based on the extent to which that support will benefit them. If a white person believes that being an advocate for civil and equal rights benefits them, it becomes a viable endeavor. This notion is expanded by Delgado and Stefancic (2017) in their contention that this behavior, on some level, is less about civil rights because it is the fair and inclusive thing to do, and more about how it further elevates majority individual (p. 49).

In terms of alter ego construction and individual narrative, the white individual in this example has the privilege to advocate, or not, based on the context of where they live and who they surround themselves with and can tailor their beliefs to what will garner the most positive reception from others. Conversely, an individual of color is not afforded this privilege and if their experience supports the belief that the maintenance of a symptom benefits them (i.e., protects them), it becomes safer to preserve that symptom than abandon it. If that is the case, it becomes a viable function of that presenting issue. For example, an intervention for a young African-American male may be to explore asserting himself and verbalizing his underlying emotions to communicate more authentically with others but, if that intervention puts the client at risk of being received as "aggressive" or "threatening," then not only is there going to be resistance, it could be argued that it is an irresponsible intervention for the clinician to employ.

Case Studies

Hero Profile: Luke Cage, a.k.a. Power Man

I was in the thick of my clinical internship when I experienced the first case where I realized that the use of superheroes had deep and impactful merit for clients. Luke was a 36-years-old and identified as an African-American male. Luke was built like a hero, muscular and stocky, and had a subdued and soft-spoken way about him. The thing I remember most fondly about Luke was his laugh. It was infectious and genuine, and he accessed it easily, even in his most somber moods. I was a novice clinician to be sure, but by the time I had met Luke, I had fallen into a therapeutic style of my own and felt *slightly* more confident in my role as a burgeoning therapist. Luke was self-referred to the agency and endorsed steadily more concerning depressive symptoms. Luke had been sent to prison two years prior for involuntary manslaughter and experienced a significant adjustment reaction in the wake of his release and subsequent probation. He struggled with how to re-integrate back into his life and felt "uneasy" about his place in his family.

Luke struggled with guilt about what he had done and though he desperately sought forgiveness, was decidedly certain that he did not deserve it. He shared that he and his younger brother had been at a bar and that they were confronted by a man who threatened and attacked his brother. Luke described his reaction as "instinct" as he recounted springing into action to come to his brother's aid. He intervened and was forced by the assailant to defend himself, landing blow after blow until the attacker was downed. When the dust settled, Luke and his brother sustained multiple injuries and their attacker was severely injured and would later die due to complications caused by his injuries. Luke explored his guilt and shared anger at his brother for exchanging threats with a man for what now Luke described as, "Meaningless; nothing … worthless shit talking." He had defended his brother, and in doing so, paid a steep price.

Luke struggled with his identity surrounding how he could have done what he did and still be a man worth being loved. In our work, we talked a great deal about comics and superheroes. Initially, Luke seemed to entertain my connections to comic book characters out of what I can only imagine was a sort of respectful tolerance or perhaps a response to my power and privilege as a white "expert" clinician. The superhero metaphor grew to become a way to unbalance the problem saturated stories that Luke shared about himself and lend itself to building and strengthening a therapeutic relationship. As it did, I began to perceive that he had created an alter ego for himself. This alter ego was an identity to fit a dominant narrative that had been written for him, about him. It was a narrative that said he was aggressive, dangerous and emotionless and he began making decisions that maintained this narrative.

For Luke, his alter ego was also based in racial stereotypes, put on him by a narrative written from a perspective of power and privilege: a white perspective. His alter ego was an angry black man who had just come out of prison and had no place in society, no place in his family and little hope of redemption. Luke identified most with the Hulk. He recurrently described himself similarly to what he felt the Hulk represented, a rage monster; unable to quell his aggression, dangerous to be around, a threat to those he loved, and void of any other ability than destruction. He began to navigate his life in ways that maintained that narrative. He shared in sessions that he could not reconcile how he can move past it because they [society] will never let that happen. "This is me now," he said. "I am a monster." External narratives told through a lens of institutionalized racism about what it means to be black in the United States, to be a black man, and to be a "black man who is a convict" infected his sense of self. He felt he had no recourse other than to placate those that would brand him that way because to defy that message of him felt "pointless" and "dangerous."

We used the exploration of superheroes as a means of reauthoring his narrative. We reframed the initial bar fight, not to excuse what happened, but to highlight the virtue of protection he felt in that moment. With support, he began to talk about himself in terms of Superman, specifically regarding a character with great strength that can be imposing and, if not used "for good," could easily become destructive. Using this new character, we began to explore the function of distancing himself from his family (i.e., his mother, wife and daughter). He identified with the underlying fear shared by many superheroes that if he lets others in, they could get hurt. This insight served to further highlight his protective nature and we used that to suggest that the function of his disconnection to others as ones seemed to be rooted in his love for them instead of their fear of him. Luke began to experience a decrease in depressive features and overall, more willingness to challenge destructive internal and external narratives of whom he was and who he could be.

Case Summary: Power Man

My internship ended before Luke's treatment concluded and I never did hear about how things ended up for him. The work I did with Luke energized me. I was amazed that comic book tropes and an affinity for superheroes could be accepted and effective in a real therapeutic context. My co-therapist and I were able to help Luke in a way that highlighted his inner hero and deconstructed, if only minimally, the complexity of a narrative that was burying his heroism and, in his mind, creating a villain. However, as I said, I was a novice clinician and did not at that time realize the intricacies that this approach entailed. I felt successful and proficient but looking back I was also woefully unaware of the limitations and potential barriers that exist in deconstructing an identity that is, and has been, subjected to repeated and systemic marginalization. Additionally, if I could do it again, I would use the character of Luke Cage with this client because he actually embodied many of the same virtues as Luke in the comics and the recently released Luke Cage series. Looking back, there is a direct connection between the two regarding their motivation to keep others safe with their power while at the same time pushing others away for fear that they might be the ones to hurt them.

By his own report, Luke's motivation to maintain his alter ego was largely rooted in placation; a conscious choice to allay the perception of him as a threat. Though stereotypes and prejudicial notions of or about prisoners both current and former are not unique to marginalized individuals, one's ethnicity, socio-economic status and societal privilege all significantly impact that individual's ability to effectively move along the continuum and their ability to re-acclimate to society post incarceration. Using superheroes as a vehicle, Luke was able to experience a new way of talking and thinking about himself in relation to his presenting symptoms, but that does not change the fact that he continues to move through a world that is not always accepting or representative of who he is. In this we also can assert that acceptance of this destructive alter ego served the function to protect himself and potentially to shield his family from the subversive paradigm of associating with the black American convict. I ask you, what is more heroic than someone who would shoulder that to protect others?

Hero Profile: Sam Wilson, a.k.a. Falcon & Mari McCabe, a.k.a Vixen

My first job out of grad school was as a clinician in a level 3 Day Treatment facility. I was assigned to a program for children ages 5–12 who presented with pervasive mental health issues and systemic barriers which significantly impacted functioning across settings. Our program had a therapeutic as well as school component to it and we treated clients six hours per day, five days per week. Sam and Mari were both assigned to my caseload as individual clients, but I also had them in many of the therapeutic groups that I facilitated. Sam was 8 years old and identified as an African-American male and Mari, 7 years old, identified as an African-American female. Both Sam and Mari had similar symptomology and historical diagnoses. They presented with irritability, low self-esteem, impulsivity, anger outbursts characterized by verbal aggression, and property destruction. Both had a history of neglect and Mari had been placed in multiple settings within the foster care system. Sam lived with his biological father and step-mother but had not had contact with his biological mother for many years due to a termination of her parental rights.

Their diagnoses historically were more reflective of the outward manifestations of their symptoms; surface behaviors that, by report, were the catalysts for the severe declination of academic functioning that warranted the removal from mainstream school and created the medical necessity for the intensity of day treatment services. In my experience in day treatment, it was common for many of the clients referred to our program to already, at their young ages, be struggling with destructive self-narratives. Sam and Mari in their own ways had created alter egos of themselves. First, there was the alter ego that was informed by the treatment setting they were in. Both had stories of being told that they "would struggle" in a less restrictive academic setting. As children often do, Sam and Mari began to play to the low expectations that they were experiencing from the adults in their lives and as they did, they became increasingly more symptomatic. Through discussion with their caretakers, I learned that during this distress, Sam and Mari had a similar experience of watching kids, who their caretakers identified as Caucasian, act out in comparable ways and receive no discipline, negative attention or re-direction.

I have seen recurrent instances that highlight a significant discrepancy in the response to and subsequent treatment of kids struggling with emotional and behavioral distress, particularly when that distress involved outward expressions of anger. It is an especially stark difference when seeing it play out between Caucasian and African-American children. In my five years working with children in various settings one thing I am certain of and need no citation for is that the threshold for outward emotional and behavioral outbursts for African-American children, especially in a school-based setting, is dramatically lower than the threshold that exists for Caucasian children presenting with the same symptoms and behaviors. I have seen this pattern play out time and time again and seen the maladaptive effects it has on both groups of children.

I began using superheroes in my groups to bridge differences among the members and begin to cultivate social skills. Sam and Mari were clients in one such group; a relatively small group, five clients in total. There was Sam, Mari and the other three kids were Caucasian, one of whom was female. We all shared an affinity for superheroes and I thought it would be a natural way to join and find commonality with one another. I began to explore with them what they felt a hero represented. What did they like about superheroes? What qualities did they aspire to emulate? I relied heavily on their knowledge of mainstream and accessible superheroes, but I neglected to account for what was, in retrospect, a massive oversight on my part given the fact that an overwhelming percentage of mainstream and "accessible" superheroes were white (I suspect 96% white; with 1% being Falcon and the remaining 3% reserved for those characters that were green, blue, raccoons, or trees).

Almost immediately, Sam and Mari were reminded that one of the most identifiable traits of a superhero is their ability to be white and that they did not fit that paradigm. They shared their favorites with the group, but their contributions were met with comments the likes of, "You can't be Black Widow, your hair is too nappy." Or, "You can be Falcon … he's black." "You can't be Captain America, though. You have to be white to be him." I made a mistake and in doing so, I set those kids up to experience another instance of marginalization and highlighted that their heroes did not represent who they are. I addressed what happened immediately and made it clear that those comments were not going to be tolerated in this group, but that was of little recompense. This was the external narrative that informed Sam and Mari's idea that they could, or rather could not, be heroes.

For both clients' individual sessions, we explored their narrative surrounding experiences they have had like what happened in the group.

Sam shared that he "knew" he could never be a hero and so there was "no point, why try? I will just be a bad guy; at least no one will be able to hurt me." Mari struggled with an additional layer of intersectionality in that she was not only under-represented as an African-American in comics; she was under-represented as a female AND under-represented as an African-American female. I sought to expose Sam and Mari to heroes that would be more representative of their culture, race and gender and if I'm honest, I was motivated to educate myself because for all my love of comics, I had a limited exposure to cross-cultural superheroes. Sam initially identified a great deal with Green Lantern, John Stewart. He was certainly taken with his powers including light constructs and flight, but what I thought was so striking is that he was most excited that John Stewart was an architect. He thought it was "so awesome" that he was a superhero AND an architect. We began to build on that moment to explore a future where he could see himself as something other than the self-proclaimed villain that he felt was all he could or wanted to be.

I was motivated by the connection Sam felt to John Stewart, but I was somewhat remiss because my initial instinct had been to stop there. I had found a super-hero that was both more representative of Sam and instituted a greater sense of connection to his inner hero, but I was curious if there were more. That is when I found it, a 2014 comic run featuring the hero Falcon titled, All New Captain America (issue No. 1), wherein Falcon assumes the mantle of Captain America (Remender, 2014). I read about Falcon's transformation into the iconic character and immediately thought of the group where my client Sam was told, "You can be Falcon … he's black. You can't be Captain America though. You have to be white to be him." I was eager to share this revelation with Sam and when I did, he looked at me in disbelief; giant smile on his face. We sat and laughed, gob smacked, Sam looking at the comic; me looking at Sam. This one event in Marvel comics created a paradigm shift and in doing so, significantly altered this boy's narrative with respect to his view of himself, his presenting issues, and his identity of himself as a young black kid; eager to be a hero.

It proved more difficult to find examples for Mari; what I would have done for the introduction of Riri Williams as Ironheart just a few years earlier. Characters like Storm and Vixen immediately came to mind, and Mari showed some interest in both. She gravitated to Storm because she liked that she was from Africa and that she was a princess. She was excited when I introduced her to Misty Knight because finally, "she has hair like me!" Over time though, I began to struggle with the female characters we explored because more and more, I began to take issue with the sexualization of female comic book characters I shared with my 7-year-old client. I had uncovered another layer of complexity to using superheroes to address complex issues related to the marginalization of my clients. Mari made comments about their figures, a concept that Delgado and Stefancic (2017) high-light as "another layer of destructive subliminal narratives of Eurocentric standards of beauty" (p. 142).

I gained a great deal of insight from my inability to help Mari in the same way as I did for Sam, or Luke. My idea to address the various problematic narratives about female superheroes was to help Mari create her own superhero. We started from the ground up and Mari decided what powers her hero would have, and she could draw her hero however she wanted. I did not specify that she needed to make her hero a female, but I was glad when she did. Mari drew her hero in her own image and named her "Midnight." We would talk about Midnight and Mari began to create adventures and villains for her; villains that were representative of stressors, trauma, and figures that had impacted her sense of self. It was not what I sought out to do and certainly a touch off from my idea of an alter ego, but she took it and made it her own and that, at the end of the day, is all I could really hope for as her clinician.

Case Summary: Falcon and Vixen

Sam and Mari both transitioned from the day treatment program and back into mainstream school. They had made an incredible amount of progress with respect to emotional expression and increased sense of selves. I never received any sort of update about Mari, as was regularly the case for day treatment clients, but Sam and his mom did call me some months later to let me know that he liked his new school and missed seeing me every day. Sam and Mari were the first kids I used this alter ego approach with and I was surprised at what I learned from it. Sam had created an alter ego that was rooted in overwhelming saturation of the idea that there was no use in trying to be anything other than a "bad guy" (i.e., property destruction, threats and verbal aggression) because the opposite for him was a hero, something that he, as a young African-American boy, felt he could not be. His alter ego served the purpose of protecting him from the barriers that he encountered, both in individual interactions and in a greater societal context, which suggested to him that his identity was that of his symptom presentation. He also began to preserve what Delgado and Stefancic (2017) assert is "the systemic prescription of a racial face, or paradigm, that perpetuates stereotypical representation in many facets of society, in this case, what a hero is and/or looks like" (p. 13).

What I learned about Mari's construction of her alter ego narrative is that I had a lot to continue to learn about how to use this approach and had not, until this case, taken into account the intersectionality of the various layers of power, privilege and marginalization my clients experience. For me, it is not so much a limitation of the approach, as a limitation of MY approach that created the criticism that I had not understood how to achieve the same efficacy with Mari as I had with African-American male clients. I realized that to understand where I fell short in using this approach was in my failure to conceptualize the approach through an intersectional lens. I needed to carefully consider and ask how variations in one domain of identity, for example race/ethnicity, become more complex when an additional domain, in Mari's case, gender, is introduced into the theoretical and empirical discussion (Azmita & Thomas, 2015). To date, the bulk of the work

I have done with this approach has been with African-American males. It is a testament to the importance of acknowledging a vital component in what it means to be a mental health professional in that our clients' stories are complex. The efficacy of an approach is only as good as the ability to abandon that approach if it is not capable of addressing that idiosyncratic complexity.

Hero Profile: Victor "Vic" Stone, a.k.a. Cyborg

Treating individuals directly is necessary to create space for the identified client to address their mental health needs, but a healthy balance between that and family therapy is essential for a Marriage and Family Therapist to engage parents and siblings in treatment that highlights and challenges the overall functioning of the family system to further support the changes made in the individual client's course of treatment. This is the capacity in which I met and worked with Vic and his family. Vic, a 13-year-old African-American male, was referred to outpatient services by his parents who were urgently seeking services to address concerns surrounding anger outbursts, defiance, declined academic functioning, property destruction and verbal/physical aggression. Vic was the product of a transracial adoption, specifically Vic's biological parents were both African-American and he was adopted in early childhood by Caucasian parents. Vic and his family lived in an affluent suburb of the metro area and his parents reported that their decision to pursue a transracial adoption was motivated by their desire to provide a loving, safe and supportive family life for a child who did not otherwise have it.

Vic was the second of three kids, having an older (16) and younger (9) sister who were both biological children of Vic's adoptive parents. Vic reported that he did not remember, nor has he had contact with, either of his biological parents and that the only family he had ever known was his adoptive family. Vic reportedly experienced disruptions to care in early childhood and was removed as a baby from his bio-parents' custody due to recurrent instances of neglect. Vic was briefly placed in foster care but was soon after adopted by his parents. Vic and his family reported that since the adoption, he has had no exposure or connection to extended biological family. Vic's parents asserted that they did their very best to "raise him the same as they did for their other children, because he was their son and that was always just the way of it." They frequently noted that a major goal was to make Vic feel loved and accepted in their family and in their community.

Vic's parents reported that around the age of 9, he began to struggle in relationships with peers and as he did, he reportedly became increasingly more reactive and agitated. His parents noted that Vic had become uncharacteristically "defiant" and "combative." Vic's distress reportedly began to manifest as "unpredictable" outward emotional expression and worsened to include more intense verbal/physical aggression and property destruction; occurring primarily at home with his parents. In school, Vic described his experience as feeling "angry" and "on edge all of the time," but for the most part, he was reportedly able to maintain good grades and was active in school sports. Over time, Vic's distress began to impact his school functioning and he began to experience recurrent instances of conflict and a dramatic declination in academic and social functioning. Vic's parents recognized the necessity for intervention and parlayed their relationship with school staff into a system of early warnings, favors and second chances for Vic to shield him from more severe disciplinary action on a scholastic level.

Treatment initially focused on individual therapy with Vic, and although he presented as shy and quiet at first, he had a great sense of humor and we connected right away through a shared affinity for comics. As I joined with Vic, he began to reveal his alter ego to me. Vic defined himself by his anger, namely his aggression. He maintained a similar self-narrative as the heroes in the previous case studies in that he saw himself as a broken, hopeless and dangerous person. Unlike previous clients though, Vic made a point to emphasize that, "he didn't care." In my clinical experience working with people of all ages, "I don't care" is a recurrent comment that sets my Spidey-sense tingling. "I don't care" has emerged as one of the most indirectly identifiable cues that there is a deep well of pain and sadness underneath what is usually a history of surface behaviors. Vic's presentation was that he wanted me to know that he was made from armor and nails and unfazed by the distance that existed between him and others, in particular with his family. He would also have me believe that all that he could be was the kind of person who hurts others so in that, it was for the best that he was alone.

As I began to form a relationship with Vic, I began to challenge the narrative that informed his alter ego, especially the fact that he didn't care. We began to explore the benefits that he felt would come out of his distancing himself from others. Above all else, the theme was that of protection for others and I used that theme to reframe the function of his alter ego as heroic. Vic and I talked many times about superheroes and in those conversations, the movie *The Dark Knight* came up several times. I told Vic, after a period of him highlighting how it benefitted others for him to be a villain, that he reminded me of Batman in the final moments of that movie. In the conclusion, Harvey Dent has been lost to his alter ego, Two-Face and Batman fears the breakdown that will ensue when Gotham finds out that The Joker was able to sway their most hopeful public figure (De La Noy & Nolan, 2008). "Where I think you play it out." I explained to Vic, "is in the same way Batman took on the role of the villain to protect Gotham, you take on the role of the villain to protect … someone. Who, do you think?"

The Batman conversation was revisited a few times, but eventually Vic was able to share that he whole-heartedly believed that if he made himself a "target," it would take the focus off his family. He shared stories of school peers referencing his sisters and reminding him, "but yeah though … they aren't like, your REAL sisters though." He shared his experience of living in a predominately white community and hearing the praise his parents had recurrently received for adopting an African-American child, when "they didn't have to." He added though, the "look they gave my parents when I struggled or screwed something up" was spiteful; blaming. Vic explained to me that, as he began to ramp up the severity and frequency of his behaviors, the look others gave his parents and sisters regarding him shifted from condemnation to something more resembling sympathy. Vic began to shape his behavior to create more of that experience for his family, even if he had to sacrifice parts of himself to do it. In Vic verbalizing these underlying microaggressions, we had uncovered a functional motivation for his symptoms that was deeply rooted in love for his family. He could be the "villain" because it was what he felt his family needed him to be.

After shifting his narrative to one more accommodating of the notion that he may not have to be a villain, we began to explore parallels between Vic and the DC hero Cyborg. Cyborg's origin story is that of a star athlete seeking to excel in order to attain his father s approval, only to have it all cut short by an accident in which his father saved his life by replacing over half of Cyborg's body with cybernetic parts (Beatty, Greenberger, Jiminez, & Wallace, 2008). Vic identified with this story because he felt it was like him being saved from an unhealthy situation by his adoptive parents, but growing up in that system, he felt "the black part of me was replaced with something else." He shared that though he had African-American peers who experienced similar layers of privilege: affluence, good schooling, access to resources and a safe community, they had what he did not have "parents that look like them." This hero resonated with him because Cyborg is noticeably different from the two worlds (man and machine) he is constantly attempting to acclimate to. For Vic, this was represented by the dissonance created by his struggle to develop his sense of self against juxtapositions of his racial (biological) identity and his familial (communal) identity.

I began to see Vic along with his parents and sisters at times, to address systemic functioning and to explore ways in which Vic is, or can be, supported in fostering a greater connection to both of his identity narratives. We began to explore the lack of space and effort that is, and has been, made in the family for conversation about race, racism and culture in the family. Vic's mother shared that they have never had any issues with race or racism because, "We don't care about the color of your [Vic's] skin; we love you and you are OUR son." After hearing this, Vic retorted with, "Then why are you afraid of me!" Vic was experiencing a double bind message; a dilemma in which "two closely communicated messages are contradictory in nature" (Klajs, 2016, p. 18). On one hand, Vic was hearing "We love you" from his family while on the other, he received a more covert message in times of anger and distress that said to him, "but we are afraid of you." Vic had incorporated this double bind messaging into his narrative and quickly attached the fear to his racial identity and framed it as they were afraid of "the angry black kid." Vic was experiencing a disconnect because to him, to believe the first message, he would have to find it in himself to disbelieve the second message. To disbelieve the more covert and visceral message, he would have to ignore the way he feels; his experience as a young black man in a racial integrate situation in which racial dynamics are not explored.

This was a pivotal moment in the therapeutic process and it led to the verbalization by Vic's parents that they felt defeated in not being able to help their son and were terrified that the world with "beat him down" because of the color of his skin. Vic's parents explored this fear in sessions and over time, acknowledged that they sought to leverage their privilege in a predominately white and affluent community to create a buffer around their son and admitted that they did not do that for their other kids in the way they have for Vic. Vic and I recognized a similar protective function to his parents pattern and Vic suggested, "Wow, you guys are superheroes too." With Vic's help, I was able to use a similar notion of the Batman metaphor to highlight the loving and positive function of the dynamics and highlight that while it served a purpose, created its own complications and maintenance of symptomology.

Case Summary: Cyborg

Vic is a particularly special client for me and in the work we did together, I saw him grow and tap into insight and abilities that he had long since convinced himself were not possible. I learned a great deal about a hero's resiliency and quiet honesty, a great deal about the complexity of racial and familial identity. Going into the treatment with Vic and his family, I had a limited knowledge of working with transracial adoption. In research to better understand the complex nature of it, I learned that in the 1990s, transracial adoption was under scrutiny for being outside of the best interest for the kids of color that were adopted by white families and that special legislation had to be passed to eliminate the barriers that existed for Caucasian parents to adopted cross-culturally (Bumpus, 2014).

Bumpus (2014) additionally explained that a "wealth of research exists that highlights the benefits and detriment to transracial adoption" (p. 2). Ultimately, there is an overwhelming need for permanent placement of children in the foster care system and her research indicated that transracial adoption, between 2006 and 2014, was a large factor in reducing the number of African-American kids stuck within that system (Bumpus, 2014). In my experience, placing kids with safe and secure families is a win; however, as in Vic's case, if there is no attunement or effort to support and foster some semblance of racial identity, it can become a difficult undertaking to achieve healthy functioning across the system. For example, by virtue of the very language Vic's parents used (i.e., color blind, we don't see color, make him comfortable), though rooted in love, advocacy and good intention, highlighted racial disparities that in turn, were covertly forbidden to talk about.

In subsequent family sessions, I explored ways in which Vic and his family could mindfully explore the complicated layers of intersectionality that when unacknowledged, stifled the love permeating throughout this system. We discussed Vic's desire to connect more with his cultural roots and ways in which they could support him in that and give him space to find his own way into doing so. Vic has recently connected with his paternal grandfather and is feeling positive, albeit unsure, about how that relationship will fit into his life. Vic and his family taught me that this superhero approach had a rich and layered capacity for change and I gained insight into the complex nature of heroes and their alter egos, both how they work together and against one another.

Conclusion

In this chapter, I have addressed potential limitations to the alter ego approach. In particular, the complexity of a client's intersectionality is a major factor that influences the efficacy of this approach because without mindfulness about that element, this approach becomes a further extension of the privilege that allows a person to ignore other layered experiences of marginalization. For me, it bears repeating that the "self of the therapist" is vital to the successful utilization of this approach. Self of the therapist is a term used by MFTs to describe the diligent and ongoing self-reflection of a practicing clinician; whether burgeoning or well established. In my experience, leaning into courageous and authentic conversation about race, power and privilege is a hard enough skill to learn how to comfortably (if it ever is comfortable) employ, much less to feel that anxiety and at times, fear, and then try to fill that vulnerable space with superheroes.

The very nature of superheroes and comics poses another interesting complication to using this approach. To challenge thematic elements of discriminatory, stereotypical and oppressive societal dynamics using superheroes is difficult to incorporate because, as I have detailed in my case studies, comic books have had a longstanding historical struggle with equitable and inclusive representation of characters that challenge the paradigm of the white superhero. Because of this pattern, the use of superheroes can easily become a reminder of just another layer of privilege that exacerbates an already visceral experience of oppression for clients of color.

I have made many mistakes in the use of this approach and I am grateful for each one of them. Each mistake resulted in authentic experiential moments in the therapeutic relationship that created movement, insight and learning which has, in turn, led to a richer understanding of how superheroes actually DO have had a a powerful place in clinical practice. I continue to strive to explore the efficacy of this approach in a more expansive way cross-culturally and am eager to talk with and learn from others to broaden the efficacy of this style of therapy.

Using superhero tropes, I was able to explore my clients' motivations, highlight the heroic resiliency that they demonstrate daily and deconstruct their negatively saturated narratives. In the process, I realized that I meet superheroes all the time. I have seen clients blossom and create heroes worthy of any comic book. Moreover, I have yet to see them give up. The clients I presented in this chapter challenged themselves and me in every therapeutic moment, and consistently made the choice to push forward and confront not only their alter egos, but the systems and mechanisms that exist to work against them and for me, THAT is the very *essence* of a superhero.

Questions for Clinical Discussion

1. What are the defining characteristics of your "alter ego" and what role does your racial/cultural identity play in the formation of your second self?

2. What would you say is your level of comfortability with initiating courageous conversations with clients and colleagues about racism, power and privilege and how might the introduction of superheroes into those conversations do that comfortability?
3. In terms of self-reflection, what are the vulnerabilities or prejudices that discussing race and racism might expose about you?
4. What can you do to create space for the similarities or differences in your and your clients' layers of intersectionality?
5. Are there ways that you or your colleagues discuss, consult on or write in ways that unwittingly ascribe elements of destructive external narratives onto clients?
6. When is it, if at all, that an "alter ego" is a positive construct?

References

Azmita, M. & Thomas, V. (2015). Intersectionality and the development of self and identity. In: *Emerging trends in the social and behavioral sciences: An interdisciplinary, searchable, and linkable resource*. Hoboken, NJ: John Wiley & Sons.

Bender, L. (Producer) & Tarantino, Q. (Director) (2004). *Kill Bill: vol. 2* [Motion picture]. Los Angeles, CA: Miramax Studios.

Beatty, S., Greenberger, R., Jiminez, P., & Wallace, D. (2008), *The DC Comics encyclopedia: The definitive guide to the characters of the DC universe*. New York: DK Publishing.

Bumpus, J. A. (2014). *Transracial adoption: Racial identity, resilience, and self-esteem of African American adoptees* [Doctoral dissertation]. Retrieved from Antioch University Department of Clinical Psychology. http://antioch.edu/etds/101.

De La Noy, K. (Producer) & Nolan, C. (Director) (2008). *The Dark Knight* [Motion picture]. Burbank, CA: Warner Bros.

Delgado, R. & Stefancic, J. (2017). *Critical race theory: An introduction* (3rd edn.). New York: New York University Press.

Feagin, J. R. (2010). *The white racial frame: Centuries of racial framing and counter-framing* (2nd edn.). New York: Routledge.

Foeman, A. (2009). Science and magic: DNA and the racial narratives that shape the social construction of race in the USA. *Intercultural Communication Studies, 18(2)*, 14–25. Retrieved from http://digitalcommons.wcupa.edu/comstudies_facpub/2

Gearing, R. E. (2004). Bracketing in research: A typology. *Qualitative Research, 14*, 1429–1452.

Hart, B. (1995). Re-authoring the stories we work by situating the narrative approach in the presence of the family of therapists. *Australian & New Zealand Journal of Family Therapy, 16(4)*, 181–189.

Klajs, K. (2016). Jay Haley: Pioneer in strategic family therapy. *Psychotherapia, 2 (177)*, 17–28

Nichols, M. P. (2010). *Family therapy: Concepts and method*. Boston, MA: Pearson Education Inc.

Remender, R. (2014). *All-new Captain America, 1(1)*.

Afterword

Lawrence C. Rubin

The journey has now come to its end. The mission is complete. You have traveled with a talented team of clinicians of all swaths and orientations, whose primary goal has been to share with you the many ways that superheroes, both literally and figuratively, can be woven into the fabric of the therapeutic relationship with children, teens, adults and families. And this particular group of clients with whom these clinicians have worked were as varied in their backgrounds, orientations and beliefs as the therapists themselves. As a result, you've had the opportunity to witness the creative and flexible way in which a simple, yet powerful metaphor, that of the superhero, provides the groundwork from which to build meaningful therapeutic change.

I am most thankful to these clinicians for their efforts but perhaps even more so to the clients who inspired them. After all, we are really only as powerful as our clients allow us to be.

And I am equally thankful to you, the reader, for taking your time and energy to journey with us.

Index

LGBTQIA+ *see* queer
Lidz, Theodore 158
life stories: re-authoring and reframing 132
Link 270
Livesay, Harry 210
Logan (2017) 13
Loki 193
Luthor, Lex 15, 141

maladaptive daydreaming (case of Jackson) 59–71
Malfoy, Draco: jealousy of Harry Potter 234, 235, 239–242
Malfoy, Lucius 234, 235, 241–242
Malfoy, Narcissa 241–242
Man-Bat 130
Mandarin 141
Manga 89
manipulation and addiction 141
Mantis 14
marriage counseling 158
marriage couple and family counseling 159
Marvel Age 186
Marvel Avengers *see* Avengers
Marvel Cinematic Universe (MCU) 183
Marvel comics 57
Marvel superheroes: creation of 185–186
Maslow, Abraham 188–189, 207
Maslow's hierarchy of needs 206
Masque 106
McCabe, Mari 300–304; *see also* Vixen
McCloud, Scott 76
meaning in life: well-being and 10, 14–15
media: gendered representations 282; impact on child identity development 38–39, 42–43; impact on interpretation of self 34–35
media representation of women 256; effect on boys' view of women 257; female stereotypes 256; lack of strong, relatable female characters 262–263
mental health disorders 141; developing resilience and strength 223–224; zombies as a metaphor for 222, 224
mental health in early childhood: *I can be a Super Friend!* scripted story 147, 149–155

mental health services: challenge of children affected by maltreatment 147–149
metaphors: for life problems that accompany SUD 141; use in narrative therapy 133, 134; for the world of the reader 84–86
Milan Systemic school 295, 296
mindfulness 110–111
Minecraft 123, 225–226
Minecraft Lego 226
Minuchin, Salvador 159, 160, 162
mirror neurons 173
mirroring process 173–174
Mittleman, Bella 158
modern mythologies: fanfiction as 266–267
monomyth model (hero's journey) 77–78, 81, 266–267
monomyth structure: therapeutic importance 78
Mood Disorder NOS 258
Moore, Alan 80
Morrison, G. 198
MRI Strategic school 295, 296
Ms. Marvel 257, 262
Mudd, Emily 158
Multidimensional Model of Racial Identity (MMRI) 278–279
multigenerational patterns of behavior 161–162
Munroe, Ororo 105; *see also* Storm
Murdock, Matt 13–14; *see also* Daredevil
music 230
My Fear Zapper CBT program 122, 125, 126

Narcotics Anonymous 134
narrative therapy: client's creative contribution 134–135; contextualized meaning-making 131–132; differing perspectives on events 294–295; externalization of problems 132, 133, 164, 265; family counseling 163–164, 165–169; fanfiction and 265–266; features of 131–133; internalization of problems 132–133; language selection 133–134; postmodern philosophy 131; poststructural philosophy 131–132;

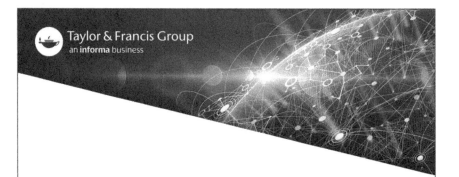